Get the eBook FREE!

(PDF, ePub, Kindle, and liveBook all included)

We believe that once you buy a book from us, you should be able to read it in any format we have available. To get electronic versions of this book at no additional cost to you, purchase and then register this book at the Manning website.

Go to https://www.manning.com/freebook and follow the instructions to complete your pBook registration.

That's it!
Thanks from Manning!

Data Analysis with Python and PySpark

JONATHAN RIOUX

MANNING

SHELTER ISLAND

For online information and ordering of this and other Manning books, please visit
www.manning.com. The publisher offers discounts on this book when ordered in quantity.
For more information, please contact

> Special Sales Department
> Manning Publications Co.
> 20 Baldwin Road
> PO Box 761
> Shelter Island, NY 11964
> Email: orders@manning.com

Manning Publications Co.
20 Baldwin Road
PO Box 761
Shelter Island, NY 11964

Development editor:	Marina Michaels
Technical development editor:	Arthur Zubarev
Review editor:	Aleksander Dragosavljević
Production editor:	Keri Hales
Copy editor:	Michele Mitchell
Proofreader:	Melody Dolab
Technical proofreader:	Alex Ott
Typesetter:	Dennis Dalinnik
Cover designer:	Marija Tudor

ISBN: 9781617297205
Printed in the United States of America

contents

iii

3 Submitting and scaling your first PySpark program 45

4 Analyzing tabular data with pyspark.sql 62

7 **Bilingual PySpark: Blending Python and SQL code   151**

8 **Extending PySpark with Python: RDD and UDFs   175**

9 **Big data is just a lot of small data: Using pandas UDFs   192**

preface

While computers have been getting more powerful and more capable of chewing though larger data sets, our appetite for consuming data grows much faster. Consequently, we built new tools to scale big data jobs across multiple machines. This does not come for free, and early tools were complicated by requiring users to manage not only the data program, but also the health and performance of the cluster of machines themselves. I recall trying to scale my own programs, only to be faced with the advice to "just sample your data set and get on with your day."

PySpark changes the game. Starting with the popular Python programming language, it provides a clear and readable API to manipulate very large data sets. Still, while in the driver's seat, you write code as if you were dealing with a single machine. PySpark sits at the intersection of powerful, expressive, and versatile. Through a powerful multidimensional data model, you can build your data programs with a clear path to scalability, regardless of the data size.

I fell in love with PySpark while working as a data scientist for building credit risk models. On the cusp of migrating our models to a new big data environment, we needed to devise a plan to intelligently convert our data products while "keeping the lights on." As the self-appointed Python guy, I got tasked to help the team become familiar with PySpark and help accelerate the transition. This love grew exponentially as I got the chance to work with a myriad of clients on different use cases. The common thread? Big data and big problems, all solvable through a powerful data model. One caveat: most of the material available for learning Spark focused on Scala and Java, with Python developers left transliterating the code to their favorite programming language. I started writing this book to promote PySpark as a great tool for data analysts. In a fortunate turn of events, the Spark project really promoted Python as a first-class citizen. Now, more than ever, you have a powerful tool for scaling your data programs.

And big data, once tamed, really feels powerful.

acknowledgments

Although my name is on the cover, this book has been a tremendous team effort, and I want to take the time to thank those who helped me along the way.

First and foremost, I want to thank my family. Writing a book is a lot of work, and with this work comes a lot of complaining. Simon, Catherine, Véronique, Jean, *merci du fond du coeur pour votre soutien. Je vous aime énormément.*

Regina, in a way, you were my very first PySpark student. Through your leadership, you literally changed everything for me career-wise. I will forever cherish the time we worked together, and I feel lucky our paths crossed when they did.

I want to thank Renata Pompas, who allowed me to use a color palette made under her supervision for the diagrams in my book. I am color-blind, and finding a set of safe colors to use that would please me and be consistent was helpful during book development. If the figures look good to you, thank her (and the fine Manning graphic designers). If they look bad, blame it on me.

Thank you to my team at EPAM, with a special shout-out to Zac, James, Nasim, Vahid, Dmitrii, Yuriy, Val, Robert, Aliaksandra, Ihor, Pooyan, Artem, Volha, Ekaterina, Sergey, Sergei, Siarhei, Kseniya, Artemii, Anatoly, Yuliya, Nadzeya, Artsiom, Denis, Yevhen, Sofiia, Roman, Mykola, Lisa, Gaurav, Megan, and so many more. From the day I announced that I was writing a book to when I wrote these words, I felt supported and encouraged. Thank you to the Laivly team, Jeff, Rod, Craig, Jordan, Abu, Brendan, Daniel, Guy, and Reid, for the opportunity to continue the adventure. I promise you that the future is bright.

A warm thank you to those who believed in my "use PySpark, you'll be grateful you did" mantra. There are too many folks to be exhaustive here, but I want to give a shout out to Mark Derry, Uma Gopinath, Tom Everett, Dhrun Lauwers, Milena Kumurdjieva, Shahid Amlani, Sam Diab, Chris Wagner, JV Eng, Chris Purtill, Naveen Pothayath, Vish Tipirneni, and Patrick Kurkiewicz.

During the writing of the book, I had the joy to geek out on PySpark with some fine podcast producers: Brian at Test and Code (https://testandcode.com/), Lior and Michael at *WHAT the Data?!* (https://podcast.whatthedatapodcast.com/), and Ben at *Profitable Python* (https://anchor.fm/profitablepythonfm). I am so humbled and grateful that you invited me to exchange with you. Thank you Alexey Grigorev for having me in your Book of the Week club on Slack—what an awesome community you've built!

I want to thank readers who provided comments on the manuscript during development, as well as the reviewers who provided excellent feedback: Alex Lucas, David Cronkite, Dianshuang Wu, Gary Bake, Geoff Clark, Gustavo Patino, Igor Vieira, Javier Collado Cabeza, Jeremy Loscheider, Josh Cohen, Kay Engelhardt, Kim Falk, Michael Kareev, Mike Jensen, Patrick A. Mol, Paul Fornia, Peter Hampton, Philippe Van Bergen, Rambabu Posa, Raushan Jha, Sergio Govoni, Sriram Macharla, Stephen Oates, and Werner Nindl.

Finally, and most importantly, I want to thank the dream team at Manning that participated in making this book a reality. There are many folks who made this experience incredible: Marjan Bace, Michael Stephens, Rebecca Rinehart, Bert Bates, Candace Gillhoolley, Radmila Ercegovac, Aleks Dragosavljević, Matko Hrvatin, Christopher Kaufmann, Ana Romac, Branko Latincic, Lucas Weber, Stjepan Jureković, Goran Ore, Keri Hales, Michele Mitchell, Melody Dolab, and the rest of the Manning production team.

Speaking of Manning, I want to thank the authors of two specific books: Noel Rappin and Robin Dunn from *wxPython in Action* (Manning, 2016; https://www.manning.com/books/wxpython-in-action), as well as Michael Fogus and Chris Houser from *The Joy of Clojure* (Manning, 2014; https://www.manning.com/books/the-joy-of-clojure-second-edition). These books triggered something in my brain and made me plunge headfirst into programming (and then data science). In a way, they were the initial spark (bad pun intended) that resulted in this book.

Finally, I want to highlight the team at Manning that helped me stay accountable on a day-to-day basis and made this book something I am proud of. Arthur Zubarev, I can't believe we live in the same city and couldn't meet! Thank you for your excellent feedback and answering my many questions. Alex Ott, I don't think I could have wished for a better technical advisor. Databricks is incredibly lucky to have you. Last, but certainly not least, I want to thank Marina Michaels for supporting me from the moment I had the idea of writing this book. Writing a book is a lot more difficult than I originally thought, but you made the whole experience enjoyable, formative, and relevant. Thank you from the bottom of my heart.

about this book

Data Analysis with Python and PySpark teaches you how to use PySpark to conduct your own big data analysis programs. It takes a practical stance on teaching both the how and why of PySpark. You'll learn about how to effectively ingest, process, and work with data at scale as well as how to reason about your own data transformation code. After reading this book, you should feel comfortable using PySpark to write your own data programs and analyses.

Who should read this book

This book is structured around increasingly complicated use cases, moving from simple data transformation to machine learning pipelines. We cover the whole cycle, from data ingestion to results consumption, adding more elements with regard to data source consumption and transformation possibilities.

This book caters mostly to data analysts, scientists, and engineers who want to scale their Python code to larger data sets. Ideally, you should have written a few data programs, either through your work or while learning to program. You'll get more out of this book if you already are comfortable using the Python programming language and ecosystem.

Spark (and PySpark, naturally) borrows a lot from object-oriented and functional programming. I do not think it's reasonable to expect complete knowledge of both programming paradigms just to use big data efficiently. If you understand Python classes, decorators, and higher-order functions, you'll have a blast using some of the more advanced constructions in the book to bend PySpark to your will. Should those concepts be foreign to you, I cover them in the context of PySpark throughout the book (when appropriate) and in the appendixes.

How this book is organized: A road map

The book is divided into three parts. Part 1, "Get Acquainted," introduces PySpark and its computation model. It also covers building and submitting a simple data program, focusing on the core operations that you certainly will use in every PySpark program you create, such as selecting, filtering, joining, and grouping data in a data frame.

Part 2, "Get Proficient," goes further into data transformation by introducing hierarchical data, a key element of scalable data programs in PySpark. We also make our programs more expressive, flexible, and performant through the judicious introduction of SQL code, an exploration of resilient distributed datasets/user-defined functions, efficient usage of pandas within PySpark, and window functions. We also explore Spark's reporting capabilities and resource management to pinpoint potential performance problems.

Finally, Part 3, "Get Confident," builds on parts 1 and 2 and covers how to build a machine learning program in PySpark. We use our data transformation tool kit to create and select features before building and evaluating a machine learning pipeline. We finish this part with creating our own machine learning pipeline components, ensuring maximum usability and readability for our ML programs.

Parts 1 and 2 have exercises throughout the chapters, as well as at the end of the chapters. Exercises at the end of a section don't require you to code; you should be able to answer the questions with what you learned.

The book was written with the idea of being read cover to cover, using the appendixes as needed. Should you want to dig directly into a topic, I still recommend covering part 1 before delving into a specific chapter. Here are the hard and soft dependencies to help you navigate the book more efficiently:

- Chapter 3 is a direct continuation of chapter 2.
- Chapter 5 is a direct continuation of chapter 4.
- Chapter 9 uses some concepts taught in chapter 8, but advanced readers can read it on its own.
- Chapters 12, 13, and 14 are best read one after the other.

About the code

This book works best with Spark version 3.1 or 3.2: Spark introduced many new functionalities in version 3, and most commercial offerings are now defaulting to this version. When appropriate, I provide backward-compatible instructions for Spark version 2.3/2.4. I do not recommend Spark 2.2 or below. I also recommend using Python version 3.6 and above (I used Python 3.8.8 for the book). Installation instructions are available in appendix A.

You can find the companion repository for the book, with data and code, at https://github.com/jonesberg/DataAnalysisWithPythonAndPySpark. When appropriate, it also contains runnable versions of the programs developed throughout the book, as well as a few optional exercises. In addition, you can get executable snippets of code from the liveBook (online) version of this book at https://livebook.manning.com/book/data-analysis-with-python-and-pyspark.

This book contains many examples of source code both in numbered listings and in line with normal text. In both cases, source code is formatted in a `fixed-width font like this` to separate it from ordinary text. Sometimes code is also in bold to highlight code that has changed from previous steps in the chapter, such as when a new feature adds to an existing line of code.

In many cases, the original source code has been reformatted; we've added line breaks and reworked indentation to accommodate the available page space in the book. In rare cases, even this was not enough, and listings include line-continuation markers (➡). Additionally, comments in the source code have often been removed from the listings when the code is described in the text. Code annotations accompany many of the listings and highlight important concepts.

liveBook discussion forum

Purchase of *Data Analysis with Python and PySpark* includes free access to liveBook, Manning's online reading platform. Using liveBook's exclusive discussion features, you can attach comments to the book globally or to specific sections or paragraphs. It's a snap to make notes for yourself, ask and answer technical questions, and receive help from the author and other users. To access the forum, go to https://livebook.manning.com/book/data-analysis-with-python-and-pyspark/discussion. You can also learn more about Manning's forums and the rules of conduct at https://livebook.manning.com/#!/discussion.

Manning's commitment to our readers is to provide a venue where a meaningful dialogue between individual readers and between readers and the author can take place. It is not a commitment to any specific amount of participation on the part of the author, whose contribution to the forum remains voluntary (and unpaid). We suggest you try asking the author some challenging questions lest his interest stray! The forum and the archives of previous discussions will be accessible from the publisher's website as long as the book is in print.

about the author

JONATHAN RIOUX uses PySpark inside and out on a daily basis. He also teaches large-scale data analysis to data scientists, engineers, and data-savvy business analysts.

Jonathan spent a decade in various analytical positions in the insurance industry before venturing into the consulting industry as a machine learning and data analysis expert. He currently works as the director of machine learning for Laivly, a company that equips friendly humans with intelligent automations and machine learning to create the best customer experiences on the planet.

about the cover illustration

The figure on the cover of *Data Analysis with Python and PySpark* is "Russien," or Russian man, taken from a book by Jacques Grasset de Saint-Sauveur, published in 1788. Each illustration is finely drawn and colored by hand.

In those days, it was easy to identify where people lived and what their trade or station in life was just by their dress. Manning celebrates the inventiveness and initiative of today's computer business with book covers based on the rich diversity of regional culture centuries ago, brought back to life by pictures from collections such as this one.

Introduction

This chapter covers

- What PySpark is
- Why PySpark is a useful tool for analytics
- The versatility of the Spark platform and its limitations
- PySpark's way of processing data

According to pretty much every news outlet, data is everything, everywhere. It's the new oil, the new electricity, the new gold, plutonium, even bacon! We call it powerful, intangible, precious, dangerous. At the same time, data itself is not enough: it is what you do with it that matters. After all, for a computer, any piece of data is a collection of zeroes and ones, and it is our responsibility, as users, to make sense of how it translates to something useful.

Just like oil, electricity, gold, plutonium, and bacon (especially bacon!), our appetite for data is growing. So much, in fact, that computers aren't following. Data is growing in size and in complexity, yet consumer hardware has been stalling a little. RAM is hovering for most laptops at around 8 to 16 GB, and SSDs are getting prohibitively expensive past a few terabytes. Is the solution for the burgeoning data analyst to triple-mortgage their life to afford top-of-the-line hardware to tackle big data problems?

Here is where Apache Spark (which I'll call Spark throughout the book) and its companion PySpark are introduced. They take a few pages of the supercomputer playbook—powerful, but manageable compute units meshed in a network of machines—and bring them to the masses. Add on top a powerful set of data structures ready for any work you're willing to throw at them, and you have a tool that will *grow* (pun intended) with you.

A goal for this book is to provide you with the tools to analyze data using PySpark, whether you need to answer a quick data-driven question or build an ML model. It covers just enough theory to get you comfortable while giving you enough opportunities to practice. Most chapters contain a few exercises to anchor what you just learned. The exercises are all solved and explained in appendix A.

1.1   What is PySpark?

What's in a name? Actually, quite a lot. Just by separating PySpark in two, you can already deduce that this will be related to Spark and Python. And you would be right!

At its core, PySpark can be summarized as being the Python API to Spark. While this is an accurate definition, it doesn't give much unless you know the meaning of Python and Spark. Still, let's break down the summary definition by first answering "What is Spark?" With that under our belt, we then will look at why Spark becomes especially powerful when combined with Python and its incredible array of analytical (and machine learning) libraries.

1.1.1   Taking it from the start: What is Spark?

According to the authors of the software, Apache Spark™, which I'll call Spark throughout this book, is a "unified analytics engine for large-scale data processing" (see https://spark.apache.org/). This is a very accurate, if a little dry, definition. As a mental image, we can compare Spark to an *analytics factory*. The raw material—here, data—comes in, and data, insights, visualizations, models, you name it, comes out.

Just like a factory will often gain more capacity by increasing its footprint, Spark can process an increasingly vast amount of data by *scaling out* (across multiple smaller machines) instead of *scaling up* (adding more resources, such as CPU, RAM, and disk space, to a single machine). RAM, unlike most things in this world, gets *more* expensive the more you buy (e.g., one stick of 128 GB is more than the price of two sticks of 64 GB). This means that, instead of buying thousands of dollars of RAM to accommodate your data set, you'll rely on multiple computers, splitting the job between them. In a world where two modest computers are less costly than one large one, scaling out is less expensive than scaling up, which keeps more money in your pockets.

> **Cloud cost and RAM**
>
> In the cloud, prices will often be more consequential. For instance, as of January 2022, a 16-Core/128-GB RAM machine can be about twice the cost of an 8 Core/64 GB of RAM machine. As the data size grows, Spark can help control costs by scaling the number of workers and executors for a given job. As an example, if you have a

data transformation job on a modest data set (a few TB), you can limit yourself to a lower number—say, five—machines, scaling up to 60 when you want to do machine learning. Some vendors, such as Databricks (see appendix B), offer *auto-scaling*, meaning that they increase and decrease the number of machines during a job depending on the pressure on the cluster. The implementation of auto-scaling/cost controlling is 100% vendor-dependent. (Check out chapter 11 for an introduction to the resources making up a Spark cluster, as well as their purpose.)

A single computer can crash or behave unpredictably at times. If instead of one you have one hundred, the chance that at least one of them goes down is now much higher.[1] Spark therefore has a lot of hoops to manage, scale, and babysit so that you can focus on what you want, which is to work with data.

This is, in fact, one of the key things about Spark: it's a good tool because of what you can do with it, but especially because of what you *don't have to do* with it. Spark provides a powerful API (*application programming interface*, the set of functions, classes, and variables provided for you to interact with) that makes it look like you're working with a cohesive source of data while also working hard in the background to optimize your program to use all the power available. You don't have to be an expert in the arcane art of distributed computing; you just need to be familiar with the language you'll use to build your program.

1.1.2 PySpark = Spark + Python

PySpark provides an entry point to Python in the computational model of Spark. Spark itself is coded in Scala.[2] The authors did a great job of providing a coherent interface between languages while preserving the idiosyncrasies of each language where appropriate. It will, therefore, be quite easy for a Scala/Spark programmer to read your PySpark program, as well as for a fellow Python programmer who hasn't jumped into the deep end (yet).

Python is a dynamic, general-purpose language, available on many platforms and for a variety of tasks. Its versatility and expressiveness make it an especially good fit for PySpark. The language is one of the most popular for a variety of domains, and currently it is a major force in data analysis and science. The syntax is easy to learn and read, and the number of libraries available means that you'll often find one (or more!) that's just the right fit for your problem.

PySpark provides access not only to the core Spark API but also to a set of bespoke functionality to scale out regular Python code, as well as pandas transformations. In Python's data analysis ecosystem, pandas is the de facto data frame library for memory-bound data frames (the entire data frame needs to reside on a single machine's memory). It's not a matter of PySpark or pandas now, but PySpark *and* pandas. Chapters 8 and 9 are dedicated to combining Python, pandas, and PySpark in one

---

[1] It can be a fun probability exercise to compute, but I will try to keep the math to a minimum.

[2] Databricks, the company behind Spark, has a project called Photon, which is a rewrite of the Spark execution engine in C++.

happy program. For those really committed to the pandas syntax (or if you have a large pandas program you want to scale to PySpark), Koalas (now called `pyspark.pandas` and part of Spark as of version 3.2.0; https://koalas.readthedocs.io/) provides a pandas-like porcelain on top of PySpark. If you are starting a new Spark program in Python, I recommend using the PySpark syntax—covered thoroughly in this book—reserving Koalas for when you want to ease the transition from pandas to PySpark. Your program will work faster and, in my opinion, will read better.

1.1.3   Why PySpark?

There is no shortage of libraries and frameworks to work with data. Why should one spend their time learning PySpark specifically?

PySpark has a lot of advantages for modern data workloads. It sits at the intersection of fast, expressive, and versatile. This section covers the many advantages of PySpark, why its value proposition goes beyond just "Spark, with Python," and when it is better to reach for another tool.

PySpark is fast

If you search for "big data" in a search engine, there is a very good chance that Hadoop will come up within the first few results. There is a good reason for this: Hadoop popularized the famous *MapReduce* framework that Google pioneered in 2004 and inspired how data is processed at scale (we touch on MapReduce in chapter 8, when talking about PySpark's low-level data structure, the resilient distributed data set).

Spark was created a few years later, sitting on Hadoop's incredible legacy. With an aggressive query optimizer, a judicious usage of RAM (reducing disk I/O; see chapter 11), and some other improvements we'll touch on in the next chapters, Spark can run up to 100 times faster than plain Hadoop. Because of the integration between the two frameworks, you can easily switch your Hadoop workflow to Spark and gain some performance boost without changing your hardware.[3]

PySpark is expressive

Beyond Python being one of the most popular and easy-to-learn languages, PySpark's API has been designed from the ground up to be easy to understand. PySpark borrows and extends the vocabulary for data manipulation from SQL. It does so in a *fluent* manner: each operation on a data frame returns a "new" data frame, so you can chain operations one after the other. Although we are just in the early stages of learning PySpark, listing 1.1 shows how readable, well-crafted PySpark looks. Even with no prior knowledge, the vocabulary choices and the consistency of the syntax makes it read like prose. We read a CSV file, create a new column that contains a value conditional to an *old column*, *filter* (using `where`), group by the values of the column, generate the count for each group, and finally write the results back to a CSV file. All these methods are covered throughout part 1 of the book, but we can already deduce what this code is doing.

---

[3]   As always, the standard disclaimer applies: not every Hadoop job will get faster in Spark. Your mileage may vary. Always test your job before making large architectural changes.

Listing 1.1 Simple ETL pipeline showing expressiveness of PySpark

```
(
    spark.read.csv("./data/list_of_numbers/sample.csv", header=True)
    .withColumn(
        "new_column", F.when(F.col("old_column") > 10, 10).otherwise(0)
    )
    .where("old_column > 8")
    .groupby("new_column")
    .count()
    .write.csv("updated_frequencies.csv", mode="overwrite")
)
```

Under the hood, Spark optimizes these operations so that we don't get an intermediate data frame after each method. Because of this, we can program our data transformation code in a very succinct and self-describing way, relying on Spark to optimize the end results—a programmer's comfort at its finest.

You will see many (more complex!) examples throughout this book. As I was writing the examples, I was pleased about how close to my initial (pen-and-paper) reasoning the code ended up looking. After understanding the fundamentals of the framework, I'm confident you'll be in the same situation.

PYSPARK IS VERSATILE

A key advantage of PySpark is its versatility: you learn one tool and use it in a variety of settings. There are two components to this versatility. First, there is the *availability* of the framework. Second, there is the diversified *ecosystem* surrounding Spark.

PySpark is everywhere. All three major cloud providers (Amazon Web Services [AWS], Google Cloud Platform [GCP], Microsoft Azure) have a managed Spark cluster as part of their offerings, which means you have a fully provisioned cluster at the click of a few buttons. You can also easily install Spark on your computer to nail down your program before scaling on a more powerful cluster. Appendix B covers how to get your local Spark running and succinctly walks you through the current main cloud offerings.

PySpark is open source. Unlike other analytical software, you aren't tied to a single company. You can inspect the source code if you're curious and even contribute if you have an idea for new functionality or find a bug. It also gives a low barrier to adoption: download, learn, profit!

Finally, Spark's ecosystem doesn't stop at PySpark. There is also an API for Scala, Java, and R, as well as a state-of-the-art SQL layer. This makes it easy to write a polyglot program in Spark. A Java software engineer can tackle the data transformation pipeline in Spark using Java, while a data scientist can build a model using PySpark.

WHERE PYSPARK FALLS SHORT

It would be awesome if PySpark was the answer to every data problem. Unfortunately, there are some caveats. None of them are deal breakers, but they are to be considered when you're selecting a tool for your next project.

PySpark isn't the right choice if you're dealing with rapid processing of (very) small data sets. Executing a program on multiple machines requires a level of coordination between the nodes, which comes with some overhead. If you're just using a single node, you're paying the price but aren't using the benefits. As an example, a PySpark shell will take a few seconds to launch; this is often more than enough time to process data that fits within your RAM. As new PySpark versions get released, though, this small data set performance gap gets narrower and narrower.

PySpark also has a small disadvantage compared to the Java and Scala API. Since Spark is at the core of a Scala program, pure Python code has to be translated to and from JVM (Java Virtual Machine, the runtime that powers Java and Scala code) instructions. Since the `DataFrame` API is available with PySpark, the differences between languages have been narrowed significantly: data frame operations are mapped to highly efficient Spark operations that work at the same speed, whether your program is written in Scala, Java, or Python. You will still witness slower operations when you're using the resilient distributed data set (RDD) data structure or when you define your Python user-defined functions. This does not mean that we will avoid them: I cover both topics in chapter 8.

Finally, while programming PySpark can feel straightforward, managing a cluster can be a little arcane. Spark is a pretty complicated piece of software; while the code base matured remarkably over the past few years, we are not yet to the point that we can manage a 100-machine cluster as easily as a single node. Understanding how Spark is configured and tuning for performance is introduced in chapter 11, and cloud options are making it easier than ever (see appendix B). For hairier problems, do what I do: befriend your operations team.

This section provided the *why* of PySpark, but also some *why not*, as knowing where and when to use PySpark is key to having a great development experience and processing performance. In the next section, we delve a little deeper into how Spark processes data and makes distributed data processing look like you're controlling a single factory.

1.2 *Your very own factory: How PySpark works*

In this section, we cover how Spark processes a program. It can be a little odd to present the workings and underpinnings of a system that we claimed, a few paragraphs ago, hides that complexity. Still, it is important to have a working knowledge of how Spark is set up, how it manages data, and how it optimizes queries. With this, you will be able to reason with the system, improve your code, and figure out quickly when it doesn't perform the way you want.

If we keep the factory analogy, we can imagine that the cluster of computers Spark is sitting on is the building. If we look at figure 1.1, we can see two different ways to interpret a data factory. On the left, we see how it looks from the outside: a cohesive unit where projects come in and results come out. This is how it will appear to you most of the time. Under the hood, it looks more like what's on the right: you have some workbenches that some workers are assigned to. The workbenches are like the computers

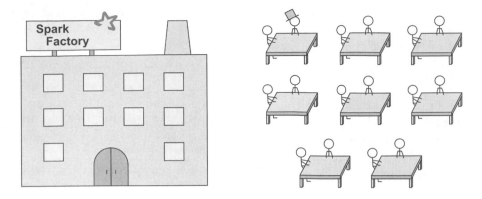

Figure 1.1 A totally relatable data factory, outside and in. Ninety percent of the time we care about the whole factory, but knowing how it's laid out helps when reflecting on our code performance.

in our Spark cluster: there is a fixed amount of them. Some modern Spark implementations, such as Databricks (see appendix B), allow for auto-scaling the number of machines at runtime. Some require more planning, especially if you run on the premises and own your hardware. The workers are called *executors* in Spark's literature: they perform the actual work on the machines/nodes.

One of the little workers looks spiffier than the other. That top hat definitely makes him stand out from the crowd. In our data factory, he's the manager of the work floor. In Spark terms, we call this the *master*.[4] The master here sits on one of the workbenches/machines, but it can also sit on a distinct machine (or even your computer!) depending on the cluster manager and deployment mode. The role of the master is crucial to the efficient execution of your program, so section 1.2.2 is dedicated to this.

> **TIP** In the cloud, you can have a *high-availability* cluster, meaning that your master will be replicated on more than one machine.

1.2.1 *Some physical planning with the cluster manager*

Upon reception of the task, which is called a *driver program* in the Spark world, the factory starts running. This doesn't mean that we get straight to processing. Before that, the cluster needs to *plan the capacity* it will allocate for your program. The entity or program taking care of this is aptly called the *cluster manager*. In our factory, this cluster manager will look at the workbenches with available space and secure as many as necessary, and then start hiring workers to fill the capacity. In Spark, it will look at the machines with available computing resources and secure what's necessary before launching the required number of executors across them.

---

4 The term *master* is getting phased out. The replacement has not been decided, but you can follow the conversation here: https://issues.apache.org/jira/browse/SPARK-32333.

NOTE   Spark provides its own cluster manager, called Standalone, but can also play well with other ones when working in conjunction with Hadoop or another big data platform. If you read about YARN, Mesos, or Kubernetes in the wild, know that they are used (as far as Spark is concerned) as cluster managers.

Any directions about capacity (machines and executors) are encoded in a Spark-Context representing the connection to our Spark cluster. If our instructions don't mention any specific capacity, the cluster manager will allocate the default capacity prescribed by our Spark installation.

As an example, let's try the following operation. Using the same sample.csv file in listing 1.1 (available in the book's repository), let's compute a simplified version of the program: return the arithmetic average of the values of old_column. Let's assume that our Spark instance has four executors, each working on its own worker node. The data processing will be approximately split between the four executors: each will have a small portion of the data frame that it will work with.

Listing 1.2   Content of the sample.csv` file

```
less data/list_of_numbers/sample.csv


old_column
1
4
4
5
7
7
7
10
14
1
4
8
```

Figure 1.2 depicts one way that PySpark could process the average of our old_column in our small data frame. I chose the average because it is not trivially distributable, unlike the sum or the count, where you sum the intermediate values from each worker. In the case of computing the average, each worker independently computes the sum of the values and their counts before moving the result—not all the data!— over to a single worker (or the master directly, when the intermediate result is really small) that will process the aggregation into a single number, the average.

For a simple example like this, mapping the thought process of PySpark is an easy and fun exercise. The size of our data and the complexity of our programs will grow and will get more complicated, and we will not be able to easily map our code to exact physical steps performed by our Spark instance. Chapter 11 covers the mechanism Spark uses to give us visibility into the work performed as well as the health of our factory.

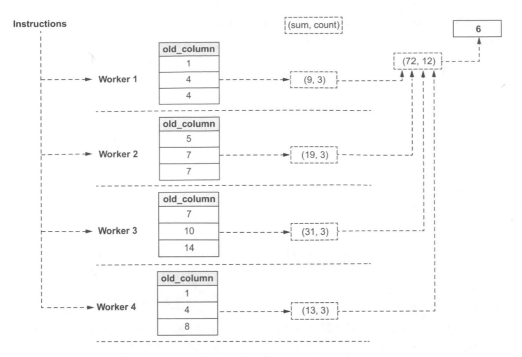

Each worker has a sample of the data and performs an intermediate step to get the sum and the count of each chunk (or partition) of the data frame.

The intermediate data, much smaller than the original data frame, is then sent to a single worker for further reduction.

We finally get our desired answer. Spark effectively hides the complexity of efficiently distributing the computation across nodes. We get our average, no fuss.

Figure 1.2   Computing the average of our small data frame, PySpark style: each worker works on a distinct piece of data. As necessary, the data gets moved/shuffled around to complete the instructions.

This section took a simple example—computing the average of a data frame of numbers—and we mapped a blueprint of the physical steps performed by Spark to give us the right answer. In the next section, we get to one of Spark's best, and most misunderstood, features: laziness. In the case of big data analysis, hard work pays off, but smart work is better!

Some language convention: Data frame vs. DataFrame

Since this book will talk about data frames more than anything else, I prefer using the noncapitalized nomenclature (i.e., "data frame"). I find this more readable than using capital letters or even "dataframe" without a space.

When referring to the PySpark object directly, I'll use `DataFrame` but with a fixed-width font. This will help differentiate between "data frame" the concept and `DataFrame` the object.

1.2.2   *A factory made efficient through a lazy leader*

This section introduces one of the most fundamental aspects of Spark: its lazy evaluation capabilities. In my time teaching PySpark and troubleshooting data scientists' programs, I would say that laziness is the concept in Spark that creates the most confusion. It's a real shame because laziness is (in part) how Spark achieves its incredible processing speed. By understanding at a high level how Spark makes laziness work, you will be able to explain a lot of its behavior and better tune for performance.

Just like in a large-scale factory, you don't go to each employee and give them a list of tasks. No, here, the master/manager is responsible for the workers. The driver is where the action happens. Think of a driver as a floor lead: you provide them your list of steps and let them deal with it. In Spark, the driver/floor lead takes your instructions (carefully written in Python code), translates them into Spark steps, and then processes them across the worker. The driver also manages which worker/table has which slice of the data, and makes sure you don't lose some bits in the process. The executor/factory worker sits atop the workers/tables and performs the actual work on the data.

As a summary:

- The master is like the factory owner, allocating resources as needed to complete the jobs.
- The driver is responsible for completing a given job. It requests resources from the master as needed.
- A worker is a set of computing/memory resources, like a workbench in our factory.
- Executors sit atop a worker and perform the work sent by the driver, like employees at a workbench.

We'll review the terminology in practice in chapter 11.

Taking the example of listing 1.1 and breaking each instruction one by one, PySpark won't start performing the work until the `write` instruction. If you use regular Python or a pandas data frame, which are not lazy (we call this *eager* evaluation), each instruction is performed one by one as it's being read.

Your floor lead/driver has all the qualities a good manager has: it's smart, cautious, and lazy. Wait, what? You read me right. *Laziness* in a programming context—and, one could argue, in the real world too—can be a very good thing. Every instruction you're providing in Spark can be classified into two categories: transformations and actions. *Actions* are what many programming languages would consider I/O. The most typical actions are the following:

- Printing information on the screen
- Writing data to a hard drive or cloud bucket
- Counting the number of records

In Spark, we'll see those instructions most often via the `show()`, `write()`, and `count()` methods on a data frame.

PySpark does not evaluate all data transformations (including reading data). A variable containing a series of data frame transformations will return almost immediately, as no data work is being performed.

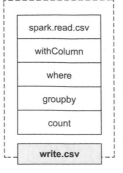

write.csv explicitly writes data to disk. An operation where PySpark actually writes or shows data is called an action and triggers the actual data work. No action, no visible result, no work. That's laziness!

Figure 1.3   Breaking down the data frame instructions as a series of transformations and one action. Each "job" Spark will perform consists of zero or more transformations and one action.

Transformations are pretty much everything else. Some examples of transformations are as follows:

- Adding a column to a table
- Performing an aggregation according to certain keys
- Computing summary statistics
- Training a machine learning model

Why the distinction, you might ask? When thinking about computation over data, you, as the developer, are only concerned about the computation leading to an action. You'll always interact with the results of an action because this is something you can see. Spark, with its lazy computation model, will take this to the extreme and avoid performing data work until an action triggers the computation chain. Before that, the driver will store your instructions. This way of dealing with computation has many benefits when dealing with large-scale data.

> **NOTE**   As we see in chapter 5, count() is a transformation when applied as an aggregation function (where it counts the number of records of each group) but an action when applied on a data frame (where it counts the number of records in a data frame).

First, storing instructions in memory takes much less space than storing intermediate data results. If you are performing many operations on a data set and are materializing the data each step of the way, you'll blow your storage much faster, although you don't need the intermediate results. We can all agree that less waste is better.

Second, by having the full list of tasks to be performed available, the driver can optimize the work between executors much more efficiently. It can use the information available at run time, such as the node where specific parts of the data are located. It can also reorder, eliminate useless transformations, combine multiple operations, and rewrite some portion of the program more effectively, if necessary.

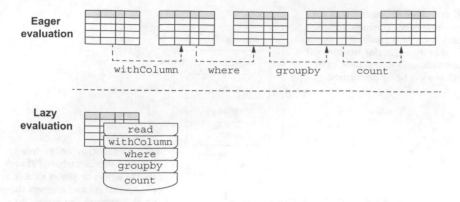

Figure 1.4   Eager versus lazy evaluation: storing (and computing on the fly) transformation saves memory by reducing the need for intermediate data frames. It also makes it easier to recreate the data frame if one of the nodes fails.

Third, should one node fail during processing—computers fail!—Spark will be able to recreate the missing chunks of data since it has the instructions cached. It'll read the relevant chunk of data and process it up to where you are without the need for you to do anything. With this, you can focus on the data-processing aspect of your code, off-loading the disaster and recovery part to Spark. Check out chapter 11 for more information about compute and memory resources, and how to monitor for failures.

Finally, during interactive development, you don't have to submit a huge block of commands and wait for the computation to happen. Instead, you can iteratively build your chain of transformation, one at a time, and when you're ready to launch the computation, you can add an action and let Spark work its magic.

Lazy computation is a fundamental aspect of Spark's operating model and part of the reason it's so fast. Most programming languages, including Python, R, and Java, are eagerly evaluated. This means that they process instructions as soon as they receive them. With PySpark, you get to use an eager language—Python—with a lazy framework—Spark. This can look a little foreign and intimidating, but you don't need to worry. The best way to learn is by doing, and this book provides explicit examples of laziness when relevant. You'll be a lazy pro in no time!

One aspect to remember is that Spark will not preserve the results of actions (or the intermediate data frames) for subsequent computations. If you submit the same program twice, PySpark will process the data twice. We use caching to change this behavior and optimize certain hot spots in our code (most noticeably when training an ML model), and chapter 11 provides you with how and when to cache (spoiler: not as often as you'd think).

NOTE   Reading data, although being I/O, is considered a transformation by Spark. In most cases, reading data doesn't perform any visible work for the user. You, therefore, won't read data until you need to perform some work on it (writing, reading, inferring schema; see chapter 6 for more information).

What's a manager without competent employees? Once the task, with its action, has been received, the driver starts allocating data to what Spark calls *executors*. Executors are processes that run computations and store data for the application. Those executors sit on what's called a *worker node*, which is the actual computer. In our factory analogy, an executor is an employee performing the work, while the worker node is a workbench where many employees/executors can work.

That concludes our factory tour. Let's summarize our typical PySpark program:

- We first encode our instructions in Python code, forming a driver program.
- When submitting our program (or launching a PySpark shell), the cluster manager allocates resources for us to use. Those will mostly stay constant (with the exception of auto-scaling) for the duration of the program.
- The driver ingests your code and translates it into Spark instructions. Those instructions are either transformations or actions.
- Once the driver reaches an action, it optimizes the whole computation chain and splits the work between executors. Executors are processes performing the actual data work, and they reside on machines labeled worker nodes.

That's it! As we can see, the overall process is quite simple, but it's obvious that Spark hides a lot of the complexity that arises from efficient distributed processing. For a developer, this means shorter and clearer code, and a faster development cycle.

1.3 What will you learn in this book?

This book will use PySpark to solve a variety of tasks that a data analyst, engineer, or scientist will encounter during their day-to-day life. We will therefore

- Read and write data from (and to) a variety of sources and formats
- Deal with messy data with PySpark's data manipulation functionality
- Discover new data sets and perform exploratory data analysis
- Build data pipelines that transform, summarize, and get insights from data in an automated fashion
- Troubleshoot common PySpark errors and how to recover from them and avoid them in the first place

After covering those fundamentals, we'll also tackle different tasks that aren't as frequent but are interesting and excellent ways to showcase the power and versatility of PySpark:

- We'll build machine learning models, from simple throwaway experiments to robust ML pipelines.
- We'll work with multiple data formats, from text to tabular to JSON.
- We'll seamlessly blend Python, pandas, and PySpark code, leveraging the strengths of each, and most importantly will scale pandas code to new territories.

We are trying to cater to many potential readers but are focusing on people with little to no exposure to Spark and/or PySpark. More seasoned practitioners might find useful analogies for when they need to explain difficult concepts and maybe learn a thing or two!

1.4 *What do I need to get started?*

The book focuses on Spark version 3.2, which is the most recent. The data frame made its appearance in Spark 1.3, so some code will work on Spark versions as old as this one. For this book, to avoid any headaches, I recommend you use Spark version 3.0 or later; if impossible, aim for the most recent version available to you.

We're assuming some basic Python knowledge; some useful concepts are outlined in appendix C. If you want a more in-depth introduction to Python, I recommend *The Quick Python Book*, by Naomi Ceder (Manning, 2018; https://www.manning.com/books/the-quick-python-book-third-edition), or *Python Workout*, by Reuven M. Lerner (Manning, 2020; https://www.manning.com/books/python-workout).

To get started, the only thing required is a working installation of Spark. It can either be on your computer or on a cloud provider (see appendix B). Most examples in the book are doable using a local installation of Spark, but some may require more horsepower and will be identified as such.

A code editor will also be very useful for writing, reading, and editing scripts as you go through the examples and craft your programs. A Python-aware editor, such as PyCharm, VS Code, or even Emacs/Vim, is nice to have but is in no way necessary. All the examples will work with Jupyter as well; check out appendix B to set up your notebook environment.

The book's code examples are available on GitHub (http://mng.bz/6ZOR), so Git will be a useful piece of software to have. If you don't know Git or don't have it handy, GitHub provides a way to download all the book's code in a zip file. Make sure you check regularly for updates!

Finally, I recommend that you have an analog way of drafting your code and schema. I am a compulsive notetaker and doodler, and even if my drawings are very basic and crude, I find that working through a new piece of software via drawings helps in clarifying my thoughts. This means rewriting less code and a happier programmer! Nothing spiffy is required: some scrap paper and a pencil will do wonders.

Summary

- PySpark is the Python API for Spark, a distributed framework for large-scale data analysis. It provides the expressiveness and dynamism of the Python programming language to Spark.
- Spark is fast: it owes its speed to a judicious usage of the RAM available and an aggressive and lazy query optimizer.
- You can use Spark in Python, Scala, Java, R, and more. You can also use SQL for data manipulation.
- Spark uses a driver that processes the instructions and orchestrates the work. The executors receive the instructions from the master and perform the work.
- All instructions in PySpark are either transformations or actions. Because Spark is lazy, only actions will trigger the computation of a chain of instructions.

Part 1

Get acquainted: First steps in PySpark

When working with a new technology, the best way to get familiar with it is to jump right in, building our intuition along the way. This first part succinctly introduces PySpark before going over two distinct use cases.

Chapter 1 introduces the technology and the computing model that power Spark.

Then, in chapters 2 and 3, we build a simple end-to-end program and learn how to structure PySpark code in a readable and intuitive fashion. We go from the data ingestion of text data to processing, to the presentation of the results, and, finally, to submitting the program in a noninteractive fashion.

Chapters 4 and 5 look at working with tabular data, the most frequently used type of data. We build on the foundation from the previous chapters (already!) to manipulate structured data to our will. At the end of part 1, you should feel comfortable about writing your own simple programs from start to finish!

Your first data
program in PySpark

This chapter covers

- Launching and using the `pyspark` shell for interactive development
- Reading and ingesting data into a data frame
- Exploring data using the `DataFrame` structure
- Selecting columns using the `select()` method
- Reshaping single-nested data into distinct records using `explode()`
- Applying simple functions to your columns to modify the data they contain
- Filtering columns using the `where()` method

Data-driven applications, no matter how complex, all boil down to what we can think of as three meta steps, which are easy to distinguish in a program:

1 We start by *loading* or reading the data we wish to work with.

2 We *transform* the data, either via a few simple instructions or a very complex machine learning model.

3 We then *export* (or *sink*) the resulting data, either into a file or by summarizing our findings into a visualization.

The next two chapters will introduce a basic workflow with PySpark via the creation of a simple ETL (*extract, transform, and load,* which is a more business-speak way of saying *ingest, transform, and export*). You will find these three simple steps repeated in every program we build in this book, from a simple summary to the most complex ML model. We will spend most of our time in the `pyspark` shell, interactively building our program one step at a time. Just like normal Python development, using the shell or REPL (I'll use the terms interchangeably) provides rapid feedback and quick progression. Once we are comfortable with the results, we will wrap our program so we can submit it in batch mode.

> **NOTE**   REPL stands for *read, evaluate, print, and loop.* In the case of Python, it represents the interactive prompt in which we input commands and read results.

Data manipulation is the most basic and important aspect of any data-driven program, and PySpark puts a lot of focus on this. It serves as the foundation of any reporting, machine learning, or data science exercise we wish to perform. This section gives you the tools to not only use PySpark to manipulate data at scale but also to think in terms of data transformation. We obviously can't cover every function provided in PySpark, but I provide a good explanation of the ones we use. I also introduce how to use the shell as a friendly reminder for those cases when you forget how something works.

Since this is your first end-to-end program in PySpark, we get our feet wet with a simple problem to solve: What are the most popular words used in the English language? Since collecting all the material ever produced in the English language would be a massive undertaking, we start with a very small sample: *Pride and Prejudice,* by Jane Austen. We first make our program work with this small sample and then scale it to ingest a larger corpus of text. I use this principle—starting with a sample of the data locally to get the structure and concepts right—when building a new program; when working in a cloud environment, this means less cost when exploring. Once I am confident about the flow of my program, I go all nodes blazing on the full data set.

Since this is our first program, and I need to introduce many new concepts, this chapter will focus on the data manipulation part of the program. Chapter 3 will cover the final computation, as well as wrapping our program and then scaling it.

> **TIP**   The book repository contains the code and data used for the examples and exercises. It is available online at http://mng.bz/6ZOR.

2.1   *Setting up the PySpark shell*

Python provides a REPL for interactive development. Since PySpark is a Python library, it also uses the same environment. It speeds up your development process by giving instantaneous feedback the moment you submit an instruction instead of forcing you to compile your program and submit it as one big monolithic block. I'll even say that using a REPL is even more useful in PySpark, since every operation can take a fair amount of time. Having a program crash midway is always frustrating, but it's even worse when you've been running a data-intensive job for a few hours.

For this chapter (and the rest of the book), I assume that you have access to a working installation of Spark, either locally or in the cloud. If you want to perform the installation yourself, appendix B contains step-by-step instructions for Linux, macOS, and Windows. If you can't install it on your computer, or prefer not to, the same appendix also provides a few cloud-powered options.

Once everything is set up, the easiest way to ensure that everything is running is by launching the PySpark shell by inputting pyspark into your terminal. You should see an ASCII-art version of the Spark logo, as well as some useful information. Listing 2.1 shows what happens on my local machine. In section 2.1.1, you'll find a less magical alternative to running pyspark as a command that will help you with integrating PySpark into an existing Python REPL.

Listing 2.1   Launching pyspark on a local machine

```
$ pyspark
```
When using PySpark locally, you most often won't have a full Hadoop cluster preconfigured. For learning purposes, this is perfectly fine.

```
Python 3.8.8 | packaged by conda-forge | (default, Feb 20 2021, 15:50:57)
[Clang 11.0.1 ] on darwin
Type "help", "copyright", "credits" or "license" for more information.
21/08/23 07:28:16 WARN Utils: Your hostname, gyarados-2.local resolves to a
    loopback address: 127.0.0.1; using 192.168.2.101 instead (on interface en0)
21/08/23 07:28:16 WARN Utils: Set SPARK_LOCAL_IP if you need to bind to another
    address
21/08/23 07:28:17 WARN NativeCodeLoader: Unable to load native-hadoop library
    for your platform... using builtin-java classes where applicable
Using Spark's default log4j profile: org/apache/spark/log4j-defaults.properties
Setting default log level to "WARN".
To adjust logging level use sc.setLogLevel(newLevel). For SparkR, use
    setLogLevel(newLevel).
Welcome to
```

Spark is indicating the level of details it'll provide to you. We will see how to configure this in section 2.1.2.

```
      ____              __
     / __/__  ___ _____/ /__
    _\ \/ _ \/ _ `/ __/  '_/
   /__ / .__/\_,_/_/ /_/\_\   version 3.2.0
      /_/
```

We are using Spark version 3.2.0.

The Spark UI is available at this address (check chapter 11 on how to use it efficiently).

```
Using Python version 3.8.8 (default, Feb 20 2021 15:50:57)
Spark context Web UI available at http:/ /192.168.2.101:4040
Spark context available as 'sc' (master = local[*], app id = local-
    1629718098205).
SparkSession available as 'spark'.

+In [1]:
```

The REPL is now ready for your input!

The pyspark shell provides an entry point for you through the variables spark and sc. More on this insection 2.1.1.

PySpark is using the Python available on your path. This will display the Python version on the master node. Since we are working locally, this is the Python installed on my machine.

No IPython? No problem!

I highly recommend you use IPython when using PySpark in interactive mode. IPython is a better frontend to the Python shell, with many useful functionalities, such as friendlier copy-and-paste and syntax highlighting. The installation instructions in appendix B include configuring PySpark to use the IPython shell.

If you don't use the IPython REPL, you will see something like this:

```
Using Python version 3.9.4 (default, Apr  5 2021 01:47:16)
Spark context Web UI available at http://192.168.0.12:4040
Spark context available as 'sc' (master = local[*], app id = local-
          1619348090080).
SparkSession available as 'spark'.
>>>
```

Appendix B also provides instructions for how to use PySpark with a Jupyter notebook interface if you prefer this user experience. In the cloud—for instance, when using Databricks—you'll most often be provided with the option to use a notebook by default.

The pyspark program provides quick and easy access to a Python REPL with PySpark preconfigured: in the last two lines of listing 2.1, we see that the variables spark and sc are preconfigured. When using my favorite code editor, I usually prefer to start with a regular python/IPython shell and add a Spark instance from said shell, like in appendix B. In the next section, we explore spark and sc as the entry points of a PySpark program by defining and instantiating them.

2.1.1 *The SparkSession entry point*

This section covers the SparkSession object and its role as the entry point to PySpark's functionality within a program. Knowing how it gets created and used removes some of the magic of getting PySpark set up. I also explain how to connect PySpark within an existing REPL, simplifying integration with Python IDEs and tooling.

   If you have a pyspark shell already launched, exit() (or Ctrl-D) will get you back to your regular terminal. Launch a python (or better yet, an ipython) shell and input the code in listing 2.2; we create the spark object by hand. This makes it very explicit that PySpark is used as a Python library and not as a separate tool. It becomes easy to mix and blend Python libraries with PySpark when you start with a Python REPL. Chapter 8 and 9 are focused on integrating Python and pandas code within PySpark's data frame.

   PySpark uses a builder pattern through the SparkSession.builder object. For those familiar with object-oriented programming, a builder pattern provides a set of methods to create a highly configurable object without having multiple constructors. In this chapter, we will only look at the happiest case, but the SparkSession builder pattern will become increasingly useful in parts 2 and 3 as we look into cluster configuration and adding dependencies to our jobs.

In listing 2.2, we start the builder pattern and then chain a configuration parameter that defined the application name. This isn't necessary, but when monitoring your jobs (see chapter 11), having a unique and well-thought-out job name will make it easier to know what's what. We finish the builder pattern with the `.getOrCreate()` method to materialize and instantiate our SparkSession.

Listing 2.2 Creating a `SparkSession` entry point from scratch

```
from pyspark.sql import SparkSession

spark = (SparkSession
         .builder
         .appName("Analyzing the vocabulary of Pride and Prejudice.")
         .getOrCreate())
```

The SparkSession entry point is located in the pyspark.sql package, providing the functionality for data transformation.

Providing a relevant appName helps in identifying which programs run on your Spark cluster (see chapter 11).

PySpark provides a builder pattern abstraction for constructing a SparkSession, where we chain the methods to configure the entry point.

NOTE By using the `getOrCreate()` method, your program will work in both interactive and batch mode by avoiding the creation of a new `SparkSession` if one already exists. Note that if a session already exists, you won't be able to change certain configuration settings (mostly related to JVM options). If you need to change the configuration of your `SparkSession`, kill everything and start from scratch to avoid any confusion.

In chapter 1, we spoke briefly about the Spark entry point called `SparkContext`, which is the liaison between your Python REPL and the Spark cluster. `SparkSession` is a superset of that. It wraps the `SparkContext` and provides functionality for interacting with the Spark SQL API, which includes the data frame structure we'll use in most of our programs. Just to prove our point, see how easy it is to get to the `SparkContext` from our `SparkSession` object—just call the `sparkContext` attribute from spark:

```
$ spark.sparkContext
# <SparkContext master=local[*] appName=Analyzing the vocabulary of [...]>
```

The `SparkSession` object is a more recent addition to the PySpark API, making its way in version 2.0. This is due to the API evolving in a way that makes more room for the faster, more versatile data frame as the main data structure over the lower-level RDD. Before that time, you had to use another object (called the `SQLContext`) to use the data frame. It's much easier to have everything under a single umbrella.

This book will focus mostly on the data frame as our main data structure. I'll discuss the RDD in chapter 8 when we discuss lower-level PySpark programming and how to embed our Python functions in our programs. In the next section, I explain how we can use Spark to provide more (or less!) information about its underpinning via the log level.

Reading older PySpark code

While this book shows modern PySpark programming, we are not living in a vacuum. Online you might face older PySpark code that uses the former `SparkContext`/`sql-Context` combo. You'll also see the `sc` variable mapped to the `SparkContext` entry point. With what we know about `SparkSession` and `SparkContext`, we can reason about old PySpark code by using the following variable assignments:

```
sc = spark.sparkContext
sqlContext = spark
```

You'll see traces of `SQLContext` in the API documentation for backward compatibility. I recommend avoiding using this, as the new `SparkSession` approach is cleaner, simpler, and more future-proof.

If you are running `pyspark` from the command line, all of this is defined for you, as seen in listing 2.1.

2.1.2   *Configuring how chatty spark is: The log level*

This section covers the log level, probably the most overlooked (and annoying) element of a PySpark program. Monitoring your PySpark jobs is an important part of developing a robust program. PySpark provides many levels of logging, from nothing at all to a full description of everything happening on the cluster. The `pyspark` shell defaults on `WARN`, which can be a little chatty when we're learning. More importantly, a non-interactive PySpark program (which is how you'll run your scripts for the most part) defaults to the oversharing `INFO` level. Fortunately, we can change the settings for your session by using the code in the next listing.

Listing 2.3   Deciding how chatty you want PySpark to be

```
spark.sparkContext.setLogLevel("KEYWORD")
```

Table 2.1 lists the available keywords you can pass to `setLogLevel` (as strings). Each subsequent keyword contains all the previous ones, with the obvious exception of `OFF`, which doesn't show anything.

Table 2.1   Log-level keywords

Keyword	Signification
OFF	No logging at all (not recommended).
FATAL	Only fatal errors. A fatal error will crash your Spark cluster.
ERROR	Will show FATAL, as well as other recoverable errors.
WARN	Add warnings (and there are quite a lot of them).
INFO	Will give you runtime information, such as repartitioning and data recovery (see chapter 1).

Table 2.1 Log-level keywords *(continued)*

Keyword	Signification
DEBUG	Will provide debug information on your jobs.
TRACE	Will trace your jobs (more verbose debug logs). Can be quite informative but very annoying.
ALL	Everything that PySpark can spit, it will spit. As useful as OFF.

NOTE When using the pyspark shell, anything chattier than WARN might appear when you're typing a command, which makes it quite hard to input commands into the shell. You're welcome to play with the log levels as you please, but we won't show any output unless it's valuable for the task at hand. Setting the log level to ALL is a *very* good way to annoy oblivious coworkers if they don't lock their computers. You didn't hear this from me.

You now have the REPL fired up and ready for your input. This is enough housekeeping for now. Let's start planning our program and get coding!

2.2 Mapping our program

This section maps the blueprint of our simple program. Taking the time to design our data analysis beforehand pays dividends since we can construct our code knowing what's coming. This will eventually speed up our coding and improve the reliability and modularity of our code. Think of it like reading the recipe when cooking: you never want to realize you're missing a cup of flour when mixing the dough!

In this chapter's introduction, we introduced our problem statement: "What are the most popular words used in the English language?" Before we can even hammer out code in the REPL, we have to start by mapping the major steps our program will need to perform:

1 *Read*—Read the input data (we're assuming a plain text file).
2 *Token*—Tokenize each word.
3 *Clean*—Remove any punctuation and/or tokens that aren't words. Lowercase each word.
4 *Count*—Count the frequency of each word present in the text.
5 *Answer*—Return the top 10 (or 20, 50, 100).

Visually, a simplified flow of our program would look like figure 2.1.

Our goal is quite lofty: the English language has produced, throughout history, an unfathomable amount of written material. Since we are learning, we'll start with a relatively small source, get our program working, and then scale it to accommodate a larger body of text. For this, I chose to use Jane Austen's *Pride and Prejudice*, since it's already in plain text and freely available. In the next section, we ingest and explore our data to start building our program.

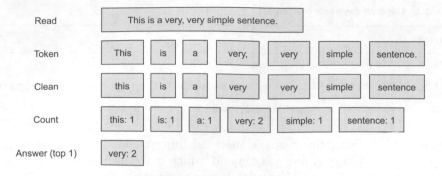

Read	This is a very, very simple sentence.

| Token | This | is | a | very, | very | simple | sentence. |

| Clean | this | is | a | very | very | simple | sentence |

| Count | this: 1 | is: 1 | a: 1 | very: 2 | simple: 1 | sentence: 1 |

| Answer (top 1) | very: 2 |

Figure 2.1   A simplified flow of our program, illustrating the five steps

Data analysis and Pareto's principle

Pareto's principle, also known as the 80/20 rule, is often summarized as "20% of the efforts will yield 80% of the results." In data analysis, we can consider that 20% to be analysis, visualization, or machine learning models, anything that provides tangible value to the recipient.

The remainder is what I call *invisible work*: ingesting the data, cleaning it, figuring out its meaning, and shaping it into a usable form. If you look at your simple steps, steps 1 to 3 can be considered invisible work: we're ingesting data and getting it ready for the counting process. Steps 4 and 5 are the visible ones that are answering our question (one could argue that only step 5 is performing visible work, but let's not split hairs here). Steps 1 to 3 are there because the data requires processing for it to be usable for our problem. The steps aren't core to our problem, but we can't do without them.

When building your project, this will be the part that will be the most time-consuming, and you might be tempted (or pressured!) to skimp on it. Always keep in mind that the data you ingest and process is the raw material of your programs, and that feeding it garbage will yield, well, garbage.

2.3   *Ingest and explore: Setting the stage for data transformation*

This section covers the three operations every PySpark program will encounter, regardless of the nature of your program: ingesting data into a structure, printing the structure (or *schema*) to see how the data is organized, and finally showing a sample of the data for review. Those operations are fundamental to any data analysis, whether it is text (this chapter and chapter 3), tabular (most chapters, but especially chapter 4 and 5), or even binary or hierarchical data (chapter 6); the general blueprint and methods will apply everywhere in your PySpark journey.

2.3.1 Reading data into a data frame with spark.read

The first step of our program is to ingest the data in a structure we can perform work in. This section introduces the basic functionality PySpark provides for reading data and how it is specialized for plain text.

Before ingesting any data, we need to choose where it's going to go. PySpark provides two main structures for storing data when performing manipulations:

- The RDD
- The data frame

The RDD was the only structure for a long time. It looks like a distributed collection of objects (or rows). I visualize this as a bag that you give orders to. You pass orders to the RDD through regular Python functions over the items in the bag.

The data frame is a stricter version of the RDD. Conceptually, you can think of it like a table, where each cell can contain one value. The data frame makes heavy usage of the concept of columns, where you operate on columns instead of on records, like in the RDD. Figure 2.2 provides a visual summary of the two structures. The data frame is now the dominant data structure, and we will almost exclusively use it in this book; chapter 8 covers the RDD (a more general and flexible structure, from which the data frame inherits) for cases that need record-by-record flexibility.

If you've used SQL in the past, you'll find that the data frame implementation takes a lot of inspiration from SQL. The module name for data organization and manipulation is even named `pyspark.sql`! Furthermore, chapter 7 teaches how to mix PySpark and SQL code within the same program.

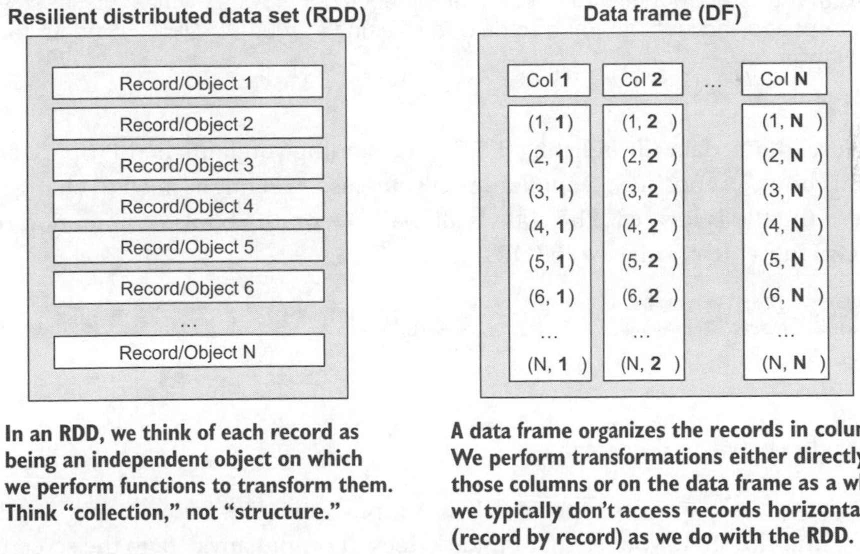

Resilient distributed data set (RDD)

| Record/Object 1 |
| Record/Object 2 |
| Record/Object 3 |
| Record/Object 4 |
| Record/Object 5 |
| Record/Object 6 |
| ... |
| Record/Object N |

Data frame (DF)

Col 1	Col 2	...	Col N
(1, 1)	(1, 2)		(1, N)
(2, 1)	(2, 2)		(2, N)
(3, 1)	(3, 2)		(3, N)
(4, 1)	(4, 2)		(4, N)
(5, 1)	(5, 2)		(5, N)
(6, 1)	(6, 2)		(6, N)
...	...		...
(N, 1)	(N, 2)		(N, N)

In an RDD, we think of each record as being an independent object on which we perform functions to transform them. Think "collection," not "structure."

A data frame organizes the records in columns. We perform transformations either directly on those columns or on the data frame as a whole; we typically don't access records horizontally (record by record) as we do with the RDD.

Figure 2.2 An RDD versus a data frame. In the RDD, we think of each record as an independent entity. With the data frame, we mostly interact with columns, performing functions on them. We still can access the rows of a data frame via RDD if necessary.

Reading data into a data frame is done through the `DataFrameReader` object, which we can access through `spark.read`. The code in listing 2.4 displays the object, as well as the methods it exposes. We recognize a few file formats: CSV stands for comma-separated values (which we'll use as early as chapter 4), JSON for JavaScript Object Notation (a popular data exchange format), and text is, well, just plain text.

Listing 2.4   The `DataFrameReader` object

```
In [3]: spark.read
Out[3]: <pyspark.sql.readwriter.DataFrameReader at 0x115be1b00>

In [4]: dir(spark.read)
Out[4]: [<some content removed>, _spark', 'csv', 'format', 'jdbc', 'json',
'load', 'option', 'options', 'orc', 'parquet', 'schema', 'table', 'text']
```

PySpark reads your data

PySpark can accommodate the different ways you can process data. Under the hood, `spark.read.csv()` will map to `spark.read.format('csv').load()`, and you may encounter this form in the wild. I usually prefer using the direct `csv` method as it provides a handy reminder of the different parameters the reader can take.

`orc` and `parquet` are also data formats that are especially well suited for big data processing. ORC (which stands for "optimized row columnar") and Parquet are competing data formats that pretty much serve the same purpose. Both are open sourced and now part of the Apache project, just like Spark.

PySpark defaults to using Parquet when reading and writing files, and we'll use this format to store our results throughout the book. I'll provide a longer discussion about the usage, advantages, and trade-offs of using Parquet or ORC as a data format in chapter 6.

Let's read our data file in listing 2.5. I am assuming you launched PySpark at the root of this book's repository. Depending on your case, you might need to change the path where the file is located. The code is all available on the book's companion repository on GitHub (http://mng.bz/6ZOR).

Listing 2.5   "Reading" our Jane Austen novel in record time

```
book = spark.read.text("./data/gutenberg_books/1342-0.txt")

book
# DataFrame[value: string]
```

We get a data frame, as expected! If you input your data frame, conveniently named book, into the shell, you see that PySpark doesn't output any data to the screen. Instead, it prints the schema, which is the name of the columns and their type. In PySpark's world, each column has a type: it represents how the value is represented by Spark's engine. By having the type attached to each column, you can instantly know what operations you can do on the data. With this information, you won't inadvertently try to add an integer to a string: PySpark won't let you add 1 to "blue." Here, we have one column, named `value`, composed of a `string`. A quick graphical representation of our data frame would look like figure 2.3: each line of text (separated by a newline character) is a record. Besides being a helpful reminder of the content of the data frame, types are integral to how Spark processes data quickly and accurately. We will explore the subject extensively in chapter 6.

Figure 2.3 A high-level logical schema of our `book` data frame, containing a `value` string column. We can see the name of the column, its type, and a small snippet of the data.

When working with data frames, we will most often worry about the logical schema, which is the organization of the data as if the data were on a single node. We use schemas to understand the data and its type (integer, string, date, etc.) for a given data frame. Spark displays the logical schema when we input the variable in the REPL: columns and types. In practice, your data frame will be distributed across multiple nodes, each one having a segment of the records. When performing data transformation and analysis, it is more convenient to work with the logical schema. Chapter 11 provides a deeper look into the logical versus physical world through *query planning*, which gives us insight into how Spark moves from high-level instruction to optimized machine instructions.

When working with a larger data frame (think hundreds or even thousands of columns), you may want to see the schema displayed more clearly. PySpark provides `printSchema()` to display the schema in a tree form. I use this method probably more than any other one as it gives you direct information on the structure of the data frame. Since `printSchema()` directly prints to the REPL with no other option, should you want to filter the schema, you can use the `dtypes` attributes of the data frame, which gives you a list of tuples (`column_name`, `column_type`). You can also access the schema programmatically (as a data structure) using the `schema` attribute (see chapter 6 for more information).

Listing 2.6 Printing the schema of our data frame

```
book.printSchema()

# root
#  |-- value: string (nullable = true)

print(book.dtypes)

# [('value', 'string')]
```

Each data frame tree starts with a root, which the columns are attached to.

We have one column value, containing strings that can be null (or None in Python terms).

The same information is stored as a list of tuples under the data frame's dtypes attribute.

In this section, we ingested our textual data into a data frame. This data frame inferred a simple columnar structure that we can explore through the variable name in the REPL, the printSchema() method, or the dtypes attribute. In the next section, we go beyond the structure to peek at the data inside.

> **Speeding up your learning by using the shell**
>
> Using the shell doesn't just apply to PySpark, but using its functionality can often save a lot of searching in the documentation. I am a big fan of using dir() on an object when I don't remember the exact method I want to apply, as I did in listing 2.4.
>
> PySpark's source code is very well documented. If you're unsure about the proper usage of a function, class, or method, you can print the __doc__ attribute or, for those using IPython, use a trailing question mark (or two, if you want more details).

Listing 2.7 Using PySpark's documentation directly in the REPL

```
# you can use `print(spark.__doc__)` if you don't have iPython.
In [292]: spark?
Type:        SparkSession
String form: <pyspark.sql.session.SparkSession object at 0x11231eb80>
File:        ~/miniforge3/envs/pyspark/lib/python3.8/site-
    packages/pyspark/sql/session.py
Docstring:
The entry point to programming Spark with the Dataset and DataFrame API.

A SparkSession can be used create :class:`DataFrame`, register
    :class:`DataFrame` as
tables, execute SQL over tables, cache tables, and read parquet files.
To create a SparkSession, use the following builder pattern:

.. autoattribute:: builder
    :annotation:

[... more content, examples]
```

2.3.2 *From structure to content: Exploring our data frame with show()*

One of the key advantages of using the REPL for interactive development is that you can peek at your work as you're performing it. Now that our data is loaded into a data frame, we can start looking at how PySpark structured our text. This section covers the most important method for looking at the data contained in a data frame, show().

In section 2.3.1, we saw that the default behavior of inputting a data frame in the shell is to provide the schema or column information of the object. While very useful, sometimes we want to take a peek at the data.

Enter the show() method, which displays a few rows of the data back to you—nothing more, nothing less. With printSchema(), this method will become one of your best friends when performing data exploration and validation. By default, it will show 20 rows and truncate long values. The code in listing 2.8 shows the default behavior of the method applied to our book data frame. For text data, the length limitation is limiting (pun intended). Fortunately, show() provides some options to display just what you need.

Listing 2.8   Showing a little data using the .show() method

```
book.show()
```

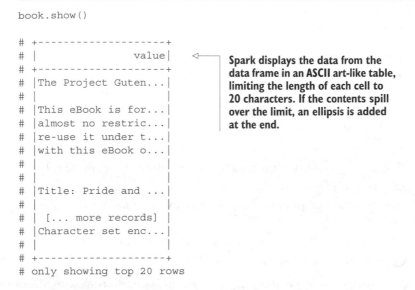

```
# +--------------------+
# |               value|
# +--------------------+
# |The Project Guten...|
# |                    |
# |This eBook is for...|
# |almost no restric...|
# |re-use it under t...|
# |with this eBook o...|
# |                    |
# |                    |
# |Title: Pride and ...|
# |                    |
# | [... more records] |
# |Character set enc...|
# |                    |
# +--------------------+
# only showing top 20 rows
```

Spark displays the data from the data frame in an ASCII art-like table, limiting the length of each cell to 20 characters. If the contents spill over the limit, an ellipsis is added at the end.

The show() method takes three optional parameters:

- n can be set to any positive integer and will display that number of rows.
- truncate, if set to true, will truncate the columns to display only 20 characters. Set to False, it will display the whole length, or any positive integer to truncate to a specific number of characters.
- vertical takes a Boolean value and, when set to True, will display each record as a small table. If you need to check records in detail, this is a very useful option.

The code in the next listing shows a more useful view of the book data frame, showing only 10 records but truncating them at 50 characters. We can see more of the text now!

Listing 2.9   Showing less length, more width with the show() method

```
book.show(10, truncate=50)

# +--------------------------------------------------+
# |                                             value|
# +--------------------------------------------------+
# |The Project Gutenberg EBook of Pride and Prejud...|
# |                                                  |
# |This eBook is for the use of anyone anywhere at...|
```

```
# |almost no restrictions whatsoever.  You may cop...|
# |re-use it under the terms of the Project Gutenb...|
# |    with this eBook or online at www.gutenberg.org|
# |                                                  |
# |                                                  |
# |                         Title: Pride and Prejudice|
# |                                                  |
# +--------------------------------------------------+
# only showing top 10 rows
```

Together, `show()` and `printSchema()` give you a complete overview of the structure and the content of the data frame. It's no surprise that those will be the methods you will reach for most often when building a data analysis at the REPL.

We can now start the real work: performing transformations on the data frame to accomplish our goal. Let's take some time to review the five steps we outlined at the beginning of the chapter:

1 **[DONE]** *Read*—Read the input data (we're assuming a plain text file).
2 *Token*—Tokenize each word.
3 *Clean*—Remove any punctuation and/or tokens that aren't words. Lowercase each word.
4 *Count*—Count the frequency of each word present in the text.
5 *Answer*—Return the top 10 (or 20, 50, 100).

In the next section, we start performing some simple column transformations to tokenize and clean the data. Our data frame will start changing right before our eyes!

Optional topic: Nonlazy Spark?

If you are coming from another data frame implementation, such as pandas or R `data.frame`, you might find it odd to see the structure of the data frame instead of a summary of the data when calling the variable. The `show()` method might be a nuisance to you.

If we take a step back and think about PySpark's use cases, it makes a lot of sense. `show()` is an action, since it performs the visible work of printing data on the screen. As savvy PySpark programmers, we want to avoid accidentally triggering the chain of computations, so the Spark developers made `show()` explicit. When building a complicated chain of transformations, triggering its execution is a lot more annoying and time-consuming than having to type the `show()` method when you're ready. This transformation-versus-action distinction also leads to more opportunities for the Spark optimizer to generate a more efficient program (see chapter 11).

That being said, there are some moments, especially when learning, when you want your data frames to be evaluated after each transformation (which we call *eager evaluation*). Since Spark 2.4.0, you can configure the `SparkSession` object to support printing to screen. We will cover how to create a `SparkSession` object in greater detail in chapter 3, but if you want to use eager evaluation in the shell, you can paste the following code in your shell:

```
from pyspark.sql import SparkSession

spark = (SparkSession.builder
                     .config("spark.sql.repl.eagerEval.enabled", "True")
                     .getOrCreate())
```

All the examples in the book assume that the data frames are evaluated lazily, but this option can be useful if you're demonstrating Spark. Use it as you see fit, but remember that Spark owes a lot of its performance to its lazy evaluation. You'll be leaving some extra horsepower on the table!

2.4 Simple column transformations: Moving from a sentence to a list of words

When ingesting our selected text into a data frame, PySpark created one record for each line of text and provided a value column of type String. To tokenize each word, we need to split each string into a list of distinct words. This section covers simple transformations using select(). We will split our lines of text into words so we can count them.

Because PySpark's code can be pretty self-explanatory, I start by providing the code in one fell swoop, and then we'll break down each step one at a time. You can see it in all its glory in the next listing.

Listing 2.10 Splitting our lines of text into arrays or words

```
from pyspark.sql.functions import split

lines = book.select(split(book.value, " ").alias("line"))

lines.show(5)

# +--------------------+
# |                line|
# +--------------------+
# |[The, Project, Gu...|
# |                  []|
# |[This, eBook, is,...|
# |[almost, no, rest...|
# |[re-use, it, unde...|
# +--------------------+
# only showing top 5 rows
```

In a single line of code (I don't count the import or the show(), which is only being used to display the result), we've done quite a lot. The remainder of this section will introduce basic column operations and explain how we can build our tokenization step as a one-liner. More specifically, we learn about the following:

- The select() method and its canonical usage, which is selecting data
- The alias() method to rename transformed columns
- Importing column functions from pyspark.sql.functions and using them

Although our example looks very specific (moving from a string to a list of words), the blueprint for using PySpark's transformation functions is very consistent: you'll see and use this pattern very frequently when transforming data frames.

2.4.1   *Selecting specific columns using select()*

This section will introduce the most basic functionality of `select()`, which is to select one or more columns from your data frame. It's a conceptually very simple method but provides the foundation for many additional operations on your data.

In PySpark's world, a data frame is made out of `Column` objects, and you perform transformations on them. The most basic transformation is the identity, where you return exactly what was provided to you. If you've used SQL in the past, you might think that this sounds like a `SELECT` statement, and you'd be right! You also get a free pass: the method name is also conveniently named `select()`.

We'll go over a quick example: selecting the only column of our `book` data frame. Since we already know the expected output, we can focus on the gymnastics for the `select()` method. The next listing provides the code for that very useful task.

> **Listing 2.11   The simplest select statement ever**

```
book.select(book.value)
```

PySpark provides for each column in its data frame a dot notation that refers to the column. This is the simplest way to select a column, as long as the name doesn't contain any funny characters: PySpark will accept `$!@#` as a column name, but you won't be able to use the dot notation for this column.

PySpark provides more than one way to select columns. I display the four most common in the next listing.

> **Listing 2.12   Selecting the `value` column from the `book` data frame**

```
from pyspark.sql.functions import col

book.select(book.value)
book.select(book["value"])
book.select(col("value"))
book.select("value")
```

The first way to select a column is the trusty dot notation we got acquainted with a few paragraphs ago. The second one uses brackets instead of the dot to name the column. It addresses the `$!@#` problem since you pass the name of the column as a string.

The third one uses the `col` function from the `pyspark.sql.functions` module. The main difference here is that you don't specify that the column comes from the `book` data frame. This will become very useful when working with more complex data pipelines in part 2 of the book. I'll use the `col` object as much as I can since I consider its usage more idiomatic and it'll prepare us for more complex use cases, such as performing column transformation (see chapter 4 and 5).

Finally, the fourth one only uses the name of the column as a string. PySpark is smart enough to infer that we mean a column here. For simple select statements (and other methods that I'll cover later), using the name of the column directly can be a viable option. That being said, it's not as flexible as the other options, and the moment your code requires column transformations, like in section 2.4.2, you'll have to use another option.

Now that we've selected our column, let's start working PySpark out. Up next is splitting the lines of text.

2.4.2 *Transforming columns: Splitting a string into a list of words*

We just saw a very simple way to select a column in PySpark. In this section, we build on this foundation by selecting a transformation of a column instead. This provides a powerful and flexible way to express our transformations, and as you'll see, this pattern will be frequently used when manipulating data.

PySpark provides a split() function in the pyspark.sql.functions module for splitting a longer string into a list of shorter strings. The most popular use case for this function is to split a sentence into words. The split() function takes two or three parameters:

- A column object containing strings
- A Java regular expression delimiter to split the strings against
- An optional integer about how many times we apply the delimiter (not used here)

Since we want to split words, we won't overcomplicate our regular expression and will use the space character to split. The next listing shows the results of our code.

Listing 2.13　Splitting our lines of text into lists of words

```
from pyspark.sql.functions import col, split

lines = book.select(split(col("value"), " "))

lines

# DataFrame[split(value,  , -1): array<string>]

lines.printSchema()

# root
#  |-- split(value,  , -1): array (nullable = true)
#  |    |-- element: string (containsNull = true)

lines.show(5)

# +--------------------+
# | split(value,  , -1)|
# +--------------------+
# |[The, Project, Gu...|
# |                  []|
# |[This, eBook, is,...|
```

```
#  |[almost, no, rest...|
#  |[re-use, it, unde...|
#  +--------------------+
# only showing top 5 rows
```

The split functions transformed our string column into an array column, containing one or more string elements. This is what we were expecting: even before looking at the data, seeing that the structure behaves according to plan is a good way to sanity-check our code.

Looking at the five rows we've printed, we can see that our values are now separated by a comma and wrapped in square brackets, which is how PySpark visually represents an array. The second record is empty, so we just see [], an empty array.

PySpark's built-in functions for data manipulations are extremely useful, and you should spend a little bit of time going over the API documentation (http://spark .apache.org/docs/latest/api/python/) to see what's available at core functionality. If you don't find exactly what you're after, chapter 6 covers how you can create your function over Column objects, and gives a deeper look into PySpark's complex data types like the array. Built-in PySpark functions are as performant as plain Spark (in Java and Scala), as they map directly to a JVM function. (See the following sidebar for more information.)

Advanced topic: PySpark's architecture and the JVM heritage

If you're like me, you might be interested to see how PySpark builds its core pyspark .sql.functions functions. If you look at the source code for split() (from the API documentation; see http://mng.bz/oa4D), you might be in for a disappointment:

```
def split(str, pattern, limit=-1):
    """ [... elided ] """
    sc = SparkContext._active_spark_context
    return Column(sc._jvm.functions.split(_to_java_column(str), pattern,
            limit))
```

It effectively refers to the split function of the sc._jvm.functions object. This has to do with how the data frame was built. PySpark uses a translation layer to call JVM functions for its core functions. This makes PySpark faster since you're not transforming your Python code into a JVM one all the time; it's already done for you. It also makes porting PySpark to another platform a little easier: if you can call the JVM functions directly, you don't have to re-implement everything.

This is one of the trade-offs of standing on the shoulders of the Spark giant. This also explains why PySpark uses JVM-base regular expressions instead of the Python ones in its built-in functions. Part 3 will expand on this subject greatly, but in the meantime, explore PySpark's source code!

With our lines of text now tokenized into words, there is a little annoyance present: Spark gave a very unintuitive name (split(value, , -1)) to our column. The next section addresses how we can rename transformed columns to our liking so we can explicitly control our columns' naming schema.

2.4.3 Renaming columns: alias and withColumnRenamed

When performing a transformation on your columns, PySpark will give a default name to the resulting column. In our case, we were blessed by the `split(value, , -1)` name after splitting our value column, using a space as the delimiter. While accurate, it's not programmer-friendly. This section provides a blueprint to rename columns, both newly created and existing, using `alias()` and `withColumnRenamed()`.

There is an implicit assumption that you'll want to rename the resulting column yourself, using the `alias()` method. Its usage isn't very complicated: when applied to a column, it takes a single parameter and returns the column it was applied to, with the new name. A simple demonstration is provided in the next listing.

Listing 2.14　Our data frame before and after the aliasing

```
book.select(split(col("value"), " ")).printSchema()
# root
#  |-- split(value,  , -1): array (nullable = true)
#  |    |-- element: string (containsNull = true)


book.select(split(col("value"), " ").alias("line")).printSchema()

# root
#  |-- line: array (nullable = true)
#  |    |-- element: string (containsNull = true)
```

Our new column is called split(value, , -1), which isn't really pretty.

We aliased our column to the name line. Much better!

`alias()` provides a clean and explicit way to name your columns after you've performed work on it. On the other hand, it's not the only renaming player in town. Another equally valid way to do so is by using the `.withColumnRenamed()` method on the data frame. It takes two parameters: the current name of the column and the wanted name of the column. Since we're already performing work on the column with `split`, chaining `alias` makes a lot more sense than using another method. Listing 2.15 shows you the two different approaches.

When writing your code, choosing between those two options is pretty easy:

- When you're using a method where you're specifying which columns you want to appear, like the `select()` method, use `alias()`.
- If you just want to rename a column without changing the rest of the data frame, use `.withColumnRenamed`. Note that, should the column not exist, PySpark will treat this method as a no-op and not perform anything.

Listing 2.15　Renaming a column, two ways

```
# This looks a lot cleaner
lines = book.select(split(book.value, " ").alias("line"))
```

```
# This is messier, and you have to remember the name PySpark assigns
      automatically
lines = book.select(split(book.value, " "))
lines = lines.withColumnRenamed("split(value,  , -1)", "line")
```

This section introduced a new set of PySpark fundamentals: we learned how to select not only plain columns but also column transformations. We also learned how to explicitly name the resulting columns, avoiding PySpark's predictable but jarring naming convention. Now we can move forward with the remainder of the operations. If we look at our five steps, we're halfway done with step 2. We have a list of words, but we need each token or word to be its own record:

1   **[DONE]** *Read*—Read the input data (we're assuming a plain text file).
2   **[IN PROGRESS]** *Token*—Tokenize each word.
3   *Clean*—Remove any punctuation and/or tokens that aren't words. Lowercase each word.
4   *Count*—Count the frequency of each word present in the text.
5   *Answer*—Return the top 10 (or 20, 50, 100).

2.4.4   *Reshaping your data: Exploding a list into rows*

When working with data, a key element in data preparation is making sure that it "fits the mold"; this means making sure that the structure containing the data is logical and appropriate for the work at hand. At the moment, each record of our data frame contains multiple words into an array of strings. It would be better to have one record for each word.

Enter the explode() function. When applied to a column containing a container-like data structure (such as an array), it'll take each element and give it its own row. This is much easier explained visually rather than using words, and figure 2.4 explains the process.

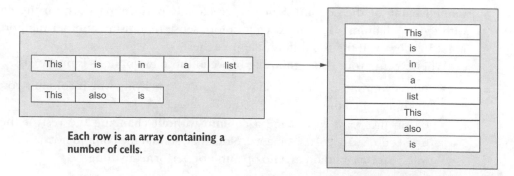

Each row is an array containing a
number of cells.

Exploding the array column creates
a record for each element of each array.

Figure 2.4   Exploding a data frame of `array[String]` into a data frame of `String`. Each element of each array becomes its own record.

The code follows the same structure as split(), and you can see the results in the next listing. We now have a data frame containing, at most, one word per row. We are almost there!

Listing 2.16 Exploding a column of arrays into rows of elements

```
from pyspark.sql.functions import explode, col

words = lines.select(explode(col("line")).alias("word"))

words.show(15)
# +----------+
# |      word|
# +----------+
# |       The|
# |   Project|
# | Gutenberg|
# |     EBook|
# |        of|
# |     Pride|
# |       and|
# |Prejudice,|
# |        by|
# |      Jane|
# |    Austen|
# |          |
# |      This|
# |     eBook|
# |        is|
# +----------+
# only showing top 15 rows
```

Before continuing our data-processing journey, we can take a step back and look at a sample of the data. Just by looking at the 15 rows returned, we can see that Prejudice, has a comma and that the cell between Austen and This contains the empty string. That gives us a good blueprint of the next steps that need to be performed before we start analyzing word frequency.

Looking back at our five steps, we can now conclude step 2, and our words are tokenized. Let's attack the third one, where we'll clean our words to simplify the counting:

1 **[DONE]** *Read*—Read the input data (we're assuming a plain text file).
2 **[DONE]** *Token*—Tokenize each word.
3 *Clean*—Remove any punctuation and/or tokens that aren't words. Lowercase each word.
4 *Count*—Count the frequency of each word present in the text.
5 *Answer*—Return the top 10 (or 20, 50, 100).

2.4.5 *Working with words: Changing case and removing punctuation*

So far, with split() and explode() our pattern has been the following: find the relevant function in pyspark.sql.functions, apply it, profit! This section will use the same winning formula to normalize the case of our words and remove punctuation, so I'll focus on the functions' behavior rather than on how to apply them. This section takes care of lowering the case (using the lower() function) and removing punctuation through the usage of a regular expression.

Let's get right to it. Listing 2.17 contains the source code to lower the case of all the words in the data frame. The code should look very familiar: we select a column transformed by lower, a PySpark function lowering the case of the data inside the column passed as a parameter. We then alias the resulting column to word_lower to avoid PySpark's default nomenclature.

Listing 2.17   Lower the case of the words in the data frame

```
from pyspark.sql.functions import lower
words_lower = words.select(lower(col("word")).alias("word_lower"))

words_lower.show()

# +-----------+
# | word_lower|
# +-----------+
# |       the|
# |    project|
# |  gutenberg|
# |      ebook|
# |         of|
# |      pride|
# |        and|
# | prejudice,|
# |         by|
# |       jane|
# |     austen|
# |           |
# |       this|
# |      ebook|
# |         is|
# |        for|
# |        the|
# |        use|
# |         of|
# |     anyone|
# +-----------+
# only showing top 20 rows
```

Next, we want to clean our words of any punctuation and other non-useful characters; in this case, we'll keep only the letters using a regular expression (see the end of the section for a reference on regular expressions [or *regex*]). This can be a little trickier: we won't improvise a full NLP (Natural Language Processing) library here, and instead rely on the functionality PySpark provides in its data manipulation toolbox. In the spirit of keeping this exercise simple, we'll keep the first contiguous group of letters as the word, and remove the rest. It will effectively remove punctuation, quotation marks, and other symbols, at the expense of being less robust with more exotic word construction. The next listing shows the code in all its splendor.

Listing 2.18   Using `regexp_extract` to keep what looks like a word

```
from pyspark.sql.functions import regexp_extract
words_clean = words_lower.select(
    regexp_extract(col("word_lower"), "[a-z]+", 0).alias("word")
)

words_clean.show()
```

> We only match for multiple lowercase characters (between a and z). The plus sign (+) will match for one or more occurrences.

```
# +---------+
# |     word|
# +---------+
# |      the|
# |  project|
# |gutenberg|
# |    ebook|
# |       of|
# |    pride|
# |      and|
# |prejudice|
# |       by|
# |     jane|
# |   austen|
# |         |
# |     this|
# |    ebook|
# |       is|
# |      for|
# |      the|
# |      use|
# |       of|
# |   anyone|
# +---------+
# only showing top 20 rows
```

Our data frame of words looks pretty regular by now, except for the empty cell between austen and this. In the next section, we cover the filtering operation by removing any empty records.

Regular expressions for the rest of us

PySpark uses regular expressions in two functions we have used so far: `regexp_extract()` and `split()`. You do not have to be a regexp expert to work with PySpark (I certainly am not). Throughout the book, each time I use a nontrivial regular expression, I'll provide a plain English definition so you can follow along.

If you are interested in building your own, the RegExr (https://regexr.com/) website is really useful, as well as the *Regular Expression Cookbook* by Steven Levithan and Jan Goyvaerts (O'Reilly, 2012).

Exercise 2.1

Given the following `exo_2_1_df` data frame, how many records will the `solution_2_1_df` data frame contain? (Note: No need to write code to solve this problem.)

```
exo_2_1_df.show()

# +-------------------+
# |            numbers|
# +-------------------+
# |    [1, 2, 3, 4, 5]|
# |[5, 6, 7, 8, 9, 10]|
# +-------------------+

solution_2_1_df = exo_2_1_df.select(explode(col("numbers")))
```

2.5   *Filtering rows*

An important data manipulation operation is filtering records according to a certain predicate. In our case, blank cells shouldn't be considered—they're not words! This section covers how to filter records from a data frame. After `select()`-ing records, filtering is probably the most frequent and easiest operation to perform on your data; PySpark provides a simple process to do so.

Conceptually, we should be able to provide a test to perform on each record. If it returns true, we keep the record. False? You're out! PySpark provides not one, but two identical methods to perform this task. You can use either `.filter()` or its alias `.where()`. This duplication is to ease the transition for users coming from other data-processing engines or libraries; some use one, some the other. PySpark provides both, so no arguments are possible! I prefer `filter()`, because w maps to more data frame methods (`withColumn()` in chapter 4 or `withColumnRenamed()` in chapter 3). If we look at the next listing, we can see that columns can be compared to values using the usual Python comparison operators. In this case, we're using "not equal," or `!=`.

Listing 2.19   Filtering rows in your data frame using `where` or `filter`

```
words_nonull = words_clean.filter(col("word") != "")

words_nonull.show()

# +---------+
# |     word|
# +---------+
# |      the|
# |  project|
# |gutenberg|
# |    ebook|
# |       of|
# |    pride|
# |      and|
```

```
# |prejudice|
# |       by|
# |     jane|
# |   austen|
# |     this|
# |    ebook|
# |       is|
# |      for|
# |      the|
# |      use|
# |       of|
# |   anyone|
# | anywhere|
# +---------+
# only showing top 20 rows
```

The blank cell is gone!

> **TIP** If you want to negate a whole expression in a `filter()` method, PySpark provides the `~` operator. We could theoretically use `filter(~(col("word") == ""))`. Look at the exercises at the end of the chapter to see them in an application. You can also use SQL-style expression; check out chapter 7 for an alternative syntax.

We could have tried to filter earlier in our program. It's a trade-off to consider: if we filtered too early, our filtering clause would have been comically complex for no good reason. Since PySpark caches all the transformations until an action is triggered, we can focus on the readability of our code and let Spark optimize our intent, like we saw in chapter 1. We'll see in chapter 3 how you can transform PySpark code so it almost reads like a series of written instructions and take advantage of the lazy evaluation.

This seems like a good time to take a break and reflect on what we have accomplished so far. If we look at our five steps, we're 60% of the way there. Our cleaning step took care of nonletter characters and filtered the empty records. We're ready for counting and displaying the results of our analysis:

1 **[DONE]** *Read*—Read the input data (we're assuming a plain text file).

2 **[DONE]** *Token*—Tokenize each word.

3 **[DONE]** *Clean*—Remove any punctuation and/or tokens that aren't words. Lowercase each word.

4 *Count*—Count the frequency of each word present in the text.

5 *Answer*—Return the top 10 (or 20, 50, 100).

In terms of PySpark operations, we covered a huge amount of ground in the data manipulation space. You can now select not only columns but transformations of columns, renaming them as you please after the fact. We learned how to break nested structures, such as arrays, into single records. Finally, we learned how to filter records using simple conditions.

We can now rest. The next chapter will cover the end of our program. We will also be looking at bringing our code into one single file, moving away from the REPL into batch mode. We'll explore options to simplify and increase the readability of our program and then finish by scaling it to a larger corpus of texts.

Summary

- Almost all PySpark programs will revolve around three major steps: reading, transforming, and exporting data.
- PySpark provides a REPL (read, evaluate, print, loop) via the `pyspark` shell where you can experiment interactively with data.
- PySpark data frames are a collection of columns. You operate on the structure using chained transformations. PySpark will optimize the transformations and perform the work only when you submit an action, such as `show()`. This is one of the pillars of PySpark's performance.
- PySpark's repertoire of functions that operate on columns is located in `pyspark.sql.functions`.
- You can select columns or transformed columns via the `select()` method.
- You can filter columns using the `where()` or `filter()` methods and by providing a test that will return `True` or `False`; only the records returning `True` will be kept.
- PySpark can have columns of nested values, like arrays of elements. In order to extract the elements into distinct records, you need to use the `explode()` method.

Additional exercises

For all exercises, assume the following:

```
from pyspark.sql import SparkSession

spark = SparkSession.builder.getOrCreate()
```

Exercise 2.2

Given the following data frame, programmatically count the number of columns that aren't strings (answer = only one column isn't a string).

`createDataFrame()` allows you to create a data frame from a variety of sources, such as a pandas data frame or (in this case) a list of lists.

```
exo2_2_df = spark.createDataFrame(
    [["test", "more test", 10_000_000_000]], ["one", "two", "three"]
)

exo2_2_df.printSchema()
# root
#  |-- one: string (nullable = true)
#  |-- two: string (nullable = true)
#  |-- three: long (nullable = true)
```

Exercise 2.3

Rewrite the following code snippet, removing the `withColumnRenamed` method. Which version is clearer and easier to read?

```
from pyspark.sql.functions import col, length

# The `length` function returns the number of characters in a string column.

exo2_3_df = (
    spark.read.text("./data/gutenberg_books/1342-0.txt")
    .select(length(col("value")))
    .withColumnRenamed("length(value)", "number_of_char")
)
```

Exercise 2.4

Assume a data frame `exo2_4_df`. The following code block gives an error. What is the problem, and how can you solve it?

```
from pyspark.sql.functions import col, greatest

exo2_4_df = spark.createDataFrame(
    [["key", 10_000, 20_000]], ["key", "value1", "value2"]
)

exo2_4_df.printSchema()
# root
#  |-- key: string (containsNull = true)
#  |-- value1: long (containsNull = true)
#  |-- value2: long (containsNull = true)

# `greatest` will return the greatest value of the list of column names,
# skipping null value

# The following statement will return an error
from pyspark.sql.utils import AnalysisException

try:
    exo2_4_mod = exo2_4_df.select(
        greatest(col("value1"), col("value2")).alias("maximum_value")
    ).select("key", "max_value")
except AnalysisException as err:
    print(err)
```

Exercise 2.5

Let's take our `words_nonull` data frame, available in the next listing. You can use the code from the repository (`code/Ch02/end_of_chapter.py`) in your REPL to get the data frame loaded.

> Listing 2.20 The `words_nonull` for the exercise

```
from pyspark.sql import SparkSession
from pyspark.sql.functions import col, split, explode, lower, regexp_extract
```

```
spark = SparkSession.builder.getOrCreate()

book = spark.read.text("./data/gutenberg_books/1342-0.txt")

lines = book.select(split(book.value, " ").alias("line"))

words = lines.select(explode(col("line")).alias("word"))

words_lower = words.select(lower(col("word")).alias("word_lower"))

words_clean = words_lower.select(
    regexp_extract(col("word_lower"), "[a-z]*", 0).alias("word")
)

words_nonull = words_clean.where(col("word") != "")
```

a) Remove all of the occurrences of the word *is*.

b) (Challenge) Using the length function, keep only the words with more than three characters.

Exercise 2.6

The where clause takes a Boolean expression over one or many columns to filter the data frame. Beyond the usual Boolean operators (>, <, ==, <=, >=, !=), PySpark provides other functions that return Boolean columns in the pyspark.sql.functions module.

A good example is the isin() method (applied on a Column object, like col(…).isin(…)), which takes a list of values as a parameter, and will return only the records where the value in the column equals a member of the list.

Let's say you want to *remove* the words is, not, the and if from your list of words, using a single where() method on the words_nonull data frame. Write the code to do so.

Exercise 2.7

One of your friends comes to you with the following code. They have no idea why it doesn't work. Can you diagnose the problem in the try block, explain why it is an error, and provide a fix?

```
from pyspark.sql.functions import col, split

try:
    book = spark.read.text("./data/gutenberg_books/1342-0.txt")
    book = book.printSchema()
    lines = book.select(split(book.value, " ").alias("line"))
    words = lines.select(explode(col("line")).alias("word"))
except AnalysisException as err:
    print(err)
```

Submitting and scaling your first PySpark program

This chapter covers

- Summarizing data using `groupby` and a simple aggregate function
- Ordering results for display
- Writing data from a data frame
- Using `spark-submit` to launch your program in batch mode
- Simplifying PySpark writing using method chaining
- Scaling your program to multiple files at once

Chapter 2 dealt with all the data preparation work for our word frequency program. We *read* the input data, *tokenized* each word, and *cleaned* our records to only keep lowercase words. If we bring out our outline, we only have steps 4 and 5 to complete:

1. **[DONE]** *Read*: Read the input data (we're assuming a plain text file).
2. **[DONE]** *Token*: Tokenize each word.
3. **[DONE]** *Clean*: Remove any punctuation and/or tokens that aren't words. Lowercase each word.
4. *Count*: Count the frequency of each word present in the text.
5. *Answer:* Return the top 10 (or 20, 50, 100).

45

After tackling those two last steps, we look at packaging our code in a single file to be able to submit it to Spark without having to launch a REPL. We also take a look at our completed program and at simplifying it by removing intermediate variables. We finish with scaling our program to accommodate more data sources.

3.1   *Grouping records: Counting word frequencies*

If you take our data frame in the same shape as it was at the end of chapter 2 (you can find the code in a single file in the book's code repository at code/Ch02/end_of_chapter.py), there is just a little more work to be done. With a data frame containing a single word per record, we just have to count the word occurrences and take the top contenders. This section shows you how to count records using the GroupedData object and perform an aggregation function—here, counting the items—on each group.

Intuitively, we count the number of each word by creating *groups*: one for each word. Once those groups are formed, we can perform an *aggregation function* on each one of them. In this specific case, we count the number of records for each group, which will give us the number of occurrences for each word in the data frame. Under the hood, PySpark represents a grouped data frame in a GroupedData object; think of it as a transitional object that awaits an aggregation function to become a transformed data frame.

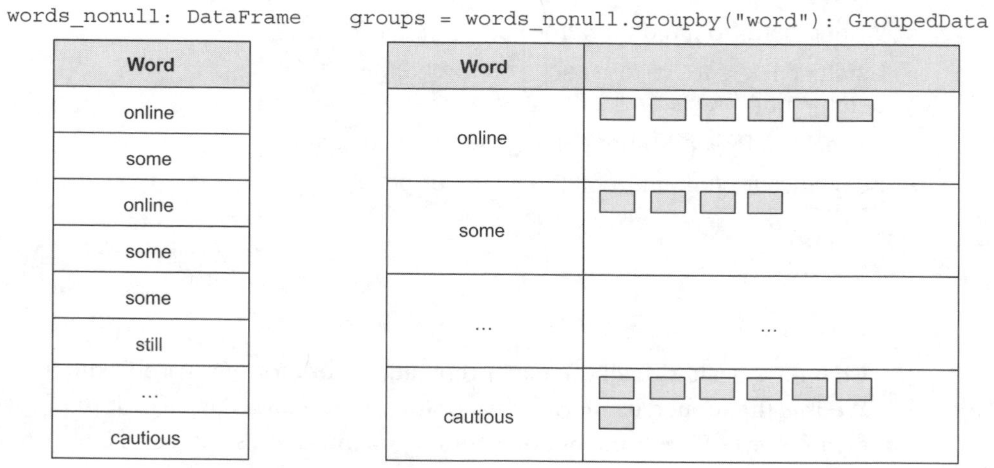

words_nonull: DataFrame   groups = words_nonull.groupby("word"): GroupedData

Word
online
some
online
some
some
still
...
cautious

Word	
online	▢ ▢ ▢ ▢ ▢ ▢
some	▢ ▢ ▢ ▢
...	...
cautious	▢ ▢ ▢ ▢ ▢ ▢ ▢ ▢

Figure 3.1   A schematic representation of our groups object. Each small box represents a record.

The easiest way to count record occurrence is to use the groupby() method, passing the columns we wish to group as a parameter. The groupby() method in listing 3.1 returns a GroupedData and awaits further instructions. Once we apply the count() method, we get back a data frame containing the grouping column word, as well as the count column containing the number of occurrences for each word.

Listing 3.1   Counting word frequencies using `groupby()` **and** `count()`

```
groups = words_nonull.groupby(col("word"))

print(groups)

# <pyspark.sql.group.GroupedData at 0x10ed23da0>

results = words_nonull.groupby(col("word")).count()

print(results)

# DataFrame[word: string, count: bigint]

results.show()

# +-------------+-----+
# |         word|count|
# +-------------+-----+
# |       online|    4|
# |         some|  203|
# |        still|   72|
# |          few|   72|
# |         hope|  122|
# [...]
# |       doubts|    2|
# |     destitute|    1|
# |     solemnity|    5|
# |gratification|    1|
# |    connected|   14|
# +-------------+-----+
# only showing top 20 rows
```

Peeking at the `results` data frame in listing 3.1, we see that the results are in no specific order. As a matter of fact, I'd be very surprised if you had the exact same order of words that I do! This has to do with how PySpark manages data. In chapter 1, we learned that PySpark distributes the data across multiple nodes. When performing a grouping function, such as `groupby()`, each worker performs the work on its assigned data. `groupby()` and `count()` are transformations, so PySpark will queue them lazily until we request an action. When we pass the `show` method to our results data frame, it triggers the chain of computation that we see in figure 3.2.

> **TIP** If you need to create groups based on the values of multiple columns, you can pass multiple columns as parameters to `groupby()`. We see this in action in chapter 5.

Because Spark is lazy, it doesn't care about the order of records unless we explicitly ask it to. Since we wish to see the top words on display, let's put a little order in our data frame and, at the same time, complete the last step of our program: return the top word frequencies.

Word	Count
same	2
cautious	1
all	6

Word	Count
same	3
none	10

Word	Count
cautious	3
same	1
all	2

Step 1: The data is unordered in each partition, after the groupby operation.

Word	Count
none	10
all	8
same	7

Step 2: Each worker sends enough summarized data to the master node for display.

Figure 3.2 A distributed group by on our `words_nonull` data frame. The work is performed in a distributed fashion until we need to assemble the results in a cohesive display via `show()`.

Exercise 3.1

Starting with the `word_nonull` seen in this section, which of the following expressions would return the number of words per letter count (e.g., there are *X* one-letter words, *Y* two-letter words, etc.)?

Assume that `pyspark.sql.functions.col, pyspark.sql.functions.length` are imported.

a `words_nonull.select(length(col("word"))).groupby("length").count()`

b `words_nonull.select(length(col("word")).alias("length")).groupby("length").count()`

c `words_nonull.groupby("length").select("length").count()`

d None of those options would work.

3.2 *Ordering the results on the screen using orderBy*

In 3.1, we explained why PySpark doesn't necessarily maintain an order of records when performing transformations. If we look at our five-step blueprint, the last step is to return the top *N* records for different values of *N*. We already know how to show a specific number of records, so this section focuses on ordering the records in a data frame before displaying them:

1 **[DONE]** *Read*: Read the input data (we're assuming a plain text file).
2 **[DONE]** *Token*: Tokenize each word.
3 **[DONE]** *Clean*: Remove any punctuation and/or tokens that aren't words. Lowercase each word.
4 **[DONE]** *Count*: Count the frequency of each word present in the text.
5 *Answer*: Return the top 10 (or 20, 50, 100).

Just like we use `groupby()` to group a data frame by the values in one or many columns, we use `orderBy()` to order a data frame by the values of one or many columns. PySpark provides two different syntaxes to order records:

- We can provide the column names as parameters, with an optional `ascending` parameter. By default, we order a data frame in ascending order; by setting `ascending` to false, we reverse the order, getting the largest values first.
- Or we can use the `Column` object directly, via the `col` function. When we want to reverse the ordering, we use the `desc()` method on the column.

PySpark orders the data frame using each column, one at a time. If you pass multiple columns (see chapter 5), PySpark uses the first column's values to order the data frame, then the second (and then third, etc.) when there are identical values. Since we have a single column—and no duplicates because of `groupby()`—the application of `orderBy()` in the next listing is simple, regardless of the syntax we pick.

Listing 3.2   Displaying the top 10 words in Jane Austen's *Pride and Prejudice*

```
results.orderBy("count", ascending=False).show(10)
results.orderBy(col("count").desc()).show(10)

# +----+-----+
# |word|count|
# +----+-----+
# | the| 4480|
# |  to| 4218|
# |  of| 3711|
# | and| 3504|
# | her| 2199|
# |   a| 1982|
# |  in| 1909|
# | was| 1838|
# |   i| 1749|
# | she| 1668|
# +----+-----+
# only showing top 10 rows
```

The list is very unsurprising: even though we can't argue with Austen's vocabulary, she isn't immune to the fact that the English language needs pronouns and other common words. In natural language processing, those words are called *stop words* and could be removed. We solved our original query and can rest easy. Should you want to get the top 20, top 50, or even top 1,000, it's easily done by changing the parameter to `show()`.

PySpark's method naming convention zoo

If you are detail-oriented, you might have noticed we used `groupby` (lowercase), but `orderBy` (lowerCamelCase, where you capitalize the first letter of each word but the first word). This seems like an odd design choice.

(continued)

groupby() is an alias for groupBy(), just like where() is an alias of filter(). I guess that the PySpark developers found that a lot of typing mistakes were avoided by accepting the two cases. orderBy() didn't have that luxury, for a reason that escapes my understanding, so we need to be mindful of this.

Part of this incoherence is due to Spark's heritage. Scala prefers camelCase for methods. On the other hand, we saw regexp_extract, which uses Python's preferred snake_case (words separated by an underscore) in chapter 2. There is no magic secret here: you'll have to be mindful of the different case conventions at play in PySpark.

Showing results on the screen is great for a quick assessment, but most of the time you'll want them to have some sort of longevity. It's much better to save those results to a file so that we'll be able to reuse them without having to compute everything each time. The next section covers writing a data frame to a file.

Exercise 3.2

Why isn't the order preserved in the following code block?

```
(
    results.orderBy("count", ascending=False)
    .groupby(length(col("word")))
    .count()
    .show(5)
)
# +------------+-----+
# |length(word)|count|
# +------------+-----+
# |          12|  199|
# |           1|   10|
# |          13|  113|
# |           6|  908|
# |          16|    4|
# +------------+-----+
# only showing top 5 rows
```

3.3 *Writing data from a data frame*

Having the data on the screen is great for interactive development, but you'll often want to export your results. For this, we write our results in a *comma-separated value* (CSV) file. I chose this format because it's a human-readable format, meaning that we can review the results of our operations.

Just like we use read() and the SparkReader to read data in Spark, we use write() and the SparkWriter object to write back our data frame to disk. In listing 3.3, I specialize the SparkWriter to export text into a CSV file, naming the output `simple_count.csv`. If we look at the results, we can see that PySpark didn't create a results.csv file. Instead, it created a directory of the same name, and put 201 files inside the directory (200 CSVs + 1 _SUCCESS file).

Listing 3.3 Writing our results in multiple CSV files, one per partition

```
results.write.csv("./data/simple_count.csv")

# The ls command is run using a shell, not a Python prompt.
# If you use IPython, you can use the bang pattern (! ls -l).
# Use this to get the same results without leaving the IPython console.

$ ls -1 ./data/simple_count.csv      ◁─── The results are written
                                          in a directory called
                                          simple_count.csv.
_SUCCESS
part-00000-615b75e4-ebf5-44a0-b337-405fccd11d0c-c000.csv
[...]                                                         We have part-00000
part-00199-615b75e4-ebf5-44a0-b337-405fccd11d0c-c000.csv  ◁── to part-00199, which
                                                             means our results are
The _SUCCESS file means the operation was successful.        split across 200 files.
```

There it is, folks! The first moment where we have to care about PySpark's distributed nature. Just like PySpark will distribute the transformation work across multiple workers, it'll do the same for writing data. While it might look like a nuisance for our simple program, it is tremendously useful when working in distributed environments. When you have a large cluster of nodes, having many smaller files makes it easy to logically distribute reading and writing the data, making it way faster than having a single massive file.

By default, PySpark will give you one file per partition. This means that our program, as run on my machine, yields 200 partitions at the end. This isn't the best for portability. To reduce the number of partitions, we apply the `coalesce()` method with the desired number of partitions. The next listing shows the difference when using `coalesce(1)` on our data frame before writing to disk. We still get a directory, but there is a single CSV file inside of it. Mission accomplished!

Listing 3.4 Writing our results under a single partition

```
results.coalesce(1).write.csv("./data/simple_count_single_partition.csv")

$ ls -1 ./data/simple_count_single_partition.csv/

_SUCCESS
part-00000-f8c4c13e-a4ee-4900-ac76-de3d56e5f091-c000.csv
```

> **NOTE** You might have realized that we're not ordering the file before writing it. Since our data here is pretty small, we could have written the words by decreasing order of frequency. If you have a large data set, this operation will be quite expensive. Furthermore, since reading is a potentially distributed operation, what guarantees that it'll get read the same way? Never assume that your data frame will keep the same ordering of records unless you explicitly ask via `orderBy()` right before the showing step.

Our workflow has been pretty interactive so far. We write one or two lines of text before showing the result to the terminal. As we get more and more confident with operating on the data frame's structure, those showings will become fewer.

Now that we've performed all the necessary steps interactively, let's look at putting our program in a single file and at refactoring opportunities.

3.4   *Putting it all together: Counting*

Interactive development is fantastic for the rapid iteration of our code. When developing programs, it's great to experiment and validate our thoughts through rapid code inputs to a shell. When the experimentation is over, it's good to bring our program into a cohesive body of code. This section takes all the code we have written in this chapter and chapter 2, and brings it into something runnable end to end.

The REPL allows you to go back in history using the directional arrows on your keyboard, just like a regular Python REPL. To make things a bit easier, I am providing the step-by-step program in the next listing. This section is dedicated to streamlining and making our code more succinct and readable.

Listing 3.5   Our first PySpark program, dubbed "Counting Jane Austen"

```python
from pyspark.sql import SparkSession
from pyspark.sql.functions import (
    col,
    explode,
    lower,
    regexp_extract,
    split,
)

spark = SparkSession.builder.appName(
    "Analyzing the vocabulary of Pride and Prejudice."
).getOrCreate()

book = spark.read.text("./data/gutenberg_books/1342-0.txt")

lines = book.select(split(book.value, " ").alias("line"))

words = lines.select(explode(col("line")).alias("word"))

words_lower = words.select(lower(col("word")).alias("word"))

words_clean = words_lower.select(
    regexp_extract(col("word"), "[a-z']*", 0).alias("word")
)

words_nonull = words_clean.where(col("word") != "")

results = words_nonull.groupby(col("word")).count()

results.orderBy("count", ascending=False).show(10)

results.coalesce(1).write.csv("./simple_count_single_partition.csv")
```

This program runs perfectly if you paste its entirety into the pyspark shell. With everything in the same file, we can make our code more friendly and make it easier for future you to come back to it. First, we adopt common import conventions when working with PySpark. We then rearrange our code to make it more readable, as seen in chapter 1.

3.4.1 *Simplifying your dependencies with PySpark's import conventions*

This section covers the general conventions when using PySpark modules. We review the most relevant import—the transformation function—and how qualifying it helps with knowing what is coming from where.

This program uses five distinct functions from the pyspark.sql.functions modules. We should probably replace this with a qualified import, which is Python's way of importing a module by assigning a keyword to it. While there is no hard rule, the common wisdom is to use F to refer to PySpark's functions. The next listing shows the before and after.

> **Listing 3.6 Simplifying our PySpark functions import**

```
# Before
from pyspark.sql.functions import col, explode, lower, regexp_extract, split

# After
import pyspark.sql.functions as F
```

Since col, explode, lower, regexp_extract, and split are all in pyspark.sql.functions, we can import the whole module. Since the new import statement imports the entirety of the pyspark.sql.functions module, we assign the keyword (or key letter) F. The PySpark community seems to have implicitly settled on using F for pyspark.sql.functions, and I encourage you to do the same. It'll make your programs consistent, and since many functions in the module share their name with pandas or Python built-in functions, you'll avoid name clashes. Each function application in the program will then be prefixed by F, just like with regular Python-qualified imports.

> **WARNING** It can be very tempting to start an import like from pyspark.sql .functions import *. Do not fall into that trap! It'll make it hard for your readers to know which functions come from PySpark and which come from regular Python. In chapter 8, where we'll use user-defined functions (UDFs), this separation will become even more important. This is a good coding hygiene rule!

In the subsequent chapters, and more specifically chapter 6, I introduce other functionality that warrants its qualified import. Whether you choose to import functions one by one or the whole qualified module depends on your use case; I usually value consistency over terseness and prefer using a qualified import for data transformation API.

We simplified our program's preamble; let's now focus on where the action is by simplifying our program flow using one of my favorite aspects of PySpark: its chaining abilities.

3.4.2 *Simplifying our program via method chaining*

If we look at the transformation methods we applied to our data frames (`select()`, `where()`, `groupBy()`, and `count()`), they all have something in common: they take a structure as a parameter—the data frame or `GroupedData` in the case of `count()`—and return a structure. All transformations can be seen as pipes that ingest a structure and return a modified structure. This section will look at method chaining and how it makes a program less verbose and thus easier to read by eliminating intermediate variables.

Our program uses intermediate variables quite a lot: every time we perform a transformation, we assign the result to a new variable. This is useful when using the shell as we keep the state of our transformation and can peek at our work at the end of every step. On the other hand, once our program works, this multiplication of variables is not as useful and can visually clutter our program.

In PySpark, every transformation returns an object, which is why we need to assign a variable to the result. This means that PySpark doesn't perform modifications *in place*. For instance, the following code block by itself in a program wouldn't do anything because we don't assign the result to a variable. In a REPL, on the other hand, you would get the return value printed as output, so this would count as work:

```
results.orderBy("word").count()
```

We can avoid intermediate variables by *chaining* the results of one method to the next. Since each transformation returns a data frame (or `GroupedData`, when we perform the `groupby()` method), we can directly append the next method without assigning the result to a variable. This means that we can eschew all but one variable assignment. The code in the next listing shows the before and after. Note that we also added the `F` prefix to our functions to respect the import convention we outlined in section 3.4.1.

Listing 3.7   Removing intermediate variables by chaining transformation methods

```
# Before
book = spark.read.text("./data/gutenberg_books/1342-0.txt")

lines = book.select(split(book.value, " ").alias("line"))

words = lines.select(explode(col("line")).alias("word"))

words_lower = words.select(lower(col("word")).alias("word"))

words_clean = words_lower.select(
    regexp_extract(col("word"), "[a-z']*", 0).alias("word")
)
```

```
words_nonull = words_clean.where(col("word") != "")

results = words_nonull.groupby("word").count()

# After
import pyspark.sql.functions as F

results = (
    spark.read.text("./data/gutenberg_books/1342-0.txt")
    .select(F.split(F.col("value"), " ").alias("line"))
    .select(F.explode(F.col("line")).alias("word"))
    .select(F.lower(F.col("word")).alias("word"))
    .select(F.regexp_extract(F.col("word"), "[a-z']*", 0).alias("word"))
    .where(F.col("word") != "")
    .groupby("word")
    .count()
)
```

It's like night and day: the "after" is much more terse and readable, and we're able to easily follow the list of steps. Visually, we can also see the difference in figure 3.3.

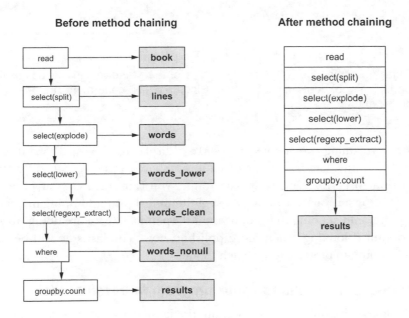

Figure 3.3 Method chaining eliminates the need for intermediate variables.

I am not saying that intermediate variables are evil and are to be avoided. But they can hinder your code readability, so you have to make sure they serve a purpose. A lot of burgeoning PySpark developers make it a habit of always writing on top of the same variable. While not dangerous in itself, it makes the code redundant and harder to reason about. If you see yourself doing something like the first two lines of the next listing, chain your methods. You'll get the same result and more aesthetically pleasing code.

Listing 3.8 Chaining for writing over the same variable

```
df = spark.read.text("./data/gutenberg_books/1342-0.txt")
df = df.select(F.split(F.col("value"), " ").alias("line"))
```
Instead of
doing this . . .

```
df = (
        spark.read.text("./data/gutenberg_books/1342-0.txt")
        .select(F.split(F.col("value"), " ").alias("line"))
    )
```
. . . you can do this—
no variable repetition!

Make your life easier by using Python's parentheses

If you look at the "after" code in listing 3.7, you'll notice that I start the right side of the equal sign with an opening parenthesis (`spark = ( [...]`). This is a trick I use when I need to chain methods in Python. If you don't wrap your result into a pair of parentheses, you'll need to add a `\` character at the end of each line, which adds visual noise to your program. PySpark code is especially prone to line breaks when you use method chaining:

```
results = spark\
        .read.text('./data/ch02/1342-0.txt')\
        ...
```

As a lazy alternative, I am a big fan of using Black as a Python code formatting tool (https://black.readthedocs.io/). It removes a lot of the guesswork involved in having your code logically laid out and consistent. Since we read code more than we write it, readability matters.

Since we are performing two actions on `results` (displaying the top 10 words on the screen and writing the data frame to a CSV file), we have to use a variable. If you only have one action to perform on your data frame, you can channel your inner code golfer[1] by not using any variable name. Most of the time, I prefer lumping my transformations together and keeping the action visually separate, like we are doing now.

Our program is looking much more polished now. The last step will be to add PySpark's plumbing to prepare it for batch mode.

3.5   *Using spark-submit to launch your program in batch mode*

If we start PySpark with the `pyspark` program, the launcher takes care of creating the `SparkSession` for us. In chapter 2, we started from a basic Python REPL, so we created our entry point and named it `spark`. This section takes our program and submits it in batch mode. It is the equivalent of running a Python script; if you only need the result and not the REPL, this will do the trick.

---

[1] Writing a program using the lowest possible number of characters.

Unlike the interactive REPL, where the choice of language triggers the program to run, as in listing 3.10, we see that Spark provides a single program, named spark-submit, to submit Spark (Scala, Java, SQL), PySpark (Python), and SparkR (R) programs. The full code for our program is available on the book's repository under code/Ch02/word_count_submit.py.

> **Listing 3.9 Submitting our job in batch mode**

```
$ spark-submit ./code/Ch03/word_count_submit.py

# [...]
# +----+-----+
# |word|count|
# +----+-----+
# | the| 4480|
# |  to| 4218|
# |  of| 3711|
# | and| 3504|
# | her| 2199|
# |   a| 1982|
# |  in| 1909|
# | was| 1838|
# |   i| 1749|
# | she| 1668|
# +----+-----+
# only showing top 10 rows
# [...]
```

TIP If you get a deluge of INFO messages, don't forget that you have control over this: use spark.sparkContext.setLogLevel("WARN") right after your spark definition. If your local configuration has INFO as a default, you'll still get a slew of messages until it catches this line, but it won't obscure your results.

Once this step is completed, we're done! Our program successfully *ingests* the book, *transforms* it into a cleaned list of word frequencies, and then *exports* it two ways: as a top-10 list on the screen and as a CSV file.

If we look at our process, we applied one transformation interactively at the time, show()-ing the process after each one. This will often be your modus operandi when working with a new data file. Once you're confident about a block of code, you can remove the intermediate variables. Out of the box, PySpark gives you a productive environment to explore large data sets interactively and provides an expressive and terse vocabulary to manipulate data. It's also easy to go from interactive development to batch deployment—you just have to define your SparkSession, if you haven't already, and you're good to go.

3.6   *What didn't happen in this chapter*

Chapter 2 and 3 were pretty dense. We learned how to read text data, process it to answer any question, display the results on the screen, and write them to a CSV file. On the other hand, there are many elements we left out on purpose. Let's quickly look at what we *didn't* do in this chapter.

Except for coalescing the data frame to write it into a single file, we didn't do much with the distribution of the data. We saw in chapter 1 that PySpark distributes data across multiple worker nodes, but our code didn't pay much attention to this. Not having to constantly think about partitions, data locality, and fault tolerance made our data discovery process much faster.

We didn't spend much time configuring PySpark. Other than providing a name for our application, no additional configuration was inputted in our `SparkSession`. It's not to say we'll never broach this, but we can start with a bare-bones configuration and tweak as we go. The subsequent chapters will customize the `SparkSession` to optimize resources (chapter 11) or create connectors to external data repositories (chapter 9).

Finally, we didn't obsess about planning the order of operations as it relates to processing, focusing instead on readability and logic. We made a point to describe our transformations as logically as they appear to us, and we're letting Spark optimize this into efficient processing steps. We could potentially reorder some and get the same output, but our program reads well, is easy to reason about, and works correctly.

This echoes the statement I made in chapter 1: PySpark is remarkable not only in what it provides, but also in what it can abstract over. You most often can write your code as a sequence of transformations that will get you to your destination most of the time. For those cases where you want a more finely tuned performance or more control over the physical layout of your data, we'll see in part 3 that PySpark won't hold you back. Because Spark is in constant evolution, there are still cases where you need to be a little more careful about how your program translates to physical execution on the cluster. For this, chapter 11 covers the Spark UI, which shows you the work being performed on your data and how you can influence processing.

3.7   *Scaling up our word frequency program*

That example wasn't big data. I'll be the first to say it.

Teaching big data processing has a catch-22. While I want to show the power of PySpark to work with massive data sets, I don't want you to purchase a cluster or rack up a massive cloud bill. It's easier to show you the ropes using a smaller set of data, knowing that we can scale using the same code.

Let's take our word-counting example: How can we scale this to a larger corpus of text? Let's download more files from Project Gutenberg and place them in the same directory:

```
$ ls -1 data/gutenberg_books

11-0.txt
1342-0.txt
1661-0.txt
2701-0.txt
30254-0.txt
84-0.txt
```

While this is not enough to claim "we're doing big data," it'll be enough to explain the general concept. If you want to scale, you can use appendix B to provision a powerful cluster on the cloud, download more books or other text files, and run the same program for a few dollars.

We modify our `word_count_submit.py` in a very subtle way. Where we `.read.text()`, we'll change the path to account for all files in the directory. The next listing shows the before and after: we are only changing the `1342-0.txt` to a `*.txt`, which is called a *glob pattern*. The `*` means that Spark selects all the `.txt` files in the directory.

Listing 3.10 Scaling our word count program using the glob pattern

```
# Before                          Here we have a single file passed as a parameter . . .
results = spark.read.text('./data/gutenberg_books/1342-0.txt')      ←

# After                  . . . and here the star (or glob) picks all the text files within the directory.
results = spark.read.text('./data/gutenberg_books/*.txt')      ←
```

NOTE You can also just pass the name of the directory if you want PySpark to ingest all the files within the directory.

The results of running the program over all the files in the directory are available in the following listing.

Listing 3.11 Results of scaling our program to multiple files

```
$ spark-submit ./code/Ch02/word_count_submit.py

+----+-----+
|word|count|
+----+-----+
| the|38895|
| and|23919|
|  of|21199|
|  to|20526|
|   a|14464|
|   i|13973|
|  in|12777|
|that| 9623|
|  it| 9099|
```

```
|  was|  8920|
+----+------+
only showing top 10 rows
```

With this, you can confidently say that you can scale a simple data analysis program using PySpark. You can use the general formula we've outlined here and modify some of the parameters and methods to fit your use case. Chapters 4 and 5 will dig a little deeper into some interesting and common data transformations, building on what we've learned here.

Summary

- You can group records using the `groupby` method, passing the column names you want to group against as a parameter. This returns a `GroupedData` object that waits for an aggregation method to return the results of computation over the groups, such as the `count()` of records.
- PySpark's repertoire of functions that operates on columns is located in `pyspark.sql.functions`. The unofficial but well-respected convention is to qualify this import in your program using the `F` keyword.
- When writing a data frame to a file, PySpark will create a directory and put one file per partition. If you want to write a single file, use the `coaslesce(1)` method.
- To prepare your program to work in batch mode via `spark-submit`, you need to create a `SparkSession`. PySpark provides a builder pattern in the `pyspark.sql` module.
- If your program needs to scale across multiple files within the same directory, you can use a glob pattern to select many files at once. PySpark will collect them in a single data frame.

Additional Exercises

For these exercises, you'll need the `word_count_submit.py` program we worked on in this chapter. You can pick it from the book's code repository (`Code/Ch03/word_count_submit.py`).

Exercise 3.3

1 By modifying the `word_count_submit.py` program, return the number of distinct words in Jane Austen's *Pride and Prejudice*. (Hint: `results` contains one record for each unique word.)
2 (Challenge) Wrap your program in a function that takes a file name as a parameter. It should return the number of distinct words.

Exercise 3.4

Taking `word_count_submit.py`, modify the script to return a sample of five words that appear only once in Jane Austen's *Pride and Prejudice*.

Exercise 3.5

1 Using the `substring` function (refer to PySpark's API or the `pyspark` shell if needed), return the top five most popular first letters (keep only the first letter of each word).

2 Compute the number of words starting with a consonant or a vowel. (Hint: The `isin()` function might be useful.)

Exercise 3.6

Let's say you want to get both the `count()` and `sum()` of a `GroupedData` object. Why doesn't this code work? Map the inputs and outputs of each method.

```
my_data_frame.groupby("my_column").count().sum()
```

Multiple aggregate function applications will be covered in chapter 4.

Analyzing tabular data with pyspark.sql

This chapter covers

- Reading delimited data into a PySpark data frame
- Understanding how PySpark represents tabular data in a data frame
- Ingesting and exploring tabular or relational data
- Selecting, manipulating, renaming, and deleting columns in a data frame
- Summarizing data frames for quick exploration

Our first example in chapters 2 and 3 worked with unstructured textual data. Each line of text was mapped to a record in a data frame, and, through a series of transformations, we counted word frequencies from one (and multiple) text files. This chapter goes deeper into data transformation, this time using structured data. Data comes in many shapes and forms: we start with *relational* (or *tabular*,[1] or row and columns) data, one of the most common formats popularized by SQL and Excel. This chapter and the next follow the same blueprint as we did with our first data analysis. We use

---

[1] If we are being very picky, tabular and relational data are not exactly the same. In chapter 5, when working with joining multiple data frames together, the differences will matter. When working with a single table, we can lump those two concepts together.

the public Canadian television schedule data to identify and measure the proportion of commercials over its total programming.

More specifically, I start by giving a primer on tabular data and how the data frame provides the necessary abstractions to represent a data table. I then specialize the `SparkReader` object once more, this time for delimited data rather than unstructured text. I then cover the most common operations on `Column` objects, processing data in a two-dimensional setting. Finally, I cover PySpark's lightweight EDA (exploratory data analysis) capabilities through the `summary()` and `describe()` methods. By the end of this chapter, you will be able to explore and change the columnar structure of a data frame. More excitingly, this knowledge will apply regardless of the data format (e.g., hierarchical data in chapter 6).

Just like with every PySpark program, we start by initializing our `SparkSession` object, as in the next listing. I also proactively import the `pyspark.sql.functions` as a qualified `F`, since we saw in chapter 3 that it helps with readability and avoiding potential name clashes for functions.

> **Listing 4.1 Creating our `SparkSession` object to start using PySpark**

```
from pyspark.sql import SparkSession
import pyspark.sql.functions as F

spark = SparkSession.builder.getOrCreate()
```

4.1 What Is tabular data?

We call data tabular when we represent it in a two-dimensional table. You have cells, each containing a single (or *simple*) value, organized into rows and columns. A good example is your grocery list: you may have one column for the item you wish to purchase, one for the quantity, and one for the expected price. Figure 4.1 provides an example of a small grocery list. We have the three columns mentioned, as well as four rows, each representing an entry in our grocery list.

Item	Quantity	Price
Banana	2	1.74
Apple	4	2.04
Carrot	1	1.09
Cake	1	10.99

Figure 4.1 My grocery list represented as tabular data. Each row represents an item, and each column represents an attribute.

The easiest analogy we can make for tabular data is the spreadsheet format: the interface provides you with a large number of rows and columns where you can input and perform computations on data. SQL databases can be thought of as tables made up of rows and columns. Tabular data is an extremely common data format, and because it's so popular and easy to reason about, it makes for a perfect first dive into PySpark's data manipulation API.

PySpark's data frame structure maps very naturally to tabular data. In chapter 2, I explain that PySpark operates either on the whole data frame structure (via methods such as select() and groupby()) or on Column objects (e.g., when using a function like split()). The data frame is *column-major,* so its API focuses on manipulating the columns to transform the data. Because of this, we can simplify how we reason about data transformations by thinking about what operations to perform and which columns will be impacted by them.

> **NOTE**   The resilient distributed dataset, briefly introduced in chapter 1, is a good example of a structure that is *row-major.* Instead of thinking about columns, you are thinking about items (rows) with attributes in which you apply functions. It's an alternative way of thinking about your data, and chapter 8 contains more information about where/when it can be useful.

4.1.1   How does PySpark represent tabular data?

In chapters 2 and 3, our data frame always contained a single column, up to the very end when we counted the occurrence of each word. In other words, we took unstructured data (a body of text), performed some transformations, and created a two-column table containing the information we wanted. Tabular data is, in a way, an extension of this, where we have more than one column to work with.

Let's take my very healthy grocery list as an example, and load it into PySpark. To make things simple, we'll encode our grocery list into a list of lists. PySpark has multiple ways to import tabular data, but the two most popular are the list of lists and the pandas data frame. In chapter 9, I briefly cover how to work with pandas. It would be a bit overkill to import a library just for loading four records (four items on our grocery list), so I kept it in a list of lists.

Listing 4.2   Creating a data frame out of our grocery list

```
my_grocery_list = [
    ["Banana", 2, 1.74],
    ["Apple", 4, 2.04],
    ["Carrot", 1, 1.09],
    ["Cake", 1, 10.99],
]
```
My grocery list is encoded in a list of lists.

```
df_grocery_list = spark.createDataFrame(
    my_grocery_list, ["Item", "Quantity", "Price"]
)
```

```
df_grocery_list.printSchema()
# root
#  |-- Item: string (nullable = true)
#  |-- Quantity: long (nullable = true)
#  |-- Price: double (nullable = true)
```
PySpark automatically inferred the type of each field from the information Python had about each value.

We can easily create a data frame from the data in our program with the `spark.createDataFrame` function, as listing 4.2 shows. Our first parameter is the data itself. You can provide a list of items (here, a list of lists), a pandas data frame, or a resilient distributed dataset, which I cover in chapter 8. The second parameter is the *schema* of the data frame. Chapter 6 covers the automatic and manual schema definitions in greater depth. In the meantime, passing a list of column names will make PySpark happy while it infers the types (`string`, `long`, and `double`, respectively) of our columns. Visually, the data frame will look like figure 4.2, although much more simplified. The master node knows about the structure of the data frame, but the actual data is represented on the worker nodes. Each column maps to data stored somewhere on our cluster that is managed by PySpark. We operate on the abstract structure and let the master delegate the work efficiently.

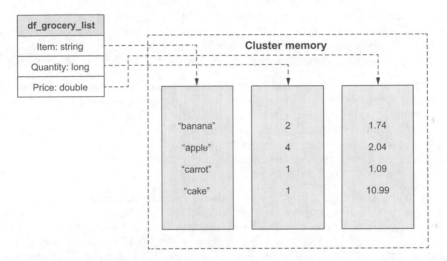

Figure 4.2   Each column of our data frame maps to some place on our worker nodes.

PySpark gladly represented our tabular data using our column definitions. This means that all the functions we've learned so far apply to our tabular data. By having one flexible structure for many data representations—we've covered text and tabular so far—PySpark makes it easy to move from one domain to another. It removes the need to learn yet another set of functions and a whole new abstraction for our data.

This section covered the look and feel of a simple two-dimensional/tabular data frame. In the next section, we ingest and process a more significant data frame. It's time for some coding!

4.2   PySpark for analyzing and processing tabular data

My grocery list was fun, but the potential for analysis work is pretty limited. We'll get our hands on a larger data set, explore it, and ask a few introductory questions that we might find interesting. This process is called *exploratory data analysis* (or EDA) and is usually the first step data analysts and scientists undertake when placed in front of new data. Our goal is to get familiar with the data discovery functions and methods, as well as with performing some basic data assembly. Being familiar with those steps will remove the awkwardness of working with data you won't see transforming before your eyes. This section shows you a blueprint you can reuse when facing new data frames until you can visually process millions of records per second.

Graphical exploratory data analysis

A lot of the EDA work you'll see in the wild incorporates charts and/or tables. Does this mean that PySpark has the option to do the same?

We saw in chapter 2 how to print a data frame so that we can view the content at a glance. This still applies to summarizing information and displaying it on the screen. If you want to export the table in an easy-to-process format (e.g., to incorporate it in a report), you can use `spark.write.csv`, making sure you coalesce the data frame in a single file. (See chapter 3 for a refresher on `coalesce()`.) By its very nature, table summaries won't be very large, so you won't risk running out of memory.

PySpark doesn't provide any charting capabilities and doesn't play with other charting libraries (like Matplotlib, seaborn, Altair, or plot.ly), and this makes a lot of sense: PySpark distributes your data over many computers. It doesn't make much sense to distribute a chart creation. The usual solution will be to transform your data using PySpark, use the `toPandas()` method to transform your PySpark data frame into a pandas data frame, and then use your favorite charting library. When using charts, I provide the code I used to generate them.

When using `toPandas()`, remember that you lose the advantages of working with multiple machines, as the data will accumulate on the driver. Reserve this operation for an aggregated or manageable data set. While this is a crude formula, I usually take the number of rows times the number of columns; if this number is over 100,000 (for a 16 GB driver), I try to reduce it further. This simple trick helps me get a sense of the size of the data I am dealing with, as well as what's possible given my driver size.

You do not want to move your data between a pandas and a PySpark data frame all the time. Reserve `toPandas()` for either discrete operations or for moving your data into a pandas data frame once and for all. Moving back and forth will yield a ton of unnecessary work in distributing and collecting the data for nothing. If you need pandas functionality on a Spark data frame, check out pandas UDFs in chapter 9.

For this exercise, we'll use some open data from the government of Canada, more specifically the CRTC (Canadian Radio-Television and Telecommunications Commission). Every broadcaster is mandated to provide a complete log of the programs and commercials showcased to the Canadian public. This gives us a lot of potential questions to answer, but we'll select just one: *What are the channels with the greatest and least proportion of commercials?*

You can download the file on the Canada Open Data portal (http://mng.bz/y4YJ); select the `BroadcastLogs_2018_Q3_M8` file. The file is 994 MB to download, which might be too large, depending on your computer. The book's repository contains a sample of the data under the data/broadcast_logs directory, which you can use in place of the original file. You also need to download the Data Dictionary in .doc form, as well as the Reference Tables zip file, unzipping them into a `ReferenceTables` directory in `data/broadcast_logs`. Once again, the examples assume that the data is downloaded under data/broadcast_logs and that PySpark is launched from the root of the repository.

Before moving to the next section, make sure you have the following. With the exception of the large `BroadcastLogs` file, the rest is in the repository:

- `data/BroadcastLogs_2018_Q3_M8.CSV` (either download from the website or use the sample from the repo)
- `data/broadcast_logs/ReferenceTables`
- `data/broadcast_logs/data_dictionary.doc`

4.3 Reading and assessing delimited data in PySpark

Now that we have tested the waters with a small synthetic tabular data set, we are ready to dive into real data. Just like in chapter 3, our first step is to read the data before we can perform exploration and transformation. This time, we read data that is a little more complex than just some unorganized text. Because of this, I cover the `Spark-Reader` usage in more detail. As the two-dimensional table is one of the most common organization formats, knowing how to ingest tabular or relational data will become second nature very quickly.

> **TIP** Relational data is often in a SQL database. Spark can read from SQL (or SQL-like) data stores very easily: check chapter 9 for an example where I read from Google BigQuery.

In this section, I start by covering the usage of the `SparkReader` for delimited data, or data that is separated by a *delimited character* (to create this second dimension), by applying it to one of the CRTC data tables. I then review the most common reader's options, so you can read other types of delimited files with ease.

4.3.1 A first pass at the SparkReader specialized for CSV files

Delimited data is a very common, popular, and tricky way of sharing data. In this section, I cover how to read the CRTC tables, which use a pretty common set of conventions for CSV files.

The CSV file format stems from a simple idea: we use *text*, separated in two-dimensional *records* (rows and columns), that are separated by two types of delimiters. Those delimiters are characters, but they serve a special purpose when applied in the context of a CSV file:

- The first one is a *row delimiter*. The row delimiter splits the file into logical records. There is one and only one record between delimiters.

- The second one is a *field delimiter*. Each record is made up of an identical number of fields, and the field delimiter tells where one field starts and ends.

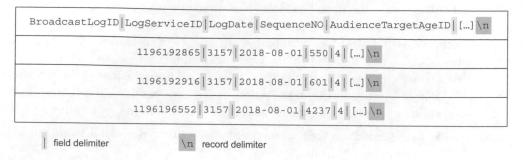

Figure 4.3   A sample of our data, highlighting the field delimiter (|) and row delimiter (\n)

The newline character (\n, when depicted explicitly) is the de facto record delimiter. It naturally breaks down the file into visual lines, where one record starts at the beginning of the line and ends, well, at the end. The comma character (,) is the most frequent field delimiter.

CSV files are easy to produce and have a loose set of rules to follow to be considered usable. Because of this, PySpark provides a whopping 25 optional parameters when ingesting a CSV file. Compare this to the two for reading text data. In listing 4.3, I use three configuration parameters: the record delimiter through sep and the presence of a header (column names) row through header, and I finally ask Spark to infer the data types for me with inferSchema (more on this in section 4.3.2). This is enough to parse our data into a data frame.

Listing 4.3   Reading our broadcasting information

```
import os

DIRECTORY = "./data/broadcast_logs"
logs = spark.read.csv(
    os.path.join(DIRECTORY, "BroadcastLogs_2018_Q3_M8.CSV"),
    sep="|",
    header=True,
    inferSchema=True,
    timestampFormat="yyyy-MM-dd",
)
```

We specify the file path where our data resides first.

Our file uses a vertical bar as delimiter/separator, so we pass | as a parameter to sep.

header takes a Boolean. When true, the first row of your file is parsed as the column names.

inferSchema takes a Boolean as well. When true, it'll pre-parse the data to infer the type of the column.

timestampFormat is used to inform the parser of the format (year, month, day, hour, minutes, seconds, microseconds) of the timestamp fields (see section 4.4.3).

While we were able to read the CSV data for our analysis, this is just one narrow example of the usage of the SparkReader. The next section expands on the most important parameters when reading CSV data and provides more detailed explanations behind the code used in listing 4.3.

4.3.2 *Customizing the SparkReader object to read CSV data files*

This section focuses on how we can specialize the `SparkReader` object to read delimited data and the most popular configuration parameters to accommodate the various declinations of CSV data.

Listing 4.4   The `spark.read.csv` function, with every parameter explicitly laid out

```
logs = spark.read.csv(
    path=os.path.join(DIRECTORY, "BroadcastLogs_2018_Q3_M8.CSV"),
    sep="|",
    header=True,
    inferSchema=True,
    timestampFormat="yyyy-MM-dd",
)
```

Reading delimited data can be a dicey business. Because of how flexible and human-editable the format is, a CSV reader needs to provide many options to cover the many use cases possible. There is also a risk that the file is malformed, in which case you will need to treat it as text and gingerly infer the fields manually. I will stay on the happy path and cover the most popular scenario: a single file, properly delimited.

THE PATH TO THE FILE YOU WANT TO READ AS THE ONLY MANDATORY PARAMETER

Just like when reading text, the only truly mandatory parameter is the `path`, which contains the file or files' path. As we saw in chapter 2, you can use a glob pattern to read multiple files inside a given directory, as long as they have the same structure. You can also explicitly pass a list of file paths if you want specific files to be read.

PASSING AN EXPLICIT FIELD DELIMITER WITH THE SEP PARAMETER

The most common variation you'll encounter when ingesting and producing CSV files is selecting the right delimiter. The comma is the most popular, but it suffers from being a popular character in text, which means you need a way to differentiate which commas are part of the text and which are delimiters. Our file uses the vertical bar character, an apt choice: it's easily reachable on the keyboard yet infrequent in text.

> **NOTE** In French, we use the comma for separating numbers between their integral part and their decimal part (e.g., `1.02` → `1,02`). This is pretty awful when in a CSV file, so most French CSVs will use the semicolon (`;`) as a field delimiter. This is one more example of why you need to be vigilant when using CSV data.

When reading CSV data, PySpark will default to using the comma character as a field delimiter. You can set the optional parameter `sep` (for separator) to the single character you want to use as a field delimiter.

QUOTING TEXT TO AVOID MISTAKING A CHARACTER FOR A DELIMITER

When working with CSVs that use the comma as a delimiter, it's common practice to *quote* the text fields to make sure any comma in the text is not mistaken for a field separator. The CSV reader object provides an optional quote parameter that defaults to the double-quote character ("). Since I am not passing an explicit value to quote, we are keeping the default value. This way, we can have a field with the value "Three | Trois", whereas without the quotation characters, we would consider this two fields. If we don't want to use any character as a quote, we need to explicitly pass the empty string to quote.

USING THE FIRST ROW AS THE COLUMN NAMES

The header optional parameter takes a Boolean flag. If set to true, it'll use the first row of your file (or files, if you're ingesting many) and use it to set your column names.

   You can also pass an explicit schema (see chapter 6) or a DDL string (see chapter 7) as the schema optional parameter if you wish to explicitly name your columns. If you don't fill any of those, your data frame will have _c* for column names, where the * is replaced with increasing integers (_c0, _c1, . . .).

INFERRING COLUMN TYPE WHILE READING THE DATA

PySpark has a schema-discovering capacity. You turn it on by setting inferSchema to True (by default, this is turned off). This optional parameter forces PySpark to go over the ingested data twice: one time to set the type of each column, and one time to ingest the data. This makes the ingestion quite a bit longer but helps us avoid writing the schema by hand (I go down to this level of detail in chapter 6). Let the machine do the work!

> **TIP** Inferring the schema can be very expensive if you have a lot of data. In chapter 6, I cover how to work with (and extract) schema information; if you read a data source multiple times, it's a good idea to keep the schema information once inferred! You can also take a small representative data set to infer the schema, followed by reading the large data set.

We are lucky enough that the government of Canada is a good steward of data and provides us with clean, properly formatted files. In the wild, malformed CSV files are legion, and you will run into errors when trying to ingest some of them. Furthermore, if your data is large, you often won't get the chance to inspect each row to fix mistakes. Chapter 6 covers some strategies to ease the pain and shows you some ways to share your data with the schema included.

   Our data frame schema, displayed in the next listing, is coherent with the documentation we've downloaded. The column names are properly displayed, and the types make sense. That's enough to get started with some exploration.

Listing 4.5   The schema of our logs data frame

```
logs.printSchema()
# root
#  |-- BroadcastLogID: integer (nullable = true)
```

```
#  |-- LogServiceID: integer (nullable = true)
#  |-- LogDate: timestamp (nullable = true)
#  |-- SequenceNO: integer (nullable = true)
#  |-- AudienceTargetAgeID: integer (nullable = true)
#  |-- AudienceTargetEthnicID: integer (nullable = true)
#  |-- CategoryID: integer (nullable = true)
#  |-- ClosedCaptionID: integer (nullable = true)
#  |-- CountryOfOriginID: integer (nullable = true)
#  |-- DubDramaCreditID: integer (nullable = true)
#  |-- EthnicProgramID: integer (nullable = true)
#  |-- ProductionSourceID: integer (nullable = true)
#  |-- ProgramClassID: integer (nullable = true)
#  |-- FilmClassificationID: integer (nullable = true)
#  |-- ExhibitionID: integer (nullable = true)
#  |-- Duration: string (nullable = true)
#  |-- EndTime: string (nullable = true)
#  |-- LogEntryDate: timestamp (nullable = true)
#  |-- ProductionNO: string (nullable = true)
#  |-- ProgramTitle: string (nullable = true)
#  |-- StartTime: string (nullable = true)
#  |-- Subtitle: string (nullable = true)
#  |-- NetworkAffiliationID: integer (nullable = true)
#  |-- SpecialAttentionID: integer (nullable = true)
#  |-- BroadcastOriginPointID: integer (nullable = true)
#  |-- CompositionID: integer (nullable = true)
#  |-- Producer1: string (nullable = true)
#  |-- Producer2: string (nullable = true)
#  |-- Language1: integer (nullable = true)
#  |-- Language2: integer (nullable = true)
```

Exercise 4.1

Let's take the following file, called sample.csv, which contains three columns:

```
Item,Quantity,Price
$Banana, organic$,1,0.99
Pear,7,1.24
$Cake, chocolate$,1,14.50
```

Complete the following code to ingest the file successfully.

```
sample = spark.read.csv([...],
                        sep=[...],
                        header=[...],
                        quote=[...],
                        inferSchema=[...]
)
```

(Note: If you want to test your code, sample.csv is available in the book's repository under data/sample.csv/sample.csv).

4.3.3   *Exploring the shape of our data universe*

When working with tabular data, especially if it comes from a SQL data warehouse, you'll often find that the data set is split between tables. In our case, our logs table contains a majority of fields suffixed by ID; those IDs are listed in other tables, and we have to link them to get the legend of those IDs. This section briefly introduces star schemas, why they are so frequently encountered, and how we can visually represent them to work with them.

Our data universe (the set of tables we are working with) follows a very common pattern in relational databases: a center table containing a bunch of IDs (or *keys*) and some ancillary tables containing a legend between each key and its value. This is called a *star schema* since it looks like a star. Star schemas are common in the relational database world because of *normalization*, a process used to avoid duplicating pieces of data and improve data integrity. Data normalization is illustrated in figure 4.4, where our center table logs contain IDs that map to the auxiliary tables called *link tables*. In the case of the CD_Category link table, it contains many fields (e.g., Category_CD and English_description) that are made available to logs when you link the tables with the Category_ID key.

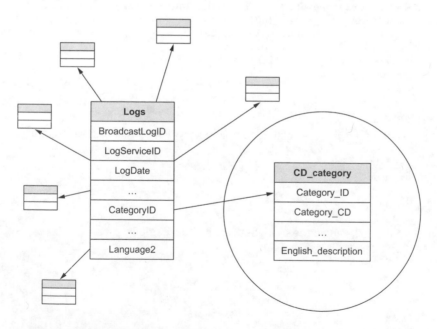

Figure 4.4   The logs table ID columns map to other tables, like the CD_category table, which links the Category_ID field.

In Spark's universe, we often prefer working with a single table instead of linking a multitude of tables to get the data. We call these *denormalized* tables, or, colloquially, *fat* tables. We start by assessing the data directly available in the logs table before plumping our table, a topic I cover in chapter 5. By looking at the `logs` table, its content, and the data documentation, we avoid linking tables that contain data with no real value for our analysis.

> **The right structure for the right work**
>
> Normalization, denormalization—what gives? Isn't this a book about data analysis?
>
> While this book isn't about data modelling, it's important to understand, at least a little, how data might be structured so that we can work with it. Normalized data has many advantages when you're working with relational information (e.g., our broadcast tables). In addition to being easier to maintain, data normalization reduces the probability of getting anomalies or illogical records in the data. On the flip side, large-scale data systems sometimes embrace denormalized tables to avoid costly join operations.
>
> When dealing with analytics, a single table containing all the data is best. However, having to link/join the data by hand can be tedious, especially when working with dozens or even hundreds of link tables (check out chapter 5 for more information about joins). Fortunately, data warehouses don't change their structure very often. If you're faced with a complex star schema one day, befriend one of the database managers. There is a very good chance they'll provide you with the information to denormalize the tables, most often in SQL, and chapter 7 will show how you can adapt the code into PySpark with minimum effort.

4.4 The basics of data manipulation: Selecting, dropping, renaming, ordering, diagnosing

It is common practice to explore and summarize the data when you first get acquainted with it. It's just like a first date with your data: you want a good overview, not to have agonize over the details. (In Québécois French, we say *s'enfarger dans les fleurs du tapis* to refer to someone who's too bogged down on the details. Translated, it means "to trip over the rug's flowers.") This section shows the most common manipulations done on a data frame in greater detail. I show how you can select, delete, rename, reorder, and create columns so you can customize how a data frame is shown. I also cover summarizing a data frame so you can have a quick diagnostic overview of the data inside your structure. No flowers required.

4.4.1 Knowing what we want: Selecting columns

So far, we've learned that typing our data frame variable into the shell prints the structure of the data frame, not the data, unless you're using eagerly evaluated Spark (referenced in chapter 2). We can also use the `show()` command to display a few records for exploration. I won't show the results, but if you try it, you'll see that the table-esque output is garbled because we are showing too many columns at once. This section reintroduces the `select()` method, which, this time, instructs PySpark on the columns you want to keep in your data frame. I also introduce how you can refer to columns when using PySpark methods and functions.

At its simplest, `select()` can take one or more column objects—or strings representing column names—and return a data frame containing only the listed columns. This way, we can keep our exploration tidy and check a few columns at a time. An example is displayed in the next listing.

Listing 4.6   Selecting five rows of the first three columns of our data frame

```
logs.select("BroadcastLogID", "LogServiceID", "LogDate").show(5, False)

# +--------------+------------+-------------------+
# |BroadcastLogID|LogServiceID|LogDate            |
# +--------------+------------+-------------------+
# |1196192316    |3157        |2018-08-01 00:00:00|
# |1196192317    |3157        |2018-08-01 00:00:00|
# |1196192318    |3157        |2018-08-01 00:00:00|
# |1196192319    |3157        |2018-08-01 00:00:00|
# |1196192320    |3157        |2018-08-01 00:00:00|
# +--------------+------------+-------------------+
# only showing top 5 rows
```

In chapter 2, you learned that `.show(5, False)` shows five rows without truncating their representation so that we can show the whole content. The `.select()` statement is where the magic happens. In the documentation, `select()` takes a single parameter, `*cols`; the `*` means that the method will accept an arbitrary number of parameters. If we pass multiple column names, `select()` will simply clump all the parameters in a tuple called `cols`.

Because of this, we can use the same de-structuring trick for selecting columns. From a PySpark perspective, the four statements in listing 4.7 are interpreted the same. Note how prefixing the list with a star removed the container so that each element becomes a parameter of the function. If this looks a little confusing to you, fear not! Appendix C provides you with a good overview of collection unpacking.

Listing 4.7   Four ways to select columns in PySpark, all equivalent in terms of results

```
# Using the string to column conversion
logs.select("BroadCastLogID", "LogServiceID", "LogDate")
logs.select(*["BroadCastLogID", "LogServiceID", "LogDate"])

# Passing the column object explicitly
logs.select(
    F.col("BroadCastLogID"), F.col("LogServiceID"), F.col("LogDate")
)
logs.select(
    *[F.col("BroadCastLogID"), F.col("LogServiceID"), F.col("LogDate")]
)
```

When explicitly selecting a few columns, you don't have to wrap them into a list. If you're already working on a list of columns, you can unpack them with a `*` prefix. This argument unpacking pattern is worth remembering as many other data frame methods taking columns as input use the same approach.

In the spirit of being clever (or lazy), let's expand our selection code to see every column in groups of three. This will give us a sense of the content. A data frame keeps track of its columns in the `columns` attributes; `logs.columns` is a Python list containing all the column names of the `logs` data frame. In the next listing, I slice the columns into groups of three to display them by small groups rather than in one fell swoop.

Listing 4.8 Peeking at the data frame in chunks of three columns

```
import numpy as np

column_split = np.array_split(
    np.array(logs.columns), len(logs.columns) // 3    ◁─
)

print(column_split)

# [array(['BroadcastLogID', 'LogServiceID', 'LogDate'], dtype='<U22'),
# [...]
# array(['Producer2', 'Language1', 'Language2'], dtype='<U22')]'

for x in column_split:
    logs.select(*x).show(5, False)

# +--------------+------------+-------------------+
# |BroadcastLogID|LogServiceID|LogDate            |
# +--------------+------------+-------------------+
# |1196192316    |3157        |2018-08-01 00:00:00|
# |1196192317    |3157        |2018-08-01 00:00:00|
# |1196192318    |3157        |2018-08-01 00:00:00|
# |1196192319    |3157        |2018-08-01 00:00:00|
# |1196192320    |3157        |2018-08-01 00:00:00|
# +--------------+------------+-------------------+
# only showing top 5 rows
# ... and more tables of three columns
```

> The array_split() function comes from the numpy package, imported as np at the beginning of this listing.

Let's take each line one at a time. We start by splitting the `logs.columns` list into approximate groups of three. To do so, we rely on a function from the `numpy` package called `array_split()`. The function takes an array and a number of desired sub-arrays, N, and returns a list of N sub-arrays. We wrap our list of columns, `logs.columns`, into an array via the `np.array` function and pass this as a first parameter. For the number of sub-arrays, we divide the number of columns by three, using an integer division, `//`.

> **TIP** To be perfectly honest, the call to `np.array` can be eschewed since `np.array_split()` can work on lists, albeit more slowly. I am still using it because if you are using a static type checker, such as mypy, you'll get a type error. Chapter 8 has a basic introduction to type checking in your PySpark program.

The last part of listing 4.8 iterates over the list of sub-arrays, using `select()`; select the columns present inside each sub-array and use `show()` to display them on the screen.

> **TIP** If you use Databricks notebooks, you can use `display(logs)` to show the `logs` data frame in an attractive table format.

This example shows how easy it is to blend Python code with PySpark. In addition to providing a trove of functions, the data frame API also exposes information, such as column names, into convenient Python structures. I won't avoid using functionality from libraries when it makes sense, but, like in listing 4.8, I'll do my best to explain what it does and why we're using it. Chapter 8 and 9 go deeper into how you can combine pure Python code in PySpark.

4.4.2 *Keeping what we need: Deleting columns*

The other side of selecting columns is choosing what not to select. We could do the full trip with `select()`, carefully crafting our list of columns to keep just the one we want. Fortunately, PySpark also provides a shorter trip: simply drop what you don't want.

Let's get rid of two columns in our current data frame in the spirit of tidying up. Hopefully, it will bring us joy:

- `BroadCastLogID` is the primary key of the table and will not serve us in answering our questions.
- `SequenceNo` is a sequence number and won't be useful either.

More will come off later when we start looking at the link tables. The code in the next listing does this simply.

Listing 4.9   Getting rid of columns using the `drop()` method

```
logs = logs.drop("BroadcastLogID", "SequenceNO")

# Testing if we effectively got rid of the columns

print("BroadcastLogID" in logs.columns)  # => False
print("SequenceNo" in logs.columns)  # => False
```

Just like `select()`, `drop()` takes a `*cols` and returns a data frame, this time excluding the columns passed as parameters. Just like every other method in PySpark, `drop()` returns a new data frame, so we overwrite our `logs` variable by assigning the result of our code.

> **WARNING** Unlike `select()`, where selecting a column that doesn't exist will return a runtime error, dropping a nonexistent column is a no-op. PySpark will simply ignore the columns it doesn't find. Be careful with the spelling of your column names!

Depending on how many columns you want to preserve, `select()` might be a neater way to keep only what you want. We can view `drop()` and `select()` as being two sides of the same coin: one drops what you specify; the other keeps what you specify. We could reproduce listing 4.9 with a `select()` method, and the next listing does just that.

Listing 4.10   Getting rid of columns, select style

```
logs = logs.select(
    *[x for x in logs.columns if x not in ["BroadcastLogID", "SequenceNO"]]
)
```

Advanced topic: An unfortunate inconsistency

In theory, you can also `select()` columns with a list without unpacking them. This code will work as expected:

```
logs = logs.select(
    [x for x in logs.columns if x not in ["BroadcastLogID", "SequenceNO"]]
)
```

This is not the case for `drop()`, where you need to explicitly unpack:

```
logs.drop(logs.columns[:])
# TypeError: col should be a string or a Column

logs.drop(*logs.columns[:])
# DataFrame[]
```

I'd rather unpack explicitly and avoid the cognitive load of remembering when it's mandatory and when it's optional.

You now know the most fundamental operations to perform on a data frame. You can select and drop columns, and with the flexibility of `select()` presented in chapters 2 and 3, you can apply functions on existing columns to transform them. The next section will cover how you can create new columns without having to rely on `select()`, simplifying your code and improving its resiliency.

NOTE   In chapter 6, we learn about restricting the data read directly from the schema definition. This is an attractive way to avoid dropping columns in the first place.

Exercise 4.2

What is the printed result of this code?

```
sample_frame.columns # => ['item', 'price', 'quantity', 'UPC']

print(sample_frame.drop('item', 'UPC', 'prices').columns)
```

   a   `['item' 'UPC']`
   b   `['item', 'upc']`
   c   `['price', 'quantity']`
   d   `['price', 'quantity', 'UPC']`
   e   Raises an error

4.4.3   *Creating what's not there: New columns with withColumn()*

Creating new columns is such a basic operation that it seems a little far-fetched to rely on select(). It also puts a lot of pressure on code readability; for instance, using drop() makes it obvious we're removing columns. It would be nice to have something that signals we're creating a new column. PySpark named this function withColumn().

Before going crazy with column creation, let's take a simple example, build what we need iteratively, and then move the data to withColumn(). Let's take the Duration column, which contains the length of each program shown.

Listing 4.11   Selecting and displaying the Duration column

```
logs.select(F.col("Duration")).show(5)

# +----------------+
# |        Duration|
# +----------------+
# |02:00:00.0000000|
# |00:00:30.0000000|
# |00:00:15.0000000|
# |00:00:15.0000000|
# |00:00:15.0000000|
# +----------------+
# only showing top 5 rows

print(logs.select(F.col("Duration")).dtypes)    ◁——  The dtypes attribute of a data
                                                       frame contains the name of the
# [('Duration', 'string')]                             column and its type, wrapped
                                                       in a tuple.
```

PySpark doesn't have a default type for time without dates or duration, so it kept the column as a string. We verified the exact type via the dtypes attribute, which returns both the name and type of a data frame's columns. A string is a safe and reasonable option, but this isn't remarkably useful for our purpose. Thanks to our peeking, we can see that the string is formatted like HH:MM:SS.mmmmmm, where

- HH is the duration in hours.
- MM is the duration in minutes.
- SS is the duration in seconds.
- mmmmmmm is the duration in microseconds.

NOTE   To match an arbitrary date/timestamp pattern, refer to the Spark documentation for date-time patterns at http://mng.bz/M2X2.

I ignore the duration in microseconds since I don't think it'll make much of a difference. The pyspark.sql.functions module (which we aliased as F) contains the substr() function that extracts a substring from a string column. In listing 4.12, I use it to extract the hours, minutes, and seconds from the Duration columns. The substr() method takes two parameters. The first gives the position of where the sub-string starts, the first character being 1, not 0 like in Python. The second gives the length of the sub-string we want to extract in a number of characters. The function application returns a string Column that I convert to an Integer via the cast() method. Finally, I provide an alias for each column so that we can easily tell which is which.

Listing 4.12   Extracting the hours, minutes, and seconds from the Duration column

```
logs.select(
    F.col("Duration"),                                              The original column,
    F.col("Duration").substr(1, 2).cast("int").alias("dur_hours"),   for sanity.
    F.col("Duration").substr(4, 2).cast("int").alias("dur_minutes"),
    F.col("Duration").substr(7, 2).cast("int").alias("dur_seconds"),
).distinct().show(
    5
)
```

To avoid seeing identical rows, I've added a distinct() to the results.

The seventh and eighth characters are the seconds.

The fourth and fifth characters are the minutes.

The first two characters are the hours.

```
# +---------------+---------+-----------+-----------+
# |       Duration|dur_hours|dur_minutes|dur_seconds|
# +---------------+---------+-----------+-----------+
# |00:10:06.0000000|        0|         10|          6|
# |00:10:37.0000000|        0|         10|         37|
# |00:04:52.0000000|        0|          4|         52|
# |00:26:41.0000000|        0|         26|         41|
# |00:08:18.0000000|        0|          8|         18|
# +---------------+---------+-----------+-----------+
# only showing top 5 rows
```

I use the distinct() method before show(), which de-dupes the data frame. This is explained further in chapter 5. I added distinct() to avoid seeing identical occurrences that would provide no additional information when displayed.

NOTE We could rely on the datetime and timedelta Python constructs through a UDF (see chapters 8 and 9). Depending on the type of UDF (simple versus vectorized), the performance can be slower or comparable to using this approach. While UDFs have their dedicated chapters, I try to use as much functionality from the PySpark API as possible, leveraging UDF when I need functionality beyond what's available.

I think that we're in good shape! Let's merge all these values into a single field: the duration of the program in seconds. PySpark can perform arithmetic with column objects using the same operators as Python, so this will be a breeze! In the next listing, we apply addition and multiplication on integer columns, just like if they were simple number values.

Listing 4.13   Creating a duration in second field from the Duration column

```
logs.select(
    F.col("Duration"),
    (
        F.col("Duration").substr(1, 2).cast("int") * 60 * 60
        + F.col("Duration").substr(4, 2).cast("int") * 60
```

```
          + F.col("Duration").substr(7, 2).cast("int")
      ).alias("Duration_seconds"),
).distinct().show(5)

# +----------------+----------------+
# |        Duration|Duration_seconds|
# +----------------+----------------+
# |00:10:30.0000000|             630|
# |00:25:52.0000000|            1552|
# |00:28:08.0000000|            1688|
# |06:00:00.0000000|           21600|
# |00:32:08.0000000|            1928|
# +----------------+----------------+
# only showing top 5 rows
```

We kept the same definitions, removed the alias, and performed arithmetic directly on the columns. There are 60 seconds in a minute, and 60 * 60 seconds in an hour. PySpark respects operator precedence, so we don't have to clobber our equation with parentheses. Overall, our code is quite easy to follow, and we are ready to add our column to our data frame.

What if we want to add a column at the end of our data frame? Instead of using `select()` on all the columns *plus* our new one, let's use `withColumn()`. Applied to a data frame, it'll return a data frame with the new column appended. The next listing takes our field and adds it to our `logs` data frame. I also include a sample of the `printSchema()` method so that you can see the column added at the end.

> ### Listing 4.14   Creating a new column with `withColumn()`

```
logs = logs.withColumn(
    "Duration_seconds",
    (
        F.col("Duration").substr(1, 2).cast("int") * 60 * 60
        + F.col("Duration").substr(4, 2).cast("int") * 60
        + F.col("Duration").substr(7, 2).cast("int")
    ),
)

logs.printSchema()

# root
#  |-- LogServiceID: integer (nullable = true)
#  |-- LogDate: timestamp (nullable = true)
#  |-- AudienceTargetAgeID: integer (nullable = true)
#  |-- AudienceTargetEthnicID: integer (nullable = true)
#  [... more columns]
#  |-- Language2: integer (nullable = true)
#  |-- Duration_seconds: integer (nullable = true)
```

Our Duration_seconds columns have been added at the end of our data frame.

WARNING   If you create a column `withColumn()` and give it a name that already exists in your data frame, PySpark will happily overwrite the column.

This is often very useful for keeping the number of columns manageable, but make sure you are seeking this effect!

We can create columns using the same expression with `select()` and with `withColumn()`. Both approaches have their use. `select()` will be useful when you're explicitly working with a few columns. When you need to create a few new ones without changing the rest of the data frame, I prefer `withColumn()`. You'll quickly gain intuition about which is easiest when faced with the choice.

> **WARNING** Creating many (100+) new columns using `withColumns()` will slow Spark down to a grind. If you need to create a lot of columns at once, use the `select()` approach. While it will generate the same work, it is less tasking on the query planner.

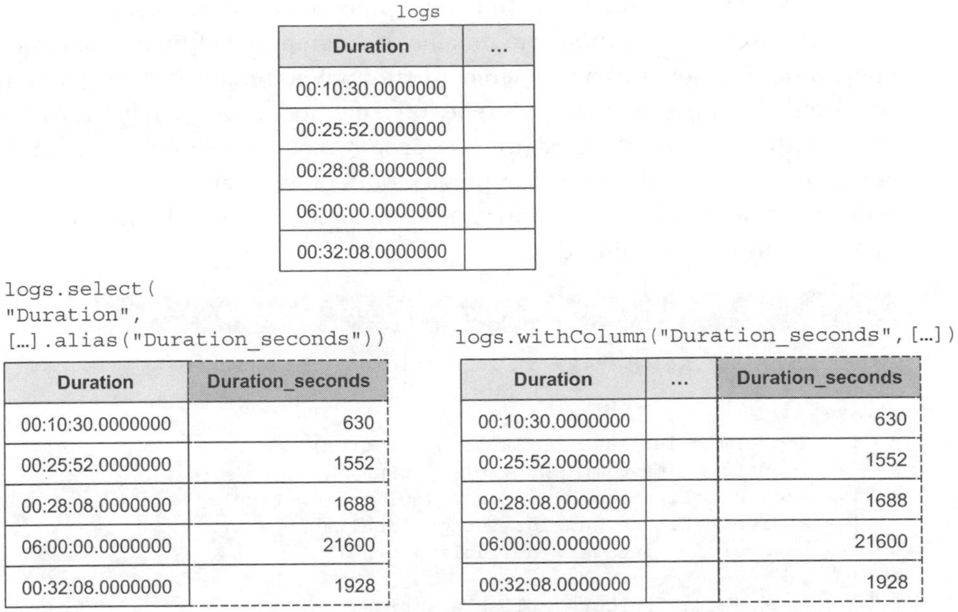

logs

Duration	...
00:10:30.0000000	
00:25:52.0000000	
00:28:08.0000000	
06:00:00.0000000	
00:32:08.0000000	

```
logs.select(
"Duration",
[…].alias("Duration_seconds"))
```

Duration	Duration_seconds
00:10:30.0000000	630
00:25:52.0000000	1552
00:28:08.0000000	1688
06:00:00.0000000	21600
00:32:08.0000000	1928

```
logs.withColumn("Duration_seconds", […])
```

Duration	...	Duration_seconds
00:10:30.0000000		630
00:25:52.0000000		1552
00:28:08.0000000		1688
06:00:00.0000000		21600
00:32:08.0000000		1928

Figure 4.5 `select()` versus `withColumn()`, visually. `withColumn()` keeps all the preexisting columns without the need the specify them explicitly.

4.4.4 Tidying our data frame: Renaming and reordering columns

This section covers how to make the order and names of the columns friendlier. It might seem a little vapid, but after a few hours of hammering code on a particularly tough piece of data, you'll be happy to have this in your toolbox.

Renaming columns can be done with `select()` and `alias()`, of course. We saw briefly in chapter 3 that PySpark provides you an easier way to do so. Enter `withColumnRenamed()`! In the following listing, I use `withColumnRenamed()` to remove the capital letters of my newly created `duration_seconds` column.

Listing 4.15   Renaming one column at a type, the `withColumnRenamed()` way

```
logs = logs.withColumnRenamed("Duration_seconds", "duration_seconds")

logs.printSchema()

# root
#  |-- LogServiceID: integer (nullable = true)
#  |-- LogDate: timestamp (nullable = true)
#  |-- AudienceTargetAgeID: integer (nullable = true)
#  |-- AudienceTargetEthnicID: integer (nullable = true)
#  [...]
#  |-- Language2: integer (nullable = true)
#  |-- duration_seconds: integer (nullable = true)
```

I'm a huge fan of having column names without capital letters. I'm a lazy typist, and pressing Shift all the time adds up! I could potentially use `withColumnRenamed()` with a `for` loop over all the columns to rename them in my data frame. The PySpark developers thought about this and offered a better way to rename all the columns of your data frame in one fell swoop. This relies on a method, `toDF()`, that returns a new data frame with the new columns. Just like `drop()`, `toDF()` takes a `*cols`, and just like `select()` and `drop()`, we need to unpack our column names if they're in a list. The code in the next listing shows how you can rename all your columns to lowercase in a single line using that method.

Listing 4.16   Batch lowercasing using the `toDF()` method

```
logs.toDF(*[x.lower() for x in logs.columns]).printSchema()

# root
#  |-- logserviceid: integer (nullable = true)
#  |-- logdate: timestamp (nullable = true)
#  |-- audiencetargetageid: integer (nullable = true)
#  |-- audiencetargetethnicid: integer (nullable = true)
#  |-- categoryid: integer (nullable = true)
#  [...]
#  |-- language2: integer (nullable = true)
#  |-- duration_seconds: integer (nullable = true)
```

If you carefully look at the code, you can see that I'm not assigning the resulting data frame. I wanted to showcase the functionality, but since we have ancillary tables with column names that match, I wanted to avoid the trouble of lowercasing every column in every table.

Our final step is *reordering* columns. Since reordering columns is equivalent to selecting columns in a different order, `select()` is the perfect method for the job. For instance, if we wanted to sort the columns alphabetically, we could use the `sorted` function on the list of our data frame columns, just like in the next listing.

Listing 4.17　Selecting our columns in alphabetical order using `select()`

```
logs.select(sorted(logs.columns)).printSchema()

# root
#  |-- AudienceTargetAgeID: integer (nullable = true)
#  |-- AudienceTargetEthnicID: integer (nullable = true)
#  |-- BroadcastOriginPointID: integer (nullable = true)
#  |-- CategoryID: integer (nullable = true)
#  |-- ClosedCaptionID: integer (nullable = true)
#  |-- CompositionID: integer (nullable = true)
#  [...]
#  |-- Subtitle: string (nullable = true)
#  |-- duration_seconds: integer (nullable = true)    <--
```

Remember that, in most programming languages, capital letters come before lowercase ones.

In this section, we covered a lot of ground: through selecting, dropping, creating, renaming, and reordering columns, we gained intuition about how PySpark manages and provides visibility over the structure of the data frame. In the next section, I cover a way to quickly explore the data in the data frame.

4.4.5　Diagnosing a data frame with describe() and summary()

When working with numerical data, looking at a long column of values isn't very useful. We're often more concerned about some key information, which may include count, mean, standard deviation, minimum, and maximum. In this section, I cover how we can quickly explore numerical columns using PySpark's `describe()` and `summary()` methods.

When applied to a data frame with no parameters, `describe()` will show summary statistics (count, mean, standard deviation, min, and max) on all numerical and string columns. To avoid screen overflow, I display the column descriptions one by one by iterating over the list of columns and showing the output of `describe()` in the next listing. Note that `describe()` will (lazily) compute the data frame but won't display it, just like any transformation, so we have to `show()` the result.

Listing 4.18　Describing everything in one fell swoop

```
for i in logs.columns:
    logs.describe(i).show()

# +-------+------------------+
# |summary|      LogServiceID|
# +-------+------------------+
# |  count|           7169318|
# |   mean|3453.8804215407936|
# | stddev|200.44137201584468|
# |    min|              3157|
# |    max|              3925|
# +-------+------------------+
#
# [...]
```

Numerical columns will display the information in a description table, like so.

```
#
# +-------+          ◁——  If the type of the column isn't
# |summary|                compatible, PySpark displays
# +-------+                only the title column.
# |  count|
# |   mean|
# | stddev|
# |    min|
# |    max|
# +-------+

# [... many more little tables]
```

It will take more time than doing everything in one fell swoop, but the output will be a lot friendlier. Since we can't compute the mean or standard deviation of a string, you'll see `null` values for those columns. Furthermore, some columns won't be displayed (you'll see time tables with only the title column), as `describe()` will only work for numerical and string columns. For a short line to type, you still get a lot!

`describe()` is a fantastic method, but what if you want more? `summary()` to the rescue!

Where `describe()` will take `*cols` as a parameter (one or more columns, the same way as `select()` or `drop()`), `summary()` will take `*statistics` as a parameter. This means that you'll need to select the columns you want to see before passing the `summary()` method. On the other hand, we can customize the statistics we want to see. By default, `summary()` shows everything `describe()` shows, adding the approximate 25-50% and 75% percentiles. The next listing shows how you can replace `describe()` for `summary()` and the result of doing so.

Listing 4.19   Summarizing everything in one fell swoop

```
for i in logs.columns:
    logs.select(i).summary().show()         ◁——  By default, we have count,
                                                  mean, stddev, min, 25%,
# +-------+------------------+                    50%, 75%, max as statistics.
# |summary|      LogServiceID|
# +-------+------------------+
# |  count|           7169318|
# |   mean|3453.8804215407936|
# | stddev|200.44137201584468|
# |    min|              3157|
# |    25%|              3291|
# |    50%|              3384|
# |    75%|              3628|
# |    max|              3925|
# +-------+------------------+
#
# [... many more slightly larger tables]     We can also pass our
                                             own, following the same
                                             nomenclature convention.
for i in logs.columns:
    logs.select(i).summary("min", "10%", "90%", "max").show()    ◁——
```

```
#  +-------+------------+
#  |summary|LogServiceID|
#  +-------+------------+
#  |    min|        3157|
#  |    10%|        3237|
#  |    90%|        3710|
#  |    max|        3925|
#  +-------+------------+
#
#  [...]
```

If you want to limit yourself to a subset of those metrics, summary() will accept a number of string parameters representing the statistic. You can input count, mean, stddev, min, or max directly. For approximate percentiles, you need to provide them in XX% format, such as 25%.

Both methods will work only on non-null values. For the summary statistics, it's the expected behavior, but the "count" entry will also count only the non-null values for each column. This is a good way to see which columns are mostly empty!

> **WARNING** describe() and summary() are two very useful methods, but they are not meant to be used for anything other than quickly peeking at data during development. The PySpark developers don't guarantee that the output will look the same from version to version, so if you need one of the outputs for your program, use the corresponding function in pyspark.sql.functions. They're all there.

This chapter covered the ingestion and discovery of a tabular data set, one of the most popular data representation formats. We built on the basics of PySpark data manipulation, covered in chapters 2 and 3, and added a new layer by working with columns. The next chapter will be the direct continuation of this one, where we will explore more advanced aspects of the data frame structure.

Summary

- PySpark uses the SparkReader object to directly read any kind of data in a data frame. The specialized CSVSparkReader is used to ingest CSV files. Just like when reading text, the only mandatory parameter is the source location.
- The CSV format is very versatile, so PySpark provides many optional parameters to account for this flexibility. The most important ones are the field delimiter, the record delimiter, and the quotation character, all of which have sensible defaults.
- PySpark can infer the schema of a CSV file by setting the inferSchema optional parameter to True. PySpark accomplishes this by reading the data twice: once for setting the appropriate types for each column and once to ingest the data in the inferred format.
- Tabular data is represented in a data frame in a series of columns, each having a name and a type. Since the data frame is a column-major data structure, the concept of rows is less relevant.

- You can use Python code to explore the data efficiently, using the column list as any Python list to expose the elements of the data frame of interest.
- The most common operations on a data frame are the selection, deletion, and creation of columns. In PySpark, the methods used are `select()`, `drop()`, and `withColumn()`, respectively.
- `select` can be used for column reordering by passing a reordered list of columns.
- You can rename columns one by one with the `withColumnRenamed()` method, or all at once by using the `toDF()` method.
- You can display a summary of the columns with the `describe()` or `summary()` methods. `describe()` has a fixed set of metrics, while `summary()` will take functions as parameters and apply them to all columns.

Additional exercises

Exercise 4.3

Reread the data in a `logs_raw` data frame (the data file is `./data/broadcast_logs-BroadcastLogs_2018_Q3_M8.CSV`), this time without passing any optional parameters. Print the first five rows of data, as well as the schema. What are the differences in terms of data and schema between `logs` and `logs_raw`?

Exercise 4.4

Create a new data frame, `logs_clean`, that contains only the columns that do not end with `ID`.

Data frame gymnastics: Joining and grouping

This chapter covers

- Joining two data frames together
- Selecting the right type of join for your use case
- Grouping data and understanding the `GroupedData` transitional object
- Breaking the `GroupedData` with an aggregation method
- Filling `null` values in your data frame

In chapter 4, we looked at how we can transform a data frame using selection, dropping, creation, renaming, reordering, and creating a summary of columns. Those operations constitute the foundation for working with a data frame in PySpark. In this chapter, I will complete the review of the most common operations you will perform on a data frame: linking or *joining* data frames, as well as grouping data (and performing operations on the `GroupedData` object). We conclude this chapter by wrapping our exploratory program into a single script we can submit, just like we performed in chapter 3. The skills learned in this chapter complete the set of fundamental operations you will use in your day-to-day work transforming data.

We use the same `logs` data frames that we left in chapter 4. In practical steps, this chapter's code enriches our table with the relevant information contained in the link tables and then summarizes it in relevant groups, using what can be considered a graduate version of the `describe()` method I show in chapter 4. If you want to catch up with a minimal amount of fuss, I provide a `checkpoint.py` script in the `code/Ch04-05` directory.

5.1 From many to one: Joining data

When working with data, we're most often working on one structure at a time. Thus far, we've explored the many ways we can slice, dice, and modify a data frame to fit our wildest desires. What happens when we need to link two sources? This section will introduce joins and how we can apply them when using a star schema setup or another set of tables where values match exactly.

Joining data frames is a common operation when working with related tables. If you've used other data-processing libraries, you might have seen the same operation called a *merge* or a *link*. Because there are multiple ways to perform joins, the next section sets a common vocabulary to avoid confusion and build understanding on solid ground.

5.1.1 What's what in the world of joins

This section covers the core blueprint of joins. I introduce the general syntax for the `join()` method, as well as the different parameters. With this, you'll recognize and know how to construct a basic join and be ready to undertake the subtlety of performing more specific join operations.

At the most basic level, a `join` operation is a way to take the data from one data frame and link it to another one according to a set of rules. To introduce the moving parts of a join, I provide a second table to be joined to our `logs` data frame in listing 5.1. I use the same parameterization of the `SparkReader.csv` as used for the `logs` table to read our new `log_identifier` table. Once the table is ingested, I filter the data frame to keep only the primary channels, as per the data documentation. With this, we should be good to go.

Listing 5.1   Exploring our first link table: `log_identifier`

```
DIRECTORY = "./data/broadcast_logs"
log_identifier = spark.read.csv(
    os.path.join(DIRECTORY, "ReferenceTables/LogIdentifier.csv"),
    sep="|",
    header=True,
    inferSchema=True,
)


log_identifier.printSchema()
# root
#  |-- LogIdentifierID: string (nullable = true)
```

This is the channel identifier.

```
#  |-- LogServiceID: integer (nullable = true)
#  |-- PrimaryFG: integer (nullable = true)

log_identifier = log_identifier.where(F.col("PrimaryFG") == 1)
print(log_identifier.count())
# 758

log_identifier.show(5)
# +---------------+------------+---------+
# |LogIdentifierID|LogServiceID|PrimaryFG|
# +---------------+------------+---------+
# |           13ST|        3157|        1|
# |         2000SM|        3466|        1|
# |           70SM|        3883|        1|
# |           80SM|        3590|        1|
# |           90SM|        3470|        1|
# +---------------+------------+---------+
# only showing top 5 rows
```

This is a Boolean flag: Is the channel primary (1) or (0)? We want only the 1s.

This is the channel key (which maps to our center table).

We have two data frames, logs and log_identifier, each containing a set of columns. We are ready to start joining!

The join operation has three major ingredients:

- Two tables, called a *left* and a *right* table, respectively
- One or more *predicates*, which are the series of conditions that determine how records between the two tables are joined
- A *method* to indicate how we perform the join when the predicate succeeds and when it fails

With these three ingredients, you can construct a join between two data frames in PySpark by filling the blueprint in listing 5.2 with the relevant keywords to accomplish the desired behavior. Every join operation in PySpark will follow the same blueprint. The next few sections will take each keyword and illustrate how they impact the end result.

> **Listing 5.2 A bare-bone recipe for a join in PySpark**

```
[LEFT].join(
    [RIGHT],
    on=[PREDICATES]
    how=[METHOD]
)
```

5.1.2 *Knowing our left from our right*

A join is performed on two tables at a time. In this section, we cover the [LEFT] and [RIGHT] blocks of listing 5.2. Knowing which table is called left and which is called right is helpful when discussing join types, so we start with this useful vocabulary.

Because of the SQL heritage in the data manipulation vocabulary, the two tables are named *left* and *right* tables. In PySpark, a neat way to remember which is which is to say that the left table is to the left of the `join()` method, whereas the right is to the right (inside the parentheses). Knowing which is which is very useful when choosing the join method. Unsurprisingly, there are a left and right join types (see section 5.1.4).

Our tables are now identified, so we can update our join blueprint as in the next listing. We now need to steer our attention to the next parameter, the predicates.

Listing 5.3   A bare-bone join in PySpark, with left and right tables filled in

```
logs.join(                          ⊲─────────────     logs is the left
        log_identifier,     ⊲────┐                     table . . .
        on=[PREDICATES]
        how=[METHOD]                              . . . and log_identifier
)                                                 is the right table.
```

5.1.3   *The rules to a successful join: The predicates*

This section covers the `[PREDICATES]` block of the join blueprint, which is the corner-stone of determining what records from the left table will match the right table. Most predicates in join operations are simple, but they can grow significantly in complexity depending on the logic you want. I introduce the simplest and most common use cases first before graduating to more complex predicates.

The predicates of a PySpark join are rules between columns of the left and right data frames. A join is performed record-wise, where each record on the left data frame is compared (via the predicates) to each record on the right data frame. If the predicates return `True`, the join is a match and is a no-match if `False`. We can think of this like a two-way `where` (see chapter 2): you match the values from one table to the other, and the (Boolean) result of the predicate block determines if it's a match.

The best way to illustrate a predicate is to create a simple example and explore the results. For our two data frames, we will build the predicate `logs["LogServiceID"] == log_identifier["LogServiceID"]`. In plain English, this translates to "match the records from the `logs` data frame to the records from the `log_identifier` data frame when the value of their `LogServiceID` column is equal."

I've taken a small sample of the data in both data frames and illustrated the result of applying the predicate in figure 5.1. There are two important points to highlight:

- If one record in the left table resolves the predicate with more than one record in the right table (or vice versa), this record will be duplicated in the joined table.

- If one record in the left or right table does not resolve the predicate with any record in the other table, it will not be present in the resulting table *unless the join method (see section 5.1.4) specifies a protocol for failed predicates.*

In our example, the 3590 record on the left is equal to the two corresponding records on the right, and we see two solved predicates with this number in our result set. On the other hand, the 3417 record does not match anything on the right, and therefore is not present in the result set. The same thing happens with the 3883 record in the right table.

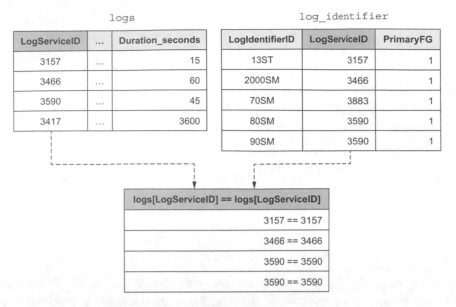

**Figure 5.1 A simple join predicate resolution between `logs` and `log_identifier`
using `LogServiceID` in both tables and equality testing in the predicate. I show only the
four successes in the result table. Our predicate is applied to a sample of our two tables:
`3590` in the left table resolves the predicate twice, while `3417` on the left and `3883` on
the right have no matches.**

You are not limited to a single test in your predicate. You can use multiple conditions by separating them with Boolean operators such as | (or) or & (and). You can also use a different test than equality. Here are two examples and their plain English translation:

- `(logs["LogServiceID"] == log_identifier["LogServiceID"]) & (logs["left_col"] < log_identifier["right_col"])`—This will only match the records that have the same `LogServiceID` on both sides *and* where the value of the `left_col` in the `logs` table is smaller than the value of the `right_col` in the `log_identifier` table.

- `(logs["LogServiceID"] == log_identifier["LogServiceID"]) | (logs["left_col"] > log_identifier["right_col"])`—This will only match the records that have the same `LogServiceID` on both sides *or* where the value of the `left_col` in the `logs` table is greater than the value of the `right_col` in the `log_identifier` table.

You can make the operations as complicated as you want. I recommend wrapping each condition in parentheses to avoid worrying about operator precedence and to facilitate the reading.

Before adding our predicate to our join in progress, I want to note that PySpark provides a few predicate shortcuts to reduce the complexity of the code. If you have multiple and predicates (such as `(left["col1"] == right["colA"]) & (left["col2"]`

> right["colB"]) & (left["col3"] != right["colC"])), you can put them into a list, such as [left["col1"] == right["colA"], left["col2"] > right["colB"], left["col3"] != right["colC"]]. This makes your intent more explicit and avoids counting parentheses for long chains of conditions.

Finally, if you are performing an "equi-join," where you are testing for equality between identically named columns, you can simply specify the name of the columns as a string or a list of strings as a predicate. In our case, it means that our predicate can only be "LogServiceID". This is what I put in the following listing.

Listing 5.4   A join in PySpark, with left and right tables and predicate

```
logs.join(
    log_identifier,
    on="LogServiceID"
    how=[METHOD]
)
```

The join method influences how you structure predicates, so section 5.1.5 revisits the whole join operation after we're done with the ingredient-by-ingredient approach. The last parameter is the how, which completes our join operation.

5.1.4   How do you do it: The join method

The last ingredient of a successful join is the how parameter, which will indicate the join method. Most books explaining joins show Venn diagrams indicating how each join colors the different areas, but I find that is only useful as a reminder, not a teaching tool. I'll review each type of join with the same tables we've used in figure 5.1 and give the result of the operation.

A join method boils down to these two questions:

- What happens when the return value of the predicates is True?
- What happens when the return value of the predicates is False?

Classifying the join methods based on the answer to these questions is an easy way to remember them.

> **TIP**   PySpark's joins are essentially the same as SQL's. If you are already comfortable with them, feel free to skip this section.

INNER JOIN

An inner join (how="inner") is the most common join. PySpark will default to an inner join if you don't pass a join method explicitly. It returns a record if the predicate is true and drops it if false. I consider an inner join the natural way to think of joins because they are very simple to reason about.

If we look at our tables, we have a table very similar to figure 5.1. The record with the LogServiceID == 3590 on the left will be duplicated because it matches two records in the right table. The result is illustrated in figure 5.2.

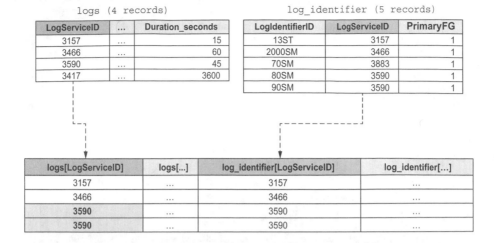

Figure 5.2　An inner join. Each successful predicate creates a joined record.

LEFT AND RIGHT OUTER JOIN

Left (how="left" or how="left_outer") and right (how="right" or how="right_outer"), as displayed in figure 5.4, are like an inner join in that they generate a record for a successful predicate. The difference is what happens when the predicate is false:

- A left (also called a *left outer*) join will add the unmatched records from the left table in the joined table, filling the columns coming from the right table with null.
- A right (also called a *right outer*) join will add the unmatched records from the right in the joined table, filling the columns coming from the left table with null.

In practice, this means that your joined table is guaranteed to contain all the records of the table that feed the join (left or right). Visually, figure 5.3 shows this. Although 3417 doesn't satisfy the predicate, it is still present in the left joined table. The same happens with 3883 and the right table. Just like an inner join, if the predicate is successful more than once, the record will be duplicated.

Left and right joins are very useful when you are not certain if the link table contains every key. You can then fill the null values (see listing 5.16) or process them knowing you didn't drop any records.

FULL OUTER JOIN

A full outer (how="outer", how="full", or how="full_outer") join is simply the fusion of a left and right join. It will add the unmatched records from the left and the right table, padding with null. It serves a similar purpose to the left and right join but is not as popular since you'll generally have one (and only one) anchor table where you want to preserve all records.

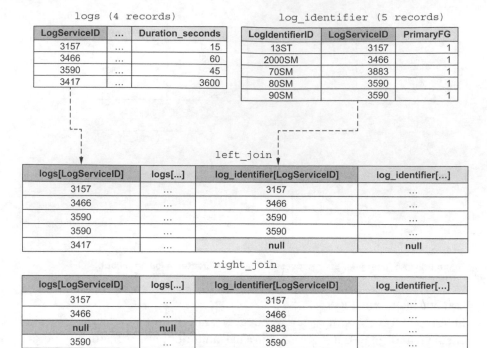

Figure 5.3   A left and right joined table. All the records of the direction table are present in the resulting table.

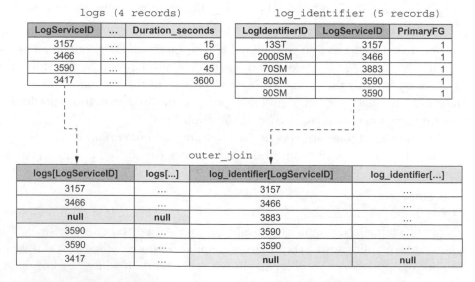

Figure 5.4   A left and right joined table. We can see all the records from both tables.

LEFT SEMI-JOIN AND LEFT ANTI-JOIN

The left semi-join and left anti-join are less popular but still quite useful nonetheless.

A left semi-join (`how="left_semi"`) is the same as an inner join, but keeps the columns in the left table. It also won't duplicate the records in the left table if they fulfill the predicate with more than one record in the right table. Its main purpose is to filter records from a table based on a predicate that is depending on another table.

A left anti-join (`how="left_anti"`) is the opposite of an inner join. It will keep only the records from the left table *that do not match the predicate with any record in the right table.* If a record from the left table matches a record from the right table, it gets dropped from the join operation.

Our blueprint join is now finalized: we are going with an inner join since we want to keep only the records where the `LogServiceID` has additional information in our `log_identifier` table. Since our join is complete, I assign the result to a new variable: `logs_and_channels`.

Listing 5.5 Our join in PySpark, with all the parameters filled in

```
logs_and_channels = logs.join(
    log_identifier,
    on="LogServiceID",
    how="inner"        ⟵———   I could have omitted the how
)                              parameter outright, since
                              inner join is the default.
```

In this section, we reviewed the different join methods and their usage. The next section covers the innocuous but important aspect of column and data frame names when joining. It'll provide a solution to the common problem of having identically named columns in both the left and right data frame.

CROSS JOIN: THE NUCLEAR OPTION

A cross join (`how="cross"`) is the nuclear option. It returns a record for every record pair, regardless of the value the predicates return. In our data frame example, our `logs` table contains four records and our `logs_identifier` five records, so the cross join will contain $4 \times 5 = 20$ records. The result is illustrated in figure 5.5.

Cross joins are seldom the operation you want, but they are useful when you want a table that contains every possible combination.

> **TIP** PySpark also provides an explicit `crossJoin()` method that takes the right data frame as a parameter.

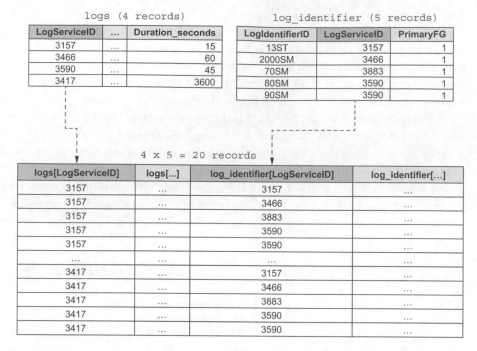

Figure 5.5 A visual example of a cross join. Each record on the left is matched to every record on the right.

The science of joining in a distributed environment

When joining data in a distributed environment, "we don't care about where data is" no longer works. To be able to process a comparison between records, the data needs to be on the same machine. If not, PySpark will move the data in an operation called a *shuffle*. As you can imagine, moving large amounts of data over the network is very slow, and we should aim to avoid this when possible.

This is one of the instances in which PySpark's abstraction model shows some weakness. Since joins are such an important part of working with multiple data sources, I introduce the syntax here so we can get things rolling. Chapter 11 discusses shuffles in greater detail.

5.1.5 Naming conventions in the joining world

This section covers how PySpark manages column and data frame names. While this applies beyond the join world, name clashing is most painful when you are trying to assemble many data frames into one. We cover how to prevent name clashing and how to treat it if you inherit an already mangled data frame.

By default, PySpark will not allow two columns to be named the same. If you create a column with withColumn() using an existing column name, PySpark will overwrite (or shadow) the column. When joining data frames, the situation is a little more complicated, as displayed in the following listing.

Listing 5.6 A join that generates two seemingly identically named columns

```
logs_and_channels_verbose = logs.join(
    log_identifier, logs["LogServiceID"] == log_identifier["LogServiceID"]
)

logs_and_channels_verbose.printSchema()

# root
# |-- LogServiceID: integer (nullable = true)           ← **This is one LogServiceID column . . .**
# |-- LogDate: timestamp (nullable = true)
# |-- AudienceTargetAgeID: integer (nullable = true)
# |-- AudienceTargetEthnicID: integer (nullable = true)
# [...]
# |-- duration_seconds: integer (nullable = true)
# |-- LogIdentifierID: string (nullable = true)         **. . . and this is another.**
# |-- LogServiceID: integer (nullable = true)           ←
# |-- PrimaryFG: integer (nullable = true)

try:
    logs_and_channels_verbose.select("LogServiceID")    **PySpark doesn't know which column we mean: is it LogServiceID or LogServiceID?**
except AnalysisException as err:
    print(err)

# "Reference 'LogServiceID' is ambiguous, could be: LogServiceID, LogServiceID.;"  ←
```

PySpark happily joins the two data frames but fails when we try to work with the ambiguous column. This is a common situation when working with data that follows the same convention for column naming. To solve this problem, in this section I show three methods, from the easiest to the most general.

First, when performing an equi-join, I prefer using the simplified syntax, since it takes care of removing the second instance of the predicate column. This only works when using an equality comparison, since the data is identical in both columns from the predicate, which prevents information loss. I show the code and schema of the resulting data frame when using a simplified equi-join in the next listing.

Listing 5.7 Using the simplified syntax for equi-joins

```
logs_and_channels = logs.join(log_identifier, "LogServiceID")

logs_and_channels.printSchema()

# root
# |-- LogServiceID: integer (nullable = true)
# |-- LogDate: timestamp (nullable = true)
# |-- AudienceTargetAgeID: integer (nullable = true)
# |-- AudienceTargetEthnicID: integer (nullable = true)
# |-- CategoryID: integer (nullable = true)
```

```
#   [...]
#   |-- Language2: integer (nullable = true)
#   |-- duration_seconds: integer (nullable = true)
#   |-- LogIdentifierID: string (nullable = true)
#   |-- PrimaryFG: integer (nullable = true)
```

No LogServiceID here: PySpark kept only the first referred column.

The second approach relies on the fact that PySpark-joined data frames remember the origin of the columns. Because of this, we can refer to the `LogServiceID` columns using the same nomenclature as before (i.e., `log_identifier["LogServiceID"]`). We can then rename this column or delete it, and thus solve our issue. I use this approach in the following listing.

Listing 5.8   Using the origin name of the column for unambiguous selection

```
logs_and_channels_verbose = logs.join(
    log_identifier, logs["LogServiceID"] == log_identifier["LogServiceID"]
)

logs_and_channels.drop(log_identifier["LogServiceID"]).select(
    "LogServiceID")

# DataFrame[LogServiceID: int]
```

By dropping one of the two duplicated columns, we can then use the name for the other without any problem.

The last approach is convenient if you use the `Column` object directly. PySpark will not resolve the origin name when you rely on `F.col()` to work with columns. To solve this in the most general way, we need to `alias()` our tables when performing the join, as shown in the following listing.

Listing 5.9   Aliasing our tables to resolve the origin

```
logs_and_channels_verbose = logs.alias("left").join(
    log_identifier.alias("right"),
    logs["LogServiceID"] == log_identifier["LogServiceID"],
)

logs_and_channels_verbose.drop(F.col("right.LogServiceID")).select(
    "LogServiceID"
)

# DataFrame[LogServiceID: int]
```

Our logs table gets aliased as left.

Our log_identifier gets aliased as right.

F.col() will resolve left and right as a prefix for the column names.

All three approaches are valid. The first one works only in the case of equi-joins, but the two others are mostly interchangeable. PySpark gives you a lot of control over the structure and naming of your data frame but requires you to be explicit.

This section packed in a lot of information about joins, a very important tool when working with interrelated data frames. Although the possibilities are endless, the syntax is simple and easy to understand: `left.join(right` decides the first parameter. `on` decides if it's a match. `how` indicates how to operate on match success and failures.

Now that the first join is done, we will link two additional tables to continue our data discovery and processing. The `CategoryID` table contains information about the types of programs, and the `ProgramClassID` table contains the data that allows us to pinpoint the commercials.

This time, we are performing `left` joins since we are not entirely certain about the existence of the keys in the link table. In listing 5.10, we follow the same process as we did for the `log_identifier` table in one fell swoop:

- We read the table using the `SparkReader.csv` and the same configuration as our other tables.
- We keep the relevant columns.
- We join the data to our `logs_and_channels` table, using PySpark's method chaining.

Listing 5.10 Linking the category and program class tables using two left joins

```
DIRECTORY = "./data/broadcast_logs"

cd_category = spark.read.csv(
    os.path.join(DIRECTORY, "ReferenceTables/CD_Category.csv"),
    sep="|",
    header=True,
    inferSchema=True,
).select(
    "CategoryID",
    "CategoryCD",
    F.col("EnglishDescription").alias("Category_Description"),
)
```
We're aliasing the EnglishDescription column to remember what it maps to.

```
cd_program_class = spark.read.csv(
    os.path.join(DIRECTORY, "ReferenceTables/CD_ProgramClass.csv"),
    sep="|",
    header=True,
    inferSchema=True,
).select(
    "ProgramClassID",
    "ProgramClassCD",
    F.col("EnglishDescription").alias("ProgramClass_Description"),
)
```
We're also aliasing here, but for the program class.

```
full_log = logs_and_channels.join(cd_category, "CategoryID", how="left").join(
    cd_program_class, "ProgramClassID", how="left"
)
```

With our table nicely augmented, let's move to our last step: summarizing the table using groupings.

Exercise 5.1

Assume two tables, `left` and `right`, each containing a column named `my_column`. What is the result of this code?

```
one = left.join(right, how="left_semi", on="my_column")
two = left.join(right, how="left_anti", on="my_column")

one.union(two)
```

Exercise 5.2

Assume two data frames, `red` and `blue`. Which is the appropriate join to use in `red.join(blue, …)` if you want to join `red` and `blue` and keep all the records satisfying the predicate?

    a Left

    b Right

    c Inner

    d Theta

    e Cross

Exercise 5.3

Assume two data frames, `red` and `blue`. Which is the appropriate join to use in `red.join(blue, …)` if you want to join `red` and `blue` and keep all the records satisfying the predicate *and* the records in the `blue` table?

    a Left

    b Right

    c Inner

    d Theta

    e Cross

5.2   *Summarizing the data via groupby and GroupedData*

When displaying data, especially large amounts of data, you'll often summarize data using statistics as a first step. Chapter 4 showed how you can use `summary()` and `display()` to compute mean, min, max, and so on over the entire data frame. How about stretching our data frame a little by summarizing it according to column contents?

    This section covers how to summarize a data frame into more granular dimensions (versus the entire data frame) via the `groupby()` method. We already grouped our text data frame in 3; this section goes deeper into the specifics of grouping. Here, I introduce the `GroupedData` object and its usage. In practical terms, we'll use `groupby()` to answer our original question: what are the channels with the greatest and least proportion of commercials? To answer this, we have to take each channel and sum the duration_seconds in two ways:

- One to get the number of seconds when the program is a commercial
- One to get the number of seconds of total programming

Our plan, before we start summing, is to identify what is considered a commercial and what is not. The documentation doesn't provide formal guidance on how to do so, so we'll explore the data and draw our conclusion. Let's group!

5.2.1 A simple groupby blueprint

In chapter 3, we performed a very simple groupby() to count the occurrences of each word. It was a simple example of grouping and counting records based on the words inside the (only) column. In this section, we expand on that simple example by grouping over many columns. I also introduce a more general notation than the count() we've used previously so that we can compute more than one summary function.

Since you are already acquainted with the basic syntax of groupby(), this section starts by presenting a full code block that computes the total duration (in seconds) of the program class. In the next listing we perform the grouping, compute the aggregate function, and present the results in decreasing order.

Listing 5.11 Displaying the most popular types of programs

```
(full_log
 .groupby("ProgramClassCD", "ProgramClass_Description")
 .agg(F.sum("duration_seconds").alias("duration_total"))
 .orderBy("duration_total", ascending=False).show(100, False)
 )

# +--------------+------------------------------------------+--------------+
# |ProgramClassCD|ProgramClass_Description                  |duration_total|
# +--------------+------------------------------------------+--------------+
# |PGR           |PROGRAM                                   |652802250     |
# |COM           |COMMERCIAL MESSAGE                        |106810189     |
# |PFS           |PROGRAM FIRST SEGMENT                     |38817891      |
# |SEG           |SEGMENT OF A PROGRAM                      |34891264      |
# |PRC           |PROMOTION OF UPCOMING CANADIAN PROGRAM    |27017583      |
# |PGI           |PROGRAM INFOMERCIAL                       |23196392      |
# |PRO           |PROMOTION OF NON-CANADIAN PROGRAM         |10213461      |
# |OFF           |SCHEDULED OFF AIR TIME PERIOD             |4537071       |
# [... more rows]
# |COR           |CORNERSTONE                               |null          |
# +--------------+------------------------------------------+--------------+
```

This small program has a few new parts, so let's review them one by one.

Our group routing starts with the groupby() method on the data frame shown in figure 5.6. A "grouped by" data frame is no longer a data frame; instead, it becomes a

logs: DataFrame

ProgramClassCD	ProgramClass_Description	...	Duration_seconds
PGR	PROGRAM	...	15
PGR	PROGRAM	...	60
COM	COMMERCIAL MESSAGE	...	45
COM	COMMERCIAL MESSAGE	...	3600
PGR	PROGRAM	...	30
PFS	PROGRAM FIRST SEGMENT	...	60
...	...	...	540
COM	COMMERCIAL MESSAGE	...	60

Figure 5.6   The original data frame, with the focus on the columns we are grouping by

GroupedData object and is displayed in all its glory in listing 5.12. This object is a transitional object: you can't really inspect it (there is no .show() method), and it's waiting for further instructions to become showable again. Illustrated, it would look like the right-hand side of figure 5.7. You have the key (or keys, if you groupby() multiple columns), and the rest of the columns are grouped inside some "cell" awaiting a summary function so that they can be promoted to a bona fide column again.

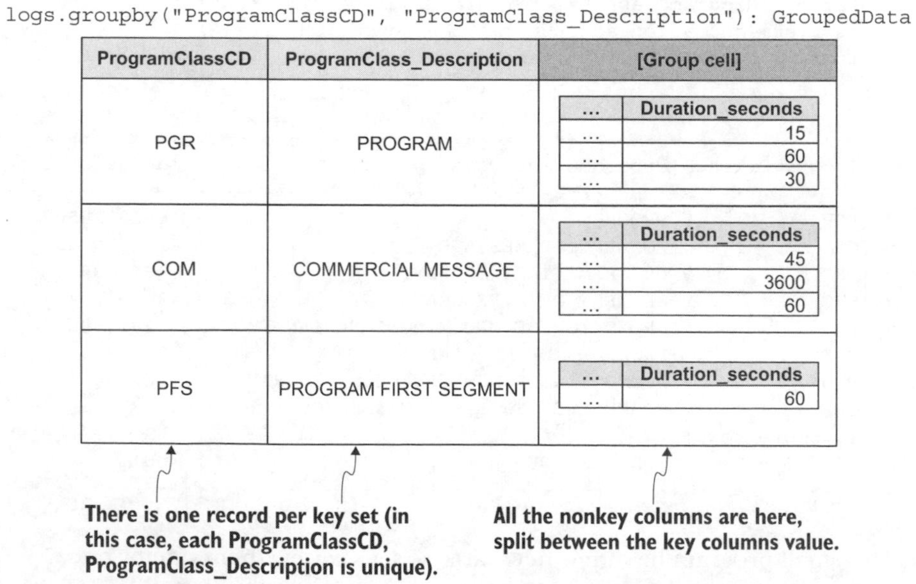

logs.groupby("ProgramClassCD", "ProgramClass_Description"): GroupedData

ProgramClassCD	ProgramClass_Description	[Group cell]
PGR	PROGRAM	... Duration_seconds ... 15 ... 60 ... 30
COM	COMMERCIAL MESSAGE	... Duration_seconds ... 45 ... 3600 ... 60
PFS	PROGRAM FIRST SEGMENT	... Duration_seconds ... 60

There is one record per key set (in this case, each ProgramClassCD, ProgramClass_Description is unique).

All the nonkey columns are here, split between the key columns value.

Figure 5.7   The GroupedData object resulting from grouping

Aggregating for the lazy

agg() also accepts a dictionary in the form {column_name: aggregation_function} where both are string. Because of this, we can rewrite listing 5.11 like so:

```
full_log.groupby("ProgramClassCD", "ProgramClass_Description").agg(
    {"duration_seconds": "sum"}
).withColumnRenamed("sum(duration_seconds)", "duration_total").orderBy(
    "duration_total", ascending=False
).show(
    100, False
)
```

This makes rapid prototyping very easy (you can, just like with column objects, use the "*" to refer to all columns). I personally don't like this approach for most cases since you don't get to alias your columns when creating them. I am including it since you will see it when reading other people's code.

Listing 5.12　A GroupedData object representation

```
full_log.groupby()
# <pyspark.sql.group.GroupedData at 0x119baa4e0>
```

In chapter 3, we brought back the GroupedData into a data frame by using the count() method, which returns the count of each group. There are a few others, such as min(), max(), mean(), or sum(). We could have used the sum() method directly, but we wouldn't have had the option of aliasing the resulting column and would have gotten stuck with sum(duration_seconds) for a name. Instead, we use the oddly named agg().

The agg() method, for aggregate (or aggregation), will take one or more *aggregate functions* from the pyspark.sql.functions module we all know and love, and apply them on each group of the GroupedData object. In figure 5.8, I start on the left with our GroupedData object. Calling agg() with an appropriate aggregate function pulls the column from the group cell, extracts the values, and performs the function, yielding the answer. Compared to using the sum() function on the groupby object, agg() trades a few keystrokes for two main advantages:

- agg() takes an arbitrary number of aggregate functions, unlike using a summary method directly. You can't chain multiple functions on GroupedData objects: the first one will transform it into a data frame, and the second one will fail.
- You can alias resulting columns so that you control their name and improve the robustness of your code.

After the application of the aggregate function on our GroupedData object, we again have a data frame. We can then use the orderBy() method to order the data by

```
logs.groupby(
    "ProgramClassCD", "ProgramClass_Description"
).agg(
    F.sum(F.col("Duration_seconds"))
): DataFrame
```

ProgramClassCD	ProgramClass_Description	Duration_seconds
PGR	PROGRAM	15 + 60 + 30 = 105
COM	COMMERCIAL MESSAGE	45 + 3600 + 60 = 3705
PFS	PROGRAM FIRST SEGMENT	60

Figure 5.8   A data frame arising from the application of the `agg()` method (aggregate function: `F.sum()` on `Duration_seconds`)

decreasing order of `duration_total`, our newly created column. We finish by showing 100 rows, which is more than what the data frame contains, so it shows everything.

Let's select our commercials. Table 5.1 shows my picks.

Table 5.1   The types of programs we'll consider as commercials

ProgramClassCD	ProgramClass_Description	duration_total
COM	COMMERCIAL MESSAGE	106810189
PRC	PROMOTION OF UPCOMING CANADIAN PROGRAM	27017583
PGI	PROGRAM INFOMERCIAL	23196392
PRO	PROMOTION OF NON-CANADIAN PROGRAM	10213461
LOC	LOCAL ADVERTISING	483042
SPO	SPONSORSHIP MESSAGE	45257
MER	MERCHANDISING	40695
SOL	SOLICITATION MESSAGE	7808

Now that we've done the hard job of identifying our commercial codes, we can start counting. The next section covers how we can flex the aggregation using custom column definitions.

agg() is not the only player in town

You can also use `groupby()`, with the `apply()` (Spark 2.3+) and `applyInPandas()` (Spark 3.0+) method, in the creatively named *split-apply-combine* pattern. We explore this powerful tool in chapter 9. Other less-used (but still useful) methods are also available. Check out the API documentation for the methods over the `GroupedData` object: http://mng.bz/aDoJ.

5.2.2 A column is a column: Using agg() with custom column definitions

When grouping and aggregating columns in PySpark, we have all the power of the `Column` object at our fingertips. This means that we can group by and aggregate on custom columns! For this section, we will start by building a definition of `duration_commercial`, which takes the duration of a program only if it is a commercial, and use this in our `agg()` statement to seamlessly compute both the total duration and the commercial duration.

If we encode the contents of table 5.1 into a PySpark definition, it gives us the next listing.

Listing 5.13   Computing only the commercial time for each program in our table

```
F.when(
    F.trim(F.col("ProgramClassCD")).isin(
        ["COM", "PRC", "PGI", "PRO", "PSA", "MAG", "LOC", "SPO", "MER", "SOL"]
    ),
    F.col("duration_seconds"),
).otherwise(0)
```

I think that the best way to describe the code this time is to literally translate it into plain English.

> **When** the field of the column `ProgramClass`, **trimmed** of spaces at the beginning and end of the field, **is in** our list of commercial codes, then take the value of the field in the column `duration_seconds`. **Otherwise**, use zero as a value.

The blueprint of the `F.when()` function is as follows. It is possible to chain multiple `when()` if we have more than one condition and to omit the `otherwise()` if we're okay with having `null` values when none of the tests are positive:

```
(
F.when([BOOLEAN TEST], [RESULT IF TRUE])
 .when([ANOTHER BOOLEAN TEST], [RESULT IF TRUE])
 .otherwise([DEFAULT RESULT, WILL DEFAULT TO null IF OMITTED])
)
```

We now have a column ready to use. While we could create the column before grouping by, using `withColumn()`, let's take it up a notch and use our definition in the `agg()` clause directly. The following listing does just that, and at the same time, gives us our answer!

Listing 5.14   Using our new column into `agg()` to compute our final answer

```
answer = (
    full_log.groupby("LogIdentifierID")
    .agg(
```

A column is a column: our F.when() function returns a column object that can be used in F.sum().

```
    F.sum(
        F.when(
            F.trim(F.col("ProgramClassCD")).isin(
                ["COM", "PRC", "PGI", "PRO", "LOC", "SPO", "MER", "SOL"]
            ),
            F.col("duration_seconds"),
        ).otherwise(0)
    ).alias("duration_commercial"),
    F.sum("duration_seconds").alias("duration_total"),
    )
    .withColumn(
        "commercial_ratio", F.col(
            "duration_commercial") / F.col("duration_total")
    )
)

answer.orderBy("commercial_ratio", ascending=False).show(1000, False)
```

```
# +--------------+-------------------+--------------+--------------------+
# |LogIdentifierID|duration_commercial|duration_total|commercial_ratio    |
# +--------------+-------------------+--------------+--------------------+
# |HPITV         |403                |403           |1.0                 |
# |TLNSP         |234455             |234455        |1.0                 |
# |MSET          |101670             |101670        |1.0                 |
# |TELENO        |545255             |545255        |1.0                 |
# |CIMT          |19935              |19935         |1.0                 |
# |TANG          |271468             |271468        |1.0                 |
# |INVST         |623057             |633659        |0.9832686034602207  |
# [...]
# |OTN3          |0                  |2678400       |0.0                 |
# |PENT          |0                  |2678400       |0.0                 |
# |ATN14         |0                  |2678400       |0.0                 |
# |ATN11         |0                  |2678400       |0.0                 |
# |ZOOM          |0                  |2678400       |0.0                 |
# |EURO          |0                  |null          |null                |
# |NINOS         |0                  |null          |null                |
# +--------------+-------------------+--------------+--------------------+
```

Wait a moment—the commercial ratio of some channels is 1.0; are some channels *only commercials*? If we look at the total duration, we can see that some channels don't broadcast much. Since one day is 86,400 seconds (24 × 60 × 60), we see that HPITV only has 403 seconds of programming in our data frame. I am not too concerned about this right now, but we always have the option to filter() our way out and remove the channels that broadcast very little (see chapter 2). Still, we accomplished our goal: we identified the channels with the most commercials. We finish this chapter with one last task: processing those null values.

5.3   *Taking care of null values: Drop and fill*

null values represent the absence of value. I think this is a great oxymoron: a value for no value? Philosophy aside, we have some nulls in our result set, and I would like them gone. This section covers the two easiest ways to deal with null values in a data frame: you can either `dropna()` the record containing them or `fillna()` the `null` with a value. In this section, we explore both options to see which is best for our analysis.

5.3.1 Dropping it like it's hot: Using dropna() to remove records with null values

Our first option is to plainly ignore the records that have `null` values. In this section, I cover the different ways to use the `dropna()` method to drop records based on the presence of `null` values.

`dropna()` is pretty easy to use. This data frame method takes three parameters:

- `how`, which can take the value `any` or `all`. If `any` is selected, PySpark will drop records where *at least one* of the fields is `null`. In the case of `all`, only the records where all fields are `null` will be removed. By default, PySpark will take the `any` mode.
- `thresh` takes an integer value. If set (its default is `None`), PySpark will ignore the `how` parameter and only drop the records with less than `thresh` non-`null` values.
- `subset` will take an optional list of columns that `dropna()` will use to make its decision.

In our case, we want to keep only the records that have a `commercial_ratio` and that are non-`null`. We just have to pass our column to the `subset` parameter, like in the next listing.

> **Listing 5.15 Dropping only the records that have a `null` `commercial_ratio` value**

```
answer_no_null = answer.dropna(subset=["commercial_ratio"])

answer_no_null.orderBy(
    "commercial_ratio", ascending=False).show(1000, False)

# +--------------+-------------------+--------------+--------------------+
# |LogIdentifierID|duration_commercial|duration_total|commercial_ratio    |
# +--------------+-------------------+--------------+--------------------+
# |HPITV         |403                |403           |1.0                 |
# |TLNSP         |234455             |234455        |1.0                 |
# |MSET          |101670             |101670        |1.0                 |
# |TELENO        |545255             |545255        |1.0                 |
# |CIMT          |19935              |19935         |1.0                 |
# |TANG          |271468             |271468        |1.0                 |
# |INVST         |623057             |633659        |0.9832686034602207  |
# [...]
# |OTN3          |0                  |2678400       |0.0                 |
# |PENT          |0                  |2678400       |0.0                 |
# |ATN14         |0                  |2678400       |0.0                 |
# |ATN11         |0                  |2678400       |0.0                 |
# |ZOOM          |0                  |2678400       |0.0                 |
# +--------------+-------------------+--------------+--------------------+

print(answer_no_null.count())  # 322
```

This option is legitimate, but it removes some records from our data frame. What if we want to keep everything? The next section covers how to replace the null values with something else.

5.3.2 *Filling values to our heart's content using fillna()*

The yin to dropna()'s yang is to provide a default value to the null values. This section covers the fillna() method to replace null values.

fillna() is even simpler than dropna(). This data frame method takes two parameters:

- The value, which is a Python int, float, string, or bool. PySpark will only fill the compatible columns; for instance, if we were to fillna("zero"), our commercial_ratio, being a double, would not be filled.
- The same subset parameter we encountered in dropna(). We can limit the scope of our filling to only the columns we want.

In concrete terms, a null value in any of our numerical columns means that the value should be zero, so the next listing fills the null values with zero.

Listing 5.16   Filling our numerical records with zero using the fillna() method

```
answer_no_null = answer.fillna(0)

answer_no_null.orderBy(
    "commercial_ratio", ascending=False).show(1000, False)

# +---------------+-------------------+--------------+--------------------+
# |LogIdentifierID|duration_commercial|duration_total|commercial_ratio    |
# +---------------+-------------------+--------------+--------------------+
# |HPITV          |403                |403           |1.0                 |
# |TLNSP          |234455             |234455        |1.0                 |
# |MSET           |101670             |101670        |1.0                 |
# |TELENO         |545255             |545255        |1.0                 |
# |CIMT           |19935              |19935         |1.0                 |
# |TANG           |271468             |271468        |1.0                 |
# |INVST          |623057             |633659        |0.9832686034602207  |
# [...]
# |OTN3           |0                  |2678400       |0.0                 |
# |PENT           |0                  |2678400       |0.0                 |
# |ATN14          |0                  |2678400       |0.0                 |
# |ATN11          |0                  |2678400       |0.0                 |
# |ZOOM           |0                  |2678400       |0.0                 |
# +---------------+-------------------+--------------+--------------------+

print(answer_no_null.count())   # 324
```

⟵ We have the two additional records that listing 5.15 dropped.

> **The return of the dict**
>
> You can also pass a dict to the `fillna()` method, with the column names as key and the values as dict values. If we were to use this method for our filling, the code would be like the following code:
>
> ```
> Filling our numerical records with zero using the fillna() method and a dict
> answer_no_null = answer.fillna(
>     {"duration_commercial": 0, "duration_total": 0, "commercial_ratio": 0}
> )
> ```
>
> Just like with `agg()`, I prefer avoiding the dict approach because I find it less readable. In this case, you can chain multiple `fillna()` to achieve the same result with better readability.

Our program is now devoid of `null` values, and we have a full list of channels and their associated ratio of commercial programming. I think it's time for a complete wrap-up of our program and to summarize what we've covered in this chapter.

5.4 What was our question again? Our end-to-end program

At the beginning of the chapter, we gave ourselves an anchor question to start exploring the data and uncover some insights. Throughout the chapter, we've assembled a cohesive data set containing the relevant information needed to identify commercial programs and ranked the channels based on how much of their programming is commercial. In listing 5.17, I've assembled all the relevant code blocks introduced in the chapter into a single program you can `spark-submit`. The code is also available in the book's repository under `code/Ch05/commercials.py`. The end-of-chapter exercises also use this code.

Not counting data ingestion, comments, or docstring, our code is a rather small hundred or so lines of code. We could play code golf (trying to shrink the number of characters as much as we can), but I think we've struck a good balance between terseness and ease of reading. Once again, we haven't paid much attention to the distributed nature of PySpark. Instead, we took a very descriptive view of our problem and translated it into code via PySpark's powerful data frame abstraction and rich function ecosystems.

This chapter is the last chapter of the first part of the book. You are now familiar with the PySpark ecosystem and how you can use its main data structure, the data frame, to ingest and manipulate two very common sources of data, textual and tabular. You know a variety and method and functions that can be applied to data frames and columns, and can apply those to your own data problem. You can also leverage the documentation provided through the PySpark docstrings, straight from the PySpark shell.

There is a lot more you can get from the plain data manipulation portion of the book. Because of this, I recommend taking the time to review the PySpark online API and become proficient in navigating its structure. Now that you have a solid understanding of the data model and how to structure simple data manipulation programs, adding new functions to your PySpark quiver will be easy.

The second part of the book builds heavily on what you've learned so far:

- We dig deeper into PySpark's data model and find opportunities to refine our code. We will also look at PySpark's column types, how they bridge to Python's types, and how to use them to improve the reliability of our code.
- We go beyond two-dimensional data frames with complex data types, such as the array, the map, and the struct, by ingesting hierarchical data.
- We look at how PySpark modernizes SQL, an influential language for tabular data manipulation, and how you can blend SQL and Python in a single program.
- We look at promoting pure Python code to run in the Spark-distributed environment. We formally introduce a lower-level structure, the resilient distributed dataset (RDD) and its row-major model. We also look at UDFs and pandas UDFs as a way to augment the functionality of the data frame.

Listing 5.17   Our full program, ordering channels by decreasing proportion of commercials

```
import os

import pyspark.sql.functions as F
from pyspark.sql import SparkSession

spark = SparkSession.builder.appName(
    "Getting the Canadian TV channels with the highest/lowest proportion of
      commercials."
).getOrCreate()

spark.sparkContext.setLogLevel("WARN")

# Reading all the relevant data sources

DIRECTORY = "./data/broadcast_logs"

logs = spark.read.csv(
    os.path.join(DIRECTORY, "BroadcastLogs_2018_Q3_M8.CSV"),
    sep="|",
    header=True,
    inferSchema=True,
)

log_identifier = spark.read.csv(
    os.path.join(DIRECTORY, "ReferenceTables/LogIdentifier.csv"),
    sep="|",
    header=True,
    inferSchema=True,
)

cd_category = spark.read.csv(
    os.path.join(DIRECTORY, "ReferenceTables/CD_Category.csv"),
    sep="|",
```

```
        header=True,
        inferSchema=True,
    ).select(
        "CategoryID",
        "CategoryCD",
        F.col("EnglishDescription").alias("Category_Description"),
    )

    cd_program_class = spark.read.csv(
        "./data/broadcast_logs/ReferenceTables/CD_ProgramClass.csv",
        sep="|",
        header=True,
        inferSchema=True,
    ).select(
        "ProgramClassID",
        "ProgramClassCD",
        F.col("EnglishDescription").alias("ProgramClass_Description"),
    )

    # Data processing

    logs = logs.drop("BroadcastLogID", "SequenceNO")

    logs = logs.withColumn(
        "duration_seconds",
        (
            F.col("Duration").substr(1, 2).cast("int") * 60 * 60
            + F.col("Duration").substr(4, 2).cast("int") * 60
            + F.col("Duration").substr(7, 2).cast("int")
        ),
    )

    log_identifier = log_identifier.where(F.col("PrimaryFG") == 1)

    logs_and_channels = logs.join(log_identifier, "LogServiceID")

    full_log = logs_and_channels.join(cd_category, "CategoryID",
        how="left").join(
        cd_program_class, "ProgramClassID", how="left"
    )

    answer = (
        full_log.groupby("LogIdentifierID")
        .agg(
            F.sum(
                F.when(
                    F.trim(F.col("ProgramClassCD")).isin(
                        ["COM", "PRC", "PGI", "PRO", "LOC", "SPO", "MER", "SOL"]
                    ),
                    F.col("duration_seconds"),
                ).otherwise(0)
            ).alias("duration_commercial"),
            F.sum("duration_seconds").alias("duration_total"),
        )
```

```
    .withColumn(
        "commercial_ratio", F.col("duration_commercial") /
     F.col("duration_total")
    )
    .fillna(0)
)

answer.orderBy("commercial_ratio", ascending=False).show(1000, False)
```

Summary

- PySpark implements seven join functionalities, using the common "what?," "on what?," and "how?" questions: cross, inner, left, right, full, left semi and left anti. Choosing the appropriate join method depends on how to process the records that resolve the predicates and those that do not.

- PySpark keeps lineage information when joining data frames. Using this information, we can avoid column naming clashes.

- You can group similar values using the groupby() method on a data frame. The method takes a number of column objects or strings representing columns and returns a GroupedData object.

- GroupedData objects are transitional structures. They contain two types of columns: the *key* columns, which are the one you "grouped by" with, and the group cell, which is a container for all the other columns. The most common way to return to a data frame is to summarize the values in the column via the agg() function or via one of the direct aggregation methods, such as count() or min().

- You can drop records containing null values using dropna() or replace them with another value with the fillna() method.

Additional exercises

Exercise 5.4

Write PySpark code that will return the result of the following code block without using a left anti-join:

```
left.join(right, how="left_anti",
    on="my_column").select("my_column").distinct()
```

Exercise 5.5

Using the data from the data/broadcast_logs/Call_Signs.csv (careful: the delimiter here is the comma, not the pipe!), add the Undertaking_Name to our final table to display a human-readable description of the channel.

Exercise 5.6

The government of Canada is asking for your analysis, but they'd like the PRC to be weighted differently. They'd like each PRC second to be considered 0.75 commercial seconds. Modify the program to account for this change.

Exercise 5.7

On the data frame returned from commercials.py, return the number of channels in each bucket based on their commercial_ratio. (Hint: look at the documentation for round on how to round a value.)

commercial_ratio	number_of_channels
1.0	
0.9	
0.8	
...	
0.1	
0.0	

Part 2

Get proficient:
Translate your ideas into code

With two different kind of programs under your belt, it's time to expand our horizons. Part 2 is about diversifying your set of tools so that no data set will have a secret for you.

Chapter 6 breaks the rows and columns mold to go multidimensional. Through JSON data, we build data frames that contain data frames themselves. This tool catapults the versatility of the Spark data frame to completely new horizons.

Chapter 7 introduces PySpark and SQL together. Together, they unlock a new level of expressiveness and succinctness in your code, allow you to scale SQL workflows at record speed, and provide a new way to reason about your analyses.

Chapters 8 and 9 cover going full Python with your PySpark code. From the resilient distributed data set, a flexible and scalable data structure, to two flavors of UDF using Python and pandas, you'll turbocharge your capabilities with full confidence.

Chapter 10 provides a new angle on your data through the introduction of window functions. Window functions are one of those things that make ordered data so much easier to work with that you'll wonder how anyone can do without them.

Finally, chapter 11 takes a break from all that coding to reflect on Spark's execution model. You'll check under the hood through the Spark UI and better understand how your instructions are being processed by the engine.

At the end of part 2, you should be able to map a clear path from data to insight, with a full toolbox at your disposal to bend your data to your will.

Multidimensional data frames: Using PySpark with JSON data

This chapter covers

- Drawing parallels between JSON documents and Python data structures
- Ingesting JSON data within a data frame
- Representing hierarchical data in a data frame through complex column types
- Reducing duplication and reliance on auxiliary tables with a document/hierarchical data model
- Creating and unpacking data from complex data types

Thus far, we have used PySpark's data frame to work with textual (chapters 2 and 3) and tabular (chapters 4 and 5) data. Both data formats were pretty different, but they fit seamlessly into the data frame structure. I believe we're ready to push the abstraction a little further by representing *hierarchical information* within a data frame. Imagine it for a moment: columns within columns, the ultimate flexibility.

This chapter is about ingesting and working with hierarchical JSON data using the PySpark data frame. JSON (JavaScript Object Notation) data rapidly took over as the dominant data format for exchanging information between a client (such as your browser) and a server. In the context of big data, JSON allows you to store more rich data types than plain scalar values compared to tabular serialization formats such as CSV. I first introduce the JSON format and how we can draw parallels to Python data structures. I go over the three container structures available for the data frame, the array, the map, and the struct, and how they are used to represent more rich data layouts. I cover how we can use them to represent multidimensional data and how the struct can represent hierarchical information. Finally, I wrap that information into a schema, a very useful construct for documenting what's in your data frame.

6.1 Reading JSON data: Getting ready for the schemapocalypse

Every data-processing job in PySpark starts with data ingestion; JSON data is no exception. This section explains what JSON is, how to use the specialized JSON reader with PySpark, and how a JSON file is represented within a data frame. After this, you'll be able to reason about your JSON data and map it to PySpark data types.

For this chapter, we use a JSON dump of information about the TV show *Silicon Valley* from TV Maze. I uploaded the data in the book's repository (under ./data/ shows), but you can download it directly from the TV Maze API (available online: http://mng.bz/g4oR). A simplified version of the JSON document is illustrated in the next listing; the main parts are numerated, and I go over each of them.

Listing 6.1   A simplified sample of the JSON object

```
                At the top level, a JSON object looks
                like a Python dictionary. Both use the
{               brackets to delimit object boundaries.
  "id":  143,                    ◄─────
  "name": "Silicon Valley",            JSON data is encoded into key-
  "type": "Scripted",                  value pairs, just like in a dictionary.
  "language": "English",               JSON keys must be strings.
  "genres": [          ◄─────
    "Comedy"                 JSON arrays can contain multiple
  ],                         values (here, we have a single string).
  "network": {       ◄─────
    "id": 8,                 Objects can be values too;
    "name": "HBO",           you can nest objects within
    "country": {             one another this way.
      "name": "United States",
      "code": "US",
      "timezone": "America/New_York"
    }
  },
  "_embedded": {           Our episodes are each
    "episodes": [    ◄─────  objects contained
      {                      within an array.
        "id": 10897,
        "name": "Minimum Viable Product",
```

```
        "season": 1,
        "number": 1,
      },
      {
        "id": 10898,
        "name": "The Cap Table",
        "season": 1,
        "number": 2,
      }
    ]
  }
}
```

My first thought when I saw the JSON data format was that it looked a lot like a Python dictionary. I still think it's a valid way to map a JSON document mentally, and the next section will explain how we can use our Python knowledge to quickly internalize JSON.

6.1.1 Starting small: JSON data as a limited Python dictionary

In this section, we cover a brief introduction to the JSON format and how we can build a mental model of the data with Python data structures. Following this, we validate our intuition by parsing a small JSON message in Python. Just like with CSV, translating your original data into PySpark structures helps tremendously in knowing how to map your data transformations; you instinctively know where a field maps to and can get to coding faster.

JSON data is a long-standing data interchange format that became massively popular for its readability and its relatively small size. JSON stands for *JavaScript Object Notation*, a fitting name considering that each JSON file can be thought of as a JavaScript object. The official JSON website (https://json.org) contains a more formal introduction to the JSON data format. Since we focus on the Python programming language, I will frame my exploration of the JSON spec through the lens of the Python family of data structures.

Looking at listing 6.1 and figure 6.1, we notice that our document starts with an opening curly bracket, {. Every valid JSON document is an *object*;[1] JavaScript uses the bracket as an object delimiter. In Python, the direct equivalent of an object, as far as JSON goes, is the dictionary. Just like a dictionary, a JSON object has keys and values. The top-level object in a JSON document is called the *root* object or element.

A JSON object—or a Python dictionary—both have keys and values. According to the JSON specification, the keys of a JSON object must be a string. Python dictionaries don't have that limitation, but we can adapt without any problems.

---

[1] According to "The JavaScript Object Notation (JSON) Data Interchange Format" (https://datatracker.ietf.org/doc/html/rfc8259) you can also have a valid JSON text with only a value (e.g., a number, a string, a Boolean, or null). For our purposes, those JSON texts are not useful as you can simply parse the value directly.

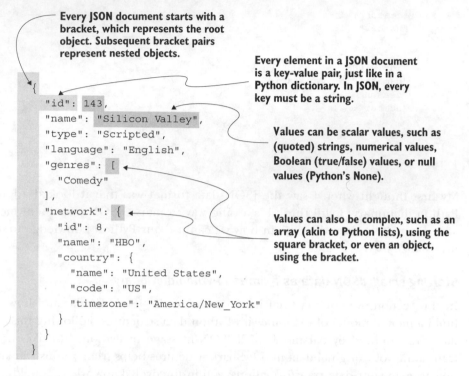

Figure 6.1   A simple JSON object, illustrating its main components: the root object, the keys, and the values. Objects use bracket delimiters and arrays/lists use square bracket delimiters. JSON uses quotes for string values but not for numerical values.

Finally, the values of a JSON object can represent a few data types:

- Strings (which use the double-quote character " as a quoting character).
- Numbers (JavaScript does not differentiate between integers and floating-point numbers).
- Booleans (`true` or `false`, which are not capitalized like in Python).
- `null`, which is akin to the Python `None`.
- Arrays, which are delimited by the square bracket [. They are akin to the Python list.
- Objects, which are delimited by the curly bracket {.

If you make the switch between the JSON and Python terms (arrays to lists and objects to dictionaries), working with JSON will be a breeze in Python. To finish our analogy, I read in the next listing: my simple JSON object using the `json` module, available in the Python standard library.

Listing 6.2   Reading a simple JSON document as a Python dictionary

```
import json          ◁──────  I import the json module,
                              available in the Python
sample_json = """{           standard library.
  "id": 143,
  "name": "Silicon Valley",
  "type": "Scripted",
  "language": "English",
  "genres": [
    "Comedy"
  ],
  "network": {
    "id": 8,
    "name": "HBO",
    "country": {
      "name": "United States",
      "code": "US",
      "timezone": "America/New_York"
    }
  }
}"""

document = json.loads(sample_json)
print(document)
# {'id': 143,                      ◁──  Our loaded document looks like a
#  'name': 'Silicon Valley',            Python dictionary with string keys.
#  'type': 'Scripted',                  Python recognized that 143 was an
#  'language': 'English',               integer and parsed the number as such.
#  'genres': ['Comedy'],
#  'network': {'id': 8,
#   'name': 'HBO',
#   'country': {'name': 'United States',
#    'code': 'US',
#    'timezone': 'America/New_York'}}}

type(document)        Our loaded document
# dict        ◁─────  is of type dict.
```

In this section, I introduced how the JSON object can be thought of as a limited Python dictionary. Keys are always strings, and values can take numerical, Boolean, string, or null values. You can also have arrays of elements or objects as values, which enables nesting and hierarchical organization of the data. Now that we understand how it works in Python, the next sections show how to read JSON data using PySpark and introduce the most complex data frame schema we've encountered so far. Before you know it, you'll conquer the schemapocalypse!

6.1.2   *Going bigger: Reading JSON data in PySpark*

This section introduces reading JSON data using the specialized JSON `SparkReader` object. We discuss the most common and useful parameters of the reader. With this information handy, you will be equipped to read JSON files into a data frame.

For this section, we will take the data introduced at the beginning of the chapter. We read the JSON document in one fell swoop, using the specialized `SparkReader` object. The result is available in the following listing.

Listing 6.3   Ingesting a JSON document using the JSON specialized `SparkReader`

```
from pyspark.sql import SparkSession

spark = SparkSession.builder.getOrCreate()

shows = spark.read.json("./data/shows/shows-silicon-valley.json")

shows.count()
# 1
```

> **The specialized SparkReader object is accessible by calling the json method on spark.read, just like with CSV or text data.**

> **The document I ingested contains only a single record.**

Two elements pop to mind when reviewing the code. First, we do not use any optional parameters. Unlike CSV data, JSON data doesn't need to worry about record delimiters or inferring data types (JSON forces the usage of string delimiters, so the value `03843` is a number, where `"03843"` is a string), which reduces the need to doctor the reading process by a fair amount. Many options are available for relaxing the JSON specification (e.g., allowing single quotes for strings, comments, or unquoted keys). If your JSON document is "up-to-spec" and you have no special need for some values not covered within the data types that JSON provided, the stock reader will work fine. When the data is less than pristine, the options to bend the reader to your will are there, ready to assist. I will introduce method options as we need them, but if you can't wait any longer, you can read the docstring for the `json` method of the `DataFrameReader` object.

The second odd thing about our data ingestion is that we only have a single record. If we take a moment to reflect on this, it makes sense: TVMaze provides the result of our query in a single document. In the PySpark world, reading JSON follows this rule: *one JSON document, one line, one record.* This means that if you want to have multiple JSON records in the same document, you need to have one document per line and no new line within your document. The JSON Lines document format (http://jsonlines.org/) has a more formal definition if you are interested. By opening the JSON document we read in listing 6.3 (a regular text editor will do), you see that we only have a single line in the file.

If you want to ingest multiple documents across multiple files, you need to set the `multiLine` (careful about the capital L!) parameter to true. This will change the JSON reading rule to the following: *one JSON document, one file, one record.* With this, you can use the glob pattern (using a `*` to refer to multiple files), as seen in chapter 3, or pass a directory containing only JSON files with the same schema as an argument to the reader. I made two more shows available in the `data/shows` directory (*Breaking Bad* and *The Golden Girls*, to cover a wide gamut). In the next listing, I read the three JSON documents in one fell swoop and show that I indeed have three records.

Listing 6.4 Reading multiple JSON documents using the `multiLine` option

```
three_shows = spark.read.json("./data/shows/shows-*.json", multiLine=True)

three_shows.count()
# 3

assert three_shows.count() == 3
```

This section covered how to import a simple JSON document in PySpark and how we can tweak the specialized JSON reader to accommodate common use cases. In the next section, we focus on how complex data types help us navigate hierarchical data within a data frame.

6.2 *Breaking the second dimension with complex data types*

This section takes the JSON data model and applies it in the context of the PySpark data frame. I go a little deeper into PySpark's complex data types: the array and the map. I take PySpark's columnar model and translate it into hierarchical data models. At the end of this section, you'll know how to represent, access, and process container types in a PySpark data frame. This will prove useful in processing hierarchical or object oriented data, like the shows data we are working with.

PySpark's ability to use complex types inside the data frame is what allows its remarkable flexibility. While you still have the tabular abstraction to work with, your cells are supercharged since they can contain more than a single value. It's just like going from 2D to 3D, and even beyond!

A *complex* type isn't complex in the Python sense: where Python uses complex data in the sense of images, maps, video files and so on, Spark uses this term to refer to data types *that contain other types*. Because of this, I also use the term *container* or *compound* type as a synonym for complex types. I find them to be less ambiguous; a container-type column contains values of other types. In Python, the main complex types are the list, the tuple, and the dictionary. In PySpark, we have the array, the map, and the struct. With these, you will be able to express an infinite amount of data layout.

> ### No type left behind: If you want to dig deeper into scalar data types
> In chapter 1 to 3, we mostly dealt with *scalar* data, which contains a single value. Those types map seamlessly to Python types; for instance, a `string` type PySpark column maps to a Python string. Because Spark borrows the Java/Scala type convention, there are some peculiarities that I introduce as we encounter them.

I think I've held the punch for long enough: behold, the next listing reveals our data frame's schema!

Listing 6.5 Nested structures with a deeper level of indentation

```
shows.printSchema()
# root
# |-- _embedded: struct (nullable = true)
# |    |-- episodes: array (nullable = true)
# |    |    |-- element: struct (containsNull = true)
# |    |    |    |-- _links: struct (nullable = true)
# |    |    |    |    |-- self: struct (nullable = true)
# |    |    |    |    |    |-- href: string (nullable = true)
# |    |    |    |-- airdate: string (nullable = true)
# |    |    |    |-- airstamp: string (nullable = true)
# |    |    |    |-- airtime: string (nullable = true)
# |    |    |    |-- id: long (nullable = true)
# |    |    |    |-- image: struct (nullable = true)
# |    |    |    |    |-- medium: string (nullable = true)
# |    |    |    |    |-- original: string (nullable = true)
# |    |    |    |-- name: string (nullable = true)
# |    |    |    |-- number: long (nullable = true)
# |    |    |    |-- runtime: long (nullable = true)
# |    |    |    |-- season: long (nullable = true)
# |    |    |    |-- summary: string (nullable = true)
# |    |    |    |-- url: string (nullable = true)
# |-- _links: struct (nullable = true)
# |    |-- previousepisode: struct (nullable = true)
# |    |    |-- href: string (nullable = true)
# |    |-- self: struct (nullable = true)
# |    |    |-- href: string (nullable = true)
# |-- externals: struct (nullable = true)
# |    |-- imdb: string (nullable = true)
# |    |-- thetvdb: long (nullable = true)
# |    |-- tvrage: long (nullable = true)
# |-- genres: array (nullable = true)
# |    |-- element: string (containsNull = true)
# |-- id: long (nullable = true)
# [and more columns...]
```

Like a JSON document, the top-level element of our data frame schema is called the root.

A complex column introduces a new level of nesting in the data frame schema.

I had to truncate the schema so that we can focus on the important point here: the *hierarchy* within the schema. PySpark took every top-level key—the keys from the root object—and parsed them as columns (see the next listing for the top-level columns). When a column had a scalar value, the type was inferred according to the JSON specification we saw in section 6.1.1.

Listing 6.6 Printing the columns of the `shows` data frame

```
print(shows.columns)

# ['_embedded', '_links', 'externals', 'genres', 'id', 'image',
#  'language', 'name', 'network', 'officialSite', 'premiered',
#  'rating', 'runtime', 'schedule', 'status', 'summary', 'type',
#  'updated', 'url', 'webChannel', 'weight']
```

In this section, I briefly introduced the schema of our ingested JSON document. The next sections will cover two complex column types that Spark provides, starting with the array, and then the map.

6.2.1 *When you have more than one value: The array*

In this section, I introduce the simplest container type in PySpark: the array. I explain where the array is most commonly used as well as the main methods to create, operate, and extract data from an array column.

In section 6.1.1, I loosely equated a JSON array to a Python list. In the PySpark world, the same follows, with an important distinction: PySpark arrays are containers for values *of the same type*. This precision has an important impact on how PySpark ingests both JSON documents and, more generally, nested structures, so I'll explain this in more detail.

In listing 6.5, the genres array points to an element item, which is of type string (I reproduced the relevant section). Like any other type within the data frame, we need to provide a complete type story for any complex type, including the array. With this loss of flexibility in what an array can contain, we gain a better grasp of the data contained within the column and can avoid hard-to-track bugs. We will refer to array columns using the Array[element] notation (e.g., Array[string] represents a column containing an array of strings):

```
|-- genres: array (nullable = true)
|    |-- element: string (containsNull = true)
```

> **WARNING** PySpark will not raise an error if you try to read an array-type column with multiple types. Instead, it will simply default to the lowest common denominator, usually the string. This way, you don't lose any data, but you will get a surprise later if your code expects an array of another type.

To work a little with the array, I select a subset of the shows data frame so as to not lose focus in this huge schema. In the next listing, I select the name and genres columns and show the record. Unfortunately, *Silicon Valley* is a single-genre show, so our array is a little too basic for my taste. Let's make it a little more interesting.

Listing 6.7 Selecting the name and genres columns

```
array_subset = shows.select("name", "genres")

array_subset.show(1, False)
# +-------------+--------+
# |name         |genres  |
# +-------------+--------+
# |Silicon Valley|[Comedy]|
# +-------------+--------+
```

Conceptually, our genres column can be thought of as containing lists of elements within each record. In chapter 2, we had a similar situation with breaking our lines

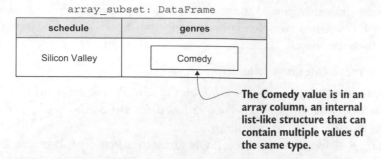

Figure 6.2   **A visual depiction of the** `array_subset` **data frame. The** `genres` **column is of type** `Array[string]`, **meaning that it contains any number of string values in a list-type container.**

into words. Visually, it looks like figure 6.2: our `Comedy` value is within a list-type structure, inside the column.

To get to the value inside the array, we need to extract them. PySpark provides a very pythonic way to work with arrays as if they were lists. In listing 6.8, I show the main ways to access the (only) element in my array. Arrays are zero-indexed when retrieving elements inside, just like Python lists. Unlike Python lists, passing an index that would go beyond the content of the list returns `null`.

Listing 6.8   Extracting elements from an array

```
import pyspark.sql.functions as F

array_subset = array_subset.select(
    "name",
    array_subset.genres[0].alias("dot_and_index"),
    F.col("genres")[0].alias("col_and_index"),
    array_subset.genres.getItem(0).alias("dot_and_method"),
    F.col("genres").getItem(0).alias("col_and_method"),
)

array_subset.show()
```

Use the dot notation and the usual square bracket with the index inside.

Instead of the index in square bracket syntax, we can use the getItem() method on the Column object.

```
# +-------------+-------------+-------------+--------------+--------------+
# |         name|dot_and_index|col_and_index|dot_and_method|col_and_method|
# +-------------+-------------+-------------+--------------+--------------+
# |Silicon Valley|       Comedy|       Comedy|        Comedy|        Comedy|
# +-------------+-------------+-------------+--------------+--------------+
```

WARNING   Although the square bracket approach looks very pythonic, you can't use it as a slicing tool. PySpark will accept only one integer as an index, so `array_subset.genres[0:10]` will fail and return an `AnalysisException` with a cryptic error message. Echoing chapter 1, PySpark is a veneer on top of Spark (Java/Scala). This provides a consistent API across languages at the expense of not always feeling integrated in the host language; here, PySpark fails to be pythonic by not allowing the slicing of arrays.

PySpark's array functions—available in the `pyspark.sql.functions` module—are almost all prefixed with the `array_` keyword (some, like `size()` in listing 6.9, can be applied to more than one complex type and therefore are not prefixed). It is therefore pretty easy to review them in one fell swoop in the API documentation (see http://mng.bz/5Kj1). Next, we use functions to create a beefier array and do a little exploration with it. In listing 6.9, I perform the following tasks:

1 I create three literal columns (using `lit()` to create scalar columns, then `make_array())` to create an array of possible genres. PySpark won't accept Python lists as an argument to `lit()`, so we have to go the long route by creating individual scalar columns before combining them into a single array. Chapter 8 covers UDFs that can return array columns.

2 I then use the function `array_repeat()` to create a column repeating the `Comedy` string we extracted in listing 6.8 five times. I finally compute the size of both columns, de-dupe both arrays, and intersect them, yielding our original `[Comedy]` array from listing 6.7.

Listing 6.9 Performing multiple operations on an array column

```
array_subset_repeated = array_subset.select(
    "name",
    F.lit("Comedy").alias("one"),
    F.lit("Horror").alias("two"),
    F.lit("Drama").alias("three"),          Creating an array from        Duplicating
    F.col("dot_and_index"),                 three columns using          the values five
).select(                                   the array() function         times within
    "name",                                                              an array using
    F.array("one", "two", "three").alias("Some_Genres"),    ◄           array_repeat()
    F.array_repeat("dot_and_index", 5).alias("Repeated_Genres"),   ◄───┘
)

array_subset_repeated.show(1, False)

# +-------------+--------------------+-------------------------------------------+
# |name         |Some_Genres         |Repeated_Genres                            |
# +-------------+--------------------+-------------------------------------------+
# |Silicon Valley|[Comedy, Horror, Drama]|[Comedy, Comedy, Comedy, Comedy, Comedy]|
# +-------------+--------------------+-------------------------------------------+

array_subset_repeated.select(
    "name", F.size("Some_Genres"), F.size("Repeated_Genres")    ◄       Computing the
).show()                                                                number of elements
                                                                       into both arrays using
# +-------------+-----------------+---------------------+                the size() function
# |         name|size(Some_Genres)|size(Repeated_Genres)|
# +-------------+-----------------+---------------------+
# |Silicon Valley|                3|                    5|
# +-------------+-----------------+---------------------+
```

```
array_subset_repeated.select(
    "name",
    F.array_distinct("Some_Genres"),
    F.array_distinct("Repeated_Genres"),
).show(1, False)
```

Removing duplicates into both arrays with the array_distinct() method. Since Some_Genres doesn't have any duplicates, the values within the array don't change.

```
# +-------------+-------------------------+-----------------------------+
# |name         |array_distinct(Some_Genres)|array_distinct(Repeated_Genres)|
# +-------------+-------------------------+-----------------------------+
# |Silicon Valley|[Comedy, Horror, Drama]  |[Comedy]                     |
# +-------------+-------------------------+-----------------------------+
```

```
array_subset_repeated = array_subset_repeated.select(
    "name",
    F.array_intersect("Some_Genres", "Repeated_Genres").alias(
        "Genres"
    ),
)
```

By intersecting both arrays using array_intersect(), the only value common to both arrays is Comedy.

```
array_subset_repeated.show()
```

```
# +-------------+-------+
# |         name| Genres|
# +-------------+-------+
# |Silicon Valley|[Comedy]|
# +-------------+-------+
```

When you want to know the position of a value in an array, you can use `array_position()`. This function takes two arguments:

- An array column to perform the search
- A value to search for within the array

It returns the cardinal position of the *value* within the *array column* (first value is 1, second value is 2, etc.). If the value does not exist, the function returns 0. I illustrate this in listing 6.10. This inconsistency between zero-based indexing (for `getItem()`) and one-based/cardinal indexing (for `array_position()`) can be confusing: I remember this difference by calling the position via `getItem()` or the square brackets *index* versus *position* for the return value of the `array_position()` function, just like in the PySpark API.

Listing 6.10   Using `array_position()` to search for `Genres` string

```
array_subset_repeated.select(
    "Genres", F.array_position("Genres", "Comedy")
).show()
```

```
# +--------+-----------------------------+
# |  Genres|array_position(Genres, Comedy)|
# +--------+-----------------------------+
# |[Comedy]|                            1|
# +--------+-----------------------------+
```

In this section, we looked at the array using our shows data frame. We saw that a PySpark array contains elements of the same time, and an array column has access to some container functions (e.g., size()) as well as a handful of array-specific functions, prefixed by array_. The next section will introduce an equally useful but much less frequently used complex type, the map.

6.2.2 *The map type: Keys and values within a column*

This section covers the map column type and where it can be used successfully. Maps are less common as a column type; reading a JSON document won't yield columns of type map, but they are nonetheless useful to represent simple key-value pairs.

A map is conceptually very close to a Python *typed* dictionary: you have keys and values just like in a dictionary, but as with the array, the keys need to be of the same type, and the values need to be of the same type (the type for the keys can be different than the type for the values). Values can be null, but keys can't, just like with Python dictionaries.

One of the easiest ways to create a map is from two columns of type array. We will do so by collecting some information about the name, language, type, and url columns into an array and using the map_from_arrays() function, like in the next listing.

Listing 6.11   Creating a map from two arrays

```
columns = ["name", "language", "type"]

shows_map = shows.select(
    *[F.lit(column) for column in columns],
    F.array(*columns).alias("values"),
)

shows_map = shows_map.select(F.array(*columns).alias("keys"), "values")

shows_map.show(1)
# +--------------------+--------------------+
# |                keys|              values|
# +--------------------+--------------------+
# |[name, language, ...|[Silicon Valley, ...|
# +--------------------+--------------------+

shows_map = shows_map.select(
    F.map_from_arrays("keys", "values").alias("mapped")
)

shows_map.printSchema()

# root
#  |-- mapped: map (nullable = false)
#  |    |-- key: string
#  |    |-- value: string (valueContainsNull = true)

shows_map.show(1, False)
```

```
# +------------------------------------------------------------------+
# |mapped                                                            |
# +------------------------------------------------------------------+
# |[name -> Silicon Valley, language -> English, type -> Scripted]|
# +------------------------------------------------------------------+
```

```
shows_map.select(
    F.col("mapped.name"),          ◁──┐   We can access the value corresponding to a key
    F.col("mapped")["name"],         ◁──   using the dot notation within the col() function.
    shows_map.mapped["name"],        ◁──
).show()                                    We can also pass the key
                                            value within brackets, as we
                                            can in a Python dictionary.
```

```
# +--------------+--------------+--------------+       Just like with the array, we can use
# |         name | mapped[name]| mapped[name]|        dot notation to get the column
# +--------------+--------------+--------------+       and then use the bracket to
# |Silicon Valley|Silicon Valley|Silicon Valley|       select the right key.
# +--------------+--------------+--------------+
```

Just like with the array, PySpark provides a few functions to work with maps under the `pyspark.sql.functions` module. Most of them are prefixed or suffixed with `map`, such as `map_values()` (which creates an array column out of the map values) or `create_map()` (which creates a map from the columns passed as a parameter, alternating between keys and values). The exercises at the end of this section and the end of the chapter provide more practice with the `map` column type.

If the `map` maps (pun intended) to a Python dictionary, why did our JSON document not have any maps? Because maps keys and values need to be the same type, respectively—something JSON objects are not forced to do—we need a more flexible container to accommodate objects. It's also much more useful to have the top-level name/value pairs as columns, like PySpark did with our `shows` data frame in listing 6.3. The next section will introduce the struct, which is the backbone of the data frame as we know it.

Null elements in arrays and maps

When defining an array or a map, you can also pass an optional parameter (`contains-Null` for the array, `valueContainsNull` for the map) that will indicate PySpark if it can accept `null` elements. This is different than the `nullable` flag at column level: here, we can mention if *any of the elements (or values)* can be `null`.

I don't use non-nullable/no-null–element columns when working with data frames, but if your data model requires it, the option is available.

Exercise 6.1

Assume the following JSON document:

```
"""{"name": "Sample name",
    "keywords": ["PySpark", "Python", "Data"]}"""
```

What is the schema once read by `spark.read.json`?

Exercise 6.2

Assume the following JSON document:

```
"""{"name": "Sample name",
    "keywords": ["PySpark", 3.2, "Data"]}"""
```

What is the schema once read by `spark.read.json`?

6.3   *The struct: Nesting columns within columns*

This section covers the struct as a column type, and also as the foundation of the data frame. We look at how we can reason about our data frame in terms of structs and how to navigate a data frame with nested structs.

The `struct` is akin to a JSON object, in the sense that the key or name of each pair is a string and that each record can be of a different type. If we take a small subset of the columns in our data frame, like in listing 6.12, we see that the `schedule` column contains two fields:

- `days`, an array of strings
- `time`, a string

Listing 6.12   The `schedule` column with an array of strings and a string

```
shows.select("schedule").printSchema()

# root
#  |-- schedule: struct (nullable = true)         ←───┐
#  |    |-- days: array (nullable = true)
#  |    |    |-- element: string (containsNull = true)
#  |    |-- time: string (nullable = true)
```

The schedule column is a struct. When looking at the nesting that rises from the column, we notice that the struct contains two named fields: days (an Array[string]) and time, a string.

The struct is very different from the array and the map in that *the number of fields and their names are known ahead of time*. In our case, the `schedule` struct column is fixed: we know that each record of our data frame will contain that `schedule` struct (or a `null` value, if we want to be pedantic), and within that struct there will be an array of strings, `days`, and a string, `time`. The array and the map enforce the types of the values, but not their numbers or names. The struct allows for more versatility of types, as long as you name each field and provide the type ahead of time.

Conceptually, I find that the easiest way to think about the struct column type is to imagine a small data frame within your column records. Using our example in listing 6.12, we can visualize that `schedule` is a data frame of two columns (`days` and `time`) trapped within the column. I illustrated the nested column analogy in figure 6.3.

Structs are able to be nested within one another. As an example, in listing 6.5 (or listing 6.13), the first field of our data frame, `_embedded`, is a struct that contains an array field, `episodes`. That array contains structs `_links`, which contains a struct `self`,

```
shows.select("schedule"): DataFrame
```

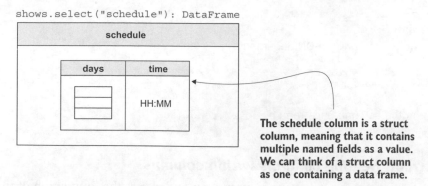

The schedule column is a struct column, meaning that it contains multiple named fields as a value. We can think of a struct column as one containing a data frame.

Figure 6.3   The `shows.select("schedule")` data frame. The column is a struct containing two named fields: `days` and `time`.

which contains a string field, `href`. We are facing a pretty confusing nesting here! Don't worry if this is still a little hard to envision; the next section will decipher the nesting dolls arrangement of structs by navigating our data frame.

6.3.1   *Navigating structs as if they were nested columns*

This section covers how to extract values from nested structs inside a data frame. PySpark provides the same convenience when working with nested columns as it would for regular columns. I cover the dot and bracket notations, and explain how PySpark treats nesting when using other complex structures. We work with the _embedded column by cleaning the useless nesting.

Before going all hands on the keyboard, we'll draft the structure of the _embedded column as a tree to get a sense of what we're working with. In the following listing, I provide the output of the `printSchema()` command, which I drew in figure 6.4.

Listing 6.13   The `_embedded` column schema

```
shows.select(F.col("_embedded")).printSchema()
# root
#  |-- _embedded: struct (nullable = true)
#  |    |-- episodes: array (nullable = true)
#  |    |    |-- element: struct (containsNull = true)
#  |    |    |    |-- _links: struct (nullable = true)
#  |    |    |    |    |-- self: struct (nullable = true)
#  |    |    |    |    |    |-- href: string (nullable = true)
#  |    |    |    |-- airdate: string (nullable = true)
#  |    |    |    |-- id: long (nullable = true)
#  |    |    |    |-- image: struct (nullable = true)
#  |    |    |    |    |-- medium: string (nullable = true)
#  |    |    |    |    |-- original: string (nullable = true)
#  |    |    |    |-- name: string (nullable = true)
#  |    |    |    |-- number: long (nullable = true)
#  |    |    |    |-- runtime: long (nullable = true)
#  |    |    |    |-- season: long (nullable = true)
```

_embedded contains a single field: episodes.

episodes is an Array[Struct]. Yes, it's possible.

Each episode is a record in the array, containing all the named fields in the struct. _links is a Struct[Struct[string]] field. PySpark will represent multiple levels of nesting without problems.

```
#  |    |    |    |-- summary: string (nullable = true)
#  |    |    |    |-- url: string (nullable = true)
```

For starters, we see in figure 6.4 that _embedded is a useless struct, as it contains only one field. In listing 6.14, I create a new top-level column called episodes that refers directly to the episodes field in the _embedded struct. For this, I use the col function and _embedded.episodes. This is consistent with the "struct as a mini data frame" mental model: you can refer to struct fields using the same notation as you would for a data frame.

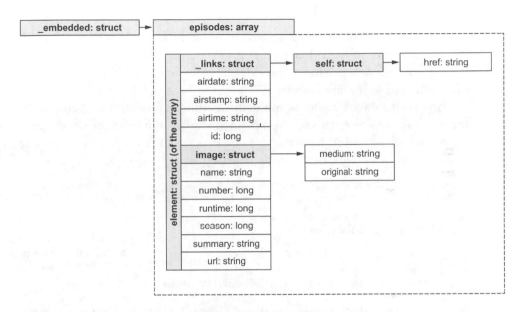

Figure 6.4   The schema for the _embedded field of our data frame

---

Listing 6.14   Promoting the fields within a struct as columns

```
shows_clean = shows.withColumn(
 "episodes", F.col("_embedded.episodes")
).drop("_embedded")

shows_clean.printSchema()
# root
#  |-- _links: struct (nullable = true)
#  |    |-- previousepisode: struct (nullable = true)
#  |    |    |-- href: string (nullable = true)
#  |    |-- self: struct (nullable = true)
#  |    |    |-- href: string (nullable = true)
#  |-- externals: struct (nullable = true)
#  |    |-- imdb: string (nullable = true)
#  [...]
```

```
# |-- episodes: array (nullable = true)
# |    |-- element: struct (containsNull = true)
# |    |    |-- _links: struct (nullable = true)
# |    |    |    |-- self: struct (nullable = true)
# |    |    |    |    |-- href: string (nullable = true)
# |    |    |-- airdate: string (nullable = true)
# |    |    |-- airstamp: string (nullable = true)
# |    |    |-- airtime: string (nullable = true)
# |    |    |-- id: long (nullable = true)
# |    |    |-- image: struct (nullable = true)
# |    |    |    |-- medium: string (nullable = true)
# |    |    |    |-- original: string (nullable = true)
# [... rest of schema]
```

> We lost the _embedded column and promoted the field of the struct (episodes) as a top-level column.

Finally, we look at drilling through structs nested in arrays. In section 6.2.1, I explained that we can refer to individual elements in the array using the index in brackets after the column reference. What about extracting the names of all the episodes, which are within the episodes array of structs?

Turns out PySpark will allow you to drill within an array and will return the subset of the struct *in array form*. This is best explained by an example: in the next listing, I extract the episodes.name field from the shows_clean data frame. Since episodes is an array of struct and name is one of the string fields, episodes.name is an array of strings.

Listing 6.15   Selecting a field in an `Array[Struct]` to create a column

```
episodes_name = shows_clean.select(F.col("episodes.name"))
episodes_name.printSchema()

# root
# |-- name: array (nullable = true)
# |    |-- element: string (containsNull = true)

episodes_name.select(F.explode("name").alias("name")).show(3, False)
# +-------------------------+
# |name                     |
# +-------------------------+
# |Minimum Viable Product   |
# |The Cap Table            |
# |Articles of Incorporation|
# +-------------------------+
```

> episodes.name refers to the name field of the elements of the episodes array.

> Since we have multiple records in the episodes array, episodes.name extracts the name field or each record in the array and packs it into an array of names. I explode (chapter 2 and section 6.5) the array to show the names clearly.

This section walked through the struct hierarchy using the same notation you would use for extracting columns from a data frame. We now can extract any field from our JSON document and know exactly what to expect. The next section will leverage our knowledge of complex data types and use that knowledge in crafting a schema. I also touch on the advantages and trade-offs of using hierarchical schemas and complex data types.

6.4   Building and using the data frame schema

In this section, I cover how to define and use a schema with a PySpark data frame. We build the schema for our JSON object programmatically and review the out-of-the-box types PySpark offers. Being able to use Python structures (serialized as JSON) means that we can manipulate our schemas just like any other data structure; we can reuse our data manipulation tool kit for manipulating our data frame's metadata. By doing this, we also address the potential slowdown from `inferSchema`, as we don't need Spark to read the data twice (once to infer the schema, once to perform the read).

In section 6.3, I explained that we can think of a struct column as a mini data frame nested in said column. The opposite also works: you can think of a data frame as having a single-struct entity, with the columns the top-level fields of the "root" struct. In any output of `printSchema()` (I reproduced the relevant part of listing 6.5 in the next listing for convenience), all the top-level fields are connected to the `root`.

Listing 6.16   A sample of the schema for the `shows` data frame

```
shows.printSchema()
# root
#  |-- _links: struct (nullable = true)
#  |    |-- previousepisode: struct (nullable = true)
#  |    |    |-- href: string (nullable = true)
#  |    |-- self: struct (nullable = true)
#  |    |    |-- href: string (nullable = true)
#  |-- externals: struct (nullable = true)
#  |    |-- imdb: string (nullable = true)
# [... rest of schema]
```

All the top-level fields (or columns) are children of a root implicit struct.

There are two syntaxes you can use to create a schema. In the next section, we review the explicit, programmatic one. PySpark also accepts a DDL-style schema, which is covered in chapter 7, where we discuss PySpark and SQL.

6.4.1   Using Spark types as the base blocks of a schema

In this section, I cover the column types in the context of a schema definition. I build the schema for our `shows` data frame from scratch and include some programmatic niceties of the PySpark schema-building capabilities. I introduce PySpark data types and how to assemble them in a struct to build your data frame schema. Decoupling the data from the schema means that you can control how your data is represented in your data frame and improve the robustness of your data transformation programs.

The data types we use to build a schema are located in the `pyspark.sql.types` module. They are such a frequent import when working with data frames that, just like `pyspark.sql.functions`, they are usually imported with the qualified prefix `T`:

```
import pyspark.sql.types as T
```

> **TIP**   Just like with functions using a capital F, the common convention is to use a capital T when importing the types module. I strongly recommend doing the same.

Within the `pyspark.sql.types`, there are two main kinds of objects. First, you have the `types` object, which represents a column of a certain type. All of those objects follow the `ValueType()` CamelCase syntax: for instance, a long column would be represented by a `LongType()` object. Most scalar types do not take any parameters (except for `DecimalType(precision, scale)`, which is used for decimal numbers that have a precise amount of precision before and after the decimal point). Complex types, such as the array and the map, take the types of their values directly in the constructor. For example, an array of strings would be `ArrayType(StringType())`, and a map of strings mapping to longs would be `MapType(StringType(), LongType())`.

Second, you have the field object; in other words, the `StructField()`. PySpark provides a `StructType()` that can contain an arbitrary number of named fields; programmatically, this translates to a `StructType()` taking a list of `StructField()`. Easy as that!

A `StructField()` contains two mandatory as well as two optional parameters:

- The `name` of the field, passed as a string
- The `dataType` of the field, passed as a type object
- (Optional) A `nullable` flag, which determines if the field can be `null` or not (by default `True`)
- (Optional) A `metadata` dictionary that contains arbitrary information, which we will use for column metadata when working with ML pipelines (in chapter 13)

> **TIP**   If you provide a reduced schema—meaning you only define a subset of the fields—PySpark will only read the defined fields. In the case where you only need a subset of columns/fields from a very wide data frame, you can save a significant amount of time!

Putting all this together, the `summary` string field of the `shows` data frame would be encoded in a StructField like so:

```
T.StructField("summary", T.StringType())
```

In listing 6.17, I've done the `_embedded` schema of the `shows` data frame. While very verbose, we gain intimate knowledge of the data frame structure. Since the data frame schemas are regular Python classes, we can assign them to variables and build our schema from the bottom up. I usually split the structs containing more than three or so fields into their own variables, so my code doesn't read like a whole block of structs interspersed with brackets.

Listing 6.17   The schema for the `_embedded` field

```
import pyspark.sql.types as T

episode_links_schema = T.StructType(
    [
```

```
        T.StructField(
            "self", T.StructType([T.StructField("href", T.StringType())])
        )
    ]
)
```

**The _links field contains a
self struct that itself contains
a single-string field: href.**

```
episode_image_schema = T.StructType(
    [
        T.StructField("medium", T.StringType()),
        T.StructField("original", T.StringType()),
    ]
)
```

**The image field is a struct of two
string fields: medium and original.**

```
episode_schema = T.StructType(
    [
        T.StructField("_links", episode_links_schema),
        T.StructField("airdate", T.DateType()),
        T.StructField("airstamp", T.TimestampType()),
        T.StructField("airtime", T.StringType()),
        T.StructField("id", T.StringType()),
        T.StructField("image", episode_image_schema),
        T.StructField("name", T.StringType()),
        T.StructField("number", T.LongType()),
        T.StructField("runtime", T.LongType()),
        T.StructField("season", T.LongType()),
        T.StructField("summary", T.StringType()),
        T.StructField("url", T.StringType()),
    ]
)
```

**Since types are Python
objects, we can pass them
to variables and use them.
Using episodes_links_schema
and episode_image_schema
makes our schema for an
episode look much cleaner.**

```
embedded_schema = T.StructType(
    [
        T.StructField(
            "_embedded",
            T.StructType(
                [
                    T.StructField(
                        "episodes", T.ArrayType(episode_schema)
                    )
                ]
            ),
        )
    ]
)
```

**It's obvious that our _embedded
column contains a single field,
episodes, which contains an array of
episodes. Using good variable names
helps with documenting our intent
without relying on comments.**

This section covered how to build a schema from the bottom up: you can use the types and field from the pyspark.sql.types module and create one field for each column. When you have a struct column, you treat it the same way: create a Struct-Type() and assign struct fields. With these simple rules, you should be able to construct any schema you need. The next section will leverage our schema to read the JSON in strict fashion.

6.4.2   *Reading a JSON document with a strict schema in place*

This section covers how to read a JSON document while enforcing a precise schema. This proves extremely useful when you want to improve the robustness of your data pipeline; it's better to know you're missing a few columns at ingestion time than to get an error later in the program. I review some convenient practices when you expect the data to fit a certain mold and how you can rely on PySpark to keep you sane in the world of messy JSON documents. As a bonus, you can expect a better performance when reading data with a schema in place, because `inferSchema` requires a pre-read of the data just to infer the schema.

If you analyzed listing 6.17 field by field, you might have realized that I defined `air-date` as a date and `airstamp` as a timestamp. In section 6.1.2, I listed the types available within a JSON document; missing from the lot were dates and timestamps. PySpark has your back on this: we can, fortunately, leverage some options of the JSON reader to read certain strings as dates and timestamps. To do so, you need to provide a full schema for your document; good thing we have one ready. In listing 6.18, I read my JSON document once more, but this time I provide an explicit schema. Note the change in type for `airdate` and `airstamp`. I also provide a new parameter, `mode`, which, when set to `FAIL-FAST`, will error if it encounters a malformed record versus the schema provided.

Because we only pass a partial schema (`embedded_schema`), PySpark will only read the defined columns. In this case, we only cover the `_embedded` struct, so that's the only part of the data frame we read. This is a convenient way to avoid reading everything before dropping unused columns.

Since our dates and timestamp in our JSON document are ISO-8601 compliant (`yyyy-MM-dd` for the date and `yyyy-MM-ddTHH:mm:ss.SSSXXX` for the timestamp), we do not have to customize the JSON `DataFrameReader` to automatically parse our values. If you are facing a nonstandard date or timestamp format, you'll need to pass the right format to `dateFormat` or `timestampFormat`. The format grammar is available on the official Spark documentation website (http://mng.bz/6ZgD).

> **WARNING** If you are using any version of Spark 2, the format followed for `dateFormat` and `timestampFormat` is different. Look for `java.text.Simple-DateFormat` if this is the case.

Listing 6.18   Reading a JSON document using an explicit partial schema

```
shows_with_schema = spark.read.json(
    "./data/shows/shows-silicon-valley.json",
    schema=embedded_schema,         ◁──
    mode="FAILFAST",         ◁──
)
```

We pass our schema to the schema parameter. Since our schema is a subset of the JSON document, we only read the defined fields.

By selecting the FAILFAST mode, our DataFrameReader will crash if our schema is incompatible.

A successful read is promising, but since I want to verify my new date and timestamp field, I drill, explode, and show the fields in the following listing.

Listing 6.19   Validating the `airdate` and `airstamp` field reading

```
for column in ["airdate", "airstamp"]:
    shows.select(f"_embedded.episodes.{column}").select(
        F.explode(column)
    ).show(5)

# +----------+
# |       col|
# +----------+
# |2014-04-06|
# |2014-04-13|
# |2014-04-20|
# |2014-04-27|
# |2014-05-04|
# +----------+
# only showing top 5 rows

# +-------------------+
# |                col|
# +-------------------+
# |2014-04-06 22:00:00|
# |2014-04-13 22:00:00|
# |2014-04-20 22:00:00|
# |2014-04-27 22:00:00|
# |2014-05-04 22:00:00|
# +-------------------+
# only showing top 5 rows
```

Everything here looks fine. What happens if the schema does not match? PySpark, even in FAILFAST, will allow absent fields in the document if the schema allows for null values. In listing 6.20, I pollute my schema, changing two StringType() to Long-Type(). I did not include the whole stack trace, but the resulting error is a Py4JJava-Error that hits it right on the head: our string value is not a bigint (or long). You won't know which one, though: the stack trace only gives what it tried to parse and what is expected.

NOTE   Py4J (https://www.py4j.org/) is a library that enables Python programs to access Java objects in a JVM. In the case of PySpark, it helps bridge the gap between the pythonic veneer and the JVM-based Spark. In chapter 2, we saw—without naming it—Py4J in action, as most pyspark.sql.functions call a _jvm function. This makes the core Spark functions as fast in PySpark as they are in Spark, at the expense of some odd errors once in a while.

Listing 6.20   Witnessing a JSON document ingestion with incompatible schema

```
from py4j.protocol import Py4JJavaError

episode_schema_BAD = T.StructType(
    [
        T.StructField("_links", episode_links_schema),
```

◁─┐ I import the relevant error
   (Py4JJavaError) to be able
   to catch and analyze it.

```
            T.StructField("airdate", T.DateType()),
            T.StructField("airstamp", T.TimestampType()),
            T.StructField("airtime", T.StringType()),
            T.StructField("id", T.StringType()),
            T.StructField("image", episode_image_schema),
            T.StructField("name", T.StringType()),
            T.StructField("number", T.LongType()),
            T.StructField("runtime", T.LongType()),
            T.StructField("season", T.LongType()),
            T.StructField("summary", T.LongType()),
            T.StructField("url", T.LongType()),
        ]
)
```

I change two fields from string to long in my schema.

```
embedded_schema2 = T.StructType(
    [
        T.StructField(
            "_embedded",
            T.StructType(
                [
                    T.StructField(
                        "episodes", T.ArrayType(episode_schema_BAD)
                    )
                ]
            ),
        )
    ]
)


shows_with_schema_wrong = spark.read.json(
    "./data/shows/shows-silicon-valley.json",
    schema=embedded_schema2,
    mode="FAILFAST",
)


try:
    shows_with_schema_wrong.show()
except Py4JJavaError:
    pass
```

PySpark will give the types of the two fields, but won't give you which field is problematic. Time for some forensic analysis, I guess.

```
# Huge Spark ERROR stacktrace, relevant bit:
#
# Caused by: java.lang.RuntimeException: Failed to parse a value for data type
#    bigint (current token: VALUE_STRING).
```

This section was a short one but is still incredibly useful. We saw how to use the schema information to create a strict contract between the data provider and the data processor (us). In practice, this kind of strict schema assertion provides a better error message when the data is not what you expect, and allows you to avoid some errors (or a wrong result) down the line.

> **FAILFAST: When do you want to get in trouble?**
>
> It seems a little paranoid to use `FAILFAST` while setting a verbose schema all by hand. Unfortunately, data is messy and people can be sloppy, and when you rely on data to make decisions, *garbage in, garbage out*.
>
> In my professional career, I've encountered data integrity problems so often when reading data that I now firmly believe that you need to diagnose them as early as possible. `FAILFAST` mode is one example: by default, PySpark will set malformed records to `null` (the `PERMISSIVE` approach). When exploring, I consider this perfectly legitimate. But I've had enough sleepless nights after a business stakeholder called me at the last minute because the "results are weird" and thus try to minimize data drama at every opportunity.

6.4.3 *Going full circle: Specifying your schemas in JSON*

This section covers a different approach to the schema definition. Instead of using the verbose constructors seen in section 6.4, I explain how you can define your schema in JSON. We're going full circle using JSON for both the data and its schema!

The `StructType` object has a handy `fromJson()` method (note the `camelCase` used here, where the first letter of the first word is not capitalized, but the others are) that will read a JSON-formatted schema. As long as we know how to provide a proper JSON schema, we should be good to go.

To understand the layout and content of a typical PySpark data frame, we use our `shows_with_schema` data frame and the `schema` attribute. Unlike `printSchema()`, which prints our schema to a standard output, `schema` returns an internal representation of the schema in terms of `StructType`. Fortunately, `StructType` comes with two methods for exporting its content into a JSON-esque format:

- `json()` will output a string containing the JSON-formatted schema.
- `jsonValue()` will return the schema as a dictionary.

In listing 6.21, I pretty-print, with the help of the `pprint` module from the standard library, a subset of the schema of the `shows_with_schema` data frame. The result is very reasonable—each element is a JSON object containing four fields:

- `name`, a string representing the name of the field
- `type`, a string (for scalar values) containing the data type (e.g., `"string"` or `"long"`) or an object (for complex values) representing the type of the field
- `nullable`, a Boolean indicating if the field can contain `null` values
- a `metadata` object containing the metadata of the field

Listing 6.21   Pretty-printing the schema

```
import pprint          ◁────────────       pprint pretty prints Python data
                                           structures into the shell. It makes reading
pprint.pprint(                             nested dictionaries much easier.
    shows_with_schema.select(
```

```
        F.explode("_embedded.episodes").alias("episode")
    )
    .select("episode.airtime")
    .schema.jsonValue()
)
# {'fields': [{'metadata': {},
#              'name': 'airtime',
#              'nullable': True,
#              'type': 'string'}],
# 'type': 'struct'}
```

These are the same parameters we pass to a `StructField`, as seen in section 6.4.1. The array, map, and struct have a slightly more involved type representation to go with their slightly more involved data representation. Rather than enumerating them out long, remember that you can have a refresher straight from your REPL by creating a dummy object and calling `jsonValue()` on it. I do it in the following listing.

> **Listing 6.22   Pretty-printing dummy complex types**

```
pprint.pprint(
    T.StructField("array_example", T.ArrayType(T.StringType())).jsonValue()
)

# {'metadata': {},
#  'name': 'array_example',
#  'nullable': True,
#  'type': {'containsNull': True, 'elementType': 'string', 'type': 'array'}}

pprint.pprint(
    T.StructField(
        "map_example", T.MapType(T.StringType(), T.LongType())
    ).jsonValue()
)

# {'metadata': {},
#  'name': 'map_example',
#  'nullable': True,
#  'type': {'keyType': 'string',
#           'type': 'map',
#           'valueContainsNull': True,
#           'valueType': 'long'}}

pprint.pprint(
    T.StructType(
        [
            T.StructField(
                "map_example", T.MapType(T.StringType(), T.LongType())
            ),
            T.StructField("array_example", T.ArrayType(T.StringType())),
        ]
    ).jsonValue()
)
```

The array types contains three elements: containsNull, elementType, and type (which is always array).

The map contains similar elements as the array, but with keyType and valueType instead of elementType and valueContainsNull (a null key does not make sense).

```
# {'fields': [{'metadata': {},
#               'name': 'map_example',
#               'nullable': True,
#               'type': {'keyType': 'string',
#                        'type': 'map',
#                        'valueContainsNull': True,
#                        'valueType': 'long'}},
#              {'metadata': {},
#               'name': 'array_example',
#               'nullable': True,
#               'type': {'containsNull': True,
#                        'elementType': 'string',
#                        'type': 'array'}}],
#  'type': 'struct'}
```

> The struct contains the same elements as the constructors: we have a type of struct and a fields element containing an JSON array of objects. Each StructField contains the same four fields as the constructor seen in section 6.3.

Finally, we can close the loop by making sure that our JSON-schema is consistent with the one currently being used. For this, we'll export the schema of `shows_with_schema` in a JSON string, load it as a JSON object, and then use `StructType.fromJson()` method to re-create the schema. As we can see in the next listing, the two schemas are equivalent.

Listing 6.23 Validating JSON schema is equal to data frame schema

```
other_shows_schema = T.StructType.fromJson(
    json.loads(shows_with_schema.schema.json())
)

print(other_shows_schema == shows_with_schema.schema)  # True
```

While this seems like a mere parlor trick, having the ability to serialize the schema of your data frame in a common format is a great help on your journey to consistent and predictable big data. You can version-control your schema and share your expectations with others. Furthermore, since JSON has a high affinity to Python dictionaries, you can use regular Python code to convert to and from any schema-definition language. (Chapter 7 contains information about DDL, a way to describe data schemas, which is what SQL databases use for defining schemas). PySpark gives you first-class access to define and access your data layout.

This section covered how PySpark organizes data within a data frame and communicates this back to you through the schema. You learned how to create one programmatically, as well as how to import and export JSON-formatted schemas. The next section explains why complex data structures make sense when analyzing large data sets.

Exercise 6.3
What is wrong with this schema?

```
schema = T.StructType([T.StringType(), T.LongType(), T.LongType()])
```

6.5 *Putting it all together: Reducing duplicate data with complex data types*

This section takes the hierarchical data model and presents the advantages in a big data setting. We look at how it helps reduce data duplication without relying on auxiliary data frames and how we can expand and contract the complex types.

When looking at a new table (or a data frame), I always ask myself, *what does each record contain?* Another way to approach this question is by completing the following sentence: each record contains a single _____.

> **TIP** Database folks sometimes call this a *primary key*. A primary key has specific implications in data base design. In my day-to-day life, I use the term *exposure record*: each record represents a single point of exposure, meaning that there is no overlap between records. This avoids domain-specific language (retail: customer or transaction; insurance: insured or policy year; banking: customer or balance at end of day). This is not an official term, but I find it very convenient, as it is portable across domains.

In the case of the shows data frame, each record contains a single *show*. When looking at the fields, we can say "each show has a (insert name of the field)." For instance, each show has an ID, a name, a URL, and so on. What about episodes? A show definitely has more than one episode. By now, I am pretty sure you see how the hierarchical data model and the complex Spark column types solve this elegantly, but let's review what the traditional "rows and columns" model has to say about this.

In the two-dimensional world, if we wanted to have a table containing shows and episodes, we would proceed with one of two scenarios.

We avoid duplication of data in a hierarchical setting with the creation of multiple tables, each one with a different exposure record. Relations are exposing that hierarchy, like the show_id field here.

shows: DataFrame

show_id	name
143	Silicon Valley

episodes: DataFrame

show_id	episode_id	name
143	1	Minimum Viable Product
143	2	The Cap Table
143	3	Articles of Incorporation

Figure 6.5 A hierarchical relationship can be expressed via a link/relation between two tables. Here, our show is linked to its episodes through a show_id key.

First, we could have a shows table linked to an episodes table, using a star schema like the one encountered in chapters 4 and 5. Visually, figure 6.5 explains how we would separate the `shows` and `episodes` hierarchical relationship using two tables. In this case, our data is *normalized*, and while we have no duplication, getting all the information we want means joining tables according to keys.

Second, we could have a joined table with scalar records (no nested structure). In our case, it becomes harder to make sense of our unit of exposure. If we look at the map and array types we'd need to "scalarize," we have shows, episodes, genres, and days. An "each episode-show-genre-day-of-airing" unit of exposure table makes little sense. In figure 6.6, I show a table with only those four records as an example. We see duplication of the data for the `show_id` and the `genre`, which provides no additional information. Furthermore, having a joined table means that the relationship between the records is lost. Is the `genre` field the genre of the show or the episode?

`shows_episodes_genre_day: DataFrame`

show_id	episode_id	genre	day
143	1	Comedy	Sunday
143	2	Comedy	Sunday
143	3	Comedy	Sunday

Both show_id and genre values are duplicated just to accommodate the hierarchical model within a two-dimensional table.

Figure 6.6   A joined representation of our `shows` hierarchical model. We witness data duplication and a loss of relationship information.

Since the beginning of the book, all of our data processing has tried to converge with having a single table. If we want to avoid data duplication, keep the relationship information, and have a single table, then we can—and should!—use the data frame's complex column types. In our `shows` data frame

- Each record represents a show.
- A show has multiple episodes (array of structs column).
- Each episode has many fields (struct column within the array).
- Each show can have multiple genres (array of string column).
- Each show has a schedule (struct column).
- Each schedule belonging to a show can have multiple days (array) but a single time (string).

Visually, it looks like figure 6.7. It's clear that the episodes, the genre, and the schedule belong to the shows, yet we can have multiple episodes without duplicating any data.

An efficient, hierarchical data model is a thing of beauty, but sometimes we need to leave our ivory tower and work on the data. The next section will show how to

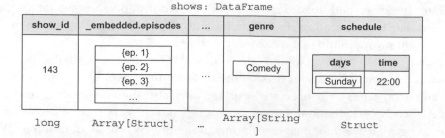

Figure 6.7 **A sample of the shows data frame showcasing the hierarchical (or object-oriented) model**

expand and contract array columns to your liking to get your Goldilocks data frame at every stage.

6.5.1 Getting to the "just right" data frame: Explode and collect

This section covers how to use explode and collect operations to go from hierarchical to tabular and back. We cover the methods to break an array or a map into discrete records and how to get the records back into the original structure.

In chapter 2, we already saw how to break an array of values into discrete records using the explode() function. We will now revisit the exploding operation by generalizing it to the map, looking at the behavior when your data frame has multiple columns, and seeing the different options PySpark provided.

In listing 6.24, I take a small subset of columns and explode the _embedded.episodes one, producing a data frame containing one record per episode. This is the same use case that we saw in chapter 2, but with more columns present. PySpark duplicates the values in the columns that aren't being exploded.

Listing 6.24 **Exploding the _embedded.episodes into 53 distinct records**

```
episodes = shows.select(
    "id", F.explode("_embedded.episodes").alias("episodes")
)
episodes.show(5, truncate=70)
```

We explode an array column creating one record per element contained in the array.

```
# +---+------------------------------------------------------------------+
# | id|                                                          episodes|
# +---+------------------------------------------------------------------+
# |143|{{{http://api.tvmaze.com/episodes/10897}}, 2014-04-06, 2014-04-07T0...|
# |143|{{{http://api.tvmaze.com/episodes/10898}}, 2014-04-13, 2014-04-14T0...|
# |143|{{{http://api.tvmaze.com/episodes/10899}}, 2014-04-20, 2014-04-21T0...|
# |143|{{{http://api.tvmaze.com/episodes/10900}}, 2014-04-27, 2014-04-28T0...|
# |143|{{{http://api.tvmaze.com/episodes/10901}}, 2014-05-04, 2014-05-05T0...|
# +---+------------------------------------------------------------------+
# only showing top 5 rows

episodes.count()  # 53
```

Explode can also happen with maps: the keys and values will be exploded in two different fields. For completeness, I'll introduce the second type of explosion: posexplode(). The "pos" stands for position: it explodes the column and returns an additional column before the data that contains the position as a long. In listing 6.25, I create a simple map from two fields in the array, then posexplode() each record. Since a map column has a key and a value field, posexplode() on a map column will generate three columns; when aliasing the result, we need to pass three parameters to alias().

> **Listing 6.25 Exploding a map using posexplode()**

```
episode_name_id = shows.select(          We build a map from two arrays:
    F.map_from_arrays(          ◄        first is the key; second is the values.
        F.col("_embedded.episodes.id"), F.col("_embedded.episodes.name")
    ).alias("name_id")
)

episode_name_id = episode_name_id.select(
    F.posexplode("name_id").alias("position", "id", "name")          ◄
)
                                                                        By position exploding, we
episode_name_id.show(5)                                                 create three columns: the
                                                                        position, the key, and the
# +--------+-----+--------------------+                                value of each element in
# |position|   id|                name|                               our map have a record.
# +--------+-----+--------------------+
# |       0|10897|Minimum Viable Pr...|
# |       1|10898|       The Cap Table|
# |       2|10899|Articles of Incor...|
# |       3|10900|    Fiduciary Duties|
# |       4|10901|       Signaling Risk|
# +--------+-----+--------------------+
# only showing top 5 rows
```

Both explode() and posexplode() will skip any null values in the array or the map. If you want to have null as records, you can use explode_outer() or posexplode_outer() the same way.

Now that we have exploded data frames, we'll do the opposite by collecting our records into a complex column. For this, PySpark provides two aggregation functions: collect_list() and collect_set(). Both work the same way: they take a column as an argument and return an array column as a result. Where collect_list() returns one array element per column record, collect_set() will return one array element per *distinct* column record, just like a Python set.

> **Listing 6.26 Collecting our results back into an array**

```
collected = episodes.groupby("id").agg(
    F.collect_list("episodes").alias("episodes")
)

collected.count()  # 1
```

```
collected.printSchema()
# |-- id: long (nullable = true)
# |-- episodes: array (nullable = true)
# |    |-- element: struct (containsNull = false)
# |    |    |-- _links: struct (nullable = true)
# |    |    |    |-- self: struct (nullable = true)
# |    |    |    |    |-- href: string (nullable = true)
# |    |    |-- airdate: string (nullable = true)
# |    |    |-- airstamp: timestamp (nullable = true)
# |    |    |-- airtime: string (nullable = true)
# |    |    |-- id: long (nullable = true)
# |    |    |-- image: struct (nullable = true)
# |    |    |    |-- medium: string (nullable = true)
# |    |    |    |-- original: string (nullable = true)
# |    |    |-- name: string (nullable = true)
# |    |    |-- number: long (nullable = true)
# |    |    |-- runtime: long (nullable = true)
# |    |    |-- season: long (nullable = true)
# |    |    |-- summary: string (nullable = true)
# |    |    |-- url: string (nullable = true)
```

Collecting an exploded map is not supported out of the box, but it's easy knowing that you can pass multiple `collect_list()` functions as an argument to `agg()`. You can then use `map_from_arrays()`. Look at listings 6.25 and 6.26 for the building blocks.

This section covered the transformation from container columns to distinct records and back. With this, we can go from hierarchical to denormalized columns and back, without relying on auxiliary tables. In the final section of the chapter, I explain how to create your own structs by creating the last missing piece of our hierarchical data model.

6.5.2   Building your own hierarchies: Struct as a function

This section concludes the chapter by showing how you can create structs within a data frame. With this last tool in your toolbox, the structure of a data frame will have no secrets for you.

To create a struct, we use the `struct()` function from the `pyspark.sql.functions` module. This function takes a number of columns as parameters (just like `select()`) and returns a struct column containing the columns passed as parameters as fields. Easy as pie!

In the next listing, I create a new struct `info` containing a few columns from the shows data frame.

> **Listing 6.27   Creating a `struct` column using the `struct` function**

```
struct_ex = shows.select(
    F.struct(                    ◁─────┐   The struct function can take one or more column
        F.col("status"), F.col("weight"), F.lit(True).alias("has_watched")
    ).alias("info")
)
```

The struct function can take one or more column objects (or column names). I passed a literal column to indicate that I've watched the show.

```
struct_ex.show(1, False)
# +-----------------+
# |info             |
# +-----------------+
# |{Ended, 96, true}|
# +-----------------+
```

**The info column is a
struct and contains the
three fields we specified.**

```
struct_ex.printSchema()
# root
#  |-- info: struct (nullable = false)
#  |    |-- status: string (nullable = true)
#  |    |-- weight: long (nullable = true)
#  |    |-- has_watched: boolean (nullable = false)
```

**The info column is a
struct and contains the
three fields we specified.**

TIP Just like with a top-level data frame, you can unpack (or select) all the columns from a struct using the star implicit column identifier, `column.*`.

This chapter introduced the power and flexibility of the data frame using a data model that is starkly incompatible with most two-dimensional data representations: the hierarchical document data model. We ingested, processed, navigated, and molded a JSON document with the same data frame and set of functions that we used for textual and tabular data. This expands the power of the data frame beyond mere rows and columns and provides an alternative to the relational model, where we duplicate data to represent when a record has multiple values for a field.

Summary

- PySpark has a specialized JSON `DataFrameReader` for ingesting JSON documents within a data frame. The default parameters will read a well-formed JSONLines document, while setting `multiLine=True` will read a series of JSON documents, each in their own files.
- JSON data can be thought of as a Python dictionary. Nested (or hierarchical) elements are allowed through arrays (Python lists) and objects (Python dictionaries).
- In PySpark, hierarchical data models are represented through complex column types. The array represents lists of elements of the same type, the map represents multiple keys and values (akin to a Python dictionary), and the struct represents an object in the JSON sense.
- PySpark provides a programatic API to build data frame schemas on top of a JSON representation. Having an explicit schema reduces the risk of having data in an incompatible type, leading to further analysis errors in the data-manipulation stage.
- Complex types can be created and broken down via the data frame API with operations such as explosion, collection, and unpacking.

Additional exercises

Exercise 6.4

Why is it a bad idea to use the period or the square bracket in a column name, given that you also use it to reach hierarchical entities within a data frame?

Exercise 6.5

Although much less common, you can create a data frame from a dictionary. Since dictionaries are so close to JSON documents, build the schema for ingesting the following dictionary. (Both JSON or PySpark schemas are valid here.)

```
dict_schema = ???
spark.createDataFrame([{"one": 1, "two": [1,2,3]}], schema=dict_schema)
```

Exercise 6.6

Using `three_shows`, compute the time between the first and last episodes for each show. Which show had the longest tenure?

Exercise 6.7

Take the `shows` data frame and extract the air date and name of each episode in two array columns.

Exercise 6.8

Given the following data frame, create a new data frame that contains a single map from one to `square`:

```
exo6_8 = spark.createDataFrame([[1, 2], [2, 4], [3, 9]], ["one", "square"])
```

Bilingual PySpark: Blending Python and SQL code

This chapter covers

- Drawing a parallel between PySpark's instruction set and the SQL vocabulary
- Registering data frames as temporary views or tables to query them using Spark SQL
- Using the catalog to create, reference, and delete registered tables for SQL querying
- Translating common data manipulations instructions from Python to SQL, and vice versa
- Using SQL-style clauses inside certain PySpark methods

My answer to the question "Python versus SQL, which one should I learn?" is "both."

When it comes to manipulating tabular data, SQL is the reigning king. For multiple decades now, it has been the workhorse language for relational databases, and even today, learning how to tame it is a worthwhile exercise. Spark acknowledges the power of SQL head-on. You can seamlessly blend SQL code within your Spark or PySpark program, making it easier than ever to migrate those old SQL ETL jobs without reinventing the wheel.

This chapter is dedicated to using SQL with, and on top of, PySpark. I cover how we can move from one language to the other. I also cover how we can use a SQL-like syntax within data frame methods to speed up your code, and some of the trade-offs you may face. Finally, we blend Python and SQL code to get the best of both worlds.

If you already have notable exposure to SQL, this chapter will be a breeze for you. Feel free to skim over the SQL-specific section (7.4), but don't skip the sections on Python and SQL interoperability (7.5 and after), as I cover some PySpark idiosyncrasies. For those new to SQL, this will be—I hope—an eye-opening moment, and you'll add another tool under your belt. If you'd like a deeper dive into SQL, *SQL in Motion*, by Ben Brumm (Manning, 2017), is a good video source. If you prefer a book, a very exhaustive reference is Joe Celko's *SQL for Smarties* (Morgan Kauffman, 2014).

Here are the imports I use in this chapter's examples:

```
from pyspark.sql import SparkSession
from pyspark.sql.utils import AnalysisException    ◁──┐  We will deal with some
import pyspark.sql.functions as F                        AnalysisException, so I
import pyspark.sql.types as T                            import it right at the start.

spark = SparkSession.builder.getOrCreate()
```

> **Spark SQL vs. ANSI SQL vs. HiveQL**
>
> Spark supports both ANSI SQL (experimentally, as of right now; see http://mng.bz/oapr) and the vast majority of HiveQL[a] as a SQL dialect. Spark SQL also has some Spark-specific functions baked in to ensure common functionality across languages.
>
> In a nutshell, Hive is a SQL-like interface that can be used over a variety of data storage options. It became very popular because it provided the ability to query files in HDFS (Hadoop Distributed File System) as if they were a table. Spark can integrate with Hive when your environment has it installed. Spark SQL also provides additional syntax to work with larger data sets, a topic covered in this chapter.
>
> Because of the amount of material and its longevity, and also because its syntax is similar to basic and intermediate queries, I usually recommend learning ANSI SQL first and then learning HiveQL as you go along. This way, your knowledge will transfer to other SQL-based products. Since Hive is not a component of Spark, I won't cover Hive-specific functionality in this book and will instead focus on SQL with Spark.
>
> ───────────
>
> [a] You can see the functionality supported (and unsupported) on the Spark website: http://mng.bz/nYMg.

7.1   *Banking on what we know: pyspark.sql vs. plain SQL*

In this section, we draw parallels between Spark's function and method names and SQL keywords. Since both share a base vocabulary, it becomes easy to read Spark and SQL code and understand their behavior. More specifically, we break down a simple set of instructions in both languages to recognize the similarities and differences.

PySpark's SQL heritage is more than skin deep: the name of the module—pyspark.sql—is a dead giveaway. PySpark developers recognized the heritage of the SQL programming language for data manipulation and used the same keywords to name their method. Let's look at a quick example in both SQL and plain PySpark and look at similarities between the keywords used. In listing 7.1, I load a CSV with information about the periodic table of elements, and I query the data set to find the number of entries with a `liquid` state per period. The code is presented both in PySpark and SQL form, and, without much context, we can see similarities. I draw the parallels between the two versions in figure 7.1.

Compared to the SQL language, PySpark's data manipulation API differs in two main ways:

- PySpark will always start with the name of the data frame you are working with. SQL refers to the table (or *target*) using a `from` keyword.
- PySpark chains the transformations and actions as methods on the data frame, whereas SQL splits them into two groups: the *operation* group and the *condition* group. The first one is before the `from` clause and operates on columns. The second is after the `from` clause and groups, filters, and orders the structure of the result table.

TIP SQL is not case-sensitive, so you can either use lowercase or uppercase.

Listing 7.1 Reading and counting the liquid elements by period

```
elements = spark.read.csv(
    "./data/elements/Periodic_Table_Of_Elements.csv",
    header=True,
    inferSchema=True,
)

elements.where(F.col("phase") == "liq").groupby("period").count().show()

-- In SQL: We assume that the data is in a table called `elements`

SELECT
  period,
  count(*)
FROM elements
WHERE phase = 'liq'
GROUP BY period;
```

Both would return the same results: one element in period four (Bromine) and one in period six (Mercury).

Whether you prefer the order of operations from PySpark or SQL will depend on how you build queries mentally and how familiar you are with the respective languages. Fortunately, PySpark makes it easy to move from one to the other, and even to work with both at once.

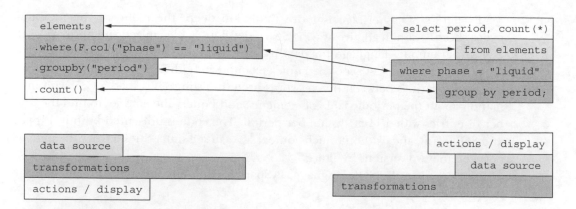

Figure 7.1   PySpark and SQL share the same keywords, but the order of operations differs. PySpark looks like an ordered list of operations (take this table, do these transformations, then finally show the result), while SQL has a more descriptive approach (show me the results from that table after performing these transformations).

7.2   Preparing a data frame for SQL

Since we can think of PySpark data frames like tables on steroids, it's not far-fetched to think about querying them using a language designed to query tables. Spark provides a full SQL API that is documented in the same fashion as the PySpark API (http://mng.bz/vozJ). The Spark SQL API also defines the functions used in the `pyspark.sql` API, such as `substr()` or `size()`.

NOTE   Spark's SQL API only covers the data manipulation subset of Spark. For instance, you won't be able to do machine learning using SQL (see chapter 13).

7.2.1   Promoting a data frame to a Spark table

In this section, I cover the simple steps to get a Spark data frame using SQL. PySpark maintains boundaries between its own name spacing and Spark SQL's name spacing; we, therefore, have to explicitly promote them.

First, let's see what happens when we don't do anything. The code in listing 7.2 shows an example.

Listing 7.2   Trying (and failing) at querying a data frame SQL style

```
try:
    spark.sql(
        "select period, count(*) from elements "
        "where phase='liq' group by period"
    ).show(5)
except AnalysisException as e:
    print(e)

# 'Table or view not found: elements; line 1 pos 29'
```

Here, PySpark doesn't make the link between the python variable `elements`, which points to the data frame, and a potential table `elements` that can be queried by Spark SQL. To allow a data frame to be queried via SQL, we need to *register* it.

When we assign a data frame to a variable, Python points to the data frame. Spark SQL does not have visibility over the variables Python assigns.

When you want to create a table/view to query with Spark SQL, use the `createOrReplaceTempView()` method. This method takes a single string parameter, which is the name of the table you want to use. This transformation will look at the data frame referenced by the Python variable on which the method was applied and will create a Spark SQL reference to the same data frame.

NOTE Although you can name the table the same name as the variable you are using, you are not forced to do so.

Once we have registered our `elements` table that points to the same data frame as our Python variable of the same name, we can query our table without any problems. Let's rerun the same code block as in listing 7.2 and see if it succeeds.

NOTE In this chapter, I use the term *table* and *view* pretty loosely. In SQL, they are distinct concepts: the table is materialized in memory and on disk, and the view is computed on the fly. Spark's temp views are conceptually closer to a view than a table. Spark SQL also has tables, but we will not be using them, and will instead read and materialize our data into a data frame.

Listing 7.3 Trying (and succeeding at) querying a data frame SQL style

```
elements.createOrReplaceTempView("elements")      ◄──┐  We register our table using the
                                                      │  createOrReplaceTempView() method
                                                      │  on the element data frame.
spark.sql(
    "select period, count(*) from elements where phase='liq' group by period"
).show(5)

# +------+--------+
# |period|count(1)|
# +------+--------+                 The same query works once
# |     6|       1|                 Spark is able to de-reference
# |     4|       1|                 the SQL view name.
# +------+--------+    ◄──┘
```

Now we have a view registered. In the case of a low number of views to manage, it's pretty easy to keep the name in memory. What about if you have dozens of views or you need to delete some? Enter the catalog, Spark's way of managing its SQL namespace.

Advanced-ish topic: Spark SQL views and persistence

PySpark has four methods to create temporary views, and they look quite similar at first glance:

- `createGlobalTempView()`
- `createOrReplaceGlobalTempView()`
- `createOrReplaceTempView()`
- `createTempView()`

We can see that there is a two-by-two matrix of possibilities:

- Do I want to replace an existing view (`OrReplace`)?
- Do I want to create a global view (`Global`)?

The first one is relatively easy to answer: if you use `createTempView` with a name already being used for another table, the method will fail. On the other hand, if you use `createOrReplaceTempView()`, Spark will replace the old table with a new one. In SQL, it is equivalent to using `CREATE VIEW` versus `CREATE OR REPLACE VIEW`. I personally always use the latter, as it mimics Python's way of doing things: when reassigning a variable, you comply.

What about `Global`? The difference between a local view and a global view has to do with how long it will last in memory. A local table is tied to your `SparkSession`, while a global table is tied to the Spark application. The differences at this time are not significant, as we are not using multiple `SparkSession`s that need to share data. In the context of data analysis with Spark, you won't deal with multiple `SparkSession`s at once, so I usually don't use the `Global` methods.

7.2.2 *Using the Spark catalog*

The Spark catalog is an object that allows working with Spark SQL tables and views. A lot of its methods have to do with managing the metadata of those tables, such as their names and the level of caching (which I'll cover in detail in chapter 11). We will look at the most basic set of functionality in this section, setting the stage for more advanced material, such as table caching (chapter 11) and UDF (chapter 8).

We can use the catalog to list the tables/views we have registered and drop them if we are done. The code in the next listing provides the simple methods to do those tasks. Since they are mostly mimicking PySpark's data frame functionality, I think that an example shows it best.

Listing 7.4   Using the catalog to display our registered view and then drop it

```
spark.catalog
```
⊲ The catalog is reached through the catalog property of our SparkSession.

```
#  <pyspark.sql.catalog.Catalog at 0x117ef0c18>

spark.catalog.listTables()
```
⊲ The listTables method gives us a list of Table objects that contain the information we want.

```
# [Table(name='elements', database=None, description=None,
#         tableType='TEMPORARY', isTemporary=True)]

spark.catalog.dropTempView("elements")

spark.catalog.listTables()

# []
```

To delete a view, we use the method **dropTempView()** and pass the name of the view as a parameter.

Our catalog now has no table for us to query.

Now that we understand how we can manage a Spark SQL view within PySpark, we can start looking at manipulating data using both languages.

7.3 SQL and PySpark

The integration between Python (through PySpark) and SQL is well thought-out and can improve the speed at which we can write code. This section focuses on using only SQL for manipulating data, with Python playing a coordinating role with the catalog and instructions. I will review the most common operations from a pure SQL and PySpark perspective to illustrate how basic manipulations are written.

For the remainder of the chapter, we will use a public data set provided by Backblaze, which provided hard-drive data and statistics. Backblaze is a company that provides cloud storage and backup. Since 2013, they have provided data on the drives in their data center, and over time have moved to a focus on failures and diagnosis. Their (clean) data is in the gigabytes range, which, although not that big yet, is certainly Spark-worthy, as it'll be more than the memory available on your home computer. Backblaze has a lot more historical data available on their website, should you want a larger data set. A convenience shell script is also provided for downloading everything in one fell swoop. For those working locally and afraid of blowing your memory, you can use Q3 2019. The syntax will differ marginally between both workflows. A computer with at least 16 GB of RAM should be able to handle all files. Backblaze provides documentation mostly in the form of SQL statements, which is perfect for what we're learning.

To get the files, you can either download them from the website (http://mng .bz/4jZa) or use the `backblaze_download_data.py` available in the code repository, which requires the `wget` package to be installed. The data needs to be in the `./data/backblaze` directory.

Listing 7.5 Downloading the data from Backblaze

```
$ pip install wget

$ python code/Ch07/download_backblaze_data.py full

# [some data download progress bars]

$ ls  data/backblaze
```

Windows users, use "dir data\backblaze".

```
__MACOSX/         data_Q2_2019.zip    data_Q4_2019/
data_Q1_2019.zip   data_Q3_2019/       data_Q4_2019.zip
data_Q2_2019/      data_Q3_2019.zip    drive_stats_2019_Q1/
```

Make sure you unzip the files into the directory before trying to read them. Unlike many other codecs (e.g., Gzip, Bzip2, Snappy, and LZO), PySpark will not decompress zip files automatically when reading them, so we need to do it ahead of time. The unzip command can be used if you are using the command line (you might need to install the tool on Linux). On Windows, I usually use Windows Explorer and unzip by hand.

The code to ingest and prep the data is pretty straightforward. We read each data source separately, and then we make sure that each data frame has the same columns as its peers. In our case, the data for the fourth quarter has two more columns than the others, so we add the missing columns. When joining the four data frames, we use a select method so that their column order is the same. We continue by casting all the columns containing a SMART measurement as a long, since they are documented as integral values. Finally, we register our data frame as a view so that we can use SQL statements on it.

Listing 7.6   Reading Backblaze data into a data frame and registering a view

```
DATA_DIRECTORY = "./data/backblaze/"

q1 = spark.read.csv(
    DATA_DIRECTORY + "drive_stats_2019_Q1", header=True, inferSchema=True
)
q2 = spark.read.csv(
    DATA_DIRECTORY + "data_Q2_2019", header=True, inferSchema=True
)
q3 = spark.read.csv(
    DATA_DIRECTORY + "data_Q3_2019", header=True, inferSchema=True
)
q4 = spark.read.csv(
    DATA_DIRECTORY + "data_Q4_2019", header=True, inferSchema=True
)

# Q4 has two more fields than the rest

q4_fields_extra = set(q4.columns) - set(q1.columns)

for i in q4_fields_extra:
    q1 = q1.withColumn(i, F.lit(None).cast(T.StringType()))
    q2 = q2.withColumn(i, F.lit(None).cast(T.StringType()))
    q3 = q3.withColumn(i, F.lit(None).cast(T.StringType()))


# if you are only using the minimal set of data, use this version
backblaze_2019 = q3

# if you are using the full set of data, use this version
backblaze_2019 = (
    q1.select(q4.columns)
    .union(q2.select(q4.columns))
    .union(q3.select(q4.columns))
```

```
        .union(q4)
)

# Setting the layout for each column according to the schema

backblaze_2019 = backblaze_2019.select(
    [
        F.col(x).cast(T.LongType()) if x.startswith("smart") else F.col(x)
        for x in backblaze_2019.columns
    ]
)

backblaze_2019.createOrReplaceTempView("backblaze_stats_2019")
```

7.4 *Using SQL-like syntax within data frame methods*

Our goal in this section is to perform a quick exploratory data analysis on a subset of
the columns presented. We will reproduce the failure rates that Backblaze computes
and identify the models with the greatest and least amount of failures in 2019.

7.4.1 *Get the rows and columns you want: select and where*

select and where are used to narrow down the columns (select) and the rows (where)
you want to keep in your data frame. In listing 7.7, I use select and where to show a few
hard drives' serial numbers that have failed at some point (failure = 1). Both select()
and where() were introduced in chapter 2 and have been used since; I want to draw the
focus once more to the differences between the SQL and Python syntax.

To use SQL within your PySpark program, use the sql method of the SparkSession
object. This method takes a string containing a SQL statement. It's as simple as that!

> **Listing 7.7   Comparing select and where in PySpark and SQL**

```
spark.sql(
    "select serial_number from backblaze_stats_2019 where failure = 1"
).show(
    5                      Since a SQL statement returns a data frame,
)              ◁─────────  we still have to show() it to see the results.

backblaze_2019.where("failure = 1").select(F.col("serial_number")).show(5)

# +-------------+
# |serial_number|
# +-------------+
# |     57GGPD9NT|
# |     ZJV02GJM|
# |     ZJV03Y00|
# |     ZDEB33GK|
# |     Z302T6CW|
# +-------------+
# only showing top 5 rows
```

Let's recap the differences between Python and SQL code using the example in listing 7.7. PySpark makes you think about how you want to chain the operations. In our

case, we start by filtering the data frame and then select the column of interest. SQL presents an alternative construction:

1 You put the columns you want to select at the beginning of your statement. This is called the *SQL operation*: `select serial_number`.
2 You add one or more tables to query, called the *target*: `from backblaze_stats_2019`.
3 You add the *conditions*, such as filtering: `where failure = 1`.

Every operation we will look at in this chapter will be classified as an operation, a target, or a condition so you can know where it fits in the statement.

As a final note, SQL has no notion of creating columns with `withColumns()` or renaming them with `withColumnRenamed`. Everything has to go through `SELECT`. In the next section, I cover grouping records together; I also take the opportunity to cover aliasing there.

> **TIP** If you have a table you want to extract as a data frame, you assign the result of a `SELECT` statement to a variable. As an example, you could do `failures = spark.sql("select serial_number . . .")`, and the resulting data frame would be assigned to the variable `failures`.

7.4.2 *Grouping similar records together: group by and order by*

The PySpark syntax for `groupby()` and `orderby()` was covered in detail in chapter 5. In this section, I introduce the SQL syntax—through a comparison with the Python syntax—by looking at the capacity, in gigabytes, of the hard drives included in the data, by model. For this, we use a little arithmetic and the `pow()` function (available in `pyspark.sql.functions`) that elevates its first argument to the power of the second. We can see similarities between the SQL and PySpark vocabulary, but once again, the order of the transformations is different.

Listing 7.8   Grouping and ordering in PySpark and SQL

```
spark.sql(
    """SELECT
        model,
        min(capacity_bytes / pow(1024, 3)) min_GB,
        max(capacity_bytes/ pow(1024, 3)) max_GB
    FROM backblaze_stats_2019
    GROUP BY 1
    ORDER BY 3 DESC"""
).show(5)

backblaze_2019.groupby(F.col("model")).agg(
    F.min(F.col("capacity_bytes") / F.pow(F.lit(1024), 3)).alias("min_GB"),
    F.max(F.col("capacity_bytes") / F.pow(F.lit(1024), 3)).alias("max_GB"),
).orderBy(F.col("max_GB"), ascending=False).show(5)
```

```
# +--------------------+--------------------+-------+
# |              model|              min_GB| max_GB|
# +--------------------+--------------------+-------+
# |       ST16000NM001G|             14902.0|14902.0|
# |  TOSHIBA MG07ACA14TA|-9.31322574615478...|13039.0|
# |HGST HUH721212ALE600|             11176.0|11176.0|
# |       ST12000NM0007|-9.31322574615478...|11176.0|
# |       ST12000NM0008|             11176.0|11176.0|
# +--------------------+--------------------+-------+
# only showing top 5 rows
```

In PySpark, once again, we look at the logical order of operations. We `groupby` the `capacity_GB` column, which is a computed column. Just like in PySpark, arithmetic operations can be performed using the usual syntax in SQL. Furthermore, the `pow()` function is also implemented in Spark SQL. If you need to see which functions can be used out of the box, the Spark SQL API doc contains the necessary information (http://mng.bz/vozJ).

To alias a column, we just add the name after the column descriptor, preceded by a space. In our case, `min(capacity_bytes / pow(1024, 3))` is aliased to `min_GB`—a much friendlier name! Some will prefer to use the keyword `as` so that the line reads `min(capacity_bytes / pow(1024, 3))` as min_GB; in Spark SQL, it's a matter of personal preference.

Grouping and ordering are conditions in SQL, so they are at the end of the statement. They both follow the same convention as PySpark:

- We provide the columns to `group by`, separated by a comma.
- For `order by`, we provide the column names to the clause with an optional `DESC` argument if we want to order by descending order (the default is `ASC` for ascending).

One thing worth noting is that we group by `1` and order by `3 DESC`. This is a shorthand way of referring to the columns in the SQL operation by position rather than name. In this case, it saves us from writing `group by capacity_bytes / pow(1024, 3)` or `order by max(capacity_bytes / pow(1024,3)) DESC` in the conditions block. We can use numerical aliases in `group by` and `order by` clauses. While they are nifty, abusing them makes your code more fragile and hard to maintain should you change the query.

Looking at the results from our query, there are some drives that report more than one capacity. Furthermore, we have some drives that report negative capacity, which is really odd. Let's focus on seeing how prevalent this is.

7.4.3 Filtering after grouping using having

Because of the order of the evaluation of operations in SQL, `where` is always applied before `group by`. What happens if we want to filter the values of columns created after the `group by` operation? We use a new keyword: `having`!

As an example, let's assume that, for each model, the maximum reported capacity is the correct one. The code in the next listing shows how we can accomplish this in both languages.

Listing 7.9   Using `having` in SQL and relying on `where` in PySpark

```
spark.sql(
    """SELECT
            model,
            min(capacity_bytes / pow(1024, 3)) min_GB,
            max(capacity_bytes/ pow(1024, 3)) max_GB
        FROM backblaze_stats_2019
        GROUP BY 1
        HAVING min_GB != max_GB
        ORDER BY 3 DESC"""
).show(5)

backblaze_2019.groupby(F.col("model")).agg(
    F.min(F.col("capacity_bytes") / F.pow(F.lit(1024), 3)).alias("min_GB"),
    F.max(F.col("capacity_bytes") / F.pow(F.lit(1024), 3)).alias("max_GB"),
).where(F.col("min_GB") != F.col("max_GB")).orderBy(
    F.col("max_GB"), ascending=False
).show(
    5
)

# +-------------------+--------------------+-------+
# |              model|              min_GB| max_GB|
# +-------------------+--------------------+-------+
# |  TOSHIBA MG07ACA14TA|-9.31322574615478...|13039.0|
# |        ST12000NM0007|-9.31322574615478...|11176.0|
# |HGST HUH721212ALN604|-9.31322574615478...|11176.0|
# |        ST10000NM0086|-9.31322574615478...| 9314.0|
# |HGST HUH721010ALE600|-9.31322574615478...| 9314.0|
# +-------------------+--------------------+-------+
# only showing top 5 rows
```

`having` is a syntax unique to SQL: it can be thought of as a `where` clause that can only be applied to aggregate fields, such as `count(*)` or `min(date)`. Since it is equivalent in functionality to `where`, `having` is in the condition block after the `group by` clause. In PySpark, we do not have `having` as a method. Since each method returns a new data frame, we do not have to have a different keyword, and can simply use `where` with the column we created instead.

NOTE   We will ignore (for now) those capacity-reporting inconsistencies. They'll come back as exercises.

So far, we've covered the most important SQL operation: selecting columns with `select`. Next, let's materialize our work, SQL-style.

7.4.4 Creating new tables/views using the CREATE keyword

Now that we have queried the data and are getting the hang of it in SQL, we might want to check our work and save some data so that we do not have to process everything from scratch the next time. For this, we can create either a table or a view, which we can then query directly.

Creating a table or a view is very easy in SQL: prefix our query by CREATE TABLE/VIEW. Here, creating a table or a view will have a different impact. If you have a Hive metastore connected, creating a table will materialize the data, whereas a view will only keep the query. To use a baking analogy, CREATE TABLE will store a cake, whereas CREATE VIEW will refer to the ingredients (the original data) and the recipe (the query).

To demonstrate this, I will reproduce the drive_days and failures that compute the number of days of operation that a model has and the number of drive failures it has had, respectively. The code in listing 7.10 shows how it is done: prefix your select query with a CREATE [TABLE/VIEW].

In PySpark, we do not have to rely on extra syntax. A newly created data frame has to be assigned to a variable and then we are good to go.

Listing 7.10 Creating a view in Spark SQL and in PySpark

```
backblaze_2019.createOrReplaceTempView("drive_stats")


spark.sql(
    """
    CREATE OR REPLACE TEMP VIEW drive_days AS
        SELECT model, count(*) AS drive_days
        FROM drive_stats
        GROUP BY model"""
)

spark.sql(
    """CREATE OR REPLACE TEMP VIEW failures AS
        SELECT model, count(*) AS failures
        FROM drive_stats
        WHERE failure = 1
        GROUP BY model"""
)

drive_days = backblaze_2019.groupby(F.col("model")).agg(
    F.count(F.col("*")).alias("drive_days")
)

failures = (
    backblaze_2019.where(F.col("failure") == 1)
    .groupby(F.col("model"))
    .agg(F.count(F.col("*")).alias("failures"))
)
```

Creating tables from data in SQL

You can also create a table from data on a hard drive or HDFS. For this, you can use a modified SQL query. Since we are reading a CSV file, we prefix our path with `csv.`:

```
spark.sql("create table q1 as select * from
    csv.`./data/backblaze/drive_stats_2019_Q1`")
```

I much prefer relying on PySpark syntax for reading and setting the schema from my data source and then using SQL, but the option is there for the taking.

7.4.5   Adding data to our table using UNION and JOIN

So far, we've seen how to query a single table at a time. In practice, you'll often get multiple tables related to one another. We already witnessed this problem by having one historical table per quarter, which needed to be stacked together (or unioned), and with our `drive_days` and `failures` tables, which each paint a single dimension of the story until they are merged (or joined).

Joins and unions are the only clauses we'll see that modify the target piece in our SQL statement. In SQL, a query is operating on a single target at a time. We already saw at the beginning of the chapter how to use PySpark to union tables together. In SQL, we follow the same blueprint: `SELECT columns FROM table1 UNION ALL SELECT columns FROM table2`.

PySpark's union() vs. SQL UNION

In SQL, `UNION` removes the duplicate records. PySpark's `union()` doesn't, which is why it's equivalent to a SQL `UNION ALL`. If you want to drop the duplicates, which is an expensive operation when working in a distributed context, use the `distinct()` function after your `union()`. This is one of the rare cases where PySpark's vocabulary doesn't follow SQL's, but it's for a good reason. Most of the time, you'll want the `UNION ALL` behavior.

It is always a good idea to make sure that your data frames have the same columns, with the same types, in the same order, before attempting a union. In the PySpark solution, we used the fact that we could extract the columns in a list to `select` the data frames in the same fashion. Spark SQL does not have a simple way to do the same, so you would have to type all the columns. This is okay when you just have a few, but we're talking hundreds here.

One easy way to circumvent this is to use the fact that a Spark SQL statement is a string. We can take our list of columns, transform it into a SQL-esque string, and be done with it. This is exactly what I did in listing 7.11. It's not a pure Spark SQL solution, but it's much friendlier than making you type all the columns one by one.

WARNING   Do not allow for plain string insertion if you are processing user input! This is the best way to have a SQL injection, where a user can craft a string that will wreak havoc on your data. For more information about SQL injections and why they can be so dangerous, review the Open Web Application Security Project article on the subject (http://mng.bz/XWdG).

Listing 7.11 Unioning tables together in Spark SQL and in PySpark

```
columns_backblaze = ", ".join(q4.columns)

q1.createOrReplaceTempView("Q1")
q2.createOrReplaceTempView("Q2")
q3.createOrReplaceTempView("Q3")
q4.createOrReplaceTempView("Q4")

spark.sql(
    """
    CREATE OR REPLACE TEMP VIEW backblaze_2019 AS
    SELECT {col} FROM Q1 UNION ALL
    SELECT {col} FROM Q2 UNION ALL
    SELECT {col} FROM Q3 UNION ALL
    SELECT {col} FROM Q4
""".format(
        col=columns_backblaze
    )
)

backblaze_2019 = (
    q1.select(q4.columns)
    .union(q2.select(q4.columns))
    .union(q3.select(q4.columns))
    .union(q4)
)
```

> We use the join() method on a separator string to create a string containing all the elements in the list, separated by ,.

> We promote our quarterly data frames to Spark SQL views so we can use them in our query.

> This is taken from listing 7.6.

Joins are equally as simple in SQL. We add a [DIRECTION] JOIN table [ON] [LEFT COLUMN] [COMPARISON OPERATOR] [RIGHT COLUMN] in the target portion of our statement. The direction is the same parameter of our how in PySpark. The on clause is a series of comparisons between columns. In the example in listing 7.12, we join the records where the value in the model column is equal (=) on both drive_days and failures tables. More than one condition? Use parentheses and logical operators (AND, OR), just like when working in Python (for more information, see chapter 5).

Listing 7.12 Joining tables in Spark SQL and in PySpark

```
spark.sql(
    """select
            drive_days.model,
            drive_days,
            failures
    from drive_days
    left join failures
    on
        drive_days.model = failures.model"""
).show(5)

drive_days.join(failures, on="model", how="left").show(5)
```

7.4.6   *Organizing your SQL code better through subqueries and common table expressions*

The last pieces of SQL syntax we will look at on their own are the subquery and the common table expression. A lot of SQL references do not talk about them until very late, which is a shame because they are (a) easy to understand and (b) very helpful in keeping your code clean. In a nutshell, they allow you to create tables local to your query. In Python, this is similar to using the `with` statement or using a function block to limit the scope of a query. I will show the function approach, as it is much more common.[1]

For our example, we will take our `drive_days` and `failures` table definitions and bundle them into a single query that will measure the models with the highest rate of failure in 2019. The code in listing 7.13 shows how we can do this using a subquery. A subquery simply replaces a table name with a standalone SQL query. In the example, we can see that the name of the table has been replaced by the `SELECT` query that formed the table. We can alias the table referred to in the subquery by adding the name at the end of the statement, after the closing parenthesis.

> **Listing 7.13   Finding drive models with highest failure rates using subqueries**

```
spark.sql(
    """
    SELECT
        failures.model,
        failures / drive_days failure_rate
    FROM (
        SELECT
            model,
            count(*) AS drive_days
        FROM drive_stats
        GROUP BY model) drive_days
    INNER JOIN (
        SELECT
            model,
            count(*) AS failures
        FROM drive_stats
        WHERE failure = 1
        GROUP BY model) failures
    ON
        drive_days.model = failures.model
    ORDER BY 2 desc
    """
).show(5)
```

Subqueries are cool but can be hard to read and debug, since you are adding complexity into the main query. This is where common table expressions, or CTEs, are especially useful. A CTE is a table definition, just like in the subquery case. The

---

[1] The `with` statement is usually used with resources that need to be cleaned up at the end. It doesn't really apply here, but I felt like the comparison was worth mentioning.

difference here is that you put them at the top of your main statement (before your main SELECT) and prefix with the word WITH. In the next listing, I take the same statement as the subquery case but use two CTE instead. These can also be considered makeshift CREATE statements that get dropped at the end of the query, just like the with keyword in Python.

Listing 7.14 Finding highest failure rates using common table expressions

```
spark.sql(
    """
    WITH drive_days as (
        SELECT
            model,
            count(*) AS drive_days
        FROM drive_stats
        GROUP BY model),
    failures as (
        SELECT
            model,
            count(*) AS failures
        FROM drive_stats
        WHERE failure = 1
        GROUP BY model)
    SELECT
        failures.model,
        failures / drive_days failure_rate
    FROM drive_days
    INNER JOIN failures
    ON
        drive_days.model = failures.model
    ORDER BY 2 desc
    """
).show(5)
```

> We can refer to drive_days and failures in our main query.

In Python, the best alternative I've found is to wrap statements in a function. Any intermediate variable created in the scope of the function would not be kept once the function returns. My version of the query using PySpark is in the next listing.

Listing 7.15 Finding the highest failure rate using Python scope rules

```
def failure_rate(drive_stats):
    drive_days = drive_stats.groupby(F.col("model")).agg(
        F.count(F.col("*")).alias("drive_days")
    )
    failures = (
        drive_stats.where(F.col("failure") == 1)
        .groupby(F.col("model"))
        .agg(F.count(F.col("*")).alias("failures"))
    )
    answer = (
        drive_days.join(failures, on="model", how="inner")
        .withColumn("failure_rate", F.col("failures") / F.col("drive_days"))
```

> We are creating intermediate data frames within the body of the function to avoid having a monster query.

> Our answer data frame uses both intermediate data frames.

```
        .orderBy(F.col("failure_rate").desc())
    )
    return answer


failure_rate(backblaze_2019).show(5)

print("drive_days" in dir())
```

We are testing if we have a variable drive_days in scope once the function returned confirms that our intermediate frames are neatly confined inside the function scope.

In this section, we transformed data using both the PySpark/Python data transformation APIs, as well as Spark SQL. PySpark gives the floor to SQL without too much ceremony. This can be very convenient if you happen to hang out with DBAs and SQL developers, as you can collaborate using their preferred language, knowing that Python is right around the corner. Everybody wins!

7.4.7   *A quick summary of PySpark vs. SQL syntax*

PySpark borrowed a lot of vocabulary from the SQL world. I think this was a very smart idea: there are generations of programmers who know SQL, and adopting the same keywords makes it easy to communicate. Where we see a lot of difference is in the order of the operations: PySpark will naturally encourage you to think about the order in which the operations should be performed. SQL follows a more rigid framework that requires you to remember if your operation belongs in the operation, the target, or the condition clause.

I find PySpark's way of treating data manipulation more intuitive, but will rely on my years of SQL experience as a data analyst when convenient. When writing SQL, I usually write my query out of order, starting with the target and building as I go. Not everything needs to be top to bottom!

So far, I've tried to keep both languages in a vacuum. We'll now break the barrier and unleash the power of Python + SQL. This will simplify how we write certain transformations and make our code easier to write and a lot less busy.

Exercise 7.1

Taking the `elements` data frame, which PySpark code is equivalent to the following SQL statement?

```
select count(*) from elements where Radioactive is not null;
```

  a `element.groupby("Radioactive").count().show()`
  b `elements.where(F.col("Radioactive").isNotNull()).groupby().count().show()`
  c `elements.groupby("Radioactive").where(F.col("Radioactive").isNotNull()).show()`
  d `elements.where(F.col("Radioactive").isNotNull()).count()`
  e None of the queries above

7.5 Simplifying our code: Blending SQL and Python

PySpark is rather accommodating when taking method and function parameters: you can pass a column name (as a string) instead of a column object (F.col()) when using groupby() (see chapter 4). In addition, there are a few methods we can use to cram a little SQL syntax into our PySpark code. You'll see that there aren't many methods in which you can use this, but it's so useful and well done that you'll end up using it all the time.

This section will build on the code we've written so far. We're going to write a function that, for a given capacity, will return the top three most reliable drives according to our failure rate. We'll leverage the code we've already written and simplify it.

7.5.1 Using Python to increase the resiliency and simplifying the data reading stage

We start by simplifying the code to read the data. The data ingestion part of the program is displayed in listing 7.16. There are a few changes compared to our original data ingestion.

First, I put all the directories in a list so that I could read them using a list comprehension. This removes some repetitive code and will also work easily if I remove or add files (if you are only using Q3 2019, you can remove the other entries in the list).

Second, since we do not need the SMART (*Self-Monitoring, Analysis, and Reporting Technology*, a monitoring system included in most hard drives; see http://mng.bz/jydV for more information.) measurements, I take the intersection of the columns instead of trying to fill in the missing columns with null values. In order to create a common intersection that will apply to any number of data sources, I use reduce, which applies the anonymous function on all the column sets, resulting in the common columns between all the data frames. (For those unfamiliar with reduce, I find the Python documentation very explicit and easy to follow: http://mng.bz/y4YG.) I also add an assertion on the common set of columns, as I want to make sure it contains the columns I need for the analysis. Assertions are a good way to short-circuit an analysis if certain conditions are not met. In this case, if I am missing one of the columns, I'd rather have my program fail early with an AssertionError than have a huge stack trace later.

Finally, I use a second reduce for unioning all the distinct data frames into a cohesive one. The same principle is used as when I created the common variables. This makes the code a lot cleaner, and it will work without any modifications should I want to add more sources or remove some.

Listing 7.16 The data ingestion part of our program

```
from functools import reduce

import pyspark.sql.functions as F
from pyspark.sql import SparkSession
```

```
spark = SparkSession.builder.getOrCreate()

DATA_DIRECTORY = "./data/backblaze/"

DATA_FILES = [
    "drive_stats_2019_Q1",
    "data_Q2_2019",
    "data_Q3_2019",
    "data_Q4_2019",
]

data = [
    spark.read.csv(DATA_DIRECTORY + file, header=True, inferSchema=True)
    for file in DATA_FILES
]

common_columns = list(
    reduce(lambda x, y: x.intersection(y), [set(df.columns) for df in data])
)

assert set(["model", "capacity_bytes", "date", "failure"]).issubset(
    set(common_columns)
)

full_data = reduce(
    lambda x, y: x.select(common_columns).union(y.select(common_columns)), data
)
```

7.5.2   *Using SQL-style expressions in PySpark*

Now that our data has been read and is in a steady state, we can process it so that it can easily answer our question. Three methods accept SQL-type statements: select-Expr(), expr(), and where()/filter(). In this section, we use SQL-style expressions when appropriate to showcase when it makes sense to fuse both languages. At the end of this section, we have code that

- Selects only the useful columns for our query
- Gets our drive capacity in gigabytes
- Computes the drive_days and failures data frames
- Joins the two data frames into a summarized one and computes the failure rate

The code is available in the following listing.

Listing 7.17   Processing our data so it's ready for the query function
---

```
full_data = full_data.selectExpr(
    "model", "capacity_bytes / pow(1024, 3) capacity_GB", "date", "failure"
)

drive_days = full_data.groupby("model", "capacity_GB").agg(
    F.count("*").alias("drive_days")
)
```

```
failures = (
    full_data.where("failure = 1")
    .groupby("model", "capacity_GB")
    .agg(F.count("*").alias("failures"))
)

summarized_data = (
    drive_days.join(failures, on=["model", "capacity_GB"], how="left")
    .fillna(0.0, ["failures"])
    .selectExpr("model", "capacity_GB", "failures / drive_days failure_rate")
    .cache()
)
```

selectExpr() is just like the select() method with the exception that it will process SQL-style operations. I am quite a fan of this method since it removes a bit of syntax when manipulating columns with functions and arithmetic. In our case, the PySpark alternative (displayed in the next listing) is a little more verbose and cumbersome to write and read, especially since we have to create a literal 1024 column to apply the pow() function.

Listing 7.18　Replacing `selectExpr()` with a regular `select()`

```
full_data = full_data.select(
    F.col("model"),
    (F.col("capacity_bytes") / F.pow(F.lit(1024), 3)).alias("capacity_GB"),
    F.col("date"),
    F.col("failure")
)
```

The second method is simply called expr(). It wraps a SQL-style expression into a column. This is kind of a generalized selectExpr() that you can use in lieu of F.col() (or the column name) when you want to modify a column. If we take our failures table from listing 7.17, we can use an expr (or *expression*) as the agg() argument. This alternative syntax is shown in the next listing. I like doing it in agg() parameters, because it saves a lot of alias().

Listing 7.19　Using a SQL expression in our `failures` data frame code

```
failures = (
    full_data.where("failure = 1")
    .groupby("model", "capacity_GB")
    .agg(F.expr("count(*) failures"))
)
```

The third method, and my favorite, is the where()/filter() method. I find the syntax for filtering in SQL much less verbose than regular PySpark; being able to use the SQL syntax as the argument of the filter() method with no ceremony is a godsend. In our final program, I am able to use full_data.where("failure = 1") instead of wrapping the column name in F.col() like we've been doing.

I reuse this convenience in the query function, which is displayed in listing 7.20. This time, I use string interpolation in conjunction with between. This doesn't save many key strokes, but it's easy to understand, and you don't get as much line noise as when using the data.capacity_GB.between(capacity_min, capacity_max) (if you prefer using the column function, you can also use this syntax: F.col("capacity_GB") .between(capacity_min, capacity_max)). At this point, it's very much a question of personal style and how familiar you are with each approach.

Listing 7.20 The most_reliable_drive_for_capacity() function

```
def most_reliable_drive_for_capacity(data, capacity_GB=2048, precision=0.25,
    top_n=3):
    """Returns the top 3 drives for a given approximate capacity.

    Given a capacity in GB and a precision as a decimal number, we keep the N
    drives where:

    - the capacity is between (capacity * 1/(1+precision)), capacity *
    (1+precision)
    - the failure rate is the lowest

    """
    capacity_min = capacity_GB / (1 + precision)
    capacity_max = capacity_GB * (1 + precision)

    answer = (
        data.where(f"capacity_GB between {capacity_min} and {capacity_max}")     ◁
        .orderBy("failure_rate", "capacity_GB", ascending=[True, False])
        .limit(top_n)        ◁
    )

    return answer
```

> I used a SQL-style expression in my where() method, without having to use any other special syntax or method.

> Since we want to return the top N results, not just show them, I use limit() instead of show().

```
most_reliable_drive_for_capacity(summarized_data, capacity_GB=11176.0).show()
# +-------------------+-----------+--------------------+
# |              model|capacity_GB|        failure_rate|
# +-------------------+-----------+--------------------+
# |HGST HUH721010ALE600|     9314.0|                 0.0|
# |HGST HUH721212ALN604|    11176.0|1.088844437497695E-5|
# |HGST HUH721212ALE600|    11176.0|1.528677999266234...|
# +-------------------+-----------+--------------------+
```

7.6   Conclusion

You do not need to learn or use SQL to effectively work with PySpark. That being said, since the data manipulation API shares so much vocabulary and functionality with SQL, you will have a much more productive time with PySpark if you have a basic understanding of the syntax and query structure.

My family speaks both English and French, and sometimes you don't always know where one language starts and one ends. I tend to think in both languages, and sometimes blend them in a single sentence. Likewise, I find that some problems are easier to solve with Python, and some are more in SQL's territory. You will find your own balance, as well, which is why it's nice to have the option. Just like spoken languages, the goal is to express your thoughts and intentions as clearly as possible while keeping your audience in mind.

Summary

- Spark provides a SQL API for data manipulation. This API supports ANSI SQL.
- Spark (and PySpark, by extension) borrows a lot of vocabulary and expected functionality from the way SQL manipulates tables. This is especially evident since the data manipulation module is called `pyspark.sql`.
- PySpark's data frames need to be registered as views or tables before they can be queried with Spark SQL. You can give them a different name than the data frame you're registering.
- PySpark's own data frame manipulation methods and functions borrow SQL functionality, for the most part. Some exceptions, such as `union()`, are present and documented in the API.
- Spark SQL queries can be inserted in a PySpark program through the `spark.sql` function, where `spark` is the running `SparkSession`.
- Spark SQL table references are kept in a `Catalog`, which contains the metadata for all tables accessible to Spark SQL.
- PySpark will accept SQL-style clauses in `where()`, `expr()`, and `selectExpr()`, which can simplify the syntax for complex filtering and selection.
- When using Spark SQL queries with user-provided input, be careful with sanitizing the inputs to avoid potential SQL injection attacks.

Additional exercises

Exercise 7.2

If we look at the code that follows, we can simplify it even further and avoid creating two tables outright. Can you write a `summarized_data` without having to use a table other than `full_data` and no join? (Bonus: Try using pure PySpark, then pure Spark SQL, and then a combo of both.)

```
full_data = full_data.selectExpr(
    "model", "capacity_bytes / pow(1024, 3) capacity_GB", "date", "failure"
)

drive_days = full_data.groupby("model", "capacity_GB").agg(
    F.count("*").alias("drive_days")
)

failures = (
    full_data.where("failure = 1")
    .groupby("model", "capacity_GB")
    .agg(F.count("*").alias("failures"))
)
```

```
summarized_data = (
    drive_days.join(failures, on=["model", "capacity_GB"], how="left")
    .fillna(0.0, ["failures"])
    .selectExpr("model", "capacity_GB", "failures / drive_days failure_rate")
    .cache()
)
```

Exercise 7.3

The analysis in the chapter is flawed in that the age of a drive is not taken into consideration. Instead of ordering the model by failure rate, order by average age at failure (assume that every drive fails on the maximum date reported if they are still alive). (Hint: Remember that you need to count the age of each drive first.)

Exercise 7.4

What is the total capacity (in TB) that Backblaze records at the beginning of each month?

Exercise 7.5

> **NOTE**   There is a much more elegant way to solve this problem that we see in chapter 10 using window functions. In the meantime, this exercise can be solved with the judicious usage of group bys and joins.

If you look at the data, you'll see that some drive models can report an erroneous capacity. In the data preparation stage, restage the full_data data frame so that the most common capacity for each drive is used.

Extending PySpark with Python: RDD and UDFs

This chapter covers

- Using the RDD as a low-level, flexible data container
- Manipulating data in the RDD using higher-order functions
- How to promote regular Python functions to UDFs to run in a distributed fashion
- How to apply UDFs on local data to ease debugging

Our journey with PySpark thus far has proven that it is a powerful and versatile data-processing tool. So far, we've explored many out-of-the-box functions and methods to manipulate data in a data frame. Recall from chapter 1 that PySpark's data frame manipulation functionality takes our Python code and applies an optimized query plan. This makes our data jobs efficient, consistent, and predictable, just like coloring within the lines. What if we need to go off-script and manipulate our data according to our own rules?

In this chapter, I cover the two mechanisms PySpark provides for distributing Python code. In other words, we move away from the set of functions and methods provided by `pyspark.sql`; instead, we build our own set of transformations in pure Python, using PySpark as a convenient distributing engine. For this, we start with the *resilient distributed dataset* (or RDD); the RDD is akin to the data frame, but distributes unordered objects rather than records and columns. This object-first approach provides more flexibility compared to the more rigid schema of the data frame. Second, I introduce UDFs, a simple way to promote regular Python functions to be used on a data frame.

The RDD, too old-school?

With the advent of the data frame, which boasts better performance and a streamlined API for common data operations (`select`, `filter`, `groupby`, `join`), the RDD fell behind in terms of popularity. Is there room for the RDD in a modern PySpark program?

While the data frame is becoming more and more flexible as the Spark versions are released, the RDD still reigns in terms of flexibility. The RDD especially shines in two use cases:

- When you have an unordered collection of Python objects that can be pickled (which is how Python calls object serialization; see http://mng.bz/M2X7)
- When you have unordered `key`, `value` pairs, like in a Python dictionary

Both use cases are covered in this chapter. The data frame should be your structure of choice by default, but know that if you find it restrictive, the RDD is waiting for you.

8.1 *PySpark, freestyle: The RDD*

This section covers the RDD. More specifically, I introduce how to reason about the data structure and the API to manipulate data it contains.

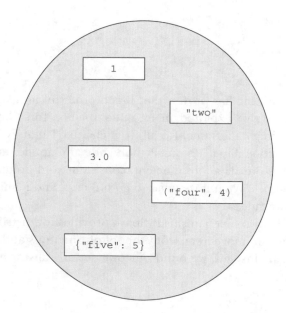

Figure 8.1 The `collection_rdd`. Each object is independent from the others in the container—no column, no structure, no schema.

Unlike the data frame, where most of our data manipulation tool kit revolved around columns, RDD revolves around objects: I think of an RDD as a bag of elements with no order or relationship to one another. Each element is independent of the other. The easiest way to experiment with a RDD is to create one from a Python list. In listing 8.1, I create a list containing multiple objects of different types, and then promote it to an RDD via the `parallelize` method. The resulting RDD is depicted in figure 8.1. The creation of the RDD takes the objects on the list, serializes (or *pickles*) them, and then distributes them between the worker nodes.

Listing 8.1 Promoting a Python list to an RDD

```
from pyspark.sql import SparkSession

spark = SparkSession.builder.getOrCreate()

collection = [1, "two", 3.0, ("four", 4), {"five": 5}]

sc = spark.sparkContext

collection_rdd = sc.parallelize(collection)

print(collection_rdd)
# ParallelCollectionRDD[0] at parallelize at PythonRDD.scala:195
```

My collection is a list of an integer, a string, a float, a tuple, and a dict.

The list gets promoted to an RDD using the parallelize method of the SparkContext.

The RDD functions and methods are under the SparkContext object, accessible as an attribute of our SparkSession. I alias it to sc for convenience.

Our collection_rdd object is effectively an RDD. PySpark returns the type of the collection when we print the object.

Compared to a data frame, the RDD is much more *freestyle* (pardon the 90s reference) in terms of what it accepts. If we were trying to store an integer, a string, a floating point number, a tuple, and a dictionary in a single column, the data frame would have (and fail) to find a common denominator to fit those different types of data.

In this section, we checked the general allure of an RDD and witnessed the flexibility it provides in ingesting many types of data into a single container abstraction. The next section covers manipulating data in the RDD; with great flexibility comes great responsibility!

8.1.1 *Manipulating data the RDD way: map(), filter(), and reduce()*

This section explains the building blocks of data manipulation using an RDD. I discuss the concept of higher-order functions and use them to transform data. I finish with a quick overview of MapReduce, a fundamental concept in large-scale data processing, and place it in the context of Spark and the RDD.

Manipulating data with an RDD feels like giving orders to an army as a general: you have full obedience from your privates/divisions in the field/cluster, but if you give an incomplete or wrong order, you'll cause havoc within your troops/RDD. Furthermore, each division has its own specific type of order it can perform, and you don't have a reminder of what's what (unlike with a data frame schema). Sounds like a fun job.

An RDD provides many methods (which you can find in the API documentation for the `pyspark.RDD` object), but we put our focus on three specific methods: `map()`, `filter()`, and `reduce()`. Together, they capture the ethos of data manipulation with an RDD; knowing how these three work will give you the necessary foundation to understand the others.

`map()`, `filter()`, and `reduce()` all take a function (that we will call f) as their only parameter and return a copy of the RDD with the desired modifications. We call functions that take other functions as parameters *higher-order functions*. They can be a little difficult to understand the first time you encounter them; fear not, after seeing them in action, you'll be very comfortable using them in PySpark (and in Python, if you look at appendix C).

APPLY ONE FUNCTION TO EVERY OBJECT: MAP

We start with the most basic and common operation: applying a Python function to every element of the RDD. For this, PySpark provides `map()`. This directly echoes the functionality of the `map()` function in Python.

The best way to illustrate `map()` is through an example. In listing 8.2, I apply a function that adds 1 to its argument in every object in the RDD. After the application of the function, via `map()`, I `collect()` each of the elements of the RDD in a Python list to print them back—or so it seems; we get an error with its companion stack trace. What's happening?

Listing 8.2   Mapping a simple function, `add_one()`, to each element

```
from py4j.protocol import Py4JJavaError


def add_one(value):            ◁──┐  A seemingly inoffensive function, add_one()
    return value + 1              │  adds 1 to the value passed as an argument.


                                          ┌  I apply my function to
collection_rdd = collection_rdd.map(add_one)  ◁──┤  every element in the RDD
                                          └  via the map() method.
try:
    print(collection_rdd.collect())    ◁──┐  collect() materializes an RDD into
except Py4JJavaError:                       │  a Python list on the master node.
    pass


# Stack trace galore! The important bit, you'll get one of the following:
# TypeError: can only concatenate str (not "int") to str
# TypeError: unsupported operand type(s) for +: 'dict' and 'int'
# TypeError: can only concatenate tuple (not "int") to tuple
```

To understand why our code is failing, we'll break down the mapping process, illustrated in figure 8.2. I apply the `add_one()` function to each element in the RDD by passing it as an argument to the `map()` method. `add_one()` is a regular Python function, applied to regular Python objects. Since we have incompatible types (e.g., `"two"` + `1` is not a legal operation in Python), three of our elements are `TypeError`. When I `collect()` the RDD to peek at the values, it explodes into a stack trace right in my REPL.

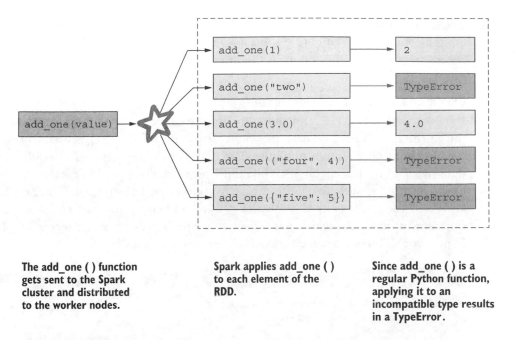

The add_one ( ) function gets sent to the Spark cluster and distributed to the worker nodes.

Spark applies add_one ( ) to each element of the RDD.

Since add_one ( ) is a regular Python function, applying it to an incompatible type results in a TypeError.

Figure 8.2 Applying the `add_one()` function to each element of the RDD via `map()`. If the function cannot be applied, an error will be raised during action time.

NOTE The RDD is a lazy collection. If you have an error in your function application, it will not be visible until you perform an action (e.g., `collect()`), just like with the data frame.

Fortunately, since we are working with Python, we can use a `try`/`except` block to prevent errors. I provide an improved `safer_add_one()` function in the next listing, which returns the original element if the function runs into a type error.

Listing 8.3 Mapping `safer_add_one()` to each element in an RDD

```
collection_rdd = sc.parallelize(collection)
```
I recreate my RDD from scratch to remove the erroneous operation in the thunk (see chapter 1 for a description of a computation thunk).

```
def safer_add_one(value):
    try:
        return value + 1
    except TypeError:
        return value
```
Our function returns the original value untouched if it encounters a TypeError.

```
collection_rdd = collection_rdd.map(safer_add_one)
```

```
print(collection_rdd.collect())
# [2, 'two', 4.0, ('four', 4), {'five': 5}]
```

⟵ **The relevant elements of the RDD have been incremented by 1.**

In summary, you use `map()` to apply a function to every element of the RDD. Because of the flexibility of the RDD, PySpark does not give you any safeguards regarding the content of the RDD. You are responsible, as the developer, for making your function robust regardless of the input. In the next section, we get to filter some elements of our RDD.

ONLY KEEP WHAT YOU WANT USING FILTER

Just like `where()`/`filter()` was one of the first methods I went over when I introduced the data frame, we have the same for the RDD. `filter()` is used to keep only the element that satisfies a predicate. The RDD version of `filter()` is a little different than the data frame version: it takes a function `f`, which applies to each object (or element) and keeps only those that return a truthful value. In listing 8.4, I filter my RDD to keep only the integer and float elements, using a lambda function. The `isinstance()` function returns `True` if the first argument's type is present in the second argument; in our case, it'll test if each element is either a `float` or an `int`.

Listing 8.4   Filtering our RDD with a lambda function

```
collection_rdd = collection_rdd.filter(
    lambda elem: isinstance(elem, (float, int))
)
```

```
print(collection_rdd.collect())
# [2, 4.0]
```

Using lambda functions like a pro

Lambda functions are a great way to reduce boilerplate when you need a simple function for only one use. At its core, a lambda function allows you to create a function without assigning it a name. In the following figure, I show the correspondence between a *named* function (using the `def` keyword) and a lambda (or *anonymous*) function using the `lambda` keyword. Both statements return a function object that can then be used: where the named function can be referred to by its name (`is_a_number`), the lambda function is usually defined where it needs to be used. In the case of the `filter()` application in listing 8.4, we could have replaced our lambda by the `is_a_number` function, but directly using a lambda function as the argument to `filter()` saves a few keystrokes.

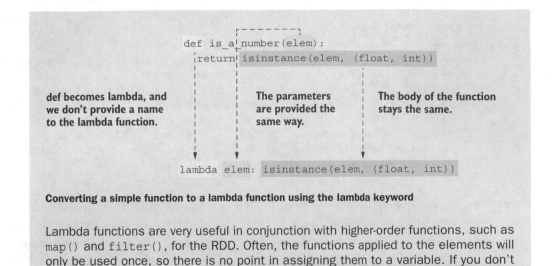

Converting a simple function to a lambda function using the lambda keyword

Lambda functions are very useful in conjunction with higher-order functions, such as `map()` and `filter()`, for the RDD. Often, the functions applied to the elements will only be used once, so there is no point in assigning them to a variable. If you don't feel comfortable using lambda functions, don't worry; it is still okay to create a small function and then apply it to your RDD.

Just like `map()`, the function passed as a parameter to `filter()` is applied to every element in the RDD. This time, though, instead of returning the result in a new RDD, we keep the original value if the result of the function is truthy. If the result is falsy, we drop the element. I show the breakdown of the `filter()` operation in figure 8.3.

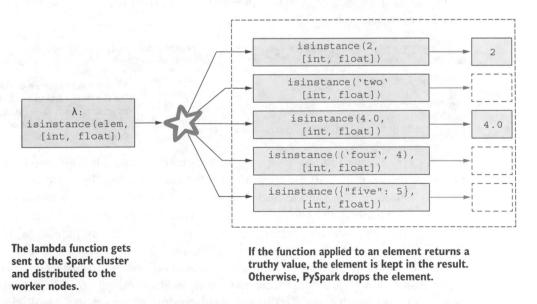

The lambda function gets sent to the Spark cluster and distributed to the worker nodes.

If the function applied to an element returns a truthy value, the element is kept in the result. Otherwise, PySpark drops the element.

Figure 8.3 Filtering our RDD to keep only `int` and `float`. Our predicate function is applied element-wise, and only the values leading to truthy predicates are kept.

> **Truthy/falsy in Python**
>
> When working with the data frame, the argument to `filter()` (the *data frame* method) needs to return a Boolean explicitly: either `True` or `False`. In this chapter, with the RDD, we follow Python's convention for Boolean testing; because of this, I avoid using absolute `True/False` when talking about filtering in the RDD since Python has its own way of determining if a value is "truthy" (it will be considered `True` by Python) or "falsy." As a reminder, `False`, `0` (the number zero in any Python numerical type), and empty sequences and collections (list, tuple, dict, set, range) are falsy. For more explanation on how Python imputes Boolean values on non-Boolean types, refer to the Python documentation (http://mng.bz/aDoz).

We can now map over and filter the elements in our RDD. How would we aggregate them into a summary value? If you think that the RDD provides yet again a very general way of summarizing the elements it contains, you are right! Ready to reduce?

TWO ELEMENTS COME IN, ONE COMES OUT: REDUCE()

This section covers the last important operation of the RDD, which enables the summarization of data (similar to `groupby()`/`agg()`) using the data frame. `reduce()`, as its name implies, is used to reduce elements in an RDD. By *reducing*, I mean taking two elements and applying a function that will return only one element. PySpark will apply the function to the first two elements, then apply it again to the result and the third element, and so on, until there are no elements left. I find the concept easier when explained visually, so figure 8.4 shows the process of summing the value of the elements in the RDD using `reduce()`. The following listing presents how to use the `reduce()` method on a data frame.

Listing 8.5   Applying the `add()` function via `reduce()`

```python
from operator import add

collection_rdd = sc.parallelize([4, 7, 9, 1, 3])

print(collection_rdd.reduce(add))    # 24
```

The operator module contains the function version or common operators, such as + (add()), so we do not have to pass a lambda a, b: a + b.

`map()`, `filter()`, and `reduce()` appear at first glance like simple concepts: they take a function and apply it to all the elements inside the collection. The result is treated differently depending on the method chosen, and `reduce()` requires a function of two arguments returning a single value. In 2004, Google used this humble concept and caused a revolution in the large-scale data processing world by publishing its Map-Reduce framework (https://research.google/pubs/pub62/). You can't argue about naming here: the name is a combination of `map()` and `reduce()`. This framework was a direct inspiration for big data frameworks, such as Hadoop and Spark. Although modern abstractions, such as the data frame, aren't as close to the original MapReduce, the ideas remain, and gaining a high-level understanding of the building blocks will make it easier to understand some higher-level design choices.

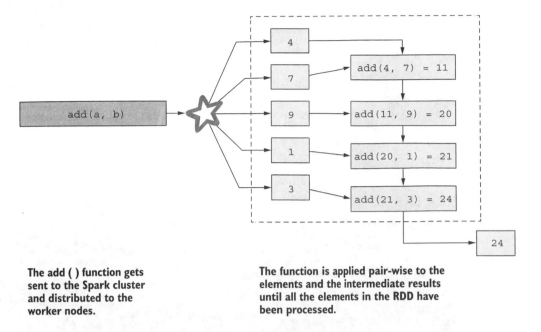

The add ( ) function gets
sent to the Spark cluster
and distributed to the
worker nodes.

The function is applied pair-wise to the
elements and the intermediate results
until all the elements in the RDD have
been processed.

Figure 8.4   Reducing our RDD by summing the values of the elements

reduce() in a distributed world

Because of PySpark's distributed nature, the data of an RDD can be distributed across multiple partitions. The `reduce()` function will be applied independently on each partition, and then each intermediate value will be sent to the master node for the final reduction. Because of this, you need to provide a commutative and associative function to `reduce()`.

A *commutative function* is a function where the order in which the arguments are applied is not important. For example, `add()` is commutative, since `a + b = b + a`. Oh the flip side, `subtract()` is not: `a - b != b - a`.

An *associative* function is a function where how the values are grouped is not important. `add()` is associative, since `(a + b) + c = a + (b + c)`. `subtract()` is not: `(a - b) - c != a - (b - c)`.

`add()`, `multiply()`, `min()`, and `max()` are both associative and commutative.

This concludes our whirlwind tour of the PySpark RDD API. We covered how the RDD applies transformations to its elements through higher-order functions such as `map()`, `filter()`, and `reduce()`. Those higher-order functions apply the functions passed as parameters to each element, making the RDD *element-major* (or *row-major*). If you are curious about the other applications of the RDD, I recommend looking at the PySpark online API documentation. Most of the methods in the RDD have a direct equivalent to the data frame or grow directly from the usage of map(), filter(), and reduce(). The next sections build on the concept of applying Python functions directly, but this time on a data frame. The fun begins!

Exercise 8.1

The PySpark RDD API provides a count() method that returns the number of elements in the RDD as an integer. Reproduce the behavior of this method using map(), filter(), and/or reduce().

Exercise 8.2

What is the return value of the following code block?

```
a_rdd = sc.parallelize([0, 1, None, [], 0.0])

a_rdd.filter(lambda x: x).collect()
```

    a [1]
    b [0, 1]
    c [0, 1, 0.0]
    d []
    e [1, []]

Optional topic: Going full circle, a data frame is an RDD!

To show the ultimate flexibility of the RDD, look at this: you can access an implicit RDD within a data frame via the rdd attribute of a data frame.

Listing 8.6   Uncovering the RDD from within a data frame using the rdd attribute

```
df = spark.createDataFrame([[1], [2], [3]], schema=["column"])

print(df.rdd)
# MapPartitionsRDD[22] at javaToPython at
#          NativeMethodAccessorImpl.java:0

print(df.rdd.collect())
# [Row(column=1), Row(column=2), Row(column=3)]
```

From a PySpark perspective, a data frame is also an RDD[Row] (from pyspark.sql .Row), where each row can be thought of as a dictionary; the key is the column name and the value is the value contained in the record. To do the opposite, you can pass the RDD to spark.createDataFrame with an optional schema. Remember that, when moving from a data frame to an RDD, you give up the schema safety of the data frame!

It can be tempting to move back and forth between a data frame and an RDD depending on the operation you wish to perform. Bear in mind that this will come at a performance cost (because you convert the data from column-major to row-major), but will also make your code harder to follow. You will also have to make sure all your Rows follow the same schema before putting your RDD into a data frame. Usually, if you need the occasional power of the RDD but with the comfort of the columnar aspect of the data frame, UDFs are the way to go. Luckily, this is the topic of the next section.

8.2 Using Python to extend PySpark via UDFs

In section 8.1, we got a taste of the flexibility of the RDD approach to data manipulation. This section takes the same question—how can we run Python code on our data?—and applies it to the data frame. More specifically, we focus on the map() transformation: for each record that comes in, one record comes out. Map-type transformations are by far the most frequent and the easiest to implement.

Unlike the RDD, the data frame has a structure enforced by columns. To address this constraint, PySpark provides the possibility of creating UDFs via the pyspark.sql.functions.udf() function. What comes in is a regular Python function, and what goes out is a function promoted to work on PySpark columns.

To illustrate this, we will mock up a data type not present in PySpark: the Fraction. Fractions are made of a numerator and a denominator. In PySpark, we'll represent this as an array of two integers. In the next listing, I create a data frame containing two columns that stand for the numerator and the denominator. I fuse the two columns in an array column via the array() function.

Listing 8.7 Creating a data frame containing a single-array column

```python
import pyspark.sql.functions as F
import pyspark.sql.types as T
```
I start the range for the denominator at 1, since a fraction with 0 for the denominator is undefined.

```python
fractions = [[x, y] for x in range(100) for y in range(1, 100)]

frac_df = spark.createDataFrame(fractions, ["numerator", "denominator"])

frac_df = frac_df.select(
    F.array(F.col("numerator"), F.col("denominator")).alias(
        "fraction"
    ),
)
```
The array() function takes two or more columns of the same type and creates a single column containing an array of the columns passed as a parameter.

```python
frac_df.show(5, False)
# +--------+
# |fraction|
# +--------+
# |[0, 1]  |
# |[0, 2]  |
# |[0, 3]  |
```

```
# |[0, 4]  |
# |[0, 5]  |
# +--------+
# only showing top 5 rows
```

To support our new makeshift fraction type, we create a few functions that provide basic functionality. This is a perfect job for Python UDFs, and I take the opportunity to introduce the two ways PySpark enables its creation.

8.2.1 *It all starts with plain Python: Using typed Python functions*

This section covers creating a Python function that will work seamlessly with a PySpark data frame. While Python and Spark usually work seamlessly together, creating and using UDFs requires a few precautions. I introduce how you can use Python-type hints to make sure your code will work seamlessly with PySpark types. At the end of this section, we will have a function to reduce a fraction and one to transform a fraction into a floating-point number.

My blueprint when creating a function destined to become a Python UDF is as follows:

1 Create and document the function.
2 Make sure the input and output types are compatible.
3 Test the function.

For this section, I provide a couple of assertions to make sure the function is behaving as expected.

Behind every UDF is a Python function, so our two functions are in listing 8.8. I introduce Python-type annotations in this code block; the rest of the section covers how they are used in this context and why they are a powerful tool when combined with Python UDFs.

Listing 8.8   Creating our three Python functions

We rely on the Fraction data type from the fractions module to avoid reinventing the wheel.

Some specific types need to be imported to be used: the standard library contains the types for scalar values, but containers like Option and Tuple need to be explicitly imported.

```
from fractions import Fraction
from typing import Tuple, Optional

Frac = Tuple[int, int]

def py_reduce_fraction(frac: Frac) -> Optional[Frac]:
    """Reduce a fraction represented as a 2-tuple of integers."""
    num, denom = frac
    if denom:
        answer = Fraction(num, denom)
        return answer.numerator, answer.denominator
    return None
```

We create a type synonym: Frac. This is equivalent to telling Python/mypy, "When you see Frac, assume it's a Tuple[int, int]" (a tuple containing two integers). This makes the type annotations easier to read.

Our function takes a Frac as an argument and returns a Optional[Frac], which translates to "either a Frac or None."

```
assert py_reduce_fraction((3, 6)) == (1, 2)
assert py_reduce_fraction((1, 0)) is None

def py_fraction_to_float(frac: Frac) -> Optional[float]:
    """Transforms a fraction represented as a 2-tuple of integers into a
     float."""
    num, denom = frac
    if denom:
        return num / denom
    return None
```

I create a few assertions to sanity check my code and make sure I get the expected behavior.

```
assert py_fraction_to_float((2, 8)) == 0.25
assert py_fraction_to_float((10, 0)) is None
```

Both functions are similar, so I'll take `py_reduce_fraction` and go through it line by line.

My function definition has a few new elements. The `frac` parameter has a `: Frac`, and we have a `-> Optional[Frac]` before the colon. Those additions are *type annotations* and are an amazing tool to make sure the function accepts and returns what we expect. Python is a dynamic language; this means that the type of an object is known at runtime. When working with PySpark's data frame, where each column has one and only one type, we need to make sure that our UDF will return consistent types. We can use type hints to ensure this.

Python's type checking can be enabled through multiple libraries; mypy is one of them. You install it via `pip install mypy`. Once installed, you can run `mypy` on your file with `mypy MY_FILE.py`. Appendix C contains a deeper introduction to the `typing` module and `mypy` and how it applies (and why it should apply) beyond a UDF. I'll add type annotation when relevant, as it can be useful documentation, in addition to making code more robust. (What does my function expect? What does it return?)

In my function definition, I announce that the `frac` function parameter is of type `Frac`, which is equivalent to a `Tuple[int, int]` or a two-element tuple containing two integers. If I get to share my code with others, this type annotation sends a signal about the input type of my function. Furthermore, mypy will complain if I try to pass an incompatible argument to my function. If I try to do `py_reduce_fraction("one half")`, mypy will tell me the following:

```
error: Argument 1 to "py_reduce_fraction" has incompatible type "str";
expected "Tuple[int, int]"
```

I can already see the type errors vanishing.

The second type annotation, located after the function arguments and prefixed with an arrow, is for the return type of the function. We recognize the `Frac`, but this time, I wrapped it into an `Optional` type.

In section 8.1, when creating functions to be distributed over the RDD, I needed to make sure that they would not trigger an error and return `None` instead. I apply the same concept here. I test for `denom` being a truthy value: if it is equal to zero, I return `None`. This is such a frequent use case that Python provides the `Optional[…]` type, which means either the type between the brackets or `None`. PySpark will accept `None` values as `null`.

Type annotations: Extra keystrokes, fewer errors

Type annotations are incredibly useful out of the box, but they are especially nifty when used with Python UDFs. Since PySpark's execution model is lazy, you'll often get your error stack trace at action time. UDF stack traces are not any harder to read than any other stack trace in PySpark—which is not saying much—but a vast majority of the bugs are because of a bad input or return value. Type annotations are not a silver bullet, but they are a great tool for avoiding and diagnosing type errors.

The rest of the function is relatively straightforward: I ingest the numerator and denominator in a `Fraction` object, which reduces the fraction. I then extract the numerator and denominator from the `Fraction` and return them as a tuple of two integers, as I promised in my return type annotation.

We have our two functions with well-defined input and output types. In the next section, I show how you promote regular Python functions to UDFs and apply them to your data frame.

8.2.2   *From Python function to UDFs using udf()*

Once you have your Python function created, PySpark provides a simple mechanism to promote to a UDF. This section covers the `udf()` function and how to use it directly to create a UDF, as well as using the decorator to simplify the creation of a UDF.

PySpark provides a `udf()` function in the `pyspark.sql.functions` module to promote Python functions to their UDF equivalents. The function takes two parameters:

- The function you want to promote
- The return type of the generated UDF

In table 8.1, I summarize the type equivalences between Python and PySpark. If you provide a return type, it must be compatible with the return value of your UDF.

Table 8.1   A summary of the types in PySpark. A star next to the `Python equivalent` column means the Python type is more precise or can contain larger values, so you need to be careful with the values you return.

Type Constructor	String representation	Python equivalent
`NullType()`	`null`	None
`StringType()`	`string`	Python's regular strings
`BinaryType()`	`binary`	bytearray
`BooleanType()`	`boolean`	bool
`DateType()`	`date`	`datetime.date` (from the `datetime` library)
`TimestampType()`	`timestamp`	`datetime.datetime` (from the `datetime` library)

Table 8.1 A summary of the types in PySpark. A star next to the `Python equivalent` **column means the Python type is more precise or can contain larger values, so you need to be careful with the values you return.** *(continued)*

Type Constructor	String representation	Python equivalent
`DecimalType(p,s)`	`decimal`	`decimal.Decimal` (from the `decimal` library)*
`DoubleType()`	`double`	float
`FloatType()`	`float`	float*
`ByteType()`	`byte` or `tinyint`	int*
`IntegerType()`	`int`	int*
`LongType()`	`long` or `bigint`	int*
`ShortType()`	`short` or `smallint`	int*
`ArrayType(T)`	N/A	list, tuple, or Numpy array (from the `numpy` library)
`MapType(K, V)`	N/A	dict
`StructType([…])`	N/A	list or tuple

In listing 8.9, I promote the `py_reduce_fraction()` function to a UDF via the `udf()` function. Just like I did with the Python equivalent, I provide a return type to the UDF (this time, an `Array` of `Long`, since `Array` is the companion type of the tuple and `Long` is the one for Python integers). Once the UDF is created, we can apply it just like any other PySpark function on columns. I chose to create a new column to showcase the before and after; in the sample shown, the fraction appears properly reduced.

Listing 8.9 Creating a UDF explicitly with the `udf()` function

I alias the "array" of long PySpark type to the SparkFrac variable.

I promote my Python function using the udf() function, passing my SparkFrac-type alias as the return type.

```
SparkFrac = T.ArrayType(T.LongType())

reduce_fraction = F.udf(py_reduce_fraction, SparkFrac)

frac_df = frac_df.withColumn(
    "reduced_fraction", reduce_fraction(F.col("fraction"))
)
```

A UDF can be used like any other PySpark column function.

```
frac_df.show(5, False)
# +--------+----------------+
# |fraction|reduced_fraction|
# +--------+----------------+
# |[0, 1]  |[0, 1]          |
# |[0, 2]  |[0, 1]          |
# |[0, 3]  |[0, 1]          |
# |[0, 4]  |[0, 1]          |
# |[0, 5]  |[0, 1]          |
# +--------+----------------+
# only showing top 5 rows
```

You also have the option of creating your Python function and promoting it as a UDF using the udf function as a decorator. *Decorators* are functions applied to other functions through the @ sign above the function definition (we call that function *decorated*). This allows for changing the behavior of a function—here, we create a UDF from a regular Python function definition—with minimal boilerplate (see appendix C for more information). In listing 8.10, I define py_fraction_to_float() (now simply called fraction_to_float()) directly as a UDF by preceding my function definition with @F.udf([return_type]). In both cases, you can access the underlying function from the UDF by calling the attribute frac.

Listing 8.10   Creating a UDF directly using the udf() decorator

```
@F.udf(T.DoubleType())                                          ◁─────────────────────┐
def fraction_to_float(frac: Frac) -> Optional[float]:
    """Transforms a fraction represented as a 2-tuple of integers into a float."""
    num, denom = frac
    if denom:                                          The decorator performs the same
        return num / denom                             function as the udf() function, but
    return None                                        returns a UDF bearing the name
                                                       of the function defined under it.


frac_df = frac_df.withColumn(
    "fraction_float", fraction_to_float(F.col("reduced_fraction"))
)


frac_df.select("reduced_fraction", "fraction_float").distinct().show(
    5, False
)
# +---------------+-------------------+
# |reduced_fraction|fraction_float     |
# +---------------+-------------------+
# |[3, 50]        |0.06               |
# |[3, 67]        |0.04477611940298507|
# |[7, 76]        |0.09210526315789473|
# |[9, 23]        |0.391304347826087  |
# |[9, 25]        |0.36               |
# +---------------+-------------------+
# only showing top 5 rows
assert fraction_to_float.func((1, 2)) == 0.5       ◁─┐ In order to perform my assertion,
                                                     │ I use the func attribute of the UDF,
                                                     │ which returns the function ready
                                                     └ to be called.
```

In this chapter, we effectively tied Python and Spark in the tightest way possible. With the RDD, you have full control over the data inside the container, but you also have the responsibility to create functions and use higher-order functions such as map(), filter(), and reduce() to process the data objects inside. For the data frame, UDFs are your best tool: you can convert a Python function to a UDF that will use columns as inputs and outputs, at the expense of a performance hit to marry the data between Spark and Python.

The next chapter takes this to the next level: we will delve into the interaction between PySpark and pandas though special types of UDFs. PySpark and pandas make an attractive combo, and having the ability to scale Pandas through the Spark framework elevates both libraries. Fun and power awaits!

Summary

- The resilient distributed dataset allows for better flexibility compared to the records and columns approach of the data frame.
- The most low-level and flexible way of running Python code within the distributed Spark environment is to use the RDD. With an RDD, you have no structure imposed on your data and need to manage type information in your program and defensively code against potential exceptions.
- The API for data processing on the RDD is heavily inspired by the MapReduce framework. You use higher-order functions such as `map()`, `filter()`, and `reduce()` on the objects of the RDD.
- The data frame's most basic Python code promotion functionality, called the (PySpark) UDF, emulates the "map" part of the RDD. You use it as a scalar function, taking `Column` objects as parameters and returning a single `Column`.

Additional exercises

Exercise 8.3

Using the following definitions, create a `temp_to_temp(value, from, to)` that takes a numerical `value` in `from` degrees and converts it to degrees.

- `C = (F - 32) * 5 / 9` (Celcius)
- `K = C + 273.15` (Kelvin)
- `R = F + 459.67` (Rankine)

Exercise 8.4

Correct the following UDF, so it doesn't generate an error.

```
@F.udf(T.IntegerType())
def naive_udf(t: str) -> str:
    return answer * 3.14159
```

Exercise 8.5

Create a UDF that adds two fractions together, and test it by adding the `reduced_fraction` to itself in the `test_frac` data frame.

Exercise 8.6

Because of the `LongType()`, the `py_reduce_fraction` (see the previous exercise) will not work if the numerator or denominator exceeds `pow(2, 63)-1` or is lower than `-pow(2, 63)`. Modify the `py_reduce_fraction` to return `None` if this is the case.

Bonus: Does this change the type annotation provided? Why?

Big data is just a lot of small data: Using pandas UDFs

This chapter covers

- Using pandas Series UDFs to accelerate column transformation compared to Python UDFs
- Addressing the cold start of some UDFs using Iterator of Series UDF
- Controlling batch composition in a split-apply-combine programming pattern
- Confidently making a decision about the best pandas UDF to use

This chapter approaches the distributed nature of PySpark a little differently. If we take a few seconds to think about it, we read data into a data frame, and Spark distributes the data across partitions on nodes. What if we could directly operate on those partitions as if they were single-node data frames? More interestingly, what if we control how those single-node partitions are created and used using a tool we know? What about pandas?

PySpark's interoperability with pandas (also colloquially called *pandas UDF*) is a huge selling point when performing data analysis at scale. pandas is the dominant in-memory Python data manipulation library, while PySpark is the dominantly distributed one. Combining both of them unlocks additional possibilities.

In this chapter, we start by scaling some basic pandas data manipulation functionality. We then look into operations on `GroupedData` and how PySpark plus Pandas implement the split-apply-combine pattern common to data analysis. We finish with the ultimate interaction between pandas and PySpark: treating a PySpark data frame like a small collection of pandas DataFrames.

This chapter obviously makes great use of the pandas (http://pandas.pydata.org) library. Extensive pandas knowledge is a nice-to-have but is in no way expected. This chapter will cover the necessary pandas skills to use in within a basic pandas UDF. If you wish to level up your pandas skills to become a pandas UDF ninja, I warmly recommend the *Pandas in Action* book by Boris Paskhaver (Manning, 2021).

> **The tale of two versions**
>
> PySpark 3.0 completely changed how we interact with the pandas UDF API and added a lot of functionality and performance improvements. Because of this, I've structured this chapter with PySpark 3.0 in mind. For those using PySpark 2.3 or 2.4, I've added some sidebars when applicable with the appropriate syntax for convenience.
>
> pandas UDF was introduced in PySpark 2.3. If you are using Spark 2.2 or a previous version, you're out of luck!

For the examples in the chapter, you need three previously unused libraries: pandas, scikit-learn, and PyArrow. If you have installed Anaconda (see appendix B), you can use `conda` to install the libraries; otherwise, you can use `pip`.[1]

If you are using Spark 2.3 or 2.4, you also need to set a flag in the conf/spark-env.sh file of your Spark root directory to account for a change in Arrow serialization format. The Spark root directory is the one we set with the `SPARK_HOME` environment variable when installing Spark, as seen in appendix B. In the conf/ directory, you should find a spark-env.sh.template file. Make a copy, name it spark-env.sh, and add this line in the file:

```
ARROW_PRE_0_15_IPC_FORMAT=1
```

This will tell PyArrow to use a serialization format compatible with a version of Spark greater than 2.0, instead of the newer one that is only compatible with Spark 3.0. The Spark JIRA ticket contains more information about this (https://issues.apache.org/jira/browse/SPARK-29367). You can also use PyArrow version 0.14 and avoid the problem altogether:

```
# Conda installation
conda install pandas scikit-learn pyarrow
```

---

[1] On Windows, sometimes you might have issues with the pip wheels. If this is the case, refer to the PyArrow documentation page for installing: https://arrow.apache.org/docs/python/install.html

```
# Pip installation
pip install pandas scikit-learn pyarrow
```

9.1 Column transformations with pandas: Using Series UDF

In this section, we cover the simplest family of pandas UDFs: the Series UDFs. This family shares a column-first focus with regular PySpark data transformation functions. All of our UDFs in this section will take a `Column` object (or objects) as input and return a `Column` object as output. In practice, they serve as the most common type of UDF and work in cases where you want to bring a functionality already implemented in pandas—or a library that plays well with pandas—and promote it to the distributed world of PySpark.

PySpark provides three types of Series UDFs. Here is a summary of them; we will explore them further in the rest of the section:

- The *Series to Series* is the simplest. It takes `Columns` objects as inputs, converts them to pandas `Series` objects (giving it its name), and returns a `Series` object that gets promoted back to a PySpark `Column` object.

- The *Iterator of Series to Iterator of Series* differs in the sense that the `Column` objects get batched into batches and then fed as Iterator objects. It takes a single `Column` object as input and returns a single `Column`. It provides performance improvements, especially when the UDF need to initialize an expensive state before working on the data (e.g., local ML models created in scikit-learn).

- The *Iterator of multiple Series to Iterator of Series* is a combination of the previous Series UDFs and can take multiple `Columns` as input, like the Series to Series UDF, yet preserves the iterator pattern from the Iterator of Series to Iterator of Series.

NOTE There is also a *Series to Scalar* UDF that is part of the Group Aggregate UDF family. See section 9.2.1 for more information. Although it looks similar to the three previously mentioned, it serves a different purpose.

Before we start exploring Series UDF, let's grab a data set to experiment with. The next section introduces how to connect PySpark to Google BigQuery's data sets to efficiently read data from a data warehouse.

9.1.1 Connecting Spark to Google's BigQuery

This section provides instructions for connecting PySpark to Google's BigQuery, where we will use the National Oceanic and Atmospheric Administration's (NOAA) Global Surface Summary of the Day (GSOD) data set. In the same vein, this provides a blueprint for connecting PySpark to other data warehouses, such as SQL or NoSQL databases. Spark has a growing list of connectors to popular data storage and processing solutions—and we can't reasonably cover all of them!—but it'll often follow the same steps as we are using with BigQuery:

1 Install and configure the connector (if necessary), following the vendor's documentation.
2 Customize the `SparkReader` object to account for the new data source type.
3 Read the data, authenticating as needed.

> **You do not need to use BigQuery**
>
> I understand that getting a GCP account just to access some data can be a little annoying. I recommend you try—it's quite representative of connecting Spark with external data sources—but should you want to simply get familiar with the contents of this chapter, skip the rest of this section and use the (Parquet) data available from the repository:
>
> ```
> gsod = (
>     reduce(
>         lambda x, y: x.unionByName(y, allowMissingColumns=True),
>         [
>             spark.read.parquet(f"./data/gsod_noaa/gsod{year}.parquet")
>             for year in range(2010, 2021)
>         ],
>     )
>     .dropna(subset=["year", "mo", "da", "temp"])
>     .where(F.col("temp") != 9999.9)
>     .drop("date")
> )
> ```

INSTALLING AND CONFIGURING THE CONNECTOR

Google BigQuery is a serverless data warehouse engine that uses a SQL dialect to rapidly process data. Google provides a number of public data sets for experimentation. In this section, we install and configure the Google Spark BigQuery connector to directly access the data made available through BigQuery.

First, you need a GCP account. Once your account is created, you need to create a service account and a service account key to tell BigQuery to give you access to the public data programmatically. To do so, select `Service Account` (under `IAM & Admin`) and click `+ Create Service Account`. Give a meaningful name to your service account. In the service account permissions menu, select `BigQuery` → `BigQuery admin` and click Continue. In the last step, click `+ CREATE KEY` and select JSON. Download the key and store it somewhere safe (see figure 9.1).

> **WARNING** Treat this key like any other password. If a malicious person steals your key, go back to the Service Accounts menu, delete this key, and create a new one.

With your account created and your key downloaded, you can now fetch the connector. The connector is hosted on GitHub (http://mng.bz/aDZz). Because it is under active development, the instructions for installation and usage might change over time.

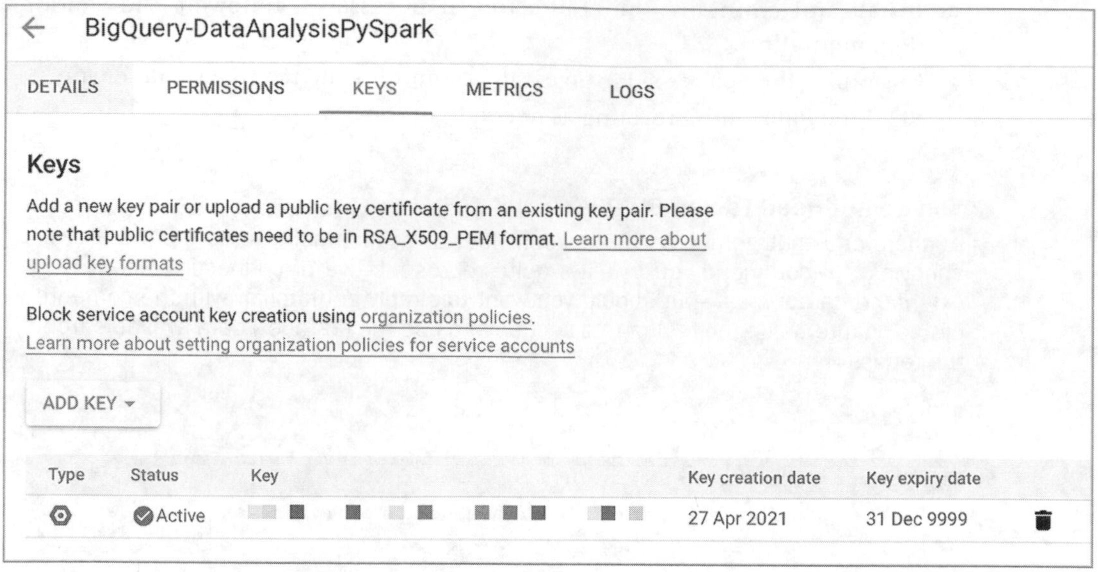

Figure 9.1   **The key under the** `BigQuery-DataAnalysisPySpark` **service account I created**

I encourage you to read its README. No need to download the connector right now: we'll let Spark take care of that during the next step.

MAKING THE CONNECTION BETWEEN PYSPARK AND BIGQUERY THROUGH THE CONNECTOR

Now we make the connection between BigQuery and our PySpark environment using the connector and the key created in the previous section. This will close the loop and directly connect our PySpark shell to BigQuery, effectively using it as an external data store.

If you use PySpark through a regular Python shell and have it running (as seen in appendix B), you need to restart your Python shell. Simply using `spark.stop()` and starting a new `SparkSession` will not work in this case, as we are adding a new dependency to our Spark installation. With a fresh Python REPL, we add, in listing 9.1, a `config` flag: `spark.jars.packages`. This instructs Spark to fetch and install external dependencies, in our case, the `com.google.cloud.spark:spark-bigquery` connector. As it is a Java/Scala dependency, we need to match the correct Spark and Scala version (at the time of writing, it is Spark 3.2, using Scala 2.12); refer to the connector's README for the latest information.

The log messages printed when the `SparkSession` gets instantiated are self-explanatory: Spark fetches the connector from Maven Central—a central repository for Java and JVM language packages, similar to Python's PyPI when you use pip—installs it, and configures it for your Spark instance. No need for manual download!

```
from pyspark.sql import SparkSession

spark = SparkSession.builder.config(
    "spark.jars.packages",
    "com.google.cloud.spark:spark-bigquery-with-dependencies_2.12:0.19.1",    ⊲─┐
).getOrCreate()
```

> I took the package version recommended for the Spark/Scala version (3.2/2.12) on my computer. Check the connector's repository for the most recent version.

```
# [...]
# com.google.cloud.spark#spark-bigquery-with-dependencies_2.12 added as a
    dependency
# :: resolving dependencies :: org.apache.spark#spark-submit-parent-77d4bbf3-
    1fa4-4d43-b5f7-59944801d46c;1.0
#    confs: [default]
#    found com.google.cloud.spark#spark-bigquery-with-
    dependencies_2.12;0.19.1 in central
# downloading https://repo1.maven.org/maven2/com/google/cloud/spark/spark-
    bigquery-with-dependencies_2.12/0.19.1/spark-bigquery-with-
    dependencies_2.12-0.19.1.jar ...
#    [SUCCESSFUL ] com.google.cloud.spark#spark-bigquery-with-
    dependencies_2.12;0.19.1!spark-bigquery-with-dependencies_2.12.jar
    (888ms)
# :: resolution report :: resolve 633ms :: artifacts dl 889ms
#    :: modules in use:
#    com.google.cloud.spark#spark-bigquery-with-dependencies_2.12;0.19.1
    from central in [default]
#    ---------------------------------------------------------------------
#    |                    |            modules            ||   artifacts   |
#    |       conf         | number| search|dwnlded|evicted|| number|dwnlded|
#    ---------------------------------------------------------------------
#    |     default        |   1   |   1   |   1   |   0   ||   1   |   1   |
#    ---------------------------------------------------------------------
# :: retrieving :: org.apache.spark#spark-submit-parent-77d4bbf3-1fa4-4d43-
    b5f7-59944801d46c
#    confs: [default]
#    1 artifacts copied, 0 already retrieved (33158kB/23ms)
```

Now that PySpark is connected to BigQuery, we simply have to read the data, using our authentication key via GCP.

Using the connector when invoking PySpark directly

If you are in an environment where you can't dynamically download dependencies (e.g., behind a corporate firewall), you can download the jar manually and add its location for the `spark.jars` config flag when instantiating your `SparkSession`. An alternative way, when using `pyspark` or `spark-submit` as a way to launch a REPL or a PySpark job, is to use the `--jars` configuration flag:

```
pyspark --jars spark-bigquery-latest.jar
spark-submit --jars spark-bigquery-latest.jar my_job_file.py
```

If you are using PySpark in the cloud, refer to your provider documentation. Each cloud provider has a different way of managing Spark dependencies and libraries.

If you use PySpark through your Python/IPython shell, you can load the library directly from Maven (Java/Scala's equivalent of PyPI) when creating your `SparkSession`.

READING THE DATA FROM BIGQUERY USING OUR SECRET KEY

We are now in the final stage before we can start creating pandas UDFs: with our environment configured, we just have to read the data. In this section, we assemble 10 years' worth of weather data located in BigQuery, which totals over 40 million records.

Reading data from BigQuery is straightforward. In listing 9.2, we use the `bigquery`-specialized `SparkReader`—provided by the connector library we embedded to our PySpark shell—which provides two options:

- The `table` parameter pointing to the table we want to ingest. The format is `project.dataset.table`; the `bigquery-public-data` is a project available to all.
- The `credentialsFile` is the JSON key downloaded in section 9.1.1. You need to adjust the path and file name according to the location of the file.

Listing 9.2   Reading the `stations` and `gsod` tables for 2010 to 2020

The stations table is available in BigQuery under
bigquery-public-data.noaa_gsod.gsodXXXX,
where XXXX is the four-digit year.

```
from functools import reduce
import pyspark.sql.functions as F
```
Since all the tables are read the same way, I abstract my reading routine in a reusable function, returning the resulting data frame.

```
def read_df_from_bq(year):
    return (
        spark.read.format("bigquery").option(
            "table", f"bigquery-public-data.noaa_gsod.gsod{year}"
        )
        # .option("credentialsFile", "bq-key.json")
        .load()
    )
```
I use the bigquery specialized reader via the format() method.

I pass my JSON service account key to the credentialsFile option to tell Google I am allowed to use the BigQuery service.

```
gsod = (
    reduce(
        lambda x, y: x.unionByName(y, allowMissingColumns=True),
        [read_df_from_bq(year) for year in range(2010, 2021)],
    )
    .dropna(subset=["year", "mo", "da", "temp"])
    .where(F.col("temp") != 9999.9)
    .drop("date")
)
```
I create a lambda function over my list comprehension of data frames to union them all.

Rather than using a looping construct, here I propose a handy pattern for unioning multiple tables in PySpark using `reduce`, also used in chapter 7. It's easier to understand the reduce operation if we break it down into discrete steps.

I start with a range of years (in my example, 2010 to 2020, including 2010 but excluding 2020). For this, I use the `range()` function.

I apply my helper function, `read_df_from_bq()`, to each year via a list comprehension, yielding a list of data frames. I don't have to worry about memory consumption as the list contains only a reference to the data frame (`DataFrame[…]`).

As a reducing function, I use a lambda function (which we used when creating one-usage functions in chapter 8) that unions two data frames by column names (with `unionByName`). `reduce` will take the first data frame in the list and union it with the second. It'll then take the result of the previous union and apply it again with the next data frame in line. The end result is a single data frame that contains every record from 2010 to 2020 inclusively.

We could do this iteratively, using a for loop. In the next listing, I show how to accomplish the same goal without using `reduce()`. Since higher-order functions usually yield cleaner code, I prefer using them instead of looping constructs where it make sense.

Listing 9.3 Reading the `gsod` data from 2010 to 2020 via a loop

```
gsod_alt = read_df_from_bq(2010)                        ◁
for year in range(2011, 2020):
    gsod_alt = gsod_alt.unionByName(
        read_df_from_bq(year), allowMissingColumns=True
    )
gsod_alt = gsod_alt.drop("date")
```

> When using a looping approach to union tables, you need an explicit starting seed. I use the table from 2010.

Because `gsod2020` has an additional `date` column that the previous years do not, `unionByName` will fill the values with `null` since we passed `True` to the `allowMissing-Columns` attribute. Instead, the date is represented in the data set via three integer columns: `year`, `mo` (for month), and `da` (for day).

> **TIP** If you are using a local Spark, loading 2010-2019 will make the examples in this chapter rather slow. I use 2018 only when working on my local instance, so I don't have to wait too long for code execution. Inversely, if you are working with a more powerful setup, you can add years to the range. The `gsod` tables go back to 1929.

In this section, we read a large amount of data from a warehouse and assembled a single data frame representing the weather information across the globe for a period of 10 years. In the next sections, I introduce the three members of the Series UDF, starting with the most common: the Series to Series UDF.

9.1.2 *Series to Series UDF: Column functions, but with pandas*

In this section, we cover the most common type of Pandas UDF: the Series to Series UDF, also called *Scalar* UDF. Series to Series UDFs are akin to most of the functions in the `pyspark.sql` model. For the most part, they work just like Python UDFs (seen in chapter 8), with one key difference: Python UDFs work on one record at a time, and you express your logic through regular Python code. Scalar UDFs work on one Series at a time, and you express your logic through pandas code. The difference is subtle, and it's easier to explain visually.

In a Python UDF, when you pass column objects to your UDF, PySpark will unpack each value, perform the computation, and then return the value for each record in a `Column` object. In a Scalar UDF, depicted in figure 9.2, PySpark will serialize (through a library called PyArrow, which we installed at the beginning of the chapter) each partitioned column into a pandas `Series` object (http://mng.bz/g4ll). You then perform the operations on the Series object directly, returning a Series of the same dimension from your UDF. From an end user perspective, they are the same functionally. Because pandas is optimized for rapid data manipulation, it is preferable to use a Series to Series UDF when you can instead of using a regular Python UDF, as it'll be much faster.

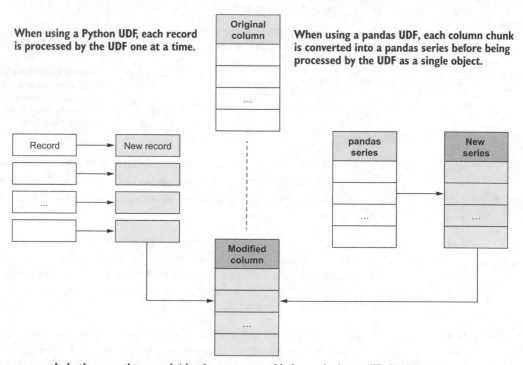

In both cases, the records/chunks are reassembled as a single, modified column.

Figure 9.2   Comparing a Python UDF to a pandas scalar UDF. The former splits a column into individual records, whereas the latter breaks them into Series.

Now armed with the "how it works" of Series to Series UDFs, let's create one ourselves. I chose to create a simple function that will transform Fahrenheit degrees to Celsius. In Canada, we use both scales depending on the usage: °F for cooking, °C for body or outside temperature. As a true Canadian, I cook my dinner at 350°F but know that 10°C is sweater weather. The function is depicted in listing 9.4. The building blocks are eerily similar, but we can pick out two main differences:

- Instead of udf(), I use pandas_udf(), again, from the pyspark.sql.functions module. Optionally (but recommended), we can pass the return type of the UDF as an argument to the pandas_udf() decorator.
- Our function signature is also different: rather than using scalar values (such as int or str), the UDF takes pd.Series and return a pd.Series.

The code within the function could be used as is for a regular Python UDF. I am (ab)using the fact that you can do arithmetic operations with a pandas Series.

Listing 9.4   Creating a pandas scalar UDF that transforms Fahrenheit into Celsius

```
import pandas as pd
import pyspark.sql.types as T


@F.pandas_udf(T.DoubleType())
def f_to_c(degrees: pd.Series) -> pd.Series:
    """Transforms Farhenheit to Celcius."""
    return (degrees - 32) * 5 / 9
```

For a scalar UDF, the biggest change happens in the decorator used. I could use the pandas_udf function directly too.

The signature for a Series to Series UDF is a function that takes one or multiple pandas.Series.

TIP If you're using a Spark 2 version, you need to add another parameter to the decorator here, as only Spark 3.0 and above recognize function signatures for pandas UDFs. The code in listing 9.4 would read @F.pandas_udf (T.DoubleType(), PandasUDFType.SCALAR). See the official PySpark documentation here: http://mng.bz/5KZz.

In listing 9.5, we apply our newly created Series to Series UDF to the temp column of the gsod data frame, which contains the temperature (in Fahrenheit) of each station-day combination. Just like with regular Python UDFs, Series to Series (and all Scalar UDF) are used like any data manipulation function. Here, I create a new column, temp_c, with withColumn() and apply the f_to_c temperature on the temp column.

Listing 9.5   Using a Series to Series UDF like any other column manipulation function

```
gsod = gsod.withColumn("temp_c", f_to_c(F.col("temp")))
gsod.select("temp", "temp_c").distinct().show(5)

# +-----+-------------------+
# | temp|             temp_c|
# +-----+-------------------+
# | 37.2| 2.8888888888888906|
# | 85.9| 29.944444444444443|
# | 53.5| 11.944444444444445|
# | 71.6| 21.999999999999996|
# |-27.6|-33.111111111111114|
# +-----+-------------------+
# only showing top 5 rows
```

Series to Series UDFs, just like regular Python UDFs, are very convenient when the record-wise transformation (or mapping) you want to apply to your data frame is not available within the stock PySpark functions (`pyspark.sql.functions`). Creating a Fahrenheit-to-Celsius converter as part of core Spark would be a little intense, so a Python or a pandas Series to Series UDF is a way to extend the core functionality with minimal fuss. Next, we see how to gain more control over the split and use the split-apply-combine pattern in PySpark.

Working with complex types in pandas UDF

PySpark has a richer data type system than pandas, which clubs strings and complex types into a catchall `object` type. Since you are dropping from PySpark into pandas during the execution of the UDF, you are solely responsible for aligning the types accordingly. This is where the return type attribute of the `pandas_udf` decorator comes in handy, as it'll help in diagnosing bugs early.

What if you want to accept or return complex types, such as the array of the struct? pandas will accept as values within a series a list of items that will be promoted to an `ArrayType` column. For `StructType` columns, you will need to replace the relevant `pd.Series` by a `pd.DataFrame`. In chapter 6, we saw that struct columns are like mini data frames, and the equivalence continues here!

9.1.3   *Scalar UDF + cold start = Iterator of Series UDF*

TIP   This is only available with PySpark 3.0+.

This section combines the other two types of Scalar UDFs: the Iterator of Series to Iterator of Series UDF and the Iterator of multiple Series to Iterator of Series. (Try to say that quickly five times!) Because they are so similar to the Series to Series UDF in their application, I will focus on the Iterator portion that gives them their power. Iterator of Series UDFs are very useful when you have an *expensive cold start* operation you need to perform. By cold start, we mean an operation we need to perform once at the beginning of the processing step, before working through the data. Deserializing a local ML model (fitted with scikit-learn or another Python modeling library) is an example: we would need to unpack and read the model once for the whole data frame, and then it could be used to process all records. Here, I'll reuse our `f_to_c` function but will add a cold start to demonstrate the usage.

Our UDF in listing 9.6 is similar to the Series to Series UDF from section 9.1.2. A few differences should be noted:

- The signature goes from `(pd.Series) -> pd.Series` to `(Iterator[pd.Series]) -> Iterator[pd.Series]`. This is consequential to using an Iterator of Series UDF.
- When working with the Series to Series UDF, we assumed that PySpark would give us one batch at a time. Here, since we are working with an Iterator of Series, we are explicitly iterating over each batch one by one. PySpark will distribute the work for us.
- Rather than using a `return` value, we `yield` so that our function returns an iterator.

Listing 9.6 Using an Iterator of Series to Iterator of Series UDF

```python
from time import sleep
from typing import Iterator

@F.pandas_udf(T.DoubleType())
def f_to_c2(degrees: Iterator[pd.Series]) -> Iterator[pd.Series]:
    """Transforms Farhenheit to Celcius."""
    sleep(5)
    for batch in degrees:
        yield (batch - 32) * 5 / 9

gsod.select(
    "temp", f_to_c2(F.col("temp")).alias("temp_c")
).distinct().show(5)
# +-----+-------------------+
# | temp|             temp_c|
# +-----+-------------------+
# | 37.2|  2.8888888888888906|
# | 85.9|  29.94444444444443|
# | 53.5|  11.94444444444445|
# | 71.6|  21.999999999999996|
# |-27.6|-33.111111111111114|
# +-----+-------------------+
# only showing top 5 rows
```

The signature is now (Iterator[pd.Series]) -> Iterator[pd.Series]. Notice the add-on of the Iterator keyword (from the typing module).

We simulate a cold start using sleep() for five seconds. The cold start will happen on each worker once, rather than for every batch.

Since we are working with an iterator here, we iterate over each batch, using yield (instead of return).

We have covered the Iterator of Series to Iterator of Series case. What about the Iterator of multiple Series to Iterator of Series? This special case is to wrap multiple columns in a single iterator. For this example, I'll assemble the year, mo, and da columns (representing the year, month, and day) into a single column. This example requires more data transformation than when using an Iterator of a single Series; I illustrate the process of data transformation in figure 9.3.

Our date assembly UDF works like this:

1 year_mo_da is an Iterator of a tuple of Series, representing all the batches of values contained in the year, mo, and da columns.
2 To access each batch, we use a for loop over the iterator, the same principle as for the Iterator of Series UDF (section 9.1.3).
3 To extract each individual series from the tuple, we use multiple assignments. In this case, year will map to the first Series of the tuple, mo to the second, and da to the third.
4 Since pd.to_datetime requests a data frame containing the year, month, and day columns, we create the data frame via a dictionary, giving the keys the relevant column names. pd.to_datetime returns a Series.
5 Finally, we yield the answer to build the Iterator of Series, fulfilling our contract.

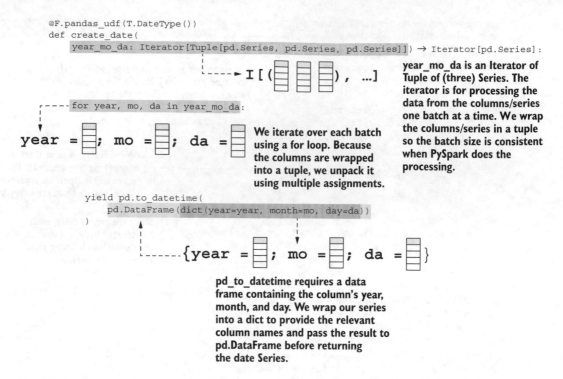

```
@F.pandas_udf(T.DateType())
def create_date(
    year_mo_da: Iterator[Tuple[pd.Series, pd.Series, pd.Series]]) -> Iterator[pd.Series]:
```

year_mo_da is an Iterator of Tuple of (three) Series. The iterator is for processing the data from the columns/series one batch at a time. We wrap the columns/series in a tuple so the batch size is consistent when PySpark does the processing.

```
for year, mo, da in year_mo_da:
```

We iterate over each batch using a for loop. Because the columns are wrapped into a tuple, we unpack it using multiple assignments.

```
yield pd.to_datetime(
    pd.DataFrame(dict(year=year, month=mo, day=da))
)
```

pd_to_datetime requires a data frame containing the column's year, month, and day. We wrap our series into a dict to provide the relevant column names and pass the result to pd.DataFrame before returning the date Series.

Figure 9.3   The transformation of three Series of values into a single date column. We iterate over each batch using a `for` loop, use multiple assignment to get the individual columns from the tuple, and pack them into a dictionary that feeds into a data frame where we can apply our `to_datetime()` function.

Listing 9.7   Assembling the date from three columns using an Iterator of multiple Series UDF

```
from typing import Tuple


@F.pandas_udf(T.DateType())
def create_date(
    year_mo_da: Iterator[Tuple[pd.Series, pd.Series, pd.Series]]
) -> Iterator[pd.Series]:
    """Merges three cols (representing Y-M-D of a date) into a Date col."""
    for year, mo, da in year_mo_da:
        yield pd.to_datetime(
            pd.DataFrame(dict(year=year, month=mo, day=da))
        )


gsod.select(
    "year", "mo", "da",
    create_date(F.col("year"), F.col("mo"), F.col("da")).alias("date"),
).distinct().show(5)
```

This concludes our overview of how to use Scalar UDFs. Scalar UDFs are very useful when you make column-level transformations, just like the functions in pyspark.sql.functions. When using any Scalar user-defined function, you need to remember that PySpark will not guarantee the order or the composition of the batches when applying it. If you follow the same "columns in, columns out" mantra we use when working with PySpark column functions, you'll do great.

> **TIP** By default, Spark will aim for 10,000 records per batch. You can customize the maximum size of each batch using the spark.sql.execution.arrow .maxRecordsPerBatch config when creating the SparkSession object; 10,000 records is a good balance for most jobs. If you are working with memory-starved executors, you might want to reduce this.

Should you need to worry about batch composition based on one or more columns, you'll learn how to apply UDFs on a GroupedData object (seen in chapter 5) to have a finer level of control over the records in the next section. We will not only create aggregate functions (e.g., sum()) but also apply functions while controlling the batches' composition.

Exercise 9.1

What are the values of WHICH_TYPE and WHICH_SIGNATURE in the following code block?

```
exo9_1 = pd.Series(["red", "blue", "blue", "yellow"])


def color_to_num(colors: WHICH_SIGNATURE) -> WHICH_SIGNATURE:
    return colors.apply(
        lambda x: {"red": 1, "blue": 2, "yellow": 3}.get(x)
    )


color_to_num(exo9_1)

# 0    1
# 1    2
# 2    2
# 3    3


color_to_num_udf = F.pandas_udf(color_to_num, WHICH_TYPE)
```

9.2 UDFs on grouped data: Aggregate and apply

This section covers UDFs in the case where you need to worry about the composition of the batches. This is useful in two cases. For completion, I provide the common names used in Spark 3 versions:

- *Group aggregate UDFs*: You need to perform aggregate functions such as count() or sum(), as we saw in chapter 5.
- *Group map UDFs*: Your data frame can be split into batches based on the values of certain columns; you then apply a function on each batch as if it were a pandas

DataFrame before combining each batch back into a Spark data frame. For instance, we could have our gsod data batched by station month and perform operations on the resulting data frames.

Both group aggregate and group map UDFs are PySpark's answer to the split-apply-combine pattern. At the core, split-apply-combine is just a series of three steps that are frequently used in data analysis:

1 *Split* your data set into logical batches (using groupby()).
2 *Apply* a function to each batch independently.
3 *Combine* the batches into a unified data set.

To be perfectly honest, I did not know this pattern's name until somebody pointed at my code one day and said, "This is some nice split-apply-combine work you did there." You probably use it intuitively as well. In the PySpark world, I see it more as a *divide and process* move, as illustrated in figure 9.4.

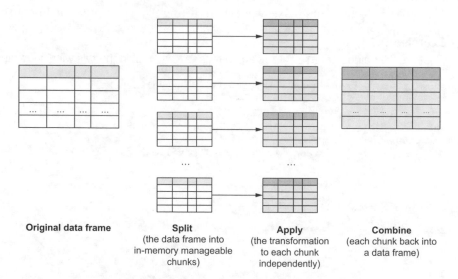

| Original data frame | Split
(the data frame into in-memory manageable chunks) | Apply
(the transformation to each chunk independently) | Combine
(each chunk back into a data frame) |

Figure 9.4   Split-apply-combine depicted visually. We batch/group the data frame and process each one with pandas before unioning them into a (Spark) data frame again.

Here, we will cover each type of UDF and illustrate how each relates to the split-apply-combine pattern. While group map and group aggregate UDFs are clubbed in the same family and both work on GroupedData objects (seen in chapter 5 when we review the groupby() method), their syntax and usage are quite different.

> **WARNING**   With great power comes great responsibility: when grouping your data frame, make sure each batch/group is "pandas-size," (i.e., it can be loaded comfortably in memory). If one or more batches is too big, you'll get an out-of-memory exception.

9.2.1 Group aggregate UDFs

> **NOTE** Only available from Spark 2.4 on. Spark 2.4 provided a `functionType` of `PandasUDFType.GROUPED_AGG` (from `pyspark.sql.functions`; see http://mng.bz/6Zmy).

This section covers the group aggregate UDF, also known as the *Series to Scalar UDF*. With such a name, we already can imagine that it shares some affinities with the Series to Series UDF seen in section 9.1.2. Unlike the Series to Series, the group aggregate UDF distills the Series received as input to a single value. In the split-apply-combine pattern, the apply stage collapses the batches into a single record based on the values of the columns we batch against.

PySpark provides the group aggregate functionality though the `groupby().agg()` pattern we learned during chapter 5. A group aggregate UDF is simply a custom aggregate function we pass as an argument to `agg()`. For this section's example, I wanted to do something a little more complex than reproducing the common aggregate functions (count, min, max, average). In listing 9.8, I compute the linear slope of the temperature for a given period using scikit-learn's `LinearRegression` object. You do not need to know scikit-learn or machine learning to follow along; I'm using basic functionality and explain each step.

> **NOTE** This is not a machine learning exercise: I am just using scikit-learn's plumbing to create a feature. Machine learning in Spark is covered in part 3 of this book. Don't take this code as robust model training!

To train a model in scikit-learn, we start by initializing the model object. In this case, I use `LinearRegression()` without any other parameters. I then `fit` the model, providing X, my feature matrix, and y, my prediction vector. In this case, since I have a single feature, I need to "reshape" my X matrix, or scikit-learn will complain about a shape mismatch. It does not change the values of the matrix whatsoever.

> **TIP** `fit()` is the common method for training an ML model. As a matter of fact, Spark ML library uses the same method when training a distributed ML model. See chapter 13 for more information.

At the end of the fit method, our `LinearRegression` object has trained a model and, in the case of a linear regression, keeps its coefficient in a `coef_` vector. Since I really only care about the coefficient, I simply extract and return it.

Listing 9.8 Creating a grouped aggregate UDF

```
from sklearn.linear_model import LinearRegression          ◁── I import the linear
                                                                 regression object from
                                                                 sklearn.linear_model.

@F.pandas_udf(T.DoubleType())
def rate_of_change_temperature(day: pd.Series, temp: pd.Series) -> float:
    """Returns the slope of the daily temperature for a given period of time."""
```

```
                  return (
I initialize the  ┌──▷  LinearRegression()
LinearRegression        .fit(X=day.astype(int).values.reshape(-1, 1), y=temp)   ◁─────┐
object.                 .coef_[0]   ◁────────┐                                         │
                  )                          │                                         │
                              Since I only have one feature,        The fit method trains the
                              I select the first value of the       model, using the day Series
                              coef_ attribute as my slope.          as a feature and the temp
                                                                    series as the prediction.
```

It's easy to apply a grouped aggregate UDF to our data frame. In listing 9.9, I groupby() the station code, name, and country, as well as the year and the month. I pass my newly created grouped aggregate function as a parameter to agg(), passing my Column objects as parameters to the UDF.

Listing 9.9   Applying our grouped aggregate UDF using agg()

```
result = gsod.groupby("stn", "year", "mo").agg(
    rate_of_change_temperature(gsod["da"], gsod["temp"]).alias(   ◁────┐
        "rt_chg_temp"                                                  │
    )                                                                  │
)                                                 Applying a grouped aggregate
                                                  UDF is the same as using a Spark
result.show(5, False)                             aggregating function: you add it as
# +------+----+---+---------------------+         an argument to the agg() method
# |stn   |year|mo |rt_chg_temp          |         of the GroupedData object.
# +------+----+---+---------------------+
# |010250|2018|12 |-0.01014397905759162 |
# |011120|2018|11 |-0.01704736746691528 |
# |011150|2018|10 |-0.013510329829648423|
# |011510|2018|03 |0.020159116598556657 |
# |011800|2018|06 |0.012645501680677372 |
# +------+----+---+---------------------+
# only showing top 5 rows
```

In this section, we created a custom aggregate function using the Series to Scalar UDF, also known at the group aggregate UDF. Following our split-apply-combine pattern, a successful group aggregate UDF usage relies on the groupby() method and uses a Series to Scalar UDF as one or more of the arguments to agg(). Like its namesake, the return value of the apply stage is a singular value, so each batch becomes a single record that gets combined in a grouped data frame. In the next section, we explore an alternative to the aggregation pattern, where the return value of the apply stage is a data frame.

9.2.2   Group map UDF

> **NOTE**   Only available from Spark 2.3+. Spark 2.3/2.4 provide a functionType of PandasUDFType.GROUPED_MAP and use the apply() method (from pyspark.sql.functions; see http://mng.bz/oa8M) and a @pandas_udf() decorator.

The second type of UDF on grouped data is the group map UDF. Unlike the group aggregate UDF, which returns a scalar value as a result over a batch, the grouped map

UDF maps over each batch and returns a (pandas) data frame that gets combined back into a single (Spark) data frame. Because of this flexibility, PySpark provides a different usage pattern (and the syntax changed greatly between Spark 2 and Spark 3; see the note at the top of this section).

Before looking at the PySpark plumbing, we focus on the pandas side of the equation. Where scalar UDFs relied on pandas Series, group map UDFs use pandas DataFrame. Each logical batch from step 1 in figure 9.4 becomes a pandas DataFrame ready for action. Our function must return a complete DataFrame, meaning that all the columns we want to display need to be returned, including the one we grouped against.

Our `scale_temperature` function in listing 9.10 looks very much like a pandas function—no `pandas_udf()` decorator (when using Spark 3) needed. pandas functions, when applied as group map UDFs, don't need any special definition. The return value data frame contains six columns: `stn`, `year`, `mo`, `da`, `temp`, and `temp_norm`. All the columns but `temp_norm` are assumed to be present in the input data frame. We create the `temp_norm` column, which holds the scaled temperature using the maximum and minimum temperature for each batch/pandas DataFrame. Since I have a division in my UDF, I am giving a reasonable value of 0.5 if the minimum temperature in my batch equals the maximum temperature. By default, pandas will give an infinite value for division by zero; PySpark will interpret this as `null`.

Listing 9.10 A group map UDF to scale temperature values

```
def scale_temperature(temp_by_day: pd.DataFrame) -> pd.DataFrame:
    """Returns a simple normalization of the temperature for a site.

    If the temperature is constant for the whole window, defaults to 0.5."""
    temp = temp_by_day.temp
    answer = temp_by_day[["stn", "year", "mo", "da", "temp"]]
    if temp.min() == temp.max():
        return answer.assign(temp_norm=0.5)
    return answer.assign(
        temp_norm=(temp - temp.min()) / (temp.max() - temp.min())
    )
```

Now that the apply is step done, the rest is a piece of cake. Just like with the group aggregate UDF, we use `groupby()` to split a data frame into manageable batches but then pass our function to the `applyInPandas()` method. The method takes a function as a first argument and a `schema` as a second. I am using the simplified DDL syntax seen in chapter 7 here; if you are more comfortable with the `StructType` syntax seen in chapter 6, it can be applied here interchangeably.

TIP Spark 2 uses the `pandas_udf()` decorator and passes the return schema as an argument, so if you're using this version, you would use the `apply()` method here.

In the next listing, we group our data frame using three columns: `stn`, `year`, and `mo`. Each batch will represent a station-month's worth of observation. My UDF has six columns in its return value; the data frame after `applyInPandas()` has the same six.

Listing 9.11   Split-apply-combing in PySpark

```
gsod_map = gsod.groupby("stn", "year", "mo").applyInPandas(
    scale_temperature,
    schema=(
        "stn string, year string, mo string, "
        "da string, temp double, temp_norm double"
    ),
)

gsod_map.show(5, False)
# +------+----+---+---+----+-------------------+
# |stn   |year|mo |da |temp|temp_norm          |
# +------+----+---+---+----+-------------------+
# |010250|2018|12 |08 |21.8|0.06282722513089001|
# |010250|2018|12 |27 |28.3|0.40314136125654443|
# |010250|2018|12 |31 |29.1|0.4450261780104712 |
# |010250|2018|12 |19 |27.6|0.36649214659685864|
# |010250|2018|12 |04 |36.6|0.8376963350785339 |
# +------+----+---+---+----+-------------------+
```

Group map UDFs are highly flexible constructs: as long as you respect the schema you provide to the `applyInPandas()`, Spark will not require that you keep the same (or any) number of records. This is as close as we will get to treating a Spark data frame like a predetermined collection (via `groupby()`) of a pandas DataFrame. If you do not care about the chunk composition but need the flexibility of "pandas DataFrame in, pandas DataFrame out," see the `mapInPandas()` method of the PySpark `DataFrame` object: it reuses the iterator pattern seen in section 9.1.3 but applies it to a full data frame instead of a number of series.

Because of that flexibility, group map UDFs are often those I see developers having the hardest time to get right. This is where your pen and paper comes in: map your inputs and outputs, taking the time to ensure that the structure of your data frame stays consistent.

The next and final section of this chapter summarizes how to decide between the cornucopia of pandas UDFs. By utilizing a few questions, you'll know which one to use, every time.

9.3   *What to use, when*

This small final section is about making the right choice regarding pandas UDFs. Because each one fills a specific use case, I think that the best way to approach this is to use the properties of each and ask ourselves a few questions about our use case. This way, there is no more hesitation!

In figure 9.5, I provide a small decision tree to follow when you hesitate about which pandas UDF to use. Here's a summary:

- If you need to control how the batches are made, you need to use a grouped data UDF. If the return value is scalar, group aggregate, or otherwise, use a group map and return a transformed (complete) data frame.
- If you only want batches, you have more options. The most flexible is `mapIn-Pandas()`, where an iterator of pandas DataFrame comes in and a transformed one comes out. This is very useful when you want to distribute a pandas/local data transformation on the whole data frame, such as with inference of local ML models. Use it if you work with most of the columns from the data frame, and use a Series to Series UDF if you only need a few columns.
- If you have a cold-start process, use a Iterator of Series/multiple Series UDF, depending on the number of columns you need within your UDF.
- Finally, if you only need to transform some columns using pandas, a Series to Series UDF is the way to go.

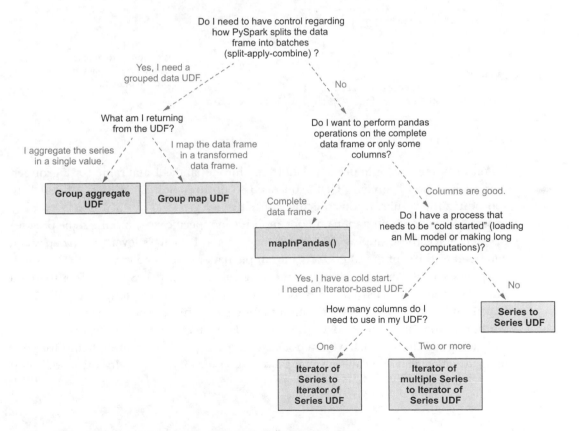

Figure 9.5   A summary of the decision-making for selecting the UDF

pandas UDFs are quite useful for extending PySpark with transformations that are not included in the pyspark.sql module. I find that they're also quite easy to understand but pretty hard to get right. I finish this chapter with a few pointers on testing out and debugging your pandas UDF.

The most important aspect of a pandas UDF (and any UDF) is that it needs to work on the nondistributed version of your data. For regular UDFs, this means passing *any argument of the type of values you expect* should yield an answer. For instance, if you divide an array of values by another one, you need to cover the case of dividing by zero. The same is true for any pandas UDF: you need to be lenient with the input you accept and strict with the output you provide.

To test your pandas UDF, my favorite strategy is to bring a sample of the data using the func() method of my UDF. This way, I can play around in the REPL until I get it just right, then promote it to my script. I show an example of the rate_of_change_-temperature() UDF, applied locally, in the next listing.

Listing 9.12   Moving one station, one month's worth of data into a local pandas DataFrame

```
gsod_local = gsod.where(
    "year = '2018' and mo = '08' and stn = '710920'"
).toPandas()


print(
    rate_of_change_temperature.func(          ◁──┐  Using func() to access
        gsod_local["da"], gsod_local["temp_norm"]  │  the underlying pandas
    )                                              │  function of our UDF
)
# -0.007830974115511494
```

When bringing a sample of your data frame into a pandas DataFrame for a grouped map or grouped aggregate UDF, you need to ensure you're getting a full batch to reproduce the results. In our specific case, since we grouped by "station", "year", "month", I brought one station and one month (one specific year/month, to be precise) of data. Since the grouping of the data happens at PySpark's level (via groupby()), you need to think of the filters for your sample data in the same way.

pandas UDFs are probably the most powerful feature PySpark offers for data manipulation. This chapter covered the most useful and frequent types. With the popularity of the Python programming language within the Spark ecosystem, I am confident that new types of optimized UDFs will make their entrance. pandas, PySpark—you no longer have to choose. Use the right tool for the job and for your data, knowing that you can leverage powerful pandas UDFs to scale your code when it make sense.

Summary

- pandas UDFs allow you to take code that works on a pandas DataFrame and scale it to the Spark data frame structure. Efficient serialization between the two data structures is ensured by PyArrow.
- We can group pandas UDFs into two main families, depending on the level of control we need over the batches. Series and Iterator of Series (and Iterator of DataFrame/mapInPandas) will batch efficiently, with the user having no control over the batch composition.
- If you need control over the contents of each batch, you can use grouped data UDFs with the split-apply-combine programming pattern. PySpark provides access to the values inside each batch of a GroupedData object, either as a Series (group aggregate UDF) or as a data frame (group map UDF).

Additional exercises

Exercise 9.2

Using the following definitions, create a temp_to_temp(value, from_temp, to_temp) that takes a numerical value in from_temp degrees and converts it to to degrees. Use a pandas UDF this time (we did the same exercise in chapter 8).

- C = (F - 32) * 5 / 9 (Celsius)
- K = C + 273.15 (Kelvin)
- R = F + 459.67 (Rankine)

Exercise 9.3

Modify the following code block to use Celsius degrees instead of Fahrenheit. How is the result of the UDF different if applied to the same data frame?

```
def scale_temperature(temp_by_day: pd.DataFrame) -> pd.DataFrame:
    """Returns a simple normalization of the temperature for a site.

    If the temperature is constant for the whole window, defaults to 0.5."""
    temp = temp_by_day.temp
    answer = temp_by_day[["stn", "year", "mo", "da", "temp"]]
    if temp.min() == temp.max():
        return answer.assign(temp_norm=0.5)
    return answer.assign(
        temp_norm=(temp - temp.min()) / (temp.max() - temp.min())
    )
```

Exercise 9.4

Complete the schema of the following code block, using scale_temperature_C from the previous exercise. What happens if we apply our group map UDF like so instead?

```
gsod_exo = gsod.groupby("year", "mo").applyInPandas(scale_temperature, schema=???)
```

Exercise 9.5

Modify the following code block to return both the intercept of the linear regression as well as the slope in an ArrayType. (Hint: The intercept is in the intercept_ attribute of the fitted model.)

```python
from sklearn.linear_model import LinearRegression


@F.pandas_udf(T.DoubleType())
def rate_of_change_temperature(day: pd.Series, temp: pd.Series) -> float:
    """Returns the slope of the daily temperature for a given period of
     time."""
    return (
        LinearRegression()
        .fit(X=day.astype("int").values.reshape(-1, 1), y=temp)
        .coef_[0]
    )
```

Your data under a different lens: Window functions

When performing data analysis or feature engineering (which is my favorite part of machine learning; see chapter 13), nothing makes me quite as happy as window functions. On first glance, they look like a watered-down version of the split-apply-combine pattern introduced in chapter 9. Then you open the blinds and bam—powerful manipulations in a short, expressive body of code.

Those who don't know window functions are bound to reimplement its functionality poorly. This has been my experience coaching data analysts, scientists, and engineers. If you find yourself struggling to

215

- Rank records
- Identify the top/bottom record according to a set of conditions
- Get a value from a previous observation in a table (e.g., using our temperature data frame from chapter 9 and asking "What was the temperature yesterday?")
- Build trended features (i.e., features that summarize past observations, such as the average of the observations for the previous week)

you will find that window functions will multiply your productivity and simplify your code.

Window functions fill a niche between group aggregate (`groupBy().agg()`) and group map UDF (`groupBy().apply()`) transformations, both seen in chapter 9. Both rely on *partitioning* to split the data frame based on a predicate. A group aggregate transformation will yield one record per grouping, while a group map UDF allows for any shape of a resulting data frame; a window function always keeps the dimensions of the data frame intact. Window functions have a secret weapon in the *window frame* that we define within a partition: it determines which records are included in the application of the function.

Window functions are mostly used for creating new columns, so they leverage some familiar methods, such as `select()` and `withColumn()`. Because we already are familiar with the syntax for adding columns, I approach this chapter differently. First, we look at how we can emulate a simple window function by relying on concepts we already know, such as the `groupby` and `join` methods. Then we get familiar with the two components of a window function: the window spec and the function itself. I then apply and dissect the three main types of window functions (summarizing, ranking, and analytical). Once you are equipped with these building blocks of window function application, we break open the window spec by introducing ordered and bounded windows and window frames. Finally, we go full circle and introduce UDF as window functions.

This chapter builds heavily on the content from chapters 5 and 9. Likewise, each section builds heavily on the one that precedes it. Window functions are themselves not complicated, but there is a lot of new terminology, and the behavior of the functions may not be intuitive at first. If you get lost, make sure you work carefully through the examples. Because the best way to learn is by doing, try the exercises throughout and at the end of the chapter. As always, answers are available in appendix A.

10.1 Growing and using a simple window function

When learning a new concept, I find that I have a much easier time when I am able to build it from basic principles, using what I already know. This is exactly what happened when I learned about window functions: I started by reproducing their behavior using a mess of SQL instructions. After I was done, it was obvious why window functions are so useful. Imagine my joy when I found them woven into PySpark, with a beautiful Python API to boot.

In this section, we follow the same path: I start by reproducing a simple window function using techniques from past chapters. Then I introduce the syntax for window functions and how they simplify your data transformation logic. My hope is that you'll get as excited as I did when window functions finally "clicked" for me.

For this section, we reuse the temperature data set from chapter 8; the data set contains weather observations for a series of stations, summarized by day. Window functions especially shine when working with time series-like data (e.g., daily observations of temperature) because you can slice the data by day, month, or year and get useful statistics. If you want to use the data from BigQuery, use the code from chapter 9, keeping as many (or as little) years of data you want. For those who prefer a local-first approach, the book's repository contains three years of data in Parquet format (see listing 10.1).

> **Listing 10.1 Reading the data necessary: GSOD NOAA weather data**

```
gsod = spark.read.parquet("./data/window/gsod.parquet")
```

Now that we're equipped with the data, let's start asking questions! The next sections illustrate the thought process behind a window function, before diving right into the terminology and the syntax.

10.1.1 *Identifying the coldest day of each year, the long way*

In this section, we emulate a simple window function through functionality we learned in previous chapters—most noticeably in chapter 5 using the `join()` method. The idea is to provide an intuitive sense for window functions and remove some of the magic surrounding them. To illustrate this, we start with simple questions to ask our data frame: *when* and *where* were the lowest temperature recorded each year? In other words, we want a data frame containing three records, one for each year and showing the station, the date (year, month, day), and the temperature of the coldest day recorded for that year.

Let's map the thought process. First, we will get a data frame containing the coldest temperature for each year. This will give us two of the columns (year, and temp) and their values. In listing 10.2, we create the `coldest_temp` data frame, which takes our historical data and groups by the year column, and we extract the minimum temp through the `min()` aggregate function applied through the `agg()`. If the syntax is a little cloudy, head to chapter 5 for a refresher on grouped data.

> **Listing 10.2 Computing the lowest temperature for each year using `groupBy()`**

```
coldest_temp = gsod.groupby("year").agg(F.min("temp").alias("temp"))
coldest_temp.orderBy("temp").show()
```

```
# +----+------+
# |year|  temp|
# +----+------+
# |2017|-114.7|
# |2018|-113.5|
# |2019|-114.7|
# +----+------+
```

People, Earth is cold!

This provides the year and the temperature, which are about 40% of the original ask. To get the other three columns (mo, da, stn), we can use a left-semi join on the original table, using the results of coldest_temp to resolve the join. In listing 10.3, we join gsod to coldest_temp using a left-semi equi-join on the year and temp columns (see chapter 5 for more information on left-semi and equi-joins!). Because coldest_temp only contains the coldest temperature for each year, the left semi-join keeps only the records from gsod that correspond to that year-temperature pair; this is equivalent to keeping only the records where the temperature was coldest for each year.

> **Listing 10.3   Using a left semi-join for computing the coldest station/day for each year**

```
coldest_when = gsod.join(
    coldest_temp, how="left_semi", on=["year", "temp"]
).select("stn", "year", "mo", "da", "temp")

coldest_when.orderBy("year", "mo", "da").show()

# +------+----+---+---+------+
# |   stn|year| mo| da|  temp|
# +------+----+---+---+------+
# |896250|2017| 06| 20|-114.7|
# |896060|2018| 08| 27|-113.5|
# |895770|2019| 06| 15|-114.7|
# +------+----+---+---+------+
```

In listing 10.2 and listing 10.3 we are performing a join between the gsod table and, well, something coming from the gsod table. A *self-join*, which is when you join a table with itself, is often considered an anti-pattern for data manipulation. While it's not technically wrong, it can be slow and make the code look more complex than it needs to be. It also looks a little odd. Joining tables make sense when you want to link data contained into two or more tables. Joining a table with itself feels redundant, as we can see in figure 10.1: the data is already in the (one) table!

Fortunately, a window function gives you the same result faster, and with less code clutter. In the next section, we'll reproduce the same data transformation using a window function, and simplify and speed up our data transformation code.

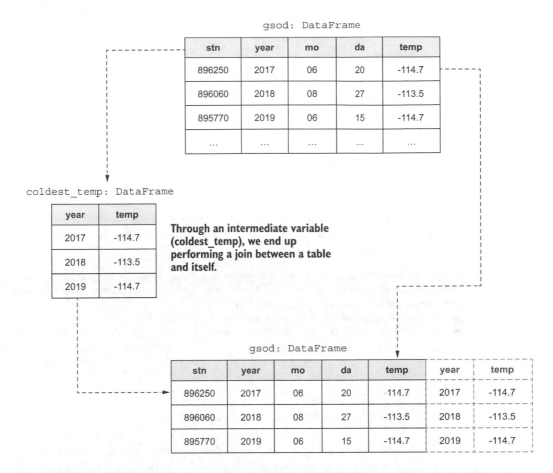

Figure 10.1 A self-join happens when a table is joined with itself. You can replace most self-joins by window functions.

10.1.2 Creating and using a simple window function to get the coldest days

This section introduces window functions by replacing the self-join example of the previous section. I introduce the `Window` object and parameterize it to split a data frame over column values. We then apply the window over a data frame, using the traditional selector approach.

At the beginning of the chapter, I drew a parallel between window functions and the split-apply-combine pattern I covered when introducing pandas group map UDF (chapter 8). To stay consistent with the `Window` function terminology, which comes from SQL (see chapter 7), I use different vocabulary for the three stages of the split-apply-combine pattern:

- Instead of splitting, we'll *partition* the data frame.
- Instead of applying, we'll *select* values *over the window*.

- The `combine`/`union` operation is implicit (i.e., not explicitly coded) in a window function.

NOTE Why use a different vocabulary here? Window functions are concepts from the SQL world, where the split-apply-combine pattern comes from the data analysis world. Different worlds, different vocabulary!

Window functions apply over a window of data split according to the values on a column. Each split, called a partition, gets the window function applied to each of its records as if they were independent data frames. The result then gets unioned back into a single data frame. In listing 10.4, I create the window, partitioning according to the values in column `year`. The `Window` class is a builder class, just like with `SparkSession.builder`: we chain the parameterization by appending methods after the `Window` class identifier. The result is a `WindowSpec` object that contains the information about the parameterization.

Listing 10.4   Creating a `WindowSpec` object by using the `Window` builder class

We import Window from pyspark.sql.window. Since it's the only object we'll use for window functions, there's no need import the whole module.

To partition according to the values of one or more columns, we pass the column name (or a Column object) to the partitionBy() method.

```
from pyspark.sql.window import Window

each_year = Window.partitionBy("year")

print(each_year)
# <pyspark.sql.window.WindowSpec object at 0x7f978fc8e6a0>
```

A `WindowSpec` object is nothing more than a blueprint for an eventual window function. In our case, in listing 10.4, we created a window specification called `each_year` that instructs the window application to split the data frame according to the values in the year column. The real magic happens when you apply the window function to your data frame. For our first window function application, I print the whole code, reproducing the self-join approach in section 10.1.1 before going through it line by line. See the difference between the window application (listing 10.6) and the left semi-join.

Listing 10.5   Using a left semi-join for computing the coldest station/day for each year

```
coldest_when = gsod.join(
    coldest_temp, how="left_semi", on=["year", "temp"]
).select("stn", "year", "mo", "da", "temp")

coldest_when.orderBy("year", "mo", "da").show()

# +------+----+---+---+------+
# |   stn|year| mo| da|  temp|
# +------+----+---+---+------+
# |896250|2017| 06| 20|-114.7|
# |896060|2018| 08| 27|-113.5|
```

```
#  |895770|2019| 06| 15|-114.7|
#  +------+----+---+---+------+
```

```
(gsod
 .withColumn("min_temp", F.min("temp").over(each_year))
  .where("temp = min_temp")
 .select("year", "mo", "da", "stn", "temp")
 .orderBy("year", "mo", "da")
 .show())
#  +----+---+---+------+------+
#  |year| mo| da|   stn|  temp|
#  +----+---+---+------+------+
#  |2017| 06| 20|896250|-114.7|
#  |2018| 08| 27|896060|-113.5|
#  |2019| 06| 15|895770|-114.7|
#  +----+---+---+------+------+
```

> We select the minimum temperature over the defined window (for each year).

It's time for some code unpacking. Through the `withColumn()` method we define a column, `min_temp`, that collects the minimum of the `temp` column. Now, rather than picking the minimum temperature of the whole data frame, the `min()` is applied *over* the window specification we defined, using the `over()` method. For each window partition, Spark computes the minimum and then broadcasts the value over each record. This is an important distinction compared to aggregating functions or UDF: in the case of a window function, *the number of records in the data frame does not change.* Although `min()` is an aggregate function, since it's applied with the `over()` method, every record in the window has the minimum value appended. The same would apply for any other aggregate function from `pyspark.sql.functions`, such as `sum()`, `avg()`, `min()`, `max()`, and `count()`.

Window functions are just methods on columns (almost)

Since a window function is applied though a method on a `Column` object, you can also apply them in a `select()`. You can also apply more than one window (or different ones) within the same `select()`. Spark won't allow you to use a window directly in a `groupby()` or `where()` method, where it'll spit an `AnalysisException`. If you want to group by or filter according to the result of a window function, "materialize" the column using `select()` or `withColumn()` before using the desired operation.

As an example, listing 10.6 could be rewritten, with the window definition put into the select. Because the window applies on a column-by-column basis, you can have multiple window applications within a select statement.

Listing 10.7 Using a window function within a `select()` method

```
gsod.select(
    "year",
    "mo",
```

continued

```
    "da",
    "stn",
    "temp",
    F.min("temp").over(each_year).alias("min_temp"),
).where(
    "temp = min_temp"
).drop(
    "min_temp"
).orderBy(
    "year", "mo", "da"
).show()
```

We drop min_temp as it served its purpose during the where clause and is no longer needed (it'll always be equal to temp in the resulting data frame).

Review the end-of-chapter exercises to experiment with multiple windows applications.

Under the hood, PySpark realizes the window spec when applied to a column. I defined a rather simple window spec here: partition the data frame according to the values of the year column. Just like with the split-apply-combine pattern, we partition the data frame according to the year column values.

> **TIP** You can partitionBy() by more than one column! Just add more column names to the partitionBy() method.

For each window partition (see the *But data frames already have partitions!* sidebar at the end of the section), we compute the aggregate function (here, min()), before broadcasting the result of each record. In plain English, we compute the minimum temperature for each year and append it as a column for each record of this year. I creatively name the new column min_temp.

Next, we need to keep only the records where the temperature is actually the minimum for the year. For this, we simply need to filter() (or where()) to keep only the records where temp = min_temp. Because the window function application gives each record a min_temp field corresponding to the minimum temperature for that year, we are back to our regular arsenal of data manipulation tricks.

That's all, folks! We have our very first window function. This was a purposefully simple example to teach the concept of a window spec, window function, and window partition. In the next section, I compare the application and speed of both approaches and explain why window functions are easier, friendlier, and faster.

But data frames already have partitions!

Once again, we're having a vocabulary problem. Since the beginning of the book, *partition* has referred to the physical splits of the data on each executor node. Now we are also using partitions with window functions to mean logical splits of the data, which may or may not be equal to the Spark physical ones.

Unfortunately, most of the literature online will not tell you which partition they refer to. But once you've internalized both Spark and window function concepts, it'll be easy to know which is which. For this chapter, I'll use *window partitions* when talking about the logical partitions made by the application of a window spec.

gsod: DataFrame

stn	year	mo	da	temp
896250	2017	06	20	-114.7
896060	2018	08	27	-113.5
895770	2019	06	15	-114.7
719200	2017	10	09	60.5
917350	2018	04	21	82.6
076470	2018	06	07	65.0
041680	2019	02	19	16.1
949110	2019	11	23	54.9

We partitioned the data set according to the column.

stn	year	mo	da	temp
896250	2017	06	20	-114.7
719200	2017	10	09	60.5

stn	year	mo	da	temp
896060	2018	08	27	-113.5
917350	2018	04	21	82.6
076470	2018	06	07	65.0

stn	year	mo	da	temp
041680	2019	02	19	16.1
949110	2019	11	23	54.9
895770	2019	06	15	-114.7

Figure 10.2 We partition the gsod data frame according to the year column and compute the minimum temperature for each partition. Each record belonging to the partition gets the minimum temperature appended. The resulting data frame contains the same number of records, but with a new column, min_temp, that contains the coldest temperature for the year.

10.1.3 Comparing both approaches

In this section, I compare both the self-join and window function approaches from a code readability perspective. We also touch on performance implications of windows versus joins. When performing data transformation and analysis, code clarity and performance are the two most important considerations for a working body of code; since we have two approaches that perform the same work, it makes sense to compare them from a clarity and performance perspective.

Compared to the self-join approach, using a window function makes your intention more clear. With a window named each_year, the code snippet F.min("temp") .over(each_year) almost reads like an English sentence. The self-join approach accomplishes the same thing, but at the expense of a slightly more cryptic code: *why am I joining this table to itself?*

Performance wise, window functions avoid potentially costly self-joins. When working with large data sets, the data frame only has to be split into window partitions before performing a function over the (smaller) partitions. When you consider that Spark's operating model is splitting large data sets across multiple nodes, it makes a lot of sense.

Finding which approach works fastest will depend on the size of the data, the memory available (see chapter 11 for an overview of how memory is used in Spark), and how complex the join/window operation is. I tend to overwhelmingly prefer window functions, as they are more clear and express my intent more clearly as well. As I repeat to myself when I code, *make it work, make it clear, then make it fast!*

Finally, and this will be the content of the next sections, window functions are much more flexible than merely computing aggregated measurements over a given window. Next, I introduce ranking and analytical functions, which provide a new window (get it?) over your data. The *summarize-and-join* approach will quickly fall short!

Exercise 10.1

Using the `gsod` data frame, which window spec that, once applied, could generate the hottest station for each day?

a `Window.partitionBy("da")`

b `Window.partitionBy("stn", "da")`

c `Window.partitionBy("year", "mo", "da")`

d `Window.partitionBy("stn", "year", "mo", "da")`

e None of the above

10.2 Beyond summarizing: Using ranking and analytical functions

In this section, I cover the two other families of functions that can be applied over a window. Both families provide additional functionality to the humble window. Together, those families of functions allow performance of a wider range of operations versus aggregate functions such as `count()`, `sum()`, or `min()`:

- The *ranking* family, which provides information about rank (first, second, all the way to last), n-tiles, and the ever so useful row number
- The *analytical* family, which, despite its namesake, covers a variety of behaviors not related to summary or ranking.

Both provide information over a window that isn't easy to obtain via other SQL-esque functionality (trying to torture the SQL language to reproduce window function behavior using only basic SQL functionality is left as an exercise if you're really into useless coding puzzles). Because they add new functionality to the window, I also cover how to order values in a data frame (which is very useful when you want to rank records).

For this section, I use a much smaller data frame—keeping 10 records and only the `stn`, `year`, `mo`, `da`, `temp`, and `count_temp` columns—so that we can see it in its entirety when `show()`ing it. I find that this helps tremendously in understanding what's happening. This new data frame is called `gsod_light` and is available (in Parquet format, a data format optimized for rapid retrieval of column data; see https://databricks.com/glossary/what-is-parquet) in the book's repository. All the examples can also be run using the original `gsod` data frame or even over more years, should you have a more powerful cluster readily available.

Listing 10.8 Reading `gsod_light` from the book's code repository

```
gsod_light = spark.read.parquet("./data/window/gsod_light.parquet")

gsod_light.show()
# +------+----+---+---+----+----------+
# |   stn|year| mo| da|temp|count_temp|
# +------+----+---+---+----+----------+
# |994979|2017| 12| 11|21.3|        21|
# |998012|2017| 03| 02|31.4|        24|
# |719200|2017| 10| 09|60.5|        11|
# |917350|2018| 04| 21|82.6|         9|
# |076470|2018| 06| 07|65.0|        24|
# |996470|2018| 03| 12|55.6|        12|
# |041680|2019| 02| 19|16.1|        15|
# |949110|2019| 11| 23|54.9|        14|
# |998252|2019| 04| 18|44.7|        11|
# |998166|2019| 03| 20|34.8|        12|
# +------+----+---+---+----+----------+
```

Now that we have a small but easy-to-reason-about data frame, let's explore ranking functions.

10.2.1 Ranking functions: Quick, who's first?

This section covers ranking functions: nonconsecutive ranks with `rank()`, consecutive ranks with `dense_rank()`, percentile ranks with `percent_rank()`, tiles with `ntile()`, and finally a bare row number with `row_number()`. Ranking functions are used for getting the top (or bottom) record for each window partition, or, more generally, for getting an order according to some column's value. For example, if you wanted to get the top three hottest days for each station/month, a ranking function would make this a walk in the park. Because ranking functions behave quite similarly to one another, they are better introduced in one fell swoop. Have no fear; I promise it won't read like a technical manual.

Ranking functions have one sole purpose in life: to rank records based on the value of a field. Because of this, we need to order the values within a window. Enter the `orderBy()` method for windows. In listing 10.9, I create a new window, `temp_per_month_asc`, which partitions the data frame according to the `mo` column, ordering each record in the partition according to the `count_temp` column. Just like when ordering a data frame, `orderBy()` will sort the values in ascending order.

> **TIP** When naming my windows, I like to give them names, so they read well when reading the code. In this case, I can read the code and know that my column will be over each month, ordering by the count of temperature recorded. No need to add a `_window` suffix.

Listing 10.9   An ordered version of the month-partitioned window

```
temp_per_month_asc = Window.partitionBy("mo").orderBy("count_temp")
```

Our window partitions are ordered by the values in the mo column.

Within each window, the records will be ordered according to the value in the count_temp column.

GOLD, SILVER, BRONZE: SIMPLE RANKING USING RANK()

This section covers the simplest and most intuitive form of ranking, using the `rank()` function. With `rank()`, each record gets a position based on the value contained in one (or more) columns. Identical values have identical ranks—just like medalists in the Olympics, where the same score/time yields the same rank (unless you cheat!).

`rank()` takes no parameters since it ranks according to the `orderBy()` method from the window spec; it would not make sense to order according to one column but rank according to another.

Listing 10.10   The `rank()` according to the value of the `count_temp` column

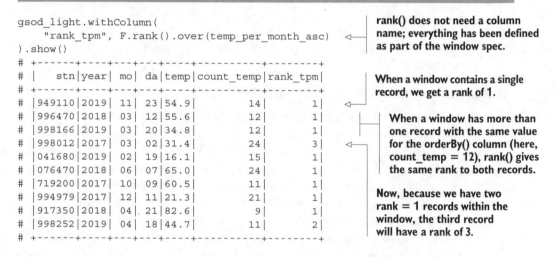

```
gsod_light.withColumn(
    "rank_tpm", F.rank().over(temp_per_month_asc)
).show()
# +------+----+---+---+----+----------+--------+
# |   stn|year| mo| da|temp|count_temp|rank_tpm|
# +------+----+---+---+----+----------+--------+
# |949110|2019| 11| 23|54.9|        14|       1|
# |996470|2018| 03| 12|55.6|        12|       1|
# |998166|2019| 03| 20|34.8|        12|       1|
# |998012|2017| 03| 02|31.4|        24|       3|
# |041680|2019| 02| 19|16.1|        15|       1|
# |076470|2018| 06| 07|65.0|        24|       1|
# |719200|2017| 10| 09|60.5|        11|       1|
# |994979|2017| 12| 11|21.3|        21|       1|
# |917350|2018| 04| 21|82.6|         9|       1|
# |998252|2019| 04| 18|44.7|        11|       2|
# +------+----+---+---+----+----------+--------+
```

rank() does not need a column name; everything has been defined as part of the window spec.

When a window contains a single record, we get a rank of 1.

When a window has more than one record with the same value for the orderBy() column (here, count_temp = 12), rank() gives the same rank to both records.

Now, because we have two rank = 1 records within the window, the third record will have a rank of 3.

The function `rank()` provides nonconsecutive ranks for each record, based on the value of the ordered value, or the column(s) provided in the `orderBy()` method of the window spec we call. In listing 10.10, for each window, the lower the `count_temp`, the lower the rank. When two records have the same ordered value, their ranks are the same. We say that the rank is nonconsecutive because, when you have multiple records that tie for a rank, the next one will be offset by the number of ties. For instance, for mo = 03, we have two records with `count_temp = 12`: both are rank 1. The next record (`count_temp = 24`) has a position of 3 rather than 2, because two records tied for the first position.

NO TIES WHEN RANKING: USING DENSE_RANK()

What if we want, say, a denser ranking that would allocate consecutive ranks for records? Enter dense_rank(). The same principle as rank() applies, where ties share the same rank, but there won't be any gap between the ranks: 1, 2, 3, and so on. This is practical when you want the second (or third, or any ordinal position) value over a window, rather than the record.

Listing 10.11   Avoiding gaps in ranking using dense_rank()

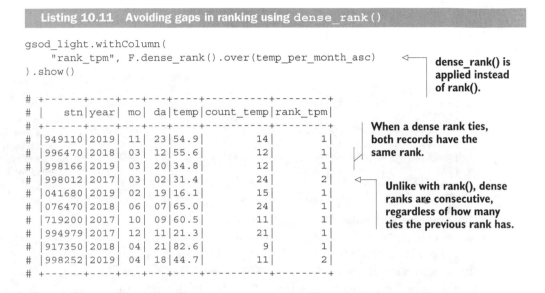

```
gsod_light.withColumn(
    "rank_tpm", F.dense_rank().over(temp_per_month_asc)    ←  dense_rank() is
).show()                                                      applied instead
                                                              of rank().

# +------+----+---+---+----+----------+--------+
# |   stn|year| mo| da|temp|count_temp|rank_tpm|
# +------+----+---+---+----+----------+--------+
# |949110|2019| 11| 23|54.9|        14|       1|           When a dense rank ties,
# |996470|2018| 03| 12|55.6|        12|       1|           both records have the
# |998166|2019| 03| 20|34.8|        12|       1|           same rank.
# |998012|2017| 03| 02|31.4|        24|       2|           Unlike with rank(), dense
# |041680|2019| 02| 19|16.1|        15|       1|           ranks are consecutive,
# |076470|2018| 06| 07|65.0|        24|       1|           regardless of how many
# |719200|2017| 10| 09|60.5|        11|       1|           ties the previous rank has.
# |994979|2017| 12| 11|21.3|        21|       1|
# |917350|2018| 04| 21|82.6|         9|       1|
# |998252|2019| 04| 18|44.7|        11|       2|
# +------+----+---+---+----+----------+--------+
```

The three remaining ranking functions, percent_rank(), ntile(), and row_number(), are more niche but still useful. I find them better explained visually.

RANKING? SCORING? PERCENT_RANK() GIVES YOU BOTH!

Ranking is usually thought of as an ordinal operation: first, second, third, and so on. What if you want something closer to a scope, perhaps even a percentage that would reflect where a record stands compared to its peers in the same window partition? Enter percent_rank().

For every window, percent_rank() will compute the percentage rank (between zero and one) based on the ordered value. For those who are mathematically inclined, the formula is as follows.

$$\frac{\text{\# records with a lower value than the current one}}{\text{\# of records in the window} - 1}$$

Listing 10.12   Computing percentage rank for every recorded temperature per year

```
temp_each_year = each_year.orderBy("temp")

gsod_light.withColumn(
    "rank_tpm", F.percent_rank().over(temp_each_year)
).show()
```

> You can create a window spec from another window spec by chaining additional methods on it. Here, I create an ordered version of each_year, which partitions the records according to year.

```
# +------+----+---+---+----+----------+------------------+
# |   stn|year| mo| da|temp|count_temp|          rank_tpm|
# +------+----+---+---+----+----------+------------------+
# |041680|2019| 02| 19|16.1|        15|               0.0|
# |998166|2019| 03| 20|34.8|        12|0.3333333333333333|
# |998252|2019| 04| 18|44.7|        11|0.6666666666666666|
# |949110|2019| 11| 23|54.9|        14|               1.0|
# |994979|2017| 12| 11|21.3|        21|               0.0|
# |998012|2017| 03| 02|31.4|        24|               0.5|
# |719200|2017| 10| 09|60.5|        11|               1.0|
# |996470|2018| 03| 12|55.6|        12|               0.0|
# |076470|2018| 06| 07|65.0|        24|               0.5|
# |917350|2018| 04| 21|82.6|         9|               1.0|
# +------+----+---+---+----+----------+------------------+
```

> For example, this record has two records in 2019 with a value of less than 44.7 and a total of four records in the window: $2 \div (4 - 1) = 0.666$.

CREATING BUCKETS BASED ON RANKS, USING NTILE()

This section covers a handy function that allows you to create an arbitrary number of buckets (called *tiles*) based on the rank of your data. You might have heard of quartiles (4 tiles), quintiles (5), deciles (10), or even percentiles (100). The ntile() computes n-tile for a given parameter n. The code in the next listing is visually depicted in figure 10.3.

Listing 10.13   Computing the two-tile value over the window

```
gsod_light.withColumn("rank_tpm", F.ntile(2).over(temp_each_year)).show()
```

```
# +------+----+---+---+----+----------+--------+
# |   stn|year| mo| da|temp|count_temp|rank_tpm|
# +------+----+---+---+----+----------+--------+
# |041680|2019| 02| 19|16.1|        15|       1|
# |998166|2019| 03| 20|34.8|        12|       1|
# |998252|2019| 04| 18|44.7|        11|       2|
# |949110|2019| 11| 23|54.9|        14|       2|
# |994979|2017| 12| 11|21.3|        21|       1|
# |998012|2017| 03| 02|31.4|        24|       1|
# |719200|2017| 10| 09|60.5|        11|       2|
# |996470|2018| 03| 12|55.6|        12|       1|
# |076470|2018| 06| 07|65.0|        24|       1|
# |917350|2018| 04| 21|82.6|         9|       2|
# +------+----+---+---+----+----------+--------+
```

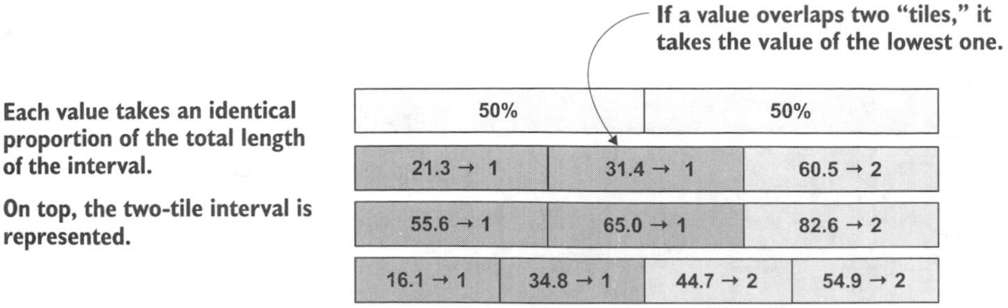

If a value overlaps two "tiles," it takes the value of the lowest one.

Each value takes an identical proportion of the total length of the interval.

On top, the two-tile interval is represented.

50%		50%

21.3 → 1	31.4 → 1	60.5 → 2
55.6 → 1	65.0 → 1	82.6 → 2

16.1 → 1	34.8 → 1	44.7 → 2	54.9 → 2

Figure 10.3 Two-tile for the three window partitions in `gsod_light`. If we consider each window to be a rectangle, each value takes the same space within that rectangle. With two tiles, the values under the 50% mark (including those overlapping) are in the first tile, whereas the ones fully over are in the second.

PLAIN ROW NUMBERS USING ROW_NUMBER()

This section covers `row_number()`, which does exactly that: given an ordered window, it'll give an increasing rank (1, 2, 3, . . .) regardless of the ties (the row number of tied records is nondeterministic, so if you need to have reproducible results, make sure you order each window so that there are no ties). This is identical to indexing each window.

Listing 10.14 Numbering records within each window partition using `row_number()`

```
gsod_light.withColumn(
    "rank_tpm", F.row_number().over(temp_each_year)
).show()

# +------+----+---+---+----+----------+--------+
# |   stn|year| mo| da|temp|count_temp|rank_tpm|
# +------+----+---+---+----+----------+--------+
# |041680|2019| 02| 19|16.1|        15|       1|
# |998166|2019| 03| 20|34.8|        12|       2|
# |998252|2019| 04| 18|44.7|        11|       3|
# |949110|2019| 11| 23|54.9|        14|       4|
# |994979|2017| 12| 11|21.3|        21|       1|
# |998012|2017| 03| 02|31.4|        24|       2|
# |719200|2017| 10| 09|60.5|        11|       3|
# |996470|2018| 03| 12|55.6|        12|       1|
# |076470|2018| 06| 07|65.0|        24|       2|
# |917350|2018| 04| 21|82.6|         9|       3|
# +------+----+---+---+----+----------+--------+
```

row_number() will give you strictly increasing ranks for every record in your window.

LOSERS FIRST: ORDERING YOUR WINDOWSPEC USING ORDERBY()

Finally, what if we want to reverse the order of our window? Unlike the `orderBy()` method on the data frame, the `orderBy()` method on a window does not have an ascending parameter we can use. We need to resort to the `desc()` method on the `Column` object directly. It's a minor annoyance that's easily solved for.

Listing 10.15   Creating a window with a descending-ordered column

```
temp_per_month_desc = Window.partitionBy("mo").orderBy(
    F.col("count_temp").desc()
)
gsod_light.withColumn(
    "row_number", F.row_number().over(temp_per_month_desc)
).show()
```

By default, a column will be ordered with ascending values. Passing the desc() method will reverse that order for that column.

```
# +------+----+---+---+----+----------+----------+
# |   stn|year| mo| da|temp|count_temp|row_number|
# +------+----+---+---+----+----------+----------+
# |949110|2019| 11| 23|54.9|        14|         1|
# |998012|2017| 03| 02|31.4|        24|         1|
# |996470|2018| 03| 12|55.6|        12|         2|
# |998166|2019| 03| 20|34.8|        12|         3|
# |041680|2019| 02| 19|16.1|        15|         1|
# |076470|2018| 06| 07|65.0|        24|         1|
# |719200|2017| 10| 09|60.5|        11|         1|
# |994979|2017| 12| 11|21.3|        21|         1|
# |998252|2019| 04| 18|44.7|        11|         1|
# |917350|2018| 04| 21|82.6|         9|         2|
# +------+----+---+---+----+----------+----------+
```

This section introduced the different types of ranking that PySpark provides in its window function API. With nonconsecutive/olympic, consecutive/dense, percent, tiles, and strict/row_number, you have a lot of options on the table when it comes to rank records. In the next section, I introduce analytic functions, which contain some of the coolest functionality of window functions: the ability to look back and ahead.

10.2.2 *Analytic functions: Looking back and ahead*

This section covers a very useful group of functions that makes it possible for you to look at the records around the record at hand. Being able to look at a previous or following record unlocks a lot of functionality when building a time series feature. For instance, when doing modeling on time series data, one of the most important features are the observations in the past. Analytic window functions are by far the easiest way to do this.

ACCESS THE RECORDS BEFORE OR AFTER USING LAG() AND LEAD()

The two most important functions in the analytic functions family are `lag(col, n=1, default=None)` and `lead(col, n=1, default=None)`, which will give you the value of the `col` column of the n-th record before and after the record you're over, respectively. If the record, offset by the lag/lead, falls beyond the boundaries of the window, Spark will default to `default`. To avoid `null` values, pass a value to the optional parameter `default`. In the next listing, I create two columns, one with a lag of one record, and one with a lag of two records. If we go beyond the window, we get `null` values since I did not provide a `default` parameter.

Listing 10.16 Getting the temperature of the previous two observations using `lag()`

```
gsod_light.withColumn(
    "previous_temp", F.lag("temp").over(temp_each_year)
).withColumn(
    "previous_temp_2", F.lag("temp", 2).over(temp_each_year)
).show()
```

> **The previous observation of the second record is the twice-previous observation of the third record, and so on.**

```
# +------+----+---+---+----+----------+-------------+---------------+
# |   stn|year| mo| da|temp|count_temp|previous_temp|previous_temp_2|
# +------+----+---+---+----+----------+-------------+---------------+
# |041680|2019| 02| 19|16.1|        15|         null|           null|
# |998166|2019| 03| 20|34.8|        12|         16.1|           null|
# |998252|2019| 04| 18|44.7|        11|         34.8|           16.1|
# |949110|2019| 11| 23|54.9|        14|         44.7|           34.8|
# |994979|2017| 12| 11|21.3|        21|         null|           null|
# |998012|2017| 03| 02|31.4|        24|         21.3|           null|
# |719200|2017| 10| 09|60.5|        11|         31.4|           21.3|
# |996470|2018| 03| 12|55.6|        12|         null|           null|
# |076470|2018| 06| 07|65.0|        24|         55.6|           null|
# |917350|2018| 04| 21|82.6|         9|         65.0|           55.6|
# +------+----+---+---+----+----------+-------------+---------------+
```

CUMULATIVE DISTRIBUTION OF THE RECORDS USING CUME_DIST()

The last analytical function we cover is `cume_dist()`, and it is similar to `percent_rank()`. `cume_dist()`, as its name indicates, provides a cumulative distribution (in the statistical sense of the term) rather than a ranking (where `percent_rank()` shines).

Just like with `percent_rank()`, I find it easier to explain via a formula:

$$\frac{\text{\# records with a lower or equal value than the current one}}{\text{\# of records in the window}}$$

In practice, I use it when doing an EDA (exploratory data analysis) of the cumulative distribution of certain variables.

Listing 10.17 `percent_rank()` and `cume_dist()` over a window

```
gsod_light.withColumn(
    "percent_rank", F.percent_rank().over(temp_each_year)
).withColumn("cume_dist", F.cume_dist().over(temp_each_year)).show()
```

```
# +------+----+---+---+----+----------+----------------+----------------+
# |   stn|year| mo| da|temp|count_temp|    percent_rank|       cume_dist|
# +------+----+---+---+----+----------+----------------+----------------+
# |041680|2019| 02| 19|16.1|        15|             0.0|            0.25|
# |998166|2019| 03| 20|34.8|        12|0.33333333333333|             0.5|
# |998252|2019| 04| 18|44.7|        11|0.66666666666666|            0.75|
# |949110|2019| 11| 23|54.9|        14|             1.0|             1.0|
# |994979|2017| 12| 11|21.3|        21|             0.0|0.33333333333333|
```

```
# |998012|2017|  03|  02|31.4|            24|            0.5|0.66666666666666|
# |719200|2017|  10|  09|60.5|            11|            1.0|             1.0|
# |996470|2018|  03|  12|55.6|            12|            0.0|0.33333333333333|
# |076470|2018|  06|  07|65.0|            24|            0.5|0.66666666666666|
# |917350|2018|  04|  21|82.6|             9|            1.0|             1.0|
# +------+----+---+---+----+----------+---------------+----------------+
```

cume_dist() is an analytic function, not a ranking function, as it does not provide a rank. Instead, it provides the cumulative density function F(x) (for those statistically inclined) for the records in the data frame.

This section introduced the cornucopia of window functions. While it reads a little like a buffet, window functions are nothing more than functions that operate over a window, just like the functions that we saw in chapters 4 and 5 apply over the whole data frame at once. Once you see them applied in the wild, it gets easy to recognize good use cases for them and reach for your new tool. In the next section, I introduce window frames, which are a powerful tool for changing which records are used in the computation of a window function.

Exercise 10.2

If you have a window where all the ordered values are the same, what is the result of applying ntile() to the window?

10.3 *Flex those windows! Using row and range boundaries*

This section goes beyond the uniform window definition for each record. I introduce how we can build static, growing, and unbounded windows based on rows and ranges. Being able to fine-tune the boundaries of a window augments the capabilities of your code by flexing the concept of static window partitions. By the end of this section, you will be fully operational with windows in PySpark.

I start this section with a seemingly harmless operation: applying an average computation over two windows identically partitioned. The only difference is that the first one is not ordered while the second one is. Surely the order of a window would have no impact on the computation of the average, right?

Check out the following listing—same window function, almost the same window (besides the ordering), different results.

Listing 10.18 Ordering a window and the computation of the average

```
not_ordered = Window.partitionBy("year")
ordered = not_ordered.orderBy("temp")
gsod_light.withColumn(
    "avg_NO", F.avg("temp").over(not_ordered)
).withColumn("avg_O", F.avg("temp").over(ordered)).show()
```

```
# +------+----+---+---+----+----------+----------------+------------------+
# |  stn|year| mo| da|temp|count_temp|          avg_NO|            avg_O|
# +------+----+---+---+----+----------+----------------+------------------+
# |041680|2019| 02| 19|16.1|        15|          37.625|              16.1|
# |998166|2019| 03| 20|34.8|        12|          37.625|             25.45|
# |998252|2019| 04| 18|44.7|        11|          37.625|31.866666666666664|
# |949110|2019| 11| 23|54.9|        14|          37.625|            37.625|
# |994979|2017| 12| 11|21.3|        21|37.7333333333334|              21.3|
# |998012|2017| 03| 02|31.4|        24|37.7333333333334|             26.35|
# |719200|2017| 10| 09|60.5|        11|37.7333333333334|37.733333333333334|
# |996470|2018| 03| 12|55.6|        12| 67.733333333333|              55.6|
# |076470|2018| 06| 07|65.0|        24| 67.733333333333|              60.3|
# |917350|2018| 04| 21|82.6|         9| 67.733333333333| 67.73333333333333|
# +------+----+---+---+----+----------+----------------+------------------+
```

All good: the average is consistent across each window, and the results are logical.

Some odd stuff is happening. It looks like each window grows, record by record, so the average changes every time.

This is fun stuff. Something with the ordering of a window messes up the computation. The official Spark API documentation informs us that when ordering is not defined, an unbounded window frame (`rowFrame`, `unboundedPreceding`, `unbounded-Following`) is used by default. When ordering is defined, a growing window frame (`rangeFrame`, `unboundedPreceding`, `currentRow`) is used by default.

The secret to deciphering the new, mysterious behavior is to understand the types of window frames we can build and how they are used. I start by introducing the different *frame sizes* (static versus growing versus unbounded) and how to reason about them before adding the second dimension, the *frame type* (range versus rows). At the end of this section, the explanation for the previous code will make perfect sense, and you will be able to flex your window skills regardless of the situation.

10.3.1 *Counting, window style: Static, growing, unbounded*

This section covers the boundaries of a window, something we call a *window frame*. I break the traditional catch-all window (where a window is equal to the whole partition) to introduce record-based boundaries. This will provide an incredible new layer of flexibility when using window functions, as it controls the scope of visibility of a record within the window. You'll be able to create window functions that only look in the past and avoid feature leakage when working with time series. This is just one of the many use cases for flexible window frames!

> **TIP** Feature leakage happens when you use future information when building a predictive model. An example of this would be to use tomorrow's rainfall to predict the total rainfall for the upcoming week. See chapters 12 and 13 for more information on features and feature leakage.

Before getting started, let's take a visual of a window: when a function is applied to it, a window spec partitions a data frame based on one or more column values and then (potentially) orders them. Spark also provides the `rowsBetween()` and `rangeBetween()` methods to create window frame boundaries. For this section, I focus on row boundaries since they are closer to what we would expect. Section 10.3.2 explains the difference between ranges versus rows.

year	mo	da	temp
2019	02	19	16.1	← `Window.unboundedPreceding`
2019	04	21	82.6	...
2019	06	07	65.0	← `-1`(row immediately before)
2019	06	15	-114.7	← `Window.currentRow`
2019	06	20	-114.7	← `1` (row immediately after)
2019	08	27	-113.5	...
2019	10	09	60.5	
2019	11	23	54.9	← `Window.unboundedFollowing`

Figure 10.4   **The different possible boundaries within a window. Some are numerical; some have reserved keywords. We count forward (up to `Window.unboundedFollowing`) when looking at records ahead, and backward (down to `Window.unboundedPreceding`) when looking at records behind.**

When using an unbounded/unordered window, we do not care about which record is which. This changes when we are using ranking or analytical functions. For a rank, a lag, or a lead, for instance, Spark will call the record being processed the `Window.currentRow`. (I keep the name of the class. Using the `currentRow` keyword makes it obvious you are working with window functions.) The record before takes a value of `-1`, and so on, until the first record, named `Window.unboundedPreceding`. The record following the current row takes a value of `1`, and so on, until the last record, named `Window.unboundedFollowing`.

> **WARNING**   *Do not* use a numerical value to represent the first or last record in a window. It makes your code harder to reason about, and you never know when the window will grow beyond that size. Internally, Spark will translate `Window.unboundedPreceding` and `Window.unboundedFollowing` to appropriate numerical values, so you don't have to.

Let's go back to listing 10.18; we can "add" boundaries to our window spec. In listing 10.19, I explicitly add the boundaries that Spark assumes when none are provided. This means that `not_ordered` and `ordered` will provide the same results whether we define the boundaries (listing 10.19) or not (listing 10.18). If I want to be very accurate, the `ordered` window spec is bounded by range, not rows, but for our data frame, it works just the same. I'll trade accuracy for ease of understanding for now, but if you apply it to the `gsod` data frame, results will differ slightly (see section 10.3.2).

Listing 10.19 Rewriting the window spec with explicit window boundaries

```
not_ordered = Window.partitionBy("year").rowsBetween(
    Window.unboundedPreceding, Window.unboundedFollowing
)
ordered = not_ordered.orderBy("temp").rangeBetween(
    Window.unboundedPreceding, Window.currentRow
)
```

◁— This window is unbounded: every record, from the first to the last, is in the window.

◁— This window is growing to the left: every record up to the current row value is included in a window.

Because the window used in the computation of `avg_NO` is *unbounded*, meaning that it spans from the first to the last record of the window, the average is consistent across the whole window. The one used in the computation of `avg_O` is *growing* on the left, meaning that the right record is bounded to the `currentRow`, where the left record is set at the first value of the window. As you move from one record to the next, the average is over more and more values. The average of the last record of the window contains all the values (because `currentRow` is the last record of the window). A *static* window frame is nothing more than a window where both records are bounded relative to the current row; for example, `rowsBetween(-1, 1)` for a window that contains the current row, the record immediately preceding, and the record immediately following.

> **WARNING** If your window spec is not ordered, using a boundary is a nondeterministic operation. Spark will not guarantee that your window will contain the same values as we are not ordering within a window before picking the boundary. This also applies if you order the data frame in a previous operation. If you use a boundary, provide an explicit ordering clause.

In practice, it is easy to know what kind of window you need. Ranking and analytical functions rely on ordered windows, since order matters in their application. Aggregate functions don't care about the ordering of values, so you *shouldn't* use them with an ordered window spec unless you want partial aggregation.

This section covered the different types of window boundaries, and partially explained the behavior of the growing average when using ordered window specs. In the next section, I introduce the last core window concept: range versus rows.

10.3.2 *What you are vs. where you are: Range vs. rows*

This section covers the subtle yet incredibly important difference between row windows versus range windows. This notion unlocks the option to build windows that care about the content of the ordered column, not just its position. Working with ranges is useful when working with dates and time, as you may want to gather windows based on time intervals that are different than the primary measure. As an example, the `gsod` data frame collects daily temperature information. What happens if we want to compare this temperature to the average of the previous month? Months have 28, 29, 30, or 31 days. This is where ranges get useful.

To start, I transform the gsod_light data frame slightly in listing 10.20. First, I convert all the dates in 2019 using F.lit(2019) as a column value so that we have a single window when breaking by year; this will give us more data to play with when using ranges. I also create a dt column that contains the date of the observation before transforming it into an integer value in the dt_num column. Range windows in PySpark work only on numerical columns; unix_timestamp() transforms the date in a number of seconds since 1970-01-01 00:00:00 UTC (the UNIX epoch). This gives us a serviceable date-like number we can use for our range windows.

Listing 10.20   Creating a date column to apply range window on

```
gsod_light_p = (
    gsod_light.withColumn("year", F.lit(2019))
    .withColumn(
        "dt",
        F.to_date(
            F.concat_ws("-", F.col("year"), F.col("mo"), F.col("da"))
        ),
    )
    .withColumn("dt_num", F.unix_timestamp("dt"))
)
gsod_light_p.show()
```

The new column is of type DateType(), which can be treated (window wise) as a number.

```
# 
# +------+----+---+---+----+----------+----------+----------+
# |   stn|year| mo| da|temp|count_temp|        dt|    dt_num|
# +------+----+---+---+----+----------+----------+----------+
# |041680|2019| 02| 19|16.1|        15|2019-02-19|1550552400|
# |998012|2019| 03| 02|31.4|        24|2019-03-02|1551502800|
# |996470|2019| 03| 12|55.6|        12|2019-03-12|1552363200|
# |998166|2019| 03| 20|34.8|        12|2019-03-20|1553054400|
# |998252|2019| 04| 18|44.7|        11|2019-04-18|1555560000|
# |917350|2019| 04| 21|82.6|         9|2019-04-21|1555819200|
# |076470|2019| 06| 07|65.0|        24|2019-06-07|1559880000|
# |719200|2019| 10| 09|60.5|        11|2019-10-09|1570593600|
# |949110|2019| 11| 23|54.9|        14|2019-11-23|1574485200|
# |994979|2019| 12| 11|21.3|        21|2019-12-11|1576040400|
# +------+----+---+---+----+----------+----------+----------+
# 
```

When using PySpark, windows must be over numerical values. Using unix_timestamp() is the easiest way to convert a date/timestamp to a number.

For a simple range window, let's compute the average of the temperatures recorded one month before and after a given day. Because our numerical date is in seconds, I'll keep things simple and say that 1 month = 30 days = 720 hours = 43,200 minutes = 2,592,000 seconds.[1] Visually, the window for a record would look like figure 10.5: for

---

[1]   If we want to be very strict on "a month is a month," check the exercises.

year	mo	da	temp	dt_num
2019	02	19	16.1	1 550 552 400
2019	03	02	31.4	1 551 502 800
2019	03	12	55.6	1 552 363 200
2019	03	20	34.8	1 553 054 400
2019	04	18	44.7	1 555 560 000
2019	04	21	82.6	1 555 819 200
2019	06	07	65.0	1 559 880 000
2019	10	09	60.5	1 570 593 600
2019	11	23	54.9	1 574 485 200
2019	12	11	21.3	1 576 040 400

```
  1 553 054 400
-     2 592 000
_____

  1 550 462 400  (left boundary)
```

← `Window.currentRow`

```
  1 553 054 400
+     2 592 000
_____

  1 555 646 400  (right boundary)
```

Figure 10.5 Displaying a window with a range of (-2_592_000, 2_592_000) (or ±30 days, in seconds)

each record, Spark computes the left and right (or lower and upper) window boundaries, and those boundaries are used to determine if a record is in the window.

In the next listing, we create a range window over 60 days (30 before, 30 after), partitioning by year; our window frame is ordered by dt_num, so we can use the rangeBetween over the number of seconds.

Listing 10.21 Computing the average temperature for a 60-day sliding window

```
ONE_MONTH_ISH = 30 * 60 * 60 * 24  # or 2_592_000 seconds
one_month_ish_before_and_after = (
    Window.partitionBy("year")
    .orderBy("dt_num")
    .rangeBetween(-ONE_MONTH_ISH, ONE_MONTH_ISH)       ◁
)

gsod_light_p.withColumn(
    "avg_count", F.avg("count_temp").over(one_month_ish_before_and_after)
).show()
```

The range becomes (current_row_value – **ONE_MONTH_ISH**, current_row_value + **ONE_MONTH_ISH**).

```
# +------+----+---+---+----+----------+----------+----------+-------------+
# |   stn|year| mo| da|temp|count_temp|        dt|    dt_num|    avg_count|
# +------+----+---+---+----+----------+----------+----------+-------------+
# |041680|2019| 02| 19|16.1|        15|2019-02-19|1550552400|        15.75|
# |998012|2019| 03| 02|31.4|        24|2019-03-02|1551502800|        15.75|
# |996470|2019| 03| 12|55.6|        12|2019-03-12|1552363200|        15.75|
# |998166|2019| 03| 20|34.8|        12|2019-03-20|1553054400|         14.8|
# |998252|2019| 04| 18|44.7|        11|2019-04-18|1555560000|10.6666666666|
# |917350|2019| 04| 21|82.6|         9|2019-04-21|1555819200|         10.0|
# |076470|2019| 06| 07|65.0|        24|2019-06-07|1559880000|         24.0|
# |719200|2019| 10| 09|60.5|        11|2019-10-09|1570593600|         11.0|
# |949110|2019| 11| 23|54.9|        14|2019-11-23|1574485200|         17.5|
# |994979|2019| 12| 11|21.3|        21|2019-12-11|1576040400|         17.5|
# +------+----+---+---+----+----------+----------+----------+-------------+
```

For each record in the window, Spark computes the range boundaries based on the current row value (from the field `dt_num`) and determines the actual window that it will aggregate over. This makes it easy to compute sliding or growing time/date windows: when working with row ranges, you can say only that "*X* records before and after." When using `Window.currentRow/unboundedFollowing/unboundedPreceding` with a range window, Spark will use the value of the record as the range boundary. If you have multiple observations for a given time, your row-based window frame will not work. Using ranges and looking at the actual values makes your window respect the context you're applying it over.

	The window is based on the position of each row. Numerical values are relative to the position of the current row.	The window is based on the value of each row. Numerical values are relative to the value of the current row.
The window stays the same size and moves as we move from record to record.	rows/ bounded	range/ bounded
The window is bounded in one direction. As we move records, it grows/shrinks in the direction in which it's not bounded.	rows/growing	range/ growing
The window contains the whole partition. It stays the same for every record within the partition.	rows/ unbounded	range/ unbounded

Figure 10.6   A matrix for the window types available in Spark

This section explained the difference between row- and range-based windows and where one is best applied versus the other. This concludes the "standard" portion of window functions. With this chapter under your belt, you should be comfortable applying window functions as part of data analyses or feature engineering operations. Before concluding this chapter, I've added an optional, bonus section that covers how we can apply UDFs over windows. With this, you'll be able to break the mold and compose your own window functions.

Exercise 10.3

If you have a data frame with 1,000,001 rows, where the ordered column `ord` is defined by `F.lit(10)`, what is the result of the following window functions?

1 `F.count("ord").over(Window.partitionBy().orderBy("ord").rowsBetween(-2, 2))`

2 `F.count("ord").over(Window.partitionBy().orderBy("ord").rangeBetween(-2, 2))`

10.4 *Going full circle: Using UDFs within windows*

This section teaches what I consider the PySpark-iest thing PySpark can do: using UDFs within windows. It uses two very Sparky things: UDFs and the split-apply-combine paradigm we learned in chapter 9. It's also something that is Python-specific, as it relies on pandas UDFs. PySpark all the way down! pandas UDFs in a window definition are useful when you need the flexibility of pandas UDFs. For instance, when you need functionality not defined in the set of window functions available in PySpark, just define UDFs to implement the functionality!

This is not a very long section, as we build on existing knowledge. For a complete refresher on pandas UDFs, refer to chapter 9. The recipe for applying a pandas UDF is very simple:

1. We need to use a *Series to Scalar* UDF (or a group aggregate UDF). PySpark will apply the UDF to every window (once per record) and put the (scalar) value as a result.
2. A UDF over *unbounded window frames* is only supported by Spark 2.4 and above.
3. A UDF over *bounded window frames* is only supported by Spark 3.0 and above.

The rest? Business as usual. In listing 10.22, I create a `median` UDF using the Spark 3-type hint notation. If you use Spark 2.4, change the decorator to `@F.pandas_udf` `("double", PandasUDFType.GROUPED_AGG)` and remove the type hints. This simple `median` function computes the median of a pandas `Series`. I then apply it twice to the `gsod_light` data frame. There is nothing remarkable to see here; it just works.

> **WARNING** Do not modify the `Series` you are passing as input. Doing so will introduce hard-to-find bugs in your code, and we saw in chapter 9 how nasty UDF bugs are.

Listing 10.22 Using a pandas UDF over window intervals

```
import pandas as pd


# Spark 2.4, use the following
# @F.pandas_udf("double", PandasUDFType.GROUPED_AGG)
@F.pandas_udf("double")
def median(vals: pd.Series) -> float:
    return vals.median()                          The UDF is applied over an
                                                  unbounded/unordered
                                                  window frame.
gsod_light.withColumn(
    "median_temp", median("temp").over(Window.partitionBy("year"))    ◁
).withColumn(
    "median_temp_g",
    median("temp").over(                          The same UDF is now
        Window.partitionBy("year").orderBy("mo", "da")    applied over a bounded/
    ),                                            ordered window frame.
).show()
```

```
#
# +------+----+---+---+----+----------+-----------+-------------+
# |   stn|year| mo| da|temp|count_temp|median_temp|median_temp_g|
# +------+----+---+---+----+----------+-----------+-------------+
# |041680|2019| 02| 19|16.1|        15|      39.75|         16.1|
# |998166|2019| 03| 20|34.8|        12|      39.75|        25.45|
# |998252|2019| 04| 18|44.7|        11|      39.75|         34.8|
# |949110|2019| 11| 23|54.9|        14|      39.75|        39.75|
# |998012|2017| 03| 02|31.4|        24|       31.4|         31.4|
# |719200|2017| 10| 09|60.5|        11|       31.4|        45.95|
# |994979|2017| 12| 11|21.3|        21|       31.4|         31.4|
# |996470|2018| 03| 12|55.6|        12|       65.0|         55.6|
# |917350|2018| 04| 21|82.6|         9|       65.0|         69.1|
# |076470|2018| 06| 07|65.0|        24|       65.0|         65.0|
# +------+----+---+---+----+----------+-----------+-------------+
#
```

Since the window is unbounded, every record within a window has the same median.

Since the window is bounded to the right, the median changes as we add more records to the window.

10.5   *Look in the window: The main steps to a successful window function*

This concludes the chapter about window functions. I encourage you to expand your data manipulation, analysis, and feature engineering arsenal to incorporate window function-based transformation. If you are stumped on how to perform a certain transformation, always remember the basic parameters of using a window function:

1 What kind of operation do I want to perform? Summarize, rank, or look ahead/behind.

2 How do I need to construct my window? Should it be bounded or unbounded? Do I need every record to have the same window value (unbounded), or should the answer depend on where the record fits within the window (bounded)? When bounding a window frame, you most often want to order it as well.

3 For bounded windows, do you want the window frame to be set according to the position of the record (row based) or the value of the record (range based)?

4 Finally, remember that a window function does not make your data frame special. After your function is applied, you can filter, group by, and even apply another, completely different, window.

As a parting gift, it seems like window functions are a favorite of data analysts and scientists' interviews. Applying window functions in PySpark will become second nature!

Summary

- Window functions are functions that are applied over a portion of a data frame called a window frame. They can perform aggregation, ranking, or analytical operations. A window function will return the data frame with the same number of records, unlike its siblings the `groupby-aggregate` operation and the group map UDF.

- A window frame is defined through a window spec. A window spec mandates how the data frame is split (`partitionBy()`), how it's ordered (`orderBy()`), and how it's portioned (`rowsBetween()`/`rangeBetween()`).

- By default, an unordered window frame will be unbounded, meaning that the window frame will be equal to the window partition for every record. An ordered window frame will grow to the left, meaning that each record will have a window frame ranging from the first record in the window partition to the current record.

- A window can be bounded by row, meaning that the records included in the window frame are tied to the row boundaries passed as parameters (with the range boundaries added to the row number of the current row), or by range, meaning that the records included in the window frame depend on the value of the current row (with the range boundaries added to the value).

Additional Exercises

Exercise 10.4

Using the following code, first identify the day with the warmest temperature for each year, and then compute the average temperature. What happens when there are more than two occurrences?

```
each_year = Window.partitionBy("year")

(gsod
 .withColumn("min_temp", F.min("temp").over(each_year))
 .where("temp = min_temp")
 .select("year", "mo", "da", "stn", "temp")
 .orderBy("year", "mo", "da")
 .show())
```

Exercise 10.5

How would you create a rank that is full, meaning that each record within a the `temp_per_month_asc` has a unique rank, using the `gsod_light` data frame? For records with an identical `orderBy()` value, the order of rank does not matter.

```
temp_per_month_asc = Window.partitionBy("mo").orderBy("count_temp")

gsod_light = spark.read.parquet("./data/window/gsod_light.parquet")
gsod_light.withColumn(
```

```
        "rank_tpm", F.rank().over(temp_per_month_asc)
    ).show()

# +------+----+---+---+----+----------+--------+
# |   stn|year| mo| da|temp|count_temp|rank_tpm|
# +------+----+---+---+----+----------+--------+
# |949110|2019| 11| 23|54.9|        14|       1|
# |996470|2018| 03| 12|55.6|        12|       1|
# |998166|2019| 03| 20|34.8|        12|       1|
# |998012|2017| 03| 02|31.4|        24|       3|
# |041680|2019| 02| 19|16.1|        15|       1|
# |076470|2018| 06| 07|65.0|        24|       1|
# |719200|2017| 10| 09|60.5|        11|       1|
# |994979|2017| 12| 11|21.3|        21|       1|
# |917350|2018| 04| 21|82.6|         9|       1|
# |998252|2019| 04| 18|44.7|        11|       2|
# +------+----+---+---+----+----------+--------+
```

These records should be 1 and 2.

Exercise 10.6

Take the gsod data frame (not the `gsod_light`) and create a new column that is `True` if the temperature at a given station is maximum for that station and a time window of seven days (before and after), and `False` otherwise.

Exercise 10.7

How would you create a window like the code that follows, but taking into account that months have different number of days? For instance, March has 31 days, but April has 30 days, so you can't do a window spec over a set number of days.

(Hint: My solution doesn't use dt_num.)

```
ONE_MONTH_ISH = 30 * 60 * 60 * 24  # or 2_592_000 seconds
one_month_ish_before_and_after = (
    Window.partitionBy("year")
    .orderBy("dt_num")
    .rangeBetween(-ONE_MONTH_ISH, ONE_MONTH_ISH)
)

gsod_light_p = (
    gsod_light.withColumn("year", F.lit(2019))
    .withColumn(
        "dt",
        F.to_date(
            F.concat_ws("-", F.col("year"), F.col("mo"), F.col("da"))
        ),
    )
    .withColumn("dt_num", F.unix_timestamp("dt"))
)

gsod_light_p.withColumn(
    "avg_count", F.avg("count_temp").over(one_month_ish_before_and_after)
).show()
```

```
# +------+----+---+---+----+----------+----------+----------+-------------+
# |   stn|year| mo| da|temp|count_temp|        dt|    dt_num|    avg_count|
# +------+----+---+---+----+----------+----------+----------+-------------+
# |041680|2019| 02| 19|16.1|        15|2019-02-19|1550552400|        15.75|
# |998012|2019| 03| 02|31.4|        24|2019-03-02|1551502800|        15.75|
# |996470|2019| 03| 12|55.6|        12|2019-03-12|1552363200|        15.75|
# |998166|2019| 03| 20|34.8|        12|2019-03-20|1553054400|         14.8|
# |998252|2019| 04| 18|44.7|        11|2019-04-18|1555560000|10.6666666666|
# |917350|2019| 04| 21|82.6|         9|2019-04-21|1555819200|         10.0|
# |076470|2019| 06| 07|65.0|        24|2019-06-07|1559880000|         24.0|
# |719200|2019| 10| 09|60.5|        11|2019-10-09|1570593600|         11.0|
# |949110|2019| 11| 23|54.9|        14|2019-11-23|1574485200|         17.5|
# |994979|2019| 12| 11|21.3|        21|2019-12-11|1576040400|         17.5|
# +------+----+---+---+----+----------+----------+----------+-------------+
```

11

Faster PySpark: Understanding Spark's query planning

This chapter covers

- How Spark uses CPU, RAM, and hard drive resources
- Using memory resources better to speed up (or avoid slowing down) computations
- Using the Spark UI to review useful information about your Spark installation
- How Spark splits a job into stages and how to profile and monitor those stages
- Classifying transformations into narrow and wide operations and how to reason about them
- Using caching judiciously and avoiding unfortunate performance drop with improper caching

Imagine the following scenario: you write a readable, well-thought-out PySpark program. When submitting your program to your Spark cluster, it runs. You wait.

How can we peek under the hood and see the progression of our program? Troubleshoot which step is taking a lot of time? This chapter is about understanding how we can access information about our Spark instance, such as its configuration and layout (CPU, memory, etc.). We also follow the execution of a program from raw Python code to optimized Spark instructions. This knowledge will remove a lot of magic from your program; you'll be in a position to know what's happening at every stage of your PySpark job. If your program takes too long, this chapter will show you where (and how) to look for the relevant information.

11.1 Open sesame: Navigating the Spark UI to understand the environment

This section covers how Spark uses allocated computing and memory resources and how we can configure how many resources are assigned to Spark. With this, you will be able to configure your jobs to use more or fewer resources, depending on how complex they are.

Stepping up from local Spark

Thus far, I have kept the data set sizes manageable to avoid needing to leverage a distributed (paid) instance of Spark. When learning a new technology (or if you are reading this book and working through the code examples), having a cloud cluster up—even if it is small—means that you are paying for something that will sit idle most of the time. When learning, experimenting, or developing small proofs of concept, don't hesitate to use Spark locally, testing on a distributed environment as you go. You'll avoid stressing out about cloud costs while ensuring your code scales healthily.

On the other hand, some of the material in the chapter relies on having Spark running on multiple machines. Because of this, if you are running Spark locally, your results will be different.

For this chapter, we go back to the word occurrences count example from chapters 2 and 3. To avoid some frantic page flipping, the code is reproduced in listing 11.1. Our program follows a pretty simple set of steps:

1 We create a `SparkSession` object to access the data frame functionality of PySpark as well as to connect to our Spark instance.

2 We create a data frame containing all the text files (line by line) within the chosen directory, and we count the occurrence of each word.

3 We show the top 10 most frequent words.

Listing 11.1 Our end-to-end program counting the occurrence of words

```
from pyspark.sql import SparkSession
import pyspark.sql.functions as F

spark = SparkSession.builder.appName(
    "Counting word occurences from a book, one more time."
).getOrCreate()
```

Like with any modern PySpark program, ours starts with creating a SparkSession and connecting to our Spark instance.

```
results = (                                              ◄──┐   results maps to a data
    spark.read.text("./data/gutenberg_books/*.txt")         │   frame from a data
    .select(F.split(F.col("value"), " ").alias("line"))     │   source plus a series
    .select(F.explode(F.col("line")).alias("word"))         │   of transformations.
    .select(F.lower(F.col("word")).alias("word"))
    .select(F.regexp_extract(F.col("word"), "[a-z']+", 0).alias("word"))
    .where(F.col("word") != "")
    .groupby(F.col("word"))                                         By show()-ing the results,
    .count()                                                        we trigger the chain of
)                                                                   transformations and
                                                                    display the top 10 most
results.orderBy(F.col("count").desc()).show(10)    ◄──┘             frequent words.
```

The work starts happening at the show() method: since it is an action, it triggers the
chain of transformations from the results variable. I do not print the results of our
program, because (a) we know it works and (b) we focus on what Spark is actually
doing under the hood.

When starting Spark, either locally or on a cluster, the program allocates compute
and memory resources for us to use. Those resources are displayed through a web
portal called the *Spark UI*. For the UI to be available, we need to create and instantiate a SparkSession, which we did at the beginning of our PySpark program. When
working locally, go to localhost:4040 to check the Spark UI landing page. If the
4040 port is currently in use, Spark will spit out a WARN Utils: Service 'SparkUI'
could not bind on port 4040. Attempting port ABCD message. Replace the 4040
after the colon with the port number listed. If you are working on a managed Spark
cluster, cloud, or on premise, refer to your provider documentation for accessing
the SparkUI.

The Spark UI landing pages (also known as the Job tab on the top menu) contain
a lot of information, which we can divide into a few sections:

- The top menu provides access to the main sections of the Spark UI, which we
  explore in this chapter.
- The timeline provides a visual overview of the activities impacting your Spark-
  Session; in our case, we see the cluster allocating resources (an executor driver,
  since we work locally) and performing our program.
- The jobs, which in our case are triggered by the show() action (depicted in the
  Spark UI as showString), are listed at the bottom of the page. In the case where
  a job is processing, it would be listed as *in progress*.

The next sections cover the different tabs of the Spark UI at a high level. We cover the
information Spark provides about its own configuration and its memory and resource
usage before plunging into understanding how our program was executed.

The top menu contains the links to the important sections of the Spark UI.

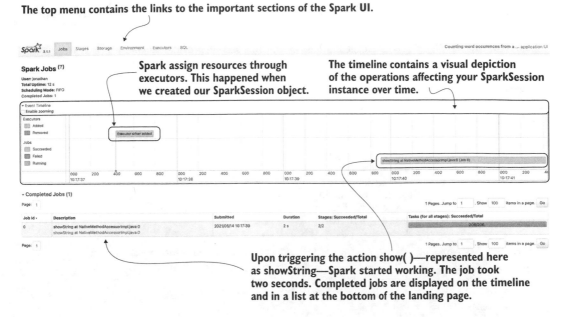

Spark assign resources through executors. This happened when we created our SparkSession object.

The timeline contains a visual depiction of the operations affecting your SparkSession instance over time.

Upon triggering the action show( )—represented here as showString—Spark started working. The job took two seconds. Completed jobs are displayed on the timeline and in a list at the bottom of the landing page.

Figure 11.1   The landing page (Jobs) for the Spark UI. We see an empty timeline because the only event that has happened is the launch of the PySpark shell.

11.1.1 Reviewing the configuration: The environment tab

This section covers the Environment tab of the Spark UI. This tab contains the configuration of the environment that our Spark instance sits on, so the information is useful for troubleshooting library problems, providing configuration information if you run into weird behavior (or a bug!), or understanding the specific behavior of a Spark instance.

The Environment tab contains all the information about how the machines on your cluster are set up. It covers information about the JVM and Scala versions installed (remember, Spark is a Scala program), as well as the options Spark is using for this session. If you want a complete description of each field (including those not listed), the Spark configuration page (http://spark.apache.org/docs/latest/configuration.html) contains a fairly readable description.

> **NOTE**   There are other sections (Hadoop Properties and Classpath Entries) that are useful if you need to pinpoint specific Hadoop or library issues or when submitting a bug, but for our purposes, we can skip them with no hard feelings.

A lot of the entries are self-explanatory, but they are, nonetheless, important when troubleshooting a PySpark job that doesn't work as planned. Other than a few identifiers, such as the application ID and name, Spark will list any configuration option and optional libraries we provide our job with in the UI. For instance, in chapter 9, the Big-Query Spark connector would be listed under `spark.jars` and `spark.repl.local.jars`.

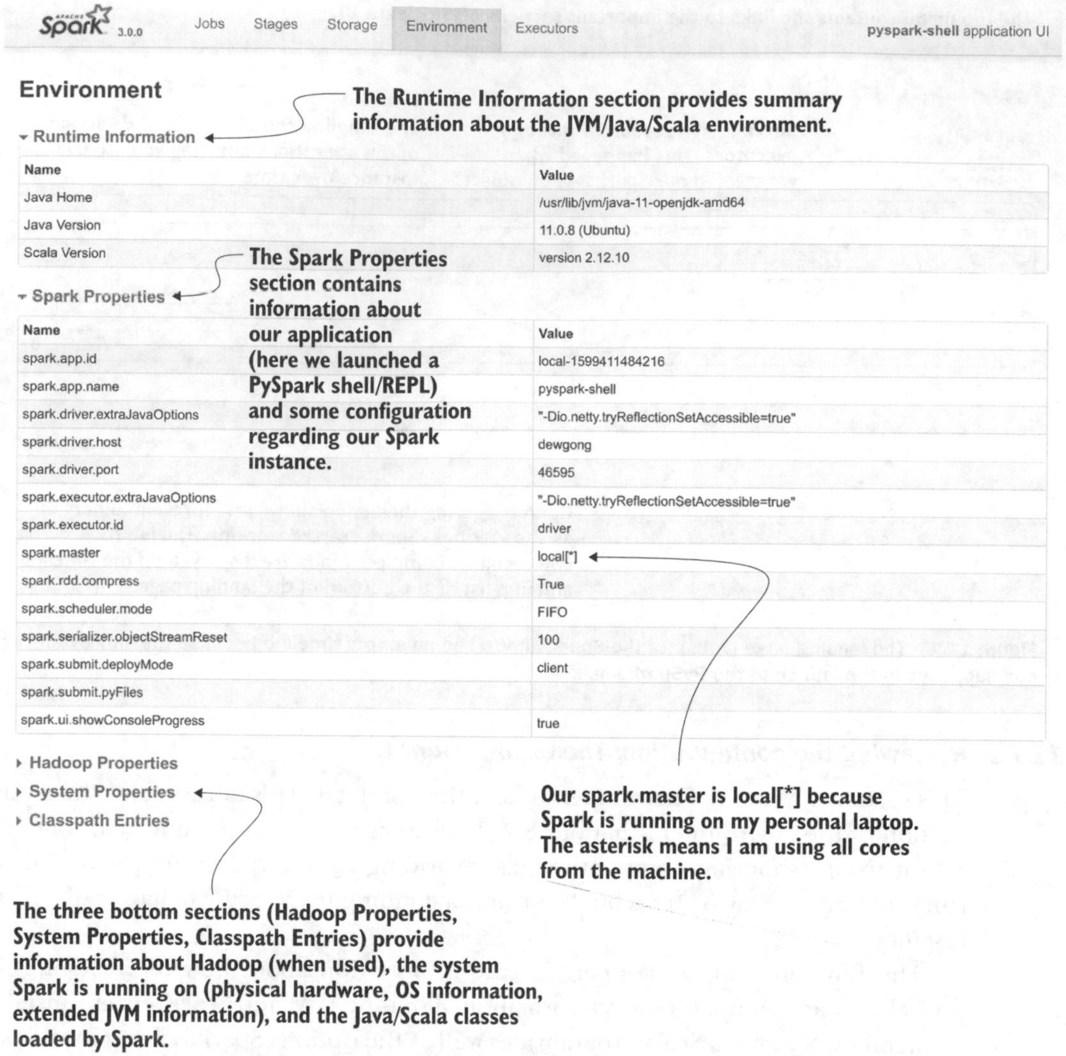

Environment

▾ Runtime Information ◄

The Runtime Information section provides summary information about the JVM/Java/Scala environment.

Name	Value
Java Home	/usr/lib/jvm/java-11-openjdk-amd64
Java Version	11.0.8 (Ubuntu)
Scala Version	version 2.12.10

▾ Spark Properties ◄

The Spark Properties section contains information about our application (here we launched a PySpark shell/REPL) and some configuration regarding our Spark instance.

Name	Value
spark.app.id	local-1599411484216
spark.app.name	pyspark-shell
spark.driver.extraJavaOptions	"-Dio.netty.tryReflectionSetAccessible=true"
spark.driver.host	dewgong
spark.driver.port	46595
spark.executor.extraJavaOptions	"-Dio.netty.tryReflectionSetAccessible=true"
spark.executor.id	driver
spark.master	local[*] ◄
spark.rdd.compress	True
spark.scheduler.mode	FIFO
spark.serializer.objectStreamReset	100
spark.submit.deployMode	client
spark.submit.pyFiles	
spark.ui.showConsoleProgress	true

▸ Hadoop Properties
▸ System Properties ◄
▸ Classpath Entries

Our spark.master is local[*] because Spark is running on my personal laptop. The asterisk means I am using all cores from the machine.

The three bottom sections (Hadoop Properties, System Properties, Classpath Entries) provide information about Hadoop (when used), the system Spark is running on (physical hardware, OS information, extended JVM information), and the Java/Scala classes loaded by Spark.

Figure 11.2   The Environment tab contains information about the hardware, OS, and libraries/software versions Spark is sitting on top of.

The only Python-specific option worth mentioning here is the `spark.submit.pyFiles`. Since we are running PySpark from the REPL, no files, per se, were submitted to Spark. When using `spark-submit` with a Python file or module, your file(s) name will be listed there.

NOTE   Python libraries installed on the cluster are not listed in the Spark UI. When working locally, installing a new library for our Spark instance is as simple as installing it on our local Python. When working on a managed cluster,

Spark provides some strategies to avoid doing it manually, which is heavily dependent on the provider. (See http://mng.bz/nYrK for more information.)

This section is more about knowing *what* you can find rather than going on a very long (and boring) description of every configuration flag. By remembering the information available in the Environment tab at a high level, you can rapidly zero in if you are facing a problem you believe is OS-, JVM-, or (Java/Scala) library-related. If we reuse the example from chapter 9, if you have a `BigQuery provider not found` error, your first reflex should be to check the Environment tab to see if the jar is listed as a dependency. It'll also provide great information when filing a bug report: you can now easily provide detailed information.

The next section covers the resources we usually care about the most when running a PySpark program: memory, CPU, and hard drive. More specifically, we review how Spark allocates resources to the executor and how to change the defaults.

11.1.2 *Greater than the sum of its parts: The Executors tab and resource management*

In this section, I review the Executors tab, which contains information about the computing and memory resources available to our Spark instance. Referring to this tab during the course of a Spark job allows you to monitor the health of your Spark installation, as well as resource usage across all nodes.

After clicking on Executors, we are presented with a summary and detailed view of all the nodes in our cluster. Since I am working locally, I see only one node that is playing the role of driver.

When considering the processing power of a cluster, we think about CPU and RAM. In figure 11.3, my cluster is made up of 12 CPU cores (`local[*]`—see section 11.1.1— gives access to all the cores of my local CPU) and 434.4 MiB (mebibytes, or 2^{20} [1,048,576] bytes, not to be confused with megabytes, which are in base 10 [10^6 or 1,000,000]). By default, Spark will allocate 1 GiB (gebibyte) of memory to the driver process. (See the sidebar at the end of this section for the formula on how to get from 1GiB to 434.4Mib.)

Spark uses RAM for three main purposes, as illustrated in figure 11.4:

- A portion of the RAM is reserved for Spark internal processing, such as user data structures, internal metadata, and safeguarding against potential out-of-memory errors when dealing with large records.
- The second portion of the RAM is used for operations (*operational memory*). This is the RAM used during data transformation.
- The last portion of the RAM is used for the storage (*storage memory*) of data. RAM access is a lot faster than reading and writing data from and to disk, so Spark will try to put as much data in memory as possible. If operational memory needs grow beyond what's available, Spark will *spill* some of the data from RAM to disk.

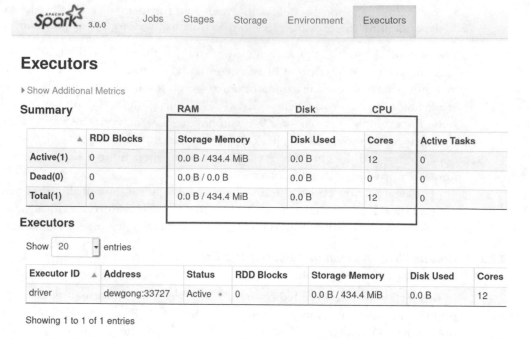

Figure 11.3   My local Spark UI Executors tab. I have 434.4 MiB of storage memory and 12 CPU cores available.

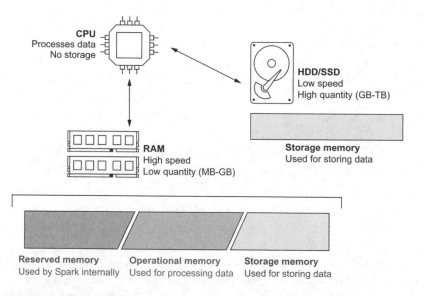

Figure 11.4   A simplified layout, or the resources Spark uses by default. Spark uses RAM as much as it can, resorting to disk when RAM is not enough (via spilling).

Spark provides a few configuration flags to change the memory and number of CPU cores available. We have access to two identical sets of parameters to define the resources our drivers and executors will have access to.

When creating the `SparkSession`, you can set the `master()` method to connect to a specific cluster manager[1] (in cluster mode) when working locally and specify the resources/number of cores to allocate from your computer. In listing 11.2, I decide to go from 12 cores to only 8 by passing `master("local[8]")` in my `SparkSession` builder object. When working locally, our (single) machine will host the driver and perform the work on the data. In the case of a Spark cluster, you'll have a driver node coordinating the work, a cluster manager, and a series of worker nodes hosting executors performing the work (see chapter 1 for a refresher).

> **NOTE** What about GPUs? As of Spark 3.0, GPU usage has been greatly simplified, but GPUs are still not common stock in Spark instances. GPU, like CPU, would be in the processing sector of the diagram. For more information, check out the RAPIDS+Spark section on the Nvidia website (https://nvidia .github.io/spark-rapids/Getting-Started/). Most, if not all, cloud providers provide the option to equip your Spark/Databricks cluster with GPU nodes.

Memory allocation is done through configuration flags; the most important when working locally is `spark.driver.memory`. This flag takes size as an attribute and is set via the `config()` method of the `SparkSession` builder object. The different abbreviations are listed in table 11.1: Spark will not accept decimal numbers, so you need to pass integer values.

Table 11.1 The different value types Spark will accept for size. You can change the 1 to another integer value.

Abbreviation	Definition
1b	1 byte
1k or 1kb	1 kibibyte = 1,024 bytes
1m or 1mb	1 mebibyte = 1,024 kibibytes
1g or 1gb	1 gibibyte = 1,024 mebibytes
1t or 1tb	1 tebibyte = 1,024 gibibytes
1p or 1pb	1 pebibyte = 1,024 tebibytes

> **WARNING** Spark uses power-of-two numbers (there are 1,024 bytes in a kibibyte, whereas there are only 1,000 bytes in a kilobytes), whereas RAM memory is usually shown in power-of-ten units.

---

[1] If you are using ephemeral clusters (i.e., spinning up a cluster for a specific job and destroying it afterward), you usually don't need to worry about cluster managers, as they are set up for you.

In listing 11.2, I combine those two options into a new SparkSession creation. If you already have Spark running, make sure you shut it down (exit the shell where you launched PySpark) and start again to make sure Spark picks up the new configuration. When working on your local machine, unless you have a strong reason to do otherwise, limit memory allocation to 50% of your total RAM to account for the other programs/tasks running at the same time. For Spark in cluster mode, the documentation recommends not going over 75% of the available RAM.

Listing 11.2   Relaunching PySpark to change the number of cores/RAM available

```
from pyspark.sql import SparkSession

spark = (
    SparkSession.builder.appName("Launching PySpark with custom options")
    .master("local[8]")                              ◁——  local[8] means that we use only
    .config("spark.driver.memory", "16g")            ◁——  eight cores for the master.
).getOrCreate()
                                                     The driver will use 16 g instead
# [... Run the program here ...]                     of the default of 1 g.
```

If you are launching PySpark using the pyspark command (e.g., when SSH-ing into a master node on a managed cloud Spark instance) or using spark-submit, you will need to pass the configuration as either command-line arguments or in the configuration file (see appendix B for more details). In our case, the Spark UI shows the configuration using command-line arguments (--conf syntax) in the java.sun.command field (see section 11.1.1). I show the result of our new SparkSession in figure 11.5.

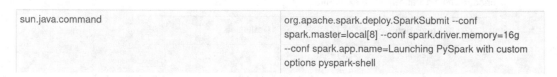

sun.java.command	org.apache.spark.deploy.SparkSubmit --conf spark.master=local[8] --conf spark.driver.memory=16g --conf spark.app.name=Launching PySpark with custom options pyspark-shell

Figure 11.5   In the Environment tab, the sun.java.command has the same configuration flags we passed in the --conf launcher syntax.

Math time! How to go from 1 GiB to 434.4 MiB

As mentioned earlier in the chapter, Spark allocates 1 GiB of memory by default to the driver program. What's the deal with 434.4 MiB? How do we go from 1 GiB of allocated memory to 434.4 MiB of usable memory?

In figure 11.4, I explained that Spark segments the memory on a node into three sections: the reserved, operational, and storage memory. The 434.4 MiB represents both the operational and storage memory. A few configuration flags are responsible for the exact memory split:

- `spark.{driver|executor}.memory` determines the total memory envelope available to the Spark driver or an executor, which I'll call `M` (by default `1g`). You can have different memory requirements for your driver versus your executor, but I usually see both values being the same.
- `spark.memory.fraction`, which I'll call `F`, sets the fraction of memory available to Spark (operational plus storage; by default `0.6`).
- `spark.memory.storageFraction`, which I'll call `S`, is the fraction of the memory available to Spark (`M x F`) and will be used predominantly for storage (by default `0.5`).

In the case of 1 GiB of RAM being provided, Spark will start by putting 300 MiB aside. The rest will be split between reserved and allocated (operational plus storage) using the `spark.memory.fraction` value: `(1 GiB - 300 MiB) * 0.6 = 434.4MiB`. This is the value shown in the Spark UI. Internally, Spark will manage the operational and storage memory using the `spark.memory.storageFraction` ratio. In our case, since the ratio is at `0.5`, the memory will be split evenly between operational and storage.

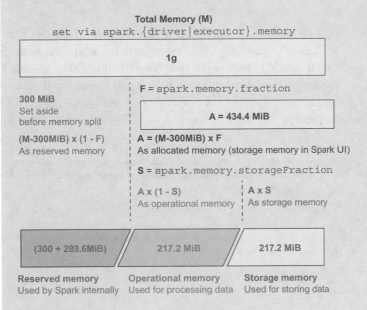

In practice, the storage can outgrow its allotted place: the `spark.memory.storage-Fraction` defines the zone where Spark will protect the data from being spilled to disk (e.g., during memory-intensive computations), but if we have more data than what fits into the storage memory, Spark will borrow from the operational memory section.

For the vast majority of your programs, it is not recommended to play with those values. While it may seem counterintuitive to use too much memory for storing data, remember that reading data from RAM makes Spark much faster than when it needs to rely on the hard drive.

In this section, we explored the configuration flags and the relevant parts of the Spark UI to review and set the CPU and memory resources. In the next section, I run some small jobs, explore the runtime information Spark provides via the Spark UI, and explain how we can use this to make better configuration and coding decisions.

11.1.3 Look at what you've done: Diagnosing a completed job via the Spark UI

This section covers the most important metrics when reviewing job performance. I introduce the concepts of jobs and stages, how Spark reports performance metrics for each stage, and how we can interpret the information the Spark UI provided to optimize our jobs.

> **NOTE** Some cloud-managed Spark jobs (such as Google Dataproc) do not provide access to the Spark UI; instead, you have a Spark History Server. The look is the same, but it won't be available *until the job you're running is done*. In the case of a PySpark shell, it means you'll have to exit the session before you can see the results.

Spark organizes the code we submit into jobs. A job is simply a series of transformations (select(), groupBy(), where(), etc.) crowned by a final action (count(), write(), show()). In chapter 1, I explained that Spark will not start working until we submit an action: each action will trigger one job. As an example, the code leading to the results data frame in listing 11.3 does not contain any action. The Spark UI does not display any job (or any sign of work, for that matter) after submitting this code in the REPL.

Listing 11.3 The chain of transformation applied to our text files

```
from pyspark.sql import SparkSession
import pyspark.sql.functions as F

spark = (
    SparkSession.builder.appName(
        "Counting word occurences from a book, one more time."
    )
    .master("local[4]")
    .config("spark.driver.memory", "8g")
    .getOrCreate()
)


results = (
    spark.read.text("./data/gutenberg_books/*.txt")
    .select(F.split(F.col("value"), " ").alias("line"))
    .select(F.explode(F.col("line")).alias("word"))
    .select(F.lower(F.col("word")).alias("word"))
    .select(F.regexp_extract(F.col("word"), "[a-z']+", 0).alias("word"))
    .where(F.col("word") != "")
    .groupby(F.col("word"))
```

```
        .count()
)

results.orderBy(F.col("count").desc()).show(10)
```

Only when we submit an action, like the show() method at the end of listing 11.3, do we see work being performed (a very fast progress bar, followed by results in the REPL window). On the Spark UI, we see one job (because there is one action), detailed in figure 11.6.

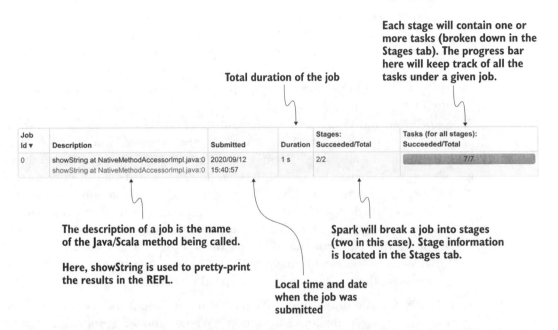

Total duration of the job

Each stage will contain one or more tasks (broken down in the Stages tab). The progress bar here will keep track of all the tasks under a given job.

Job Id ▼	Description	Submitted	Duration	Stages: Succeeded/Total	Tasks (for all stages): Succeeded/Total
0	showString at NativeMethodAccessorImpl.java:0 showString at NativeMethodAccessorImpl.java:0	2020/09/12 15:40:57	1 s	2/2	7/7

The description of a job is the name of the Java/Scala method being called.

Here, showString is used to pretty-print the results in the REPL.

Local time and date when the job was submitted

Spark will break a job into stages (two in this case). Stage information is located in the Stages tab.

Figure 11.6   The Completed Jobs table on the Jobs tab of the Spark UI with our one completed job. Our word count, with a single action, is listed as one job.

Each job is internally broken down into stages, which are units of work being performed on the data. What goes into a stage depends on how the query optimizer decides to split the work. Section 11.1.4 goes into greater detail about how the stages are constructed and how we can influence them. Our simple program has three steps:

1   Stage 0 reads the data from all (six) text files present in the directory and performs all the transformations (split, explode, lowercase, extract the regular expression, filter). It then groups by and counts the word frequency for each partition independently.

2   Spark then *exchanges* (or shuffles) the data across each node to prepare for the next stage. Because the data is very small once grouped by (and we only need 10 records to show), all the data gets back to one node in a single partition.

3 Finally, during stage 1, we compute the total word count for the 10 selected records and display the records in table form.

This two-staged approach to group by/count works because counting the number of records is commutative and associative. Chapter 8 covers commutativity and associativity and why they matter for Spark.

In the Completed Stages table (we've now moved to the *Stages* tab of the Spark UI), Spark provides four main metrics related to the memory consumption:

- *Input* is the amount of data read from source. Our program reads 4.1 MiB of data. This seems like an inevitable cost: we need to read the data in order to perform work. If you have control over the format and organization of your input data, you can achieve a significant performance boost.

- *Output* is the counterpoint to input: it represents the data our program outputs as the result of the action. Since we print to terminal, we have no value at the end of stage 1.

- *Shuffle read* and *shuffle write* are part of the `shuffling` (or exchange; see figure 11.7) operation. Shuffling rearranges the memory on a Spark worker to prepare for the next stage. In our case, we needed to write 965.6 KiB at the end of stage 0 to prepare for stage 1. In stage 1, we only read 4.8 KiB since we asked for just 10 records. Since Spark lazily optimized the whole job, it knows right from the start that we need only the count for 10 words; at exchange time (between stage 0 and 1), the driver only kept the relevant 5 words for each file, dropping the required data to answer our action by 99.5% (from 965.6 to 4.8 KiB). When working with massive files and `show()`-ing the content (by default 20 records), this results in significant speed increases!

This is all very relevant information. We gained insight about the memory consumption for our job (transformations plus action). We saw how we can measure the time each task takes, the time spent in garbage collection, and the amount of data ingested and how that data gets sent around between each stages. The next section will pay attention to the actual operations spent on the data, which are encoded in a plan. We're getting close to Spark's secret sauce!

Exercise 11.1

If we were to add 10 more files to our word count program, without making any change to the code, would that change (a) the number of jobs or (b) the number of stages? Why?

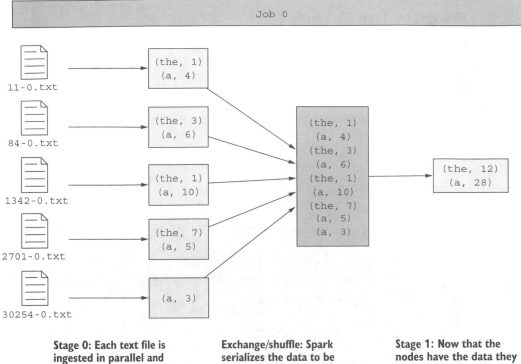

Job 0

11-0.txt → (the, 1) (a, 4)

84-0.txt → (the, 3) (a, 6)

1342-0.txt → (the, 1) (a, 10)

2701-0.txt → (the, 7) (a, 5)

30254-0.txt → (a, 3)

(the, 1) (a, 4) (the, 3) (a, 6) (the, 1) (a, 10) (the, 7) (a, 5) (a, 3)

→ (the, 12) (a, 28)

Stage 0: Each text file is ingested in parallel and the words are grouped by/counted.

At the end of stage 0, each node has a data frame containing the word count for the data present on that node.

Exchange/shuffle: Spark serializes the data to be exchanged between workers for the next stage. (For the sample job, rather than exchanging across all nodes, we centralize the results.)

Stage 1: Now that the nodes have the data they need for the next stage, processing can continue.

Stage 1 takes each data frame from stage 0 and adds the count to get the total count for each word, before returning the top words and their count.

Figure 11.7 The two stages of job 0, with the summary statistics for each stage. The size of the data ingested is listed in *input*, the data outputted as *output*, and we see the intermediate data movement as *shuffle*. We can use these values to infer how large of a data set are we processing.

11.1.4 *Mapping the operations via Spark query plans: The SQL tab*

This section covers the different plans that Spark goes through, from code to actual work on the data. We take our word count example, which we've used since the beginning of the chapter, break it down into stages, and then break those stages into steps. This is a key tool for understanding what's happening during your job at a lower level than what you wrote as code and is the first thing you should do when you feel that your code is slow or not performing as expected.

Head to the SQL tab of the Spark UI and click on the description of the job. You should see a long chain of boxes representing the different stages.

Details for Query 0

Submitted Time: 2020/10/12 11:17:53
Duration: 2 s
Succeeded Jobs: 0

☐ Show the Stage ID and Task ID that corresponds to the max metric

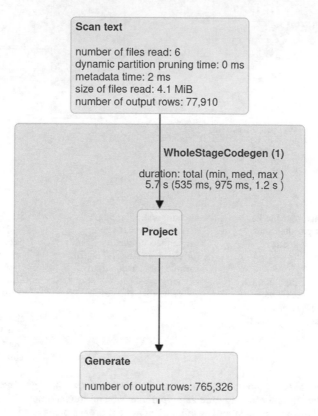

Scan text

number of files read: 6
dynamic partition pruning time: 0 ms
metadata time: 2 ms
size of files read: 4.1 MiB
number of output rows: 77,910

WholeStageCodegen (1)

duration: total (min, med, max)
5.7 s (535 ms, 975 ms, 1.2 s)

Project

Generate

number of output rows: 765,326

Figure 11.8   The chain of transformations on our data frame, encoded and optimized by Spark. Our code instructions on the `results` data frame are represented in stages that are illustrated and described when you hover over each box.

If you hover over one of the `Scan Text`, `Project`, or `Generate` boxes (like in figure 11.9), a black box with information about what happened during that step appears. In the case of the first box, called `Scan text`, we see that Spark performs a `FileScan text` operation over all the files we passed as an argument to `spark.read.text()`.

We know that Spark ingests our (Python, although the process works for every host language) code and translates it into Spark instructions (see chapter 1). Those

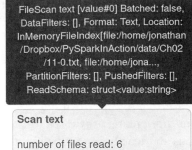

FileScan text [value#0] Batched: false, DataFilters: [], Format: Text, Location: InMemoryFileIndex[file:/home/jonathan /Dropbox/PySparkInAction/data/Ch02 /11-0.txt, file:/home/jona...], PartitionFilters: [], PushedFilters: [], ReadSchema: struct<value:string>

Scan text

number of files read: 6
dynamic partition pruning time: 0 ms
metadata time: 2 ms
size of files read: 4.1 MiB
number of output rows: 77,910

Figure 11.9 When hovering over one of the `Scan Text`, `Project`, or `Generate` boxes, a black overlay appears containing a textual representation of the transformation undertaken (called a *plan*) during that step. Most of the time we only see the beginning and end of the plan because of space constraints.

instructions are encoded into a *query plan* and then sent to the executors for processing. Because of this, the performance of PySpark, when using the data frame API, is very similar to the Spark Scala API.

> **WARNING** If you recall chapter 8, you'll remember that the translation analogy does not work when working with an RDD. In that case, PySpark will serialize the data and apply Python code, similar to when we apply a Python UDF.

How do we access this query plan? Glad you asked! Spark does not present a single query plan, but four distinct types of plans created in a sequential fashion. We see them in logical order in figure 11.10.

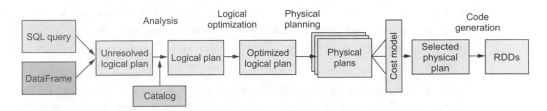

Figure 11.10 Spark optimizes jobs using a multitiered approach: unresolved logical plan, logical plan, optimized logical plan, and physical plan. The (selected) physical plan is the one applied to the data.

To see the four (full) plans in action without hovering over multiple boxes, we have two main options:

- In the Spark UI, at the very bottom of the SQL tab for our job, we can click on `Details`, where the plans will be displayed textually.
- We can also print them in the REPL, via the data frame's `explain()` method. In that case, we would not have the final action for our plan since an action usually returns a pythonic value (number, string, or `None`), none of which has an `explain` value.

This concludes the high-level overview of the SQL tab in the Spark UI. The next section will break down both the plans provided by the Spark UI and the `explain()` method, and how we interpret them.

11.1.5 *The core of Spark: The parsed, analyzed, optimized, and physical plans*

This section covers the four plans Spark goes into while performing a job. Understanding the key concepts and vocabulary from those plans provides a ton of information about how the job is structured and gives us an idea about the data journey across the cluster as the executors process the data.

> **NOTE** The Spark documentation is not very consistent on the nomenclature of plans. Because I am a fan of using single adjectives, I rely on the vocabulary from the Spark UI, dropping the "logical" for the first three plans. I'll use *parsed*, *analyzed*, *optimized*, and *physical* for the four stages in figure 11.10.

Before jumping into the gist of each plan, it's important to understand why Spark undergoes a whole planning process for a job. Managing and processing large data sources across multiple machines comes with its own set of challenges. On top of optimizing each node for high-speed processing via adequate usage of RAM, CPU, and HDD resources (see figure 11.4), Spark also needs to work through the complexity of managing the data across nodes (see section 11.2.1 for more details).

A plan is displayed in the Spark UI via the `explain()` data frame method as a tree of steps that are performed in the data. We read a plan, regardless of its type, from the most nested line to the least nested one: for most jobs, this will mean reading from the bottom to the top. In listing 11.4, the parsed plan looks very much like a translation of our Python code into Spark operations. We recognize most operations (`explode`, `regexp_extract`, `filter`) in the plan. Grouping data is called `Aggregate` in the plans, and selecting data is called `Project` (i.e., "I am projecting," not "My project is overdue").

> **TIP** By default, `explain()` will only print the physical plan. If you want to see everything, use `explain(extended=True)`. The documentation for the `explain()` method explains other options for formatting and statistics.

Listing 11.4 The parsed logical plan for our job

```
.groupby(F.col("word"))

== Parsed Logical Plan ==
GlobalLimit 6                        results.show(5, False)                          .count()
+- LocalLimit 6                 ←
   +- Project [cast(word#9 as string) AS word#27, cast(count#13L as string)
      AS count#28]
      +- Aggregate [word#9], [word#9, count(1) AS count#13L]
         +- Filter NOT (word#9 = )                              .where(F.col("word") != "")
            +- Project [regexp_extract(word#7, [a-z']+, 0) AS word#9]   ←

                    .select(F.regexp_extract(F.col("word"), "[a-z']+", 0).alias("word"))
```

```
                                    +- Project [lower(word#5) AS word#7]        ◁──────────────
select(F.explode(F.col("line"))        +- Project [word#5]
        .alias("word")).                  +- Generate explode(line#2), false, [word#5]
                                             +- Project [split(value#0,  , -1) AS line#2]   ◁─────
results = spark.read.text("./data/  ┌─▷        +- Relation[value#0] text
   gutenberg_books/1342-0.txt")      │                         .select(F.split(F.col("value"), " ").alias("line"))

                                                          .select(F.lower(F.col("word")).alias("word"))
```

NOTE Spark needs unique column names when working with data frames, which is why we see the #X (where X is a number) in the plans. For instance, `lower(word#5) AS word#7` still refers to the `word` column, but Spark assigns an increasing number after the pound sign.

Moving from the parsed logical plan to the analyzed logical plan does not change much operation wise. On the other hand, Spark now knows the schema of our resulting data frame: `word: string, count: string`.

Listing 11.5 The analyzed plan for our word count job

```
== Analyzed Logical Plan ==              The resulting data frame has two columns: word
word: string, count: string  ◁──┤       (a string column) and count (also a string, because
GlobalLimit 6                            we are show()-ing the result to the terminal).
+- LocalLimit 6
   +- Project [cast(word#9 as string) AS word#27, cast(count#13L as string)
      AS count#28]
      +- Aggregate [word#9], [word#9, count(1) AS count#13L]
         +- Filter NOT (word#9 = )
            +- Project [regexp_extract(word#7, [a-z']+, 0) AS word#9]
               +- Project [lower(word#5) AS word#7]
                  +- Project [word#5]
                     +- Generate explode(line#2), false, [word#5]
                        +- Project [split(value#0,  , -1) AS line#2]
                           +- Relation[value#0] text
```

The analyzed plan then gets optimized via multiple heuristics and rules based on how Spark performs operations. In the next listing, we recognize the same operations as the two previous plans (parsed and analyzed), but we don't have that one-to-one mapping anymore. Let's look at the differences in greater detail.

Listing 11.6 The optimized plan for our word count job

```
== Optimized Logical Plan ==
GlobalLimit 6
+- LocalLimit 6
   +- Aggregate [word#9], [word#9, cast(count(1) as string) AS count#28]
      +- Project [regexp_extract(lower(word#5), [a-z']+, 0) AS word#9]
         +- Filter NOT (regexp_extract(lower(word#5), [a-z']+, 0) = )
            +- Generate explode(line#2), [0], false, [word#5]
               +- Project [split(value#0,  , -1) AS line#2]
                  +- Relation[value#0] text
```

First, the explode() operation does not have a projection (see Project [word#5] in the analyzed plan). Nothing is too surprising here: this column is only used in the chain of computation and does not need to be selected/projected explicitly. Spark also does not keep the project step for the casting of the count as string; the casting happens during the aggregation.

Second, the regexp_extract() and lower() operations are lumped into a single step. Because both are narrow operations that operate on each record independently (see listing 11.7), Spark can perform the two transformations in a single pass over the data.

Finally, Spark duplicates the (regexp_extract(lower(word#5), [a-z']+, 0) =) step: it performs it during the Filter step and then again during the Project step. Because of this, the Filter and Project steps of the analyzed plan are inverted. This might look counterintuitive at first: since the data is in memory, Spark believes that performing the filter (even if it means just throwing some CPU cycles away) ahead of time yields better performance.

Finally, the optimized plan gets converted into actual steps that the executor will perform: this is called the *physical plan* (in the sense that Spark will actually perform this work on the data, not that you'll see your cluster doing jumping jacks). The physical plan is very different from the others.

Listing 11.7   The physical plan (actual processing steps) for our word count job

```
== Physical Plan ==
CollectLimit 6
+- *(3) HashAggregate(keys=[word#9], functions=[count(1)], output=[word#9,
      count#28])
   +- Exchange hashpartitioning(word#9, 200), true, [id=#78]
      +- *(2) HashAggregate(keys=[word#9], functions=[partial_count(1)],
                     output=[word#9, count#17L])
         +- *(2) Project [regexp_extract(lower(word#5), [a-z']+, 0) AS word#9]
            +- *(2) Filter NOT (regexp_extract(lower(word#5), [a-z']+, 0) = )
               +- Generate explode(line#2), false, [word#5]
                  +- *(1) Project [split(value#0,  , -1) AS line#2]
                     +- FileScan text [value#0] Batched: false, DataFilters: [],
                        Format: Text,
                        Location: InMemoryFileIndex[file:[...]/data/
gutenberg_books/1342-0.txt],
                        PartitionFilters: [], PushedFilters: [],
                        ReadSchema: struct<value:string>
```

Spark trades the logical relations for an actual reading of the file (FileScan text). Spark does not actually care much about the actual data for the three previous logical plans; it is only worried about getting the column names and types, and Spark will coordinate the reading of the data. If we have multiple files (like in our case), Spark will split the files between the executors so that each one reads what's needed. Neat!

We also have some numbers prefixed by an asterisk—*(1) to *(3)—which corresponds to the WholeStageCodegen of the Spark UI SQL schema seen in figure 11.8. A

`WholeStageCodegen` is a stage where each operation happens on the same pass over the data. For our example, we have three:

- Splitting the value
- Filtering out the empty words, extracting the words, and pre-aggregating the word counts (like we saw in section 11.1.3)
- Aggregating the data into a final data frame

The translation from Python instructions to a Spark physical plan is not always so clear, but even for complex PySpark programs, I follow the same blueprint of looking at the parsed plan and following the transformations all the way to the physical plan. This information, combined with the Spark instance overview, proves invaluable when you need to diagnose what's happening under the hood. If you are a detective, the Spark UI and its multiple tabs are just like having both the weapon from the crime and a confession letter.

This section covered an overview of the Spark UI. This portal provides invaluable information about the configuration of your Spark instance, the resources available, and the different jobs in progress or completed. In the next section, I cover a few important concepts useful to understanding Spark's processing performance, as well as a few pitfalls and false friends that hinder your data jobs.

> **Exercise 11.2**
>
> If you use `results.explain(extended=True)` in the REPL and look at the analyzed plan, the schema will read `word: string, count: bigint`, and there is no `Global-Limit/LocalLimit 6`. Why are the two plans (`explain()` versus Spark UI) different?

11.2 *Thinking about performance: Operations and memory*

In this section, I cover some basic concepts about distributed data processing using PySpark. More specifically, I give a foundation on how to think about your program to simplify the logic and speed up the processing. Regardless of if you use the data frame API or rely on lower-level RDD operations (see chapter 8), you'll gain useful vocabulary to describe the logic of your program and hints for troubleshooting a seemingly slow program.

For this section, I use some of the data sets we've already encountered in previous chapters. I cover two important basic concepts when designing, coding, and profiling data pipelines.

First, I introduce the concept of *narrow* versus *wide* operation. Each transformation performed on a data frame (or an RDD) can be classified as either of these. Balancing narrow and wide operations is a tricky yet important aspect of making your data pipeline run faster.

Second, I discuss *caching* as a performance strategy and when it's the right thing to do. Caching a data frame changes how Spark thinks about and optimizes the code for data transformation; by understanding the benefits and trade-offs, you will know when it's appropriate to use it.

11.2.1 Narrow vs. wide operations

In this section, I introduce the concept of narrow and wide transformation. I show how they display in the Spark UI and how thinking about the order of your transformations can matter for your program performance.

In chapter 1, I explained that Spark will lazily think the transformation into a plan until an action is triggered. Once the action is submitted, the query optimizer will review the steps of the plan and reorganize them in a way that's most efficient. We saw this in action with the optimized plan of listing 11.6, where we not only lumped the regexp_extract() and lower() operations into a single step, but duplicated that step (once for filtering, and once for the actual transformation).

Spark knows it can do that because regexp_extract() and lower() are both narrow transformations. Simply put, a narrow transformation is a transformation on records that is indifferent to the actual data location. In other words, a transformation is considered narrow if it applies to each record independently. Our two previous examples are obviously narrow: extracting a regular expression or changing the case of a column can be done on a record-by-record basis; the order of the records and their physical location on the cluster do not matter.

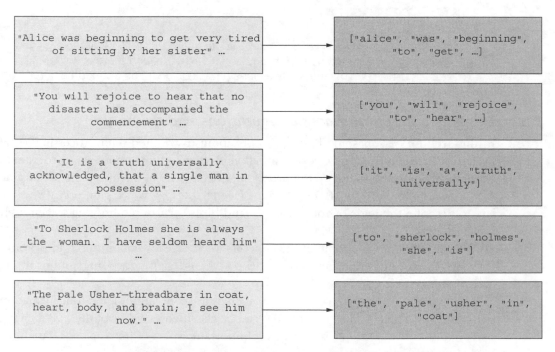

The data from each partition can be processed independently;
there is no need for any worker to exchange data.

Figure 11.11   A narrow transformation will apply without requiring the records to move across nodes. Spark can parallelize the operations across each nodes.

Narrow transformations are very convenient when working in a distributed setting: they do not require any exchanging (or shuffling) of the records. Because of this, Spark will often club many sequential narrow transformations together into a single step. Since the data is sitting in RAM (or on the hard drive), reading the data only once (by performing multiple operations on each record) usually yields better performance than reading the same data multiple times and performing one operation each time. PySpark (versions 2.0 and above) can also leverage specialized CPU (and since Spark 3.0, GPU) instructions that speed up data transformation.[2]

One important caveat of narrow transformations is, well, that they cannot do everything. For instance, grouping a data frame based on the value of some records, getting the maximum value of a column, and joining two data frames based on a predicate require the data to be logically organized for the operation to succeed. The three previous examples are called wide transformations. Unlike their narrow counterpart, wide transformations need the data to be laid in a certain way between the multiple nodes. For this, Spark uses an exchange step to move the data for the operation to complete.

In the word count example, the group by/count transformation was split into two stages, separated by an exchange. In the pre-exchange stage, Spark grouped the data on a node-by-node basis, so we ended the stage with each partition being grouped (see figure 11.12). Spark then exchanged the data across nodes—in our case, because the partition group by reduced the data size considerably, everything went to a single CPU core—and then finished the grouping. Spark was even clever enough to realize that we needed only five records, so it read only what was needed during the `shuffle read` operation (see section 11.1.3). Smart!

Since we need to exchange/send data to the network, wide operations incur a performance cost not present in narrow operations. Part of making a data transformation program swift is understanding the balance between narrow and wide operations and how we can leverage the nature of both in our program.

Spark's query optimizer is getting smarter and smarter in reorganizing operations to maximize each narrow stage. In listing 11.8, I add three transformations to the word count example:

- I keep only the words with over eight letters.
- I group by the word length.
- I count the sum of the frequencies.

[2] One example is via using SIMD (*single instruction, multiple data*) instructions and loop unrolling. If you are interested in knowing more, look at the release notes of the Spark Tungsten project.

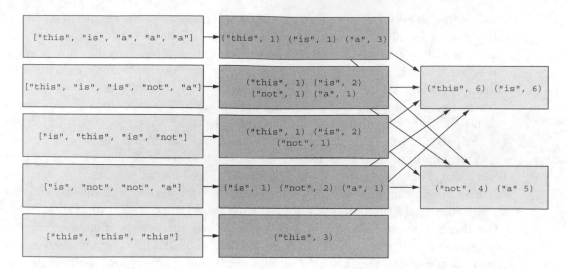

In the case of a wide operation, PySpark may attempt to perform work on each node independently (here, pre-grouping the data on each partition to reduce the amount of data to shuffle).

The data then gets exchanged (or shuffled) so the grouping operation can complete. The number of nodes where the data gets shuffled to depends on the resulting size (we show two nodes here).

Figure 11.12   A wide transformation can happen in two stages because Spark needs to exchange data across nodes. Spark calls those necessary exchange operations *shuffles*.

Listing 11.8   A more complex word count illustrating the narrow versus wide operations

```
results = (
    spark.read.text("./data/gutenberg_books/*.txt")
    .select(F.split(F.col("value"), " ").alias("line"))
    .select(F.explode(F.col("line")).alias("word"))
    .select(F.lower(F.col("word")).alias("word"))
    .select(F.regexp_extract(F.col("word"), "[a-z']+", 0).alias("word"))
    .where(F.col("word") != "")
    .groupby(F.col("word"))
    .count()
    .where(F.length(F.col("word")) > 8)
    .groupby(F.length(F.col("word")))
    .sum("count")
)

results.show(5, False)
# Output not shown for brievty.

results.explain("formatted")

# == Physical Plan ==
# * HashAggregate (12)
# +- Exchange (11)
#    +- * HashAggregate (10)
```

```
#          +- * HashAggregate (9)
#             +- Exchange (8)
#                +- * HashAggregate (7)
#                   +- * Project (6)
#                      +- * Filter (5)
#                         +- Generate (4)
#                            +- * Project (3)
#                               +- * Filter (2)
#                                  +- Scan text  (1)


# (1) Scan text
# Output [1]: [value#16766]
# Batched: false
# Location: InMemoryFileIndex [file:/.../data/gutenberg_books/11-0.txt, ... 5
      entries]
# ReadSchema: struct<value:string>


# (2) Filter [codegen id : 1]
# Input [1]: [value#16766]
# Condition : ((size(split(value#16766,  , -1), true) > 0) AND
      isnotnull(split(value#16766,  , -1)))


# [...]


# (11) Exchange
# Input [2]: [length(word#16775)#16806, sum#16799L]
# Arguments: hashpartitioning(length(word#16775)#16806, 200),
      ENSURE_REQUIREMENTS, [id=#2416]


# (12) HashAggregate [codegen id : 4]
# Input [2]: [length(word#16775)#16806, sum#16799L]
# Keys [1]: [length(word#16775)#16806]
# Functions [1]: [sum(count#16779L)]
# Aggregate Attributes [1]: [sum(count#16779L)#16786L]
# Results [2]: [length(word#16775)#16806 AS length(word)#16787,
      sum(count#16779L)#16786L AS sum(count)#16788L]
```

This is a good example of a poorly written program: I don't need to group by words to then group again by word frequency. If we look at the physical plan, two things jump out.

First, PySpark is smart enough to club the `.where(F.length(Fcol("word")) > 8)` with the two previously identified narrow transformations. Second, PySpark is not smart enough to understand that the first `groupby()` is unnecessary. We have some potential room for improvement here. In listing 11.9, I modify the last few instructions, so my program accomplishes the same thing with less instruction. By removing the (useless) intermediate `groupby()`, I bring back the number of steps to three (check the codegen IDs) and therefore reduce the amount of work PySpark will have to perform.

Listing 11.9 Reorganizing our extended word count program to avoid double counting

```
results_bis = (
    spark.read.text("./data/gutenberg_books/*.txt")
    .select(F.split(F.col("value"), " ").alias("line"))
```

```
        .select(F.explode(F.col("line")).alias("word"))
        .select(F.lower(F.col("word")).alias("word"))
        .select(F.regexp_extract(F.col("word"), "[a-z']+", 0).alias("word"))
        .where(F.col("word") != "")
        .where(F.length(F.col("word")) > 8)
        .groupby(F.length(F.col("word")))
        .count()
)

results_bis.show(5, False)
# Output not shown for brievty.

results_bis.explain("formatted")
# == Physical Plan ==
# * HashAggregate (9)
# +- Exchange (8)
#    +- * HashAggregate (7)
#       +- * Project (6)
#          +- * Filter (5)
#             +- Generate (4)
#                +- * Project (3)
#                   +- * Filter (2)
#                      +- Scan text   (1)


# (1) Scan text
# Output [1]: [value#16935]
# Batched: false
# Location: InMemoryFileIndex [file:/Users/jonathan/Library/Mobile
#     Documents/com~apple~CloudDocs/PySparkInAction/data/gutenberg_books/
#     11-0.txt, ... 5 entries]
# ReadSchema: struct<value:string>

# (2) Filter [codegen id : 1]
# Input [1]: [value#16935]
# Condition : ((size(split(value#16935,  , -1), true) > 0) AND
#     isnotnull(split(value#16935,  , -1)))

# [...]

# (5) Filter [codegen id : 2]
# Input [1]: [word#16940]
# Condition : ((isnotnull(word#16940) AND NOT
#     (regexp_extract(lower(word#16940), [a-z']+, 0) = )) AND
#     (length(regexp_extract(lower(word#16940), [a-z']+, 0)) > 8))

# [...]

# (9) HashAggregate [codegen id : 3]
# Input [2]: [length(word#16944)#16965, count#16960L]
# Keys [1]: [length(word#16944)#16965]
# Functions [1]: [count(1)]
# Aggregate Attributes [1]: [count(1)#16947L]
# Results [2]: [length(word#16944)#16965 AS length(word)#16949,
#     count(1)#16947L AS count#16948L]
```

Without going into bona fide benchmarking, a quick invocation of timeit (available on the iPython shell/Jupyter notebook) shows that the simplified program yields the same result approximately 54% faster. This is not surprising—via the physical plan (also available in the Spark UI), we know that the simplified version does less work and the code is more focused:

```
# Your results will vary.

%timeit results.show(5, False)
920 ms ± 46.7 ms per loop (mean ± std. dev. of 7 runs, 1 loop each)

%timeit results_bit.show(5, False)
427 ms ± 4.14 ms per loop (mean ± std. dev. of 7 runs, 1 loop each)
```

While this example might seem a little far-fetched, data pipelines tend to have this "append-only" code pattern, where you add more requirements, more work, and more code at the end of your chain of transformation. Using the information made available via the plans (both logical and physical), you can analyze the actual physical steps your code is going through and better understand the performance applications. This is not always easy to figure out when reading a complex data pipeline; multiple points of view help.

This section covered the concepts of narrow and wide transformations. We saw how to differentiate between the two and the implications of using them in our programs. We finally learned, in a practical way, how Spark reorganizes and clubs together narrow operations when optimizing query plans. In the next section, I introduce the single most misunderstood feature of PySpark: caching.

Exercise 11.3

For the following operations, identify if they are narrow or wide and why.

a df.select(…)
b df.where(…)
c df.join(…)
d df.groupby(…)
e df.select(F.max(…).over(…))

11.2.2 *Caching a data frame: Powerful, but often deadly (for perf)*

This section covers the caching of a data frame. I introduce what it is, how it works in Spark, and, most importantly, why you should be very careful about using it. Learning how, and especially when, to cache data is key to making your programs faster, but also to not making them slower than what they need to be.

I showed in figure 11.4 that Spark splits memory into three zones: reserved, operational, and storage. By default, each PySpark job (transformations plus actions) is independent of one another. For instance, if we `show()` the `results` data frame of our word count example five times, Spark will read the data from source and transform the data frame five times. While this seems like a highly inefficient way of working, bear in mind that data pipelines most often "flow" the data from one transformation to the next (hence the pipeline analogy); keeping intermediate states is useless and wasteful.

Caching changes this. A cached data frame will be serialized to the storage memory, which means that retrieving it will be speedy. The trade-off is that you take up RAM space on your cluster. In the case of very large data frames, that means that some data might spill to disk (leading to a slower retrieval) and that your cluster might run slower if you are using memory-heavy processing.

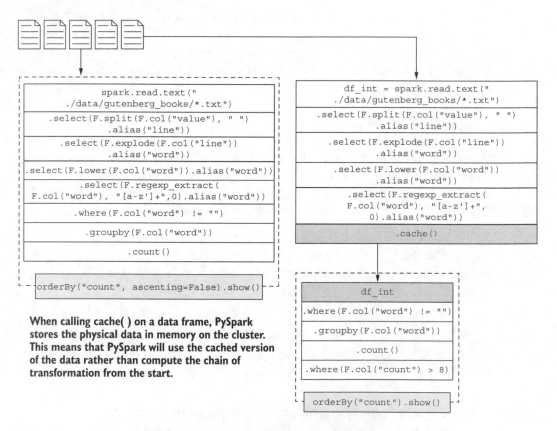

Figure 11.13 Caching a data frame in our word count program. In this case, the second action does not compute the chain of transformations from the `spark.read` operation and leverages the cached `df_int` data frame instead.

To cache a data frame, you call its `cache()` method. Because it is a transformation, `cache()` will not do anything immediately and waits for an action to be called. Once you submit an action, Spark will compute the whole data frame and cache it to memory, using disk space if needed.

Storage

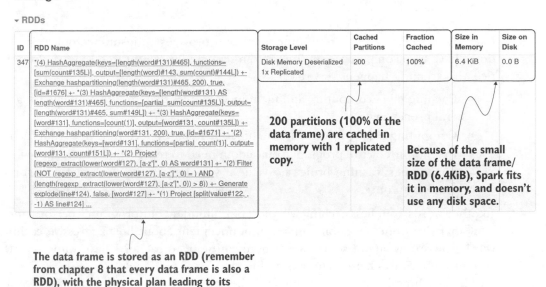

The data frame is stored as an RDD (remember from chapter 8 that every data frame is also a RDD), with the physical plan leading to its creation as its name.

200 partitions (100% of the data frame) are cached in memory with 1 replicated copy.

Because of the small size of the data frame/ RDD (6.4KiB), Spark fits it in memory, and doesn't use any disk space.

Figure 11.14 The `results` data frame, successfully cached. Because of the size, everything fits into the RAM.

In the Executors tab, you can also check how much memory storage is being used. An uncached data frame will take a little space (because each executor keeps the instructions to recompute a data frame on the fly), but nowhere as much as caching the data frame.

> ### Persisting: Caching, but with more control
>
> By default, a data frame will be cached using the `MEMORY_AND_DISK` policy, which means that the storage RAM will be used as a priority, falling back to disk if we run out of memory. An RDD will use the `MEMORY_ONLY` policy, which means that it won't use the disk at all for storage. If we don't have enough storage RAM, Spark will recompute the RDD from scratch (negating the effects of caching).
>
> If you want more control over how your data is cached, you can use the `persist()` method, passing the level (as a string) as a parameter. Beyond `MEMORY_ONLY` and `MEMORY_AND_DISK`, you can also opt for `DISK_ONLY`, which foregoes RAM to go straight to disk. You can also add a `_2` suffix (e.g., `MEMORY_ONLY_2`), which will use the same heuristic but duplicate each partition over two nodes.

(continued)

If you can afford the RAM, I suggest using it as much as possible. RAM access is orders of magnitude faster than disk. The actual decision will depend on your Spark instance configuration.

Caching looks like a very useful functionality: it provides an insurance policy, so you don't have to recompute a data frame from scratch if you want to backtrack. In practice, this scenario happens very rarely:

- Caching takes computing and memory resources that are not available for general processing.
- Computing a data frame can sometimes be faster than retrieving it from cache.
- In a noninteractive program, you seldom need to reuse a data frame more than a few times: caching brings no value if you don't reuse the exact data frame more than once.

In other words, mindless caching will most often hinder your program's performance. Now that I've done my public service announcement about how aggressive caching will harm you, what are some cases where you want to cache? I have witnessed two common use cases where caching is useful.

First, caching is useful when you are experimenting with a data frame that (a) fits into memory and (b) needs to refer to the *entire* cached data frame more than a few times. In the case of interactive development (where you are using the REPL to iterate quickly over the same data frame), caching will provide a noticeable increase in speed because you won't have to read from source every time.

Second, caching is extremely useful when you are training an ML model on Spark. ML model fitting will use the training data set multiple times, and recomputing it from scratch is unwieldy. In chapter 13, you'll notice that I casually cache my data frames before training.

As a rule of thumb, before caching, ask yourself this: Do I need this whole piece of data more than a handful of times? In most noninteractive data-processing programs, the answer will be no, and caching will do more harm than good. In the case where the answer is yes, experiment with the different levels of caching (RAM versus disk versus both) to see which one fits your program/Spark instance the most.

This section has covered the dark art of caching and why less is more. In this chapter, I introduced the Spark UI and uncovered the information Spark provides at runtime (and after the fact) to help you make better decisions about the performance of your programs. Having this handy while you are constructing a data pipeline will provide invaluable feedback on the behavior of your code and help you make better performance decisions.

Before ending the chapter, I want to stress that obsessing about performance right from the start won't do you any good. Spark provides many optimizations out of the box—which you can see when analyzing the logical and physical plans—and will provide good performance. When writing a PySpark program, make it *work* first, then make it *clean*, and then make it *fast*, using the Spark UI to help you along the way. Data pipelines, whether they are for ETL or ML, gain a lot from being easy to reason about. Shedding a few minutes of a program is not worth it if it takes you a day to decipher what the program does!

Summary

- Spark uses RAM (or memory) to store data (storage memory), as well as for processing (operational memory) data. Providing enough memory is paramount in the fast processing of Spark jobs and can be configured in the `SparkSession` initialization.

- The Spark UI provides useful information about cluster configuration. This includes memory, CPU, libraries, and OS information.

- A Spark job consists of a series of transformations and one action. Job progress is available in the Job tab of the Spark UI when processing.

- A job is split into stages, which are the logical units of work on a cluster. Stages are split by exchange operations, which are when the data moves around worker nodes. We can look at the stages and steps via the SQL tab in the Spark UI and via the `explain()` method over the resulting data frame.

- A stage consists of narrow operations that are optimized as a unit. Wide operations may require a shuffle/exchange if the necessary data is not local to a node.

- Caching moves data from the source to the storage memory (with an option to spill to disk if there isn't enough memory available). Caching interferes with Spark's ability to optimize and is usually not needed in a pipeline-like program. It is appropriate when reusing a data frame multiple times, such as during ML training.

Part 3

Get confident: Using machine learning with PySpark

Parts 1 and 2 were all about data transformation, but we're going to go above and beyond that by tackling scalable machine learning in part 3. While not a complete treatment of machine learning in itself, this part will give you the foundation to write your own ML programs in a robust and repeatable fashion.

Chapter 12 sets the stage for machine learning by building features, curated bits of information to use for the training process. Feature engineering itself is akin to purposeful data transformation. Get ready to use the skills learned in parts 1 and 2!

Chapter 13 introduces ML pipelines, Spark's way to encapsulate ML workflows in a robust and repeatable way. Now, more importantly than ever, good code structure makes or breaks ML programs, so this tool will keep you sane as you build your models.

Finally, chapter 14 extends the ML pipeline abstraction by creating our own components. With this, your ML workflows will be infinitely versatile without compromising robustness and predictability.

At the end of part 3, you'll be ready to scale your ML programs. Bring in the big data—time for some big insights!

Setting the stage: Preparing features for machine learning

12

This chapter covers

- How investing in a solid data manipulation foundation makes data preparation a breeze
- Addressing big data quality problems with PySpark
- Creating custom features for your ML model
- Selecting compelling features for your model
- Using transformers and estimators as part of the feature engineering process

I get excited doing machine learning, but not for the reasons most people do. I love getting into a new data set and trying to solve a problem. Each data set sports its own problems and idiosyncrasies, and getting it "ML ready" is extremely satisfying. Building a model gives purpose to data transformation; you ingest, clean, profile, and torture the data for a higher purpose: solving a real-life problem. This chapter focuses on the most important stage of machine learning regarding your use case: exploring, understanding, preparing, and giving purpose to your data. More specifically, we focus on preparing a data set by cleaning the data, creating new *features*, which are fields that will serve in training the model (chapter 13), and then looking at selecting a curated set of features based on how promising they look. At the end of the chapter, we will have a clean data set with well-understood features that will be ready for machine learning.

This is not a masterclass in machine learning

This chapter and the next assume a little familiarity with machine learning. I explain the concepts as I go along, but I can't cover the full modeling process, as it would be a book on its own. Furthermore, we can't reasonably learn about honing our intuition about data and modeling in a single chapter. Consider this section one way to proceed to get a model, and I encourage you to experiment with this data set (and others!) to build your own intuition.

If you are interested in learning more about machine learning, I strongly recommend *Introduction to Statistical Learning* by Gareth James, Daniela Witten, Trevor Hastie, and Robert Tibshirani (Springer, 2021, freely available online at https://www.statlearning .com). It uses R, but the concepts transcend languages. For a more practical (and Python-based) introduction, I enjoyed *Real-World Machine Learning* by Henrik Brink, Joseph W. Richards, and Mark Fetherolf (Manning, 2016).

12.1 Reading, exploring, and preparing our machine learning data set

This section covers the ingestion and exploration of our machine learning data set. More specifically, we'll review the content of our data frame, look at incoherences, and prepare our data for feature engineering.

For our ML model, I chose a data set of 20,057 dish names that contain 680 columns characterizing the ingredient list, the nutritional content, and the category of the dish. Our goal here is to predict if this dish is a dessert. It is a simple, mostly unambiguous question—you can probably classify a dish as a dessert or not just by reading the name—which makes it perfect for a simple ML model.

At their core, data cleanup, exploration, and feature preparation are purpose-driven data transformation. Because the data is a CSV file, we reuse the content from chapters 4 and 5. We will use schema information to determine the type of data each column contains (chapter 6), and even use UDFs (chapters 8 and 9) for some specialized column transformations. All of the skills learned thus far will be put to good use!

The data set is available online on Kaggle, an online community for ML enthusiasts that hosts modeling competitions, as well as interesting data sets (https://www.kaggle .com/hugodarwood/epirecipes). I also included the data in the book's companion repository (under `data/recipes/epi_r.csv`). We start our program by setting our `SparkSession` (listing 12.1): we are allocating 8 gibibytes of RAM to my driver (see chapter 11 for more information about how Spark allocates memory). The code in listing 12.2 reads the data frame (using the CSV specialized `SparkReader` object seen in chapter 4) and prints the dimensions of the data frame: 20,057 rows and 680 columns.

We will track those dimensions as we clean the data frame to see how many records are impacted or filtered out.

Listing 12.1 Starting our `SparkSession` for our machine learning program

```
from pyspark.sql import SparkSession
import pyspark.sql.functions as F
import pyspark.sql.types as T

spark = (
    SparkSession.builder.appName("Recipes ML model - Are you a dessert?")
    .config("spark.driver.memory", "8g")
    .getOrCreate()
)
```

Listing 12.2 Ingesting our data set and printing the dimension and schema

```
food = spark.read.csv(
    "./data/recipes/epi_r.csv", inferSchema=True, header=True
)
```

```
print(food.count(), len(food.columns))
# 20057 680
```
Our data set starts with 20,057 rows and 680 columns.

```
food.printSchema()
# root
#  |-- title: string (nullable = true)
#  |-- rating: string (nullable = true)
#  |-- calories: string (nullable = true)
#  |-- protein: double (nullable = true)
#  |-- fat: double (nullable = true)
#  |-- sodium: double (nullable = true)
#  |-- #cakeweek: double (nullable = true)
#  |-- #wasteless: double (nullable = true)
#  |-- 22-minute meals: double (nullable = true)
#  |-- 3-ingredient recipes: double (nullable = true)
#  |-- 30 days of groceries: double (nullable = true)
#  ...
#  |-- créme de cacao: double (nullable = true)
#  |-- crêpe: double (nullable = true)
#  |-- cr??me de cacao: double (nullable = true)
# ... and many more columns
```

Some of the columns contains undesirable characters, such as a # ...

... or a space ...

or some invalid characters!

Before we even start looking at the data, let's make our life easier by standardizing the names of our columns. The next section will show a trick to rename the whole data frame in one fell swoop.

12.1.1 *Standardizing column names using toDF()*

In this section, we process all the column names to give them a uniform look and facilitate their subsequent usage. We will remove anything that isn't a letter or a number, standardize the spaces and other separators to use the underscore (_) character, and replace the ampersand (&) with its English equivalent and. While not mandatory, this will help us in writing a clearer program and improving the consistency of our column names by reducing typos and mistakes.

Just by looking at the schema in section 12.1, we can already see some not-so-desirable column names. While #cakeweek is relatively easy to type, crêpe might be a little harder if you don't have a French keyboard, and don't get me started on cr??me de cacao! When working with data, I like my columns to all be lowercase, with underscores between the words.

To do so, listing 12.3 has a simple Python function, sanitize_column_name(), that will take a "dirty" column name and return it clean. The function is then applied to all the columns in my data frame in one fell swoop, using the toDF() method introduced in chapter 4. toDF(), when used to rename the columns of a data frame, takes as parameters *N* strings, where *N* is the number of columns in our data frame. Since we can access the columns of our data frame via food.columns, a quick list comprehension takes care of renaming everything. I also unpack my list into distinct attributes using the star operator (see appendix C for more details). Having a consistent column naming scheme will make subsequent code easier to write, read, and maintain in the long run: I treat column names like variables in a regular program.

Listing 12.3   Sanitizing my columns in one operation

```
def sanitize_column_name(name):
    """Drops unwanted characters from the column name.

    We replace spaces, dashes and slashes with underscore,
    and only keep alphanumeric characters."""
    answer = name
    for i, j in ((" ", "_"), ("-", "_"), ("/", "_"), ("&", "and")):
        answer = answer.replace(i, j)
    return "".join(
        [
            char
            for char in answer
            if char.isalpha() or char.isdigit() or char == "_"
        ]
    )
```

> I iterate over the characters I want to get rid of, replacing them with something more consistent.

> We only keep letters, numbers, and underscores.

```
food = food.toDF(*[sanitize_column_name(name) for name in food.columns])
```

With this out of the way, we can now start exploring the data. In this section, we ingested and cleaned the column names of our data, making the data frame friendlier to work with. In the next section, we'll classify our columns as different kinds of features, assess the quality of our data, and fill in the gaps.

12.1.2 *Exploring our data and getting our first feature columns*

This section covers digging into our data and encoding our first machine learning features. I introduce the main kind of machine learning features and how to easily keep track of those that we feed into our model training. While we are iteratively exploring data and creating ML features, keeping a tally of the ones we think are promising is the best way for us to stay organized and keep our code organized. At this stage, think of your code as a collection of lab notes: the tidier they are, the easier it'll be to review your work and then production-ize your results!

Exploring data for machine learning is similar to exploring data when performing a transformation in the sense that we manipulate the data to uncover some inconsistencies, patterns, or gaps. Because of this, all the material in previous chapters applies here. Talk about convenience! On the other hand, machine learning has a few idiosyncrasies that impact how we reason about and prepare data. In listing 12.4, I print a summary table for each of the columns in our `food` data frame. This takes a while but gives us a decent summary of the data contained in each column. Unlike single-node data processing, PySpark cannot necessarily assume that a column will fit into memory, so we can't go crazy with charts and extensive data profiling tools.

> **Listing 12.4 Creating a summary table of all our columns**

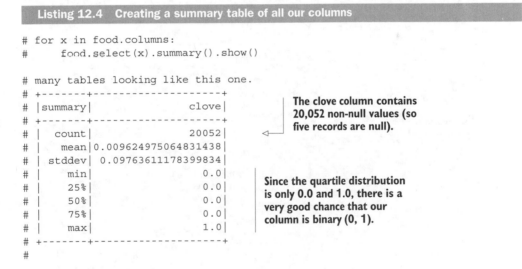

```
# for x in food.columns:
#     food.select(x).summary().show()

# many tables looking like this one.
# +-------+--------------------+
# |summary|               clove|
# +-------+--------------------+
# |  count|               20052|
# |   mean|0.009624975064831438|
# | stddev| 0.09763611178399834|
# |    min|                 0.0|
# |    25%|                 0.0|
# |    50%|                 0.0|
# |    75%|                 0.0|
# |    max|                 1.0|
# +-------+--------------------+
#
```

The clove column contains 20,052 non-null values (so five records are null).

Since the quartile distribution is only 0.0 and 1.0, there is a very good chance that our column is binary (0, 1).

> **TIP** One of the best tips when processing data in PySpark is recognizing that your data is small enough to be gathered into a single node. For pandas DataFrames, you can use the excellent `pandas-profiling` library to automate a lot of the data profiling if your data is pandas size (https://github.com/pandas-profiling/pandas-profiling). Remember: your Python knowledge doesn't go away when you use PySpark!

In our summary data, we are looking at numerical columns. In machine learning, we classify numerical features into two categories: *categorical* or *continuous*. A categorical feature is when your column takes a discrete number, such as the month of the year (1 to 12). A continuous feature is when the column can have infinite possibilities, such as the price of an item. We can subdivide the categorical family into three main types:

- *Binary* (or *dichotomous*), when you have only two choices (0/1, true/false)
- *Ordinal,* when the categories have a certain ordering (e.g., the position in a race) that matters
- *Nominal,* when the categories have no specific ordering (e.g., the color of an item)

Identifying your variables as categorical (with the proper subtype) or continuous has a direct impact on the data preparation and, down the road, the performance of your ML model (use the decision tree in figure 12.1 to assist you). Proper identification is dependent on the context (what does the column mean?) and how you want to encode its meaning. You'll develop a stronger intuition as you develop more ML programs. Don't worry if you don't get it right the first time; you can always come back and touch up your feature types. In chapter 13, we introduce ML pipelines, which provide a nice abstraction for feature preparation, making it easy to evolve your ML code over time.

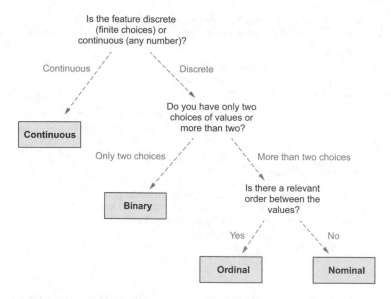

Figure 12.1   The different types of numerical features in a decision tree. Answer the questions to get which feature you are!

Looking at our summary data, it seems that we have a lot of potentially binary columns. In the case of the `clove` column, the minimum and three quartile values are all zero. To verify this, we'll group the entire data frame and collect a set of distinct values. If we have only two values for a given column, binary it is! In listing 12.5, we create a temporary data frame, `is_binary`, to identify the binary columns. We collect the results into a pandas DataFrame—since the resulting data frame has only one row—and un-pivot the result using the `unstack()` method available through pandas (PySpark has no easy way to un-pivot). Most columns are binary. I am personally not convinced about `cakeweek` and `wasteless`. Time to investigate!

Listing 12.5   Identifying the binary columns from our data frame

```
import pandas as pd

pd.set_option("display.max_rows", 1000)       ◁─── pandas will display a handful of rows at
                                                    a time. Setting this option will print at
                                                    most 1,000 rows, which will be helpful
                                                    when exploring data.
is_binary = food.agg(
    *[
        (F.size(F.collect_set(x)) == 2).alias(x)       ◁───
        for x in food.columns
    ]
).toPandas()

is_binary.unstack()       ◁───

# title                    0    False
# rating                   0    False
# calories                 0    False
# protein                  0    False
# fat                      0    False
# sodium                   0    False
# cakeweek                 0    False
# wasteless                0    False
# 22_minute_meals          0    True
# 3_ingredient_recipes     0    True
# ... the rest are all = True
```

unstack un-pivots a pandas DataFrame, making a wide data frame easier to analyze in the terminal.

collect_set() will create a set of the distinct values as an array, and size() returns the length of the array. Two distinct values means that it's probably binary.

This section covered the main types of numerical features we encounter in machine learning and identified the binary features in our data frame. In the next section, we'll perform some analysis on the remaining columns and establish our base set of features.

12.1.3 *Addressing data mishaps and building our first feature set*

In this section, we investigate some seemingly incoherent features and, following our findings, clean our data set. We also identify our first feature set, along with each feature type. This section is an example of forensic data exploration, a tremendously important part of a data analyst and scientist's job. In this case, some columns are not consistent compared to other related (binary) columns. We explore the content of the suspicious columns, address the gaps, and continue our exploration. The result? A more consistent, more robust feature set that will lead to a better ML model.

At the end of section 12.1.2, we concluded that the vast majority of our feature columns in our data set were binary. Furthermore, there were two columns that were suspicious: `cakeweek` and `wasteless`. In the next listing, I display the discrete values both columns can take and then show the records where one of them contains a nonbinary value.

Listing 12.6   Identifying the distinct values for our two suspicious columns

```
food.agg(*[F.collect_set(x) for x in ("cakeweek", "wasteless")]).show(
    1, False
)

# +----------------------------------+---------------------+
# |collect_set(cakeweek)             |collect_set(wasteless)|
# +----------------------------------+---------------------+
# |[0.0, 1.0, 1188.0, 24.0, 880.0]   |[0.0, 1.0, 1439.0]   |
# +----------------------------------+---------------------+

food.where("cakeweek > 1.0 or wasteless > 1.0").select(
    "title", "rating", "wasteless", "cakeweek", food.columns[-1]
).show()

# +--------------------+--------------------+---------+--------+------+
# |               title|              rating|wasteless|cakeweek|turkey|
# +--------------------+--------------------+---------+--------+------+
# |"Beet Ravioli wit...| Aged Balsamic Vi...|      0.0|   880.0|   0.0|
# |"Seafood ""Catapl...|            Vermouth|   1439.0|    24.0|   0.0|
# |"""Pot Roast"" of...| Aunt Gloria-Style "|      0.0|  1188.0|   0.0|
# +--------------------+--------------------+---------+--------+------+
```

> I print the first few records and the last records to see potential data alignment problems.

For three records, it seems like our data set had a bunch of quotation marks along with some commas that confused PySpark's otherwise robust parser. In our case, since we have a small number of records affected, I did not bother with realigning the data and deleted them outright. I keep the null values as well.

Should a large number of records be *misaligned*, where the CSV records boundaries that do not align consistently with what you'd expect, you can try to read the record as text and use a UDF to extract the relevant information manually, before saving the results into a better data format such as Parquet (see chapter 6 and 10). There is no silver bullet for problematic CSV data, unfortunately.

Listing 12.7   Keeping only the legit values for `cakeweek` and `wasteless`

```
food = food.where(
    (
        F.col("cakeweek").isin([0.0, 1.0])
        | F.col("cakeweek").isNull()
    )
    & (
        F.col("wasteless").isin([0.0, 1.0])
        | F.col("wasteless").isNull()
    )
)

print(food.count(), len(food.columns))

# 20054 680
```

> This reads as follows: "'if cakeweek and wasteless are both either 0.0, 1.0, or null.'"

> We lost three records, as expected.

In listing 12.7, I check my filtering by printing the dimensions of my data frame. It's not a perfect way to know if my code is bug-free, but it helps to validate that I'm removing only the three offending records. If something goes wrong data-wise, this information can help to pinpoint where in the code our data went wrong. For instance, if after filtering the data frame I lost 10,000 records when I expected to lose only three, this would tell me that I might be heavy-handed with my filtering.

Now that we have identified two binary-in-hiding feature columns, we can identify our feature set and our target variable. The *target* (or *label*) is the column containing the value we want to predict. In our case, the column is aptly named `dessert`. In listing 12.8, I create all-caps variables containing the four main sets of columns I care about:

- The *identifiers*, which are the column(s) that contain the information unique to each record
- The *targets*, which are the column(s) (most often one) that contain the value we wish to predict
- The *continuous* columns, containing continuous features
- The *binary* columns, containing binary features

The data set does not seem to contain categorical variables.

Listing 12.8 Creating four top-level variables

```
IDENTIFIERS = ["title"]

CONTINUOUS_COLUMNS = [
    "rating",
    "calories",
    "protein",
    "fat",
    "sodium",
]

TARGET_COLUMN = ["dessert"]        ◁──  Although I have only one
                                        target, I find it convenient
                                        to put it into a list to be
                                        consistent with the other
                                        VARIABLES.

BINARY_COLUMNS = [
    x
    for x in food.columns
    if x not in CONTINUOUS_COLUMNS
    and x not in TARGET_COLUMN
    and x not in IDENTIFIERS
]
```

I like to keep track of my features through variables instead of deleting them from my data frame. It removes some of the guesswork when you get the data ready for the model training—which columns are features, again?—and it serves as lightweight documentation when reading your code the next time. It's basic, but it serves our purpose well here.

In this section, we rapidly cleaned our data. In practice, this stage will take more than half your time when building an ML model. Fortunately, data cleaning is principled data manipulation, so you can leverage everything in the PySpark tool kit you've built so far. We also identified our features and their type and grouped them into lists, which makes it easier to reference in the next sections. In the next section, we'll take care of removing useless records and filling the `null` values of the binary features.

12.1.4   *Weeding out useless records and imputing binary features*

This section covers the deletion of useless records, those that provide no information to our ML model. In our case, this means removing two types of records:

- Those where all the features are `null`
- Those where the target is `null`

Furthermore, we will impute, meaning that we will provide a *default value* for, our binary features. Since each of them are `0/1`, where zero is `False` and one is `True`, we equate `null` to `False` and fill zero as a default value. Given the context of our model, this is a reasonable assumption. Those operations are common to every ML model. We always face a point where we want to ensure every record will provide some sort of information to our ML model. I like to perform this early in the process, as filtering completely `null` records needs to happen before any imputation. Once you've filled `null` values on certain columns, you won't know which record was entirely `null`.

Keep some lab notes!

In this section and the next, we do quite a bit of yo-yoing. I did my best to relatively order the data-cleaning portion of our program. In all honesty, when building the original script for this chapter, I rearranged many sections as I profiled and examined the data. Your own attempt at cleaning the data would have certainly yielded a very different program.

Data preparation for machine learning is part art, part science. Intuition and experience come into play; you will end up recognizing some data patterns and create a personal library of strategies to deal with them. Because of this, it's crucial to document your steps to make it easier on your future self (and your colleagues!) when you pull that code back. I keep a notebook by my side when cleaning data, and I make sure to collect my "lab" notes in a format that will be easy to share.

The code in listing 12.9 uses the `dropna()` method, seen in chapter 5 with two subsets. The first one is *every column but the name of the recipe* (stored in the `IDENTIFIERS` variable). The second one is the `TARGET_COLUMN`. We lose five records in the process. Because of the low number of records lost, I won't bother with *manual labeling*, or manually inputting the values for each record according to my best judgment. Labeling is always a labor-intensive operation, but sometimes, for instance, when your target is spotty or you have very little data,[1] you can't get around it. Robert (Munro)

---

[1]   You would probably not be using PySpark if this were the case.

Monarch dedicates a complete book on the topic in *Human-in-the-Loop Machine Learning* (Manning, 2021).

Listing 12.9 Removing the records that have only `null` values

```
food = food.dropna(
    how="all",
    subset=[x for x in food.columns if x not in IDENTIFIERS],    ◁
)

food = food.dropna(subset=TARGET_COLUMN)    ◁

print(food.count(), len(food.columns))
# 20049 680    ◁
```

I can use the feature group variables instead of having to remember which column is which.

We lose five records in the process (20,054 - 5 = 20,049).

As a second step, I impute a default value to all my binary columns. As a rule of thumb, 1 means `True` and 0 means `False`. In the context of our binary variable (presence of an ingredient or classification of the dish according to a certain label), an absence of a value can be thought of as being conceptually closer to false than true, so we'll default every binary feature column to `0.0`.

Listing 12.10 Setting a default value of `0.0` to every binary feature column

```
food = food.fillna(0.0, subset=BINARY_COLUMNS)

print(food.where(F.col(BINARY_COLUMNS[0]).isNull()).count())   # => 0
```

This section covered the filtration of useless records using `dropna()`, as well as the imputation of binary features according to a scalar value. In the next section, we look at continuous columns by exploring their distribution and checking the ranges of values.

12.1.5 Taking care of extreme values: Cleaning continuous columns

This section covers the analysis of continuous values in the context of feature preparation. More specifically, we review the distribution of numerical columns to account for extreme or unrealistic values. Many ML models don't deal well with extreme values (see chapter 13, when we discuss feature normalization). Just like we did with binary columns, taking the time to assess the fit of our numerical columns will pay dividends since we will not feed the wrong information to our ML model.

> **WARNING** In this section, we process extreme values using the knowledge we have about the data. We do not build a blanket blueprint to be applied regardless of the situation. Careless data transformation can introduce anomalies in your data, so be sure to take the time to understand the problem at hand.

Before we can start exploring the distribution of our continuous features, we need to make sure they are properly typed (see chapter 6 for a refresher on types). Looking back at our schema in listing 12.2, because of some data misalignment, PySpark inferred the type of the `rating` and `calories` column as a string, where they should have been numerical. In listing 12.11, a simple UDF takes a string column and returns `True` if the value is a floating-point number (or a `null`—PySpark will allow `null` values in a `Double` column) and `False` otherwise. I am doing this more as an exploration than as a bona fide cleaning step; since a string value in any of those two columns means that the data is misaligned, I will drop the record rather than try to fix it.

The UDF looks rather complicated, but if we take it slowly, it's very simple. I return `True` right off the bat if the value is `null`. If I have a non-`null` value, I try to cast the value as a Python `float`. If it fails, `False` it is!

Listing 12.11 Non-numerical values in the `rating` and `calories` columns

```python
from typing import Optional


@F.udf(T.BooleanType())
def is_a_number(value: Optional[str]) -> bool:
    if not value:
        return True
    try:
        _ = float(value)          # The underscore means
    except ValueError:            # "perform the work, but I
        return False              # don't care about the result."
    return True


food.where(~is_a_number(F.col("rating"))).select(
    *CONTINUOUS_COLUMNS
).show()

# +---------+------------+-------+----+------+
# |   rating|    calories|protein| fat|sodium|          We have one
# +---------+------------+-------+----+------+          last rogue
# | Cucumber| and Lemon "|   3.75|null|  null|          record!
# +---------+------------+-------+----+------+
```

We have a single remaining rogue record (damn those pesky unaligned CSVs!) that I remove in the next listing before confidently casting the columns as a double. Our continuous feature columns are now all numerical.

Listing 12.12 Casting the `rating` and `calories` columns into double

```python
for column in ["rating", "calories"]:
    food = food.where(is_a_number(F.col(column)))
    food = food.withColumn(column, F.col(column).cast(T.DoubleType()))

print(food.count(), len(food.columns))

# 20048 680          One record lost!
```

Now we want to look at the actual values to remove any ridiculous values that would break the computation of the average. We repeat the summary table displayed in rapid fire during our initial data exploration (listing 12.4) in listing 12.13. We immediately see that some dishes are over the top!

Just like with binary features, we need to use our judgment for the best course of action to address this data quality issue. I could filter the records once more, but this time, I'll cap the values to the 99th percentile, avoiding extreme (and potentially wrong) values.

Listing 12.13 Looking at the values in our continuous feature columns

```
food.select(*CONTINUOUS_COLUMNS).summary(
    "mean",
    "stddev",
    "min",
    "1%",
    "5%",
    "50%",
    "95%",
    "99%",
    "max",
).show()

# +-------+------------------+------------------+------------------+
# |summary|            rating|          calories|           protein|
# +-------+------------------+------------------+------------------+
# |   mean| 3.714460295291301|6324.0634571930705|100.17385283565179|
# | stddev|1.3409187660508959|359079.83696340164|3840.6809971287403|
# |    min|               0.0|               0.0|               0.0|
# |     1%|               0.0|              18.0|               0.0|
# |     5%|               0.0|              62.0|               0.0|
# |    50%|             4.375|             331.0|               8.0|
# |    95%|               5.0|            1318.0|              75.0|
# |    99%|               5.0|            3203.0|             173.0|
# |    max|               5.0|        3.0111218E7|          236489.0|
# +-------+------------------+------------------+------------------+

# +-------+------------------+-----------------+
# |summary|               fat|           sodium|
# +-------+------------------+-----------------+
# |   mean| 346.9398083953107|6226.927244193346|
# | stddev| 20458.04034412409|333349.5680370268|
# |    min|               0.0|              0.0|
# |     1%|               0.0|              1.0|
# |     5%|               0.0|              5.0|
# |    50%|              17.0|            294.0|
# |    95%|              85.0|           2050.0|
# |    99%|             207.0|           5661.0|
# |    max|         1722763.0|       2.767511E7|
# +-------+------------------+-----------------+
```

In the next listing, I hardcode the `maximum` acceptable values for each column, and then I apply those maximums iteratively to my food data frame.

Listing 12.14   Imputing the average value for four continuous columns

```
maximum = {
    "calories": 3203.0,
    "protein": 173.0,
    "fat": 207.0,
    "sodium": 5661.0,
}
```

I hardcode the values here to make sure my analysis is consistent across runs. If the data changes, I might want to recheck if the 99th percentile is still a good measure before automating the imputation, but I am comfortable with those exact values for the time being.

```
for k, v in maximum.items():
    food = food.withColumn(
        k,
        F.when(F.isnull(F.col(k)), F.col(k)).otherwise(
            F.least(F.col(k), F.lit(v))
        ),
    )
```

Because I want to preserve the null values, I keep them through a when clause. The least function will only apply to non-null records.

There is no surefire way to take care of outliers or identify them in the first place; 5,661 mg of sodium is still criminally high, but more realistic considering some outrageous recipes available in the wild. In this chapter, I won't come back to it, but this would be one instance where I'd leave some breadcrumbs after completing a full cycle to tweak my approach.

> **NOTE** What about `null` imputation here, like we did on for the binary features? PySpark provides a convenient mechanism through the `Imputer` estimator. We see this useful topic in section 12.3.1.

In this section, we imputed `null` records globally on our data set. We also cleaned the categorical feature columns using a small UDF. In the next section, we head back to binary columns to remove low-occurring features.

12.1.6 *Weeding out the rare binary occurrence columns*

In this section, I remove the columns that are not present enough in the data set to be considered reliable predictors. Binary features with only a few zeroes or ones are not helpful in classifying a recipe as a dessert: if every recipe (or no recipe) has a certain feature as true, then that feature does not *discriminate* properly, meaning that our model has no use for it.

Rarely occurring features are an annoyance when building a model, as the machine can pick up a signal that is there by chance. For example, if you are flipping a fair coin and get heads and use that as a feature for a model predicting the next flip, you might get a dummy model that will predict 100% heads. It'll work perfectly until you get tails. In the same vein, you want to have enough representation for each feature that goes into your model.

For this model, I choose 10 to be my threshold. I do not want binary features with less than 10 of `0.0` or `1.0` in my model. In listing 12.15, I compute the sum of each binary column; this will give me the number of 1.0 since the sum of the ones is equal to their count. If the count of the ones/sum of a column is below 10 or above the number of records minus 10, I collect the column name to remove it.

Listing 12.15 Removing the binary features that happen too little or too often

```
inst_sum_of_binary_columns = [
    F.sum(F.col(x)).alias(x) for x in BINARY_COLUMNS
]

sum_of_binary_columns = (
    food.select(*inst_sum_of_binary_columns).head().asDict()    ◁──────┐
)

num_rows = food.count()
too_rare_features = [
    k
    for k, v in sum_of_binary_columns.items()
    if v < 10 or v > (num_rows - 10)
]

len(too_rare_features)  # => 167

print(too_rare_features)
# ['cakeweek', 'wasteless', '30_days_of_groceries',
# [...]
#  'yuca', 'cookbooks', 'leftovers']

BINARY_COLUMNS = list(set(BINARY_COLUMNS) - set(too_rare_features))    ◁──
```

> Since a row is just like a Python dictionary, I can bring the row back to the driver and process it locally.

> Rather than deleting the columns from the data frame, I just remove them from my **BINARY_COLUMNS** list.

We removed 167 features that are either too rare or too frequent. While this number seems high, some of the features are very precise for a data set with a few thousand recipes. When creating your own model, you will certainly want to play around with different values to see if some parameters are still too rare to provide reliable predictions.

In this section, we removed rare binary features, reducing our feature space by 167 elements. In the next section, we look at creating custom features that might improve the predictive power of our model. We also generate and refine new features using a combination of those that already exist.

12.2 Feature creation and refinement

This section covers two important steps of model building: *feature creation* (also called *feature engineering*) and *refinement*. Feature creation and refinement are where the data scientists can express their judgment and creativity. Our ability to encode meaning and recognize patterns in the data means that our model can more easily pick up on the signal. We could potentially spend a lot of time crafting more and more sophisticated features. Since my goal is to provide an end-to-end model using PySpark, we look at the following:

- Creating a few custom features using our continuous feature columns
- Measuring correlation over original and generated continuous features

These are by no means the only ways we could approach this, but the steps give a good overview of what can be done in PySpark.

12.2.1 Creating custom features

In this section, we look at creating new features from the data we have at hand. Doing so can improve our model interpretability and predictive power. I show one example of feature preparation that places a few continuous features on the same scale as our binary ones.

Fundamentally, creating a custom feature in PySpark is nothing more than creating a new column, with a little more thought and notes on the side. Manual feature creation is one of the secret weapons of a data scientist: you can embed business knowledge into highly custom features that can improve your model's accuracy and interpretability. As an example, we'll take the `protein` and `fat` columns representing the quantity (in grams) of protein and fat in the recipe, respectively. With the information in those two columns, I create two features representing the percentage of calories attributed to each macro nutriment.

Listing 12.16 Creating new features that compute calories attributable to protein and fat

```
food = food.withColumn(
    "protein_ratio", F.col("protein") * 4 / F.col("calories")
).withColumn(
    "fat_ratio", F.col("fat") * 9 / F.col("calories")
)

food = food.fillna(0.0, subset=["protein_ratio", "fat_ratio"])

CONTINUOUS_COLUMNS += ["protein_ratio", "fat_ratio"]
```

There are 4 kcal per grams of protein and 9 kcal per grams of fat.

I add the two columns in my set of continuous features.

By creating these two columns, I integrate new knowledge into my data. Without adding the energy per gram of fat and protein, nothing in the data set would have provided this. The model could have drawn a relationship between the actual quantity of fat/proteins and the total calories count independently, but we're making this more obvious by allowing the model to have access to the ratio of protein/fat (and carbs; see the sidebar at the end of this section) directly.

Before we get to modeling, we'll want to remove the correlation between our continuous variables and assemble all our features into a single, clean entity. This section was extremely short, but keep this lesson close to you when building a model: you can embed new knowledge into your data set by creating custom features. In PySpark, creating new features is done simply by creating columns with the information you want; this means you can create simple or highly sophisticated features.

Why not do the same with carbs? Avoiding multicollinearity

Without going too deep into how food translates, I did not compute a carbs ratio as a custom feature. Beyond the fact that the total amount of carbs is not provided (and that carbs absorption is a little more complex), we have to consider the *linear dependence* (or *multicollinearity*) of our variables when working with certain types of models.

A linear dependence between variables happens when you have one column that can be represented as a linear combination of others. You might be tempted to approximate the ratio of calories coming from carbs using the formula

Total calories = 4 * (g of carbs) + 4 * (g of proteins) + 9 * (g of fat)

or using a ratio-based approach:

1 = (% of calories from carbs) + (% of calories from proteins) + (% of calories from fat)

In both cases, we introduce a linear dependency: we (and the machine) can compute the values of a column using nothing but the values of other columns. When using a model that has a linear component, such as the linear regression and the logistic regression, this will cause problems with your model's accuracy (either under- or over-fitting).

Multicollinearity can happen even if you pay attention to your variable selection. For more information, I recommend referring to *Introduction to Statistical Learning* (Springer, 2021), section 3.3.3.

12.2.2 *Removing highly correlated features*

In this section, we take our set of continuous variables and look at the correlation between them in order to improve our model accuracy and explainability. I explain how PySpark builds a correlation matrix and the `Vector` and `DenseMatrix` objects and how we can extract data from those objects for decision making.

Correlation in linear models is not always bad; as a matter of fact, you want your features to be correlated with your target (this provides predictive power). On the other hand, we want to avoid correlation between features for two main reasons:

- If two features are highly correlated, it means that they provide almost the same information. In the context of machine learning, this can confuse the fitting algorithm and create model or numerical instability.
- The more complex your model, the more complex the maintenance. Highly correlated features rarely provide improved accuracy, yet complicate the model. Simple is better.

For computing correlation between variables, PySpark provides the `Correlation` object. `Correlation` has a single method, `corr`, that computes the correlation between features in a `Vector`. Vectors are like PySpark arrays but with a special representation optimized for ML work (see chapter 13 for a more detailed introduction). In listing 12.17, I use the `VectorAssembler` transformer on the `food` data frame to create a new column, `continuous_features`, that contains a `Vector` of all our continuous features.

A transformer is a preconfigured object that, as its name indicates, transforms a data frame. Independently, it looks like unnecessary complexity, but it shines when applied within a pipeline. I cover transformers in greater detail in chapter 13.

Listing 12.17   Assembling feature columns into a single `Vector` column

```
from pyspark.ml.feature import VectorAssembler

continuous_features = VectorAssembler(
    inputCols=CONTINUOUS_COLUMNS, outputCol="continuous_features"
)

vector_food = food.select(CONTINUOUS_COLUMNS)
for x in CONTINUOUS_COLUMNS:
    vector_food = vector_food.where(~F.isnull(F.col(x)))

vector_variable = continuous_features.transform(vector_food)

vector_variable.select("continuous_features").show(3, False)

# +-----------------------------------------------------------------+
# |continuous_features                                              |
# +-----------------------------------------------------------------+
# |[2.5,426.0,30.0,7.0,559.0,0.28169014084507044,0.14788732394366197]  |
# |[4.375,403.0,18.0,23.0,1439.0,0.17866004962779156,0.5136476426799007]|
# |[3.75,165.0,6.0,7.0,165.0,0.14545454545454545,0.38181818181818183]  |
# +-----------------------------------------------------------------+
# only showing top 3 rows

vector_variable.select("continuous_features").printSchema()

# root
#  |-- continuous_features: vector (nullable = true)
```

> Vector columns cannot have null values (and they don't make sense when computing correlation), so we remove them through a series of where() (see chapter 4).

> **NOTE**   Correlation will not work well if you blend categorical and/or binary features together. Choosing the appropriate dependency measure depends on your model, your interpretability needs, and your data. See, for instance, the Jaccard distance measure for noncontinuous data.

In listing 12.18, I apply the `Correlation.corr()` function on my continuous feature vector and export the correlation matrix into an easily interpretable pandas DataFrame. PySpark returns the correlation matrix in a `DenseMatrix` column type, which is like a two-dimensional vector. In order to extract the values in an easy-to-read format, we have to do a little method juggling:

1   We extract a single record as a list of `Row` using `head()`.
2   A `Row` is like an ordered dictionary, so we can access the first (and only) field containing our correlation matrix using list slicing.
3   A `DenseMatrix` can be converted into a pandas-compatible array by using the `toArray()` method on the matrix.
4   We can directly create a pandas DataFrame from our Numpy array. Inputting our column names as an index (in this case, they'll play the role of "row names") makes our correlation matrix very readable.

Listing 12.18 Creating a correlation matrix in PySpark

```
from pyspark.ml.stat import Correlation

correlation = Correlation.corr(
    vector_variable, "continuous_features"
)

correlation.printSchema()

# root
#  |-- pearson(binary_features): matrix (nullable = false)

correlation_array = correlation.head()[0].toArray()

correlation_pd = pd.DataFrame(
    correlation_array,
    index=CONTINUOUS_COLUMNS,
    columns=CONTINUOUS_COLUMNS,
)

print(correlation_pd.iloc[:, :4])

#                    rating  calories   protein       fat
# rating           1.000000 -0.019631 -0.020484 -0.027028
# calories        -0.019631  1.000000  0.958442  0.978012
# protein         -0.020484  0.958442  1.000000  0.947768
# fat             -0.027028  0.978012  0.947768  1.000000
# sodium          -0.032499  0.938167  0.936153  0.914338
# protein_ratio   -0.026485  0.029879  0.121392  0.086444
# fat_ratio       -0.010696 -0.007470  0.000260  0.029411

print(correlation_pd.iloc[:, 4:])

#                   sodium  protein_ratio  fat_ratio
# rating          -0.032499      -0.026485  -0.010696
# calories         0.938167       0.029879  -0.007470
# protein          0.936153       0.121392   0.000260
# fat              0.914338       0.086444   0.029411
# sodium           1.000000       0.049268  -0.005783
# protein_ratio    0.049268       1.000000   0.111694
# fat_ratio       -0.005783       0.111694   1.000000
```

The corr method takes a data frame and a Vector column reference as a parameter and generates a single-row, single-column data frame containing the correlation matrix.

Since the data frame is small enough to be brought locally, we extract the first record with head() and the first column via an index slice, and we export the matrix as a NumPy array via toArray().

The resulting DenseMatrix (shown as matrix in the schema) is not easily accessible by itself.

The easiest way to interpret the correlation matrix is to create a pandas DataFrame. We can pass out column names as both index and columns for easy interpretability.

The correlation matrix gives the correlation between each field of the vector. The diagonal is always 1.0 because each variable is perfectly correlated with itself.

When working with summary measures, such as the correlation of hypothesis tests, PySpark will often delegate the extraction of values to a simple NumPy or pandas conversion. Instead of remembering a different series of method juggling for each scenario, I use the REPL and the inline documentation:

1   Look at the schema of your data frame and the documentation of the method/ function used: matrix or vector? They are NumPy arrays in disguise.
2   Since your data frame will always fit in memory, bring the desired records and extract the structures using head(), take(), and the methods available on Row objects.

3 Finally, wrap your data in a pandas DataFrame, a list, or your structure of choice.

Once again, our CONTINUOUS_COLUMNS variable avoided a ton of typing and potential errors, which helps in keeping track of our features when manipulating our data frame.

The last step from our correlation computation is to assess which variables we want to keep and which we want to drop. There is no absolute threshold for keeping or removing correlated variables (nor is there a protocol for which variable to keep). From the correlation matrix in listing 12.18, we see high correlation between sodium, calories, protein, and fat. Surprisingly, we see little correlation between our custom features and the columns that contributed to their creation. In my lab notes, I'd collect the following action items:

- Explore the relationship between calorie count and the ratio of macro nutriments (and sodium). Is there a pattern there, or is the calorie count (or size of portions) just all over the place?
- Is the calorie/protein/fat/sodium content related to the "dessert-ness" of the recipes? I can't imagine a dessert being very salty.
- Run the model with all features, then with calories and protein removed. What is the impact on performance?

The correlation analysis raised more questions than it answered. This is a very good thing: data quality is a complicated thing to assess. By keeping track of elements to explore in greater detail, we can move quickly to modeling and have a (crude) benchmark to anchor our next modeling cycles. We refactor our Python programs, and ML models are no exception!

In this section, I covered how PySpark computes the correlation between variables and provides the results in a matrix. We saw the Vector and Matrix objects and how we can extract values from them. Finally, we assessed the correlation between our continuous variables and made a decision about their inclusion in our first model. In the next section, we get into preparing our features for machine learning with the usage of transformers and estimators.

12.3 *Feature preparation with transformers and estimators*

This section provides an overview of transformers and estimators in the context of feature preparation. We use transformers and estimators as an abstraction over common operations in machine learning modeling. We explore two relevant examples of transformers and estimators:

- Null imputation, where we provide a value to replace null occurrences in a column (e.g., the mean)
- Scaling features, where we normalize the values of a column, so they are on a more logical scale (e.g., between zero and one)

Transformers and estimators are powerful on their own but are especially relevant in the context of ML pipelines, introduced in chapter 13.

We saw an example of a transformer in section 12.2.2 through the `VectorAssembler` object. The best way to think about a transformer is by translating its behavior into a function. In figure 12.2, I compare a `VectorAssembler` to a function `assemble_vector()` that performs the same work, which is to create a `Vector` named after the argument to `outputCol`, which contains all the values in the columns passed to `inputCols`. Don't focus on the actual work here, but more on the mechanism of application.

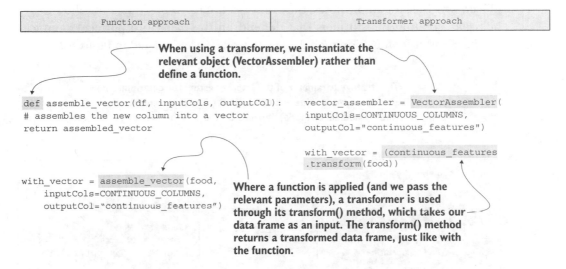

Figure 12.2 Comparing a function applied on a data frame to a transformer. The transformer object separates parameterization (at instantiation) and application on the data (via the `transform()` method).

The function is applied to the data frame, along with the parameterization, and returns a transformed data frame.

The transformer object has a two-staged process. First, when instantiating the transformer, we provide the parameters necessary for its application, but *not* the data frame on which it'll be applied. This echoes the separation of data and instructions we saw in chapter 1. Then, we use the instantiated transformer's `transform()` method on the data frame to get a transformed data frame.

TIP We could reproduce that two-staged process using the `transform()` method and a transform-enabled function. See appendix C for an introduction to the topic.

This separation of instructions and data is key in creating serializable ML pipelines, which leads to easier ML experiments and model portability. Chapter 13 covers this topic in greater detail when we build our model.

Estimators are like a transformers factory. The next two sections introduce estimators through the usage of `Imputer` and `MinMaxScaler`.

12.3.1 *Imputing continuous features using the Imputer estimator*

In this section, we cover the `Imputer` estimator and introduce the concept of an estimator. Estimators are the main abstraction used by Spark for any data-dependent transformation, including ML models, so they are pervasive in any ML code using PySpark.

At the core, an estimator is a transformer-generating object. We instantiate an estimator object just like a transformer by providing the relevant parameters to its constructor. To apply an estimator, we call the `fit()` method, which returns a `Model` object, which is, for all purposes, the same as a transformer. Estimators allow for automatically creating transformers that depend on the data. As a perfect example, the `Imputer` and its companion model, `ImputerModel`, are depicted in figure 12.3.

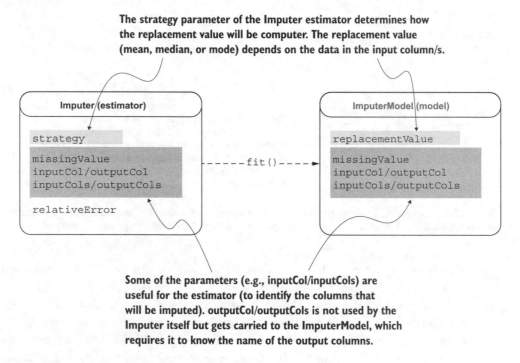

The strategy parameter of the Imputer estimator determines how the replacement value will be computer. The replacement value (mean, median, or mode) depends on the data in the input column/s.

Some of the parameters (e.g., inputCol/inputCols) are useful for the estimator (to identify the columns that will be imputed). outputCol/outputCols is not used by the Imputer itself but gets carried to the ImputerModel, which requires it to know the name of the output columns.

Figure 12.3   The `Imputer` and its companion transformer/model, `ImputerModel`. When `fit()` is called on an instantiated estimator, a fully parameterized transformer (called Model) is created.

As an example, we want our `Imputer` to impute the mean value to every record in the `calories`, `protein`, `fat`, and `sodium` columns when the record is null. We would parameterize the `Imputer` object like in the next listing, providing the relevant parameters seen in figure 12.3 (the `missingValue` and `relativeError` are okay with their default parameters).

Listing 12.19 Instantiating and applying the `Imputer` to create an `ImputerModel`

```
from pyspark.ml.feature import Imputer

OLD_COLS = ["calories", "protein", "fat", "sodium"]
NEW_COLS = ["calories_i", "protein_i", "fat_i", "sodium_i"]

imputer = Imputer(
    strategy="mean",
    inputCols=OLD_COLS,
    outputCols=NEW_COLS,
)

imputer_model = imputer.fit(food)

CONTINUOUS_COLUMNS = (
    list(set(CONTINUOUS_COLUMNS) - set(OLD_COLS)) + NEW_COLS
)
```

We use the mean of each column to fill the null values.

Since we have four columns to impute, we pass their name to inputCols.

I give an _i suffix to every variable to give me a visual cue about how they were created.

The ImputerModel object is created as a result of the fit() method being called with the food data frame.

I adjust the **CONTINUOUS_COLUMNS** variable to account for the new column names.

WARNING If a transformer or an estimator has `inputCol`/`outputCol` *and* `inputCols`/`outputCols` as parameters, it means they can be applied on either one or many columns. You can only choose one of those options. When in doubt, review the signature and the documentation for the object.

We apply the resulting `ImputerModel` just like with any transformer by using the `transform()` method. In the next listing, we see that `calories` is correctly imputed to approximately 475.52 calories. Neat!

Listing 12.20 Using the `ImputerModel` object just like a transformer

```
food_imputed = imputer_model.transform(food)

food_imputed.where("calories is null").select("calories", "calories_i").show(
    5, False
)
# +--------+-----------------+
# |calories|calories_i       |
# +--------+-----------------+
# |null    |475.5222194325885|
# |null    |475.5222194325885|
# |null    |475.5222194325885|
# |null    |475.5222194325885|
# |null    |475.5222194325885|
# +--------+-----------------+
# only showing top 5 rows
```

Our Imputer works as expected: null calories means 475.52 calories_i.

Estimators and transformers will make a comeback in chapter 13, as they are the building blocks of ML pipelines. In this section, we reviewed the estimator and its relationship to the transformer through the `Imputer`. In the next section, we see another example through the `MinMaxScaler`.

> **Model or model: It depends on the angle you see it from**
>
> Although we are covering this topic in greater detail in chapter 13, there is a clash of words between model (like a machine learning model) and `Model`, the output of a fitted estimator.
>
> In Spark's world, an estimator is a data-dependent construction that, upon calling the `fit()` method, yields a `Model` object. This means that any ML model (lowercase "m") available in PySpark is an estimator that we `fit()` on the data to get a trained `Model` object.
>
> On the flip side, although our `ImputerModel` is a `Model` object (capital "M"), it is not really an ML model. For PySpark, we used the `fit()` method with some data to generate a `Model` object, so the definition stands as far as Spark is concerned.

12.3.2 *Scaling our features using the MinMaxScaler estimator*

This section covers variable scaling using the `MinMaxScaler` transformer. Scaling variables means performing a mathematical transformation on the variables so that they are all on the same numeric scale. When using a linear model, having scaled features means that your model coefficients (the weight of each feature) are comparable. This provides a tremendous boost to the interpretability of the model, a useful asset to have when assessing model performance. For some types of models, such as neural nets, scaled features also help with model performance.

As an example, if you have a variable that contains a number between 0.0 and 1.0 and another that contains a number between 1,000.0 and 2,500.0, if they both have the same model coefficient (let's say 0.48), you might be tempted to think that both are equally important. In reality, the second variable is much more important because 0.48 times something in the thousands is much higher than 0.48 times something between zero and one.

To choose the right scaling algorithm, we need to look at our variables as a whole. Since we have so many binary variables, it is convenient to have every variable be between zero and one. Our `protein_ratio` and `fat_ratio` are ratios between zero and one too! PySpark provides the `MinMaxScaler` for this use case: for each value in the input column, it creates a normalized output between `0.0` and `1.0` (further options for the `MinMaxScaler` are introduced in chapter 13).

In listing 12.21, we create a `MinMaxScaler` estimator and provide the vector column input and output columns as strings. This follows the same steps as the `Imputer/ImputerModel`.

min and max represent the minimum and maximum values the resulting column should take and are passed verbatim to the MinMaxScalerModel. When the fit( ) method is called, the estimator computes the min and max of the column (named E_min and E_max).

The formula is then applied on each value of the column when we call the transform( ) method of the MinMaxScalerModel.

Rescaled(e) = (e - E_min) / (E_max - E_min) * (max - min) + min

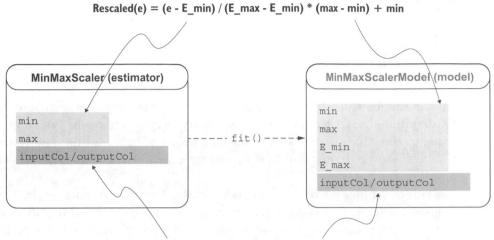

Here, the estimator/model can only be applied to a single column at a time, so we don't see the plural versions of the inputCol/outputCol combo.

Figure 12.4 The `MinMaxScaler` and its companion model, the `MinMaxScalerModel`—the same model of operation as the `Imputer` estimator

Listing 12.21 Scaling our nonscaled continuous variables

```
from pyspark.ml.feature import MinMaxScaler

CONTINUOUS_NB = [x for x in CONTINUOUS_COLUMNS if "ratio" not in x]

continuous_assembler = VectorAssembler(
    inputCols=CONTINUOUS_NB, outputCol="continuous"
)

food_features = continuous_assembler.transform(food_imputed)

continuous_scaler = MinMaxScaler(
    inputCol="continuous",
    outputCol="continuous_scaled",
)

food_features = continuous_scaler.fit(food_features).transform(
    food_features
)
```

```
food_features.select("continuous_scaled").show(3, False)
# +--------------------------------------------------------...+
# |continuous_scaled                                        ...|
# +--------------------------------------------------------...+
# |[0.5,0.13300031220730565,0.17341040462427745,0.0338164...|
# |[0.875,0.12581954417733376,0.10404624277456646,0.11111...|
# |[0.75,0.051514205432407124,0.03468208092485549,0.03381...|
# +--------------------------------------------------------...+
# only showing top 3 rows
```

> **TIP**   For your own models, check the `pyspark.ml.feature` module for other scalers. `StandardScaler`, which normalizes your variables by subtracting the mean and then dividing by the standard deviation, is also a favorite among data scientists.

All the variables in our `continuous_scaled` vector are now between zero and one. Our continuous variables are ready; our binary variables are ready. I think we are now ready to assemble our data set for machine learning! In this section, we reviewed the `MinMaxScaler` estimator and how we can scale variables so that they have the same amplitude.

This concludes the data preparation chapter. From a raw data set, we tamed the column names; explored the data; set a target; encoded columns into binary and continuous features; created bespoke features; and selected, imputed, and scaled some features. Is the work done? Not by a long shot!

In the next chapter, we'll finally get to modeling. At the same time, we will revisit our program through the ML pipeline abstraction, which will provide the necessary flexibility to put the science in data science and experiment with multiple scenarios. We set the stage, now let's model!

Summary

- A big part of creating a machine learning model is data manipulation. For this, everything we've learned within `pyspark.sql` can be leveraged.
- The first step in creating an ML model is assessing data quality and addressing potential data problems. Moving from large data sets in PySpark to small summaries in pandas or plain Python speeds up data discovery and assessment.
- Feature creation and selection can either be done manually using the PySpark data manipulation API or by leveraging some `pyspark.ml`-specific constructors, such as the correlation matrix.
- Multiple common feature engineering patterns, like imputing and scaling features, are provided through PySpark transformers and estimators.

Robust machine learning with ML Pipelines

13

This chapter covers

- Using transformers and estimators to transform data into ML features
- Assembling features into a vector through an ML pipeline
- Training a simple ML model
- Evaluating a model using relevant performance metrics
- Optimizing a model using cross-validation
- Interpreting a model's decision-making process through feature weights

In the previous chapter, we set the stage for machine learning: from a raw data set, we tamed the data and crafted features based on our exploration and analysis of the data. Looking back at the data transformation steps from chapter 12, we performed the following work, resulting in a data frame named food_features:

1 Read a CSV file containing dish names and multiple columns as feature candidates
2 Sanitized the column names (lowered the case and fixed the punctuation, spacing, and nonprintable characters)

3 Removed illogical and irrelevant records

4 Filled the `null` values of binary columns to `0.0`

5 Capped the amounts for `calories`, `protein`, `fat`, and `sodium` to the 99th percentile

6 Created ratio features (number of calories from a macro over number of calories for the dish)

7 Imputed the `mean` of continuous features

8 Scaled continuous features between `0.0` and `1.0`

TIP If you want to catch up with the code from chapter 12, I included the code that leads to `food_features` in the book's repository under `./code/Ch12/end_of_chapter.py`.

In this chapter, we continue our journey to a robust ML training program. We delve deeper into transformers and estimators, this time in the context of an ML pipeline. With this new tool, we first train and evaluate our initial model. We then learn about *customizing* an ML pipeline at runtime, using cross-validation, a popular ML optimization technique, for optimizing our model parameters. Finally, we briefly discuss model interpretability by extracting the model coefficients (the weights attributed to each parameter) from our ML pipeline.

ML pipelines are how PySpark implements ML capabilities. They provide better code organization and flexibility, at the expense of a little preparation up front. This chapters starts by explaining what an ML pipeline is, using the dessert prediction data set we created in chapter 12. We review just enough theory about transformers, estimators, and ML pipelines to get us started.

13.1 *Transformers and estimators: The building blocks of ML in Spark*

This section covers the two main components of ML pipelines: transformers and estimators. We take a second look at transformers and estimators in the context of reusable and parameterizable building blocks. From a 36,000 feet view, an ML pipeline is an ordered list of transformers and estimators. This section goes from that high-level overview to a more in-depth understanding. However, it is crucial that we understand not only how to create, but also how to modify those building blocks to use ML pipelines with optimal efficiency.

Transformers and estimators are very useful classes for ML modeling. When we train an ML model, we get back a *fitted* model, which is akin to a new program that we did not code explicitly. This new data-driven program then has one sole purpose: taking a properly formatted data set and transforming it by appending a prediction column. In this section, we see that transformers and estimators not only provide a useful abstraction for ML modeling, but they also provide portability through serialization and deserialization. This means that you can train and save your ML model and deploy it in another environment.

To illustrate how a transformer and an estimator are parameterized, we will use a transformer and an estimator defined and used in chapter 12:

- `continuous_assembler`—a `VectorAssembler` transformer that takes five columns and creates a Vector column to be used for model training
- `consinuous_scaler`—a `MinMaxScaler` estimator that scales values contained in a Vector column, returning values between `0` and `1` for each element in the vectors

For convenience, I include the relevant code in the following listing. We start with the transformer and then build on it to introduce the estimator.

Listing 13.1 The `VectorAssembler` and `MinMaxScaler` example

```
CONTINUOUS_NB = ["rating", "calories_i", "protein_i", "fat_i", "sodium_i"]

continuous_assembler = VectorAssembler(
    inputCols=CONTINUOUS_NB, outputCol="continuous"
)

continuous_scaler = MinMaxScaler(
    inputCol="continuous",
    outputCol="continuous_scaled",
)
```

13.1.1 Data comes in, data comes out: The Transformer

This section formally introduces the transformer as the first building block of an ML pipeline. We introduce the general transformer blueprint and how to access and modify its parameterization. This added context on the transformer plays a crucial role when we want to run experiments with our ML code or optimize our ML models (see section 13.3.3).

In our `VectorAssembler` transformer example, introduced in figure 13.1, we provide two arguments to the constructor: `inputCols` and `outpulCol`. These arguments provide the necessary functionality to create a fully functional `VectorAssembler` transformer. This transformer's sole purpose—through its `transform()` method—is to take the values in `inputCols` (assembled values) and return a single column, named `outputCol`, that contains a vector of all the assembled values.

The parameterization of a transformer is called *Params* (capital P). When instantiating a transformers class, just like with any Python class, we pass the parameters we want as arguments, making sure to explicitly specify each keyword. Once the transformer has been instantiated, PySpark provides us with a set of methods to extract and modify Params. The next two sections cover retrieving and modifying Params after the transformer's instantiation.

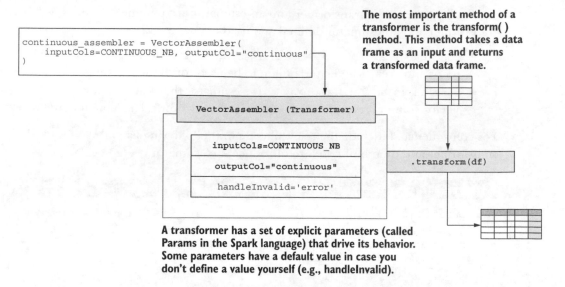

Figure 13.1   The `continuous_assembler` **transformer, along with its Params. The transformer uses the** `transform()` **method to apply a predefined transformation to the data frame, passed as input.**

Peeking at the signature of `VectorAssembler`: Keyword-only arguments

If you look at the signature for `VectorAssembler` (and pretty much every transformer and estimator in the `pyspark.ml` modules), you'll see an asterisk at the beginning of the parameters list:

```
class pyspark.ml.feature.VectorAssembler(*, inputCols=None,
outputCol=None, handleInvalid='error')
```

In Python, every parameter after the asterisk (*) is called a *keyword-only argument*, meaning that we need to mention the keyword. For instance, we couldn't do `Vector-Assembler("input_column", "output_column")`. For more information, refer to PEP (Python Enhancement Proposal) 3102 at http://mng.bz/4jKV.

As a fun add-on, Python also supports *positional-only parameters* with the slash (/) character. See PEP 570 (http://mng.bz/QWqj).

PEEKING UNDER THE HOOD: GETTING AND EXPLAINING THE PARAMS

Looking back at figure 13.1, the instantiation of `VectorAssembler` accepted three arguments: `inputCols`, `outputCol`, and `handleInvalid`. We also hinted that the configuration of a transformer (and estimator, by the same occasion) class instance relied on Params, which drove the behavior of the transformers. In this section, we explore Params, highlight their similarities and differences compared to regular class attributes, and address why those differences matter. You might think, "Well, I know how to get attributes out of a Python class, and transformers are Python classes." While that is correct, transformers (and estimators) follow a more Java/ Scala-like design, and I recommend not skipping over this section. It's short and useful and will allow you to avoid headaches when working with ML pipelines.

First, let's do what any Python developer would do and access one of the attributes of the transformer directly. In listing 13.2, we see that accessing the `outputCol` attribute of `continuous_assembler` does not yield `continuous`, like when we passed to the constructor. Instead, we get a reference to an object called a Param (class `pyspark.ml.param.Param`), which wraps each of our transformer's attributes.

> **Listing 13.2 Accessing a transformer's parameters to yield a `Param`**

```
print(continuous_assembler.outputCol)
# VectorAssembler_e18a6589d2d5__outputCol   ◁─┤
```
Rather than returning the continuous value passed as an argument to outputCol, we get an object called a Param.

To directly access the value of a specific param, we use a *getter* method, which is simply putting the word `get`, followed by the name of our Param in CamelCase. In the case of `outputCol`, shown in the next listing, the getter method is called `getOutput-Col()` (note the capital O).

> **Listing 13.3 Accessing the value of the `outputCol` Param through `getOutputCol()`**

```
print(continuous_assembler.getOutputCol())  # => continuous
```

So far, Params seem like they add boilerplate with little benefit. `explainParam()` changes this. This method provides documentation about the Param as well as the value. This is best explained by an example, and we see the output of explaining the `outputCol` Param in listing 13.4.

> **TIP** If you want to see all the Params at once, you can also use the pluralized version, `explainParams()`. This method takes no argument and will return a newline-delimited string of all the Params.

The string output contains the following:

- The name of the Param: `outputCol`
- A short description of the Param: `output column name`
- The `default` value of the Param: `VectorAssembler_e18a6589d2d5__output`, used if we don't explicitly pass a value ourselves
- The current value of the Param: `continuous`

> **Listing 13.4 Explaining the `outputCol` Param with `explainParam`**

This is the name and a short description of the outputCol Param.

We defined a value for outputCol.

```
print(continuous_assembler.explainParam("outputCol"))
# outputCol: output column name.
# (default: VectorAssembler_e18a6589d2d5__output, current: continuous)  ◁─
```

In this section, we addressed the relevant information of our transformer's Params. The ideas in this section also apply to estimators (see section 13.1.2). In the next section, we stop looking at Params, and we start changing them. Transformers will have no secret from us!

> **What about the plain `getParam()` method?**
> Transformers (and estimators) provide the plain `getParam()`. It simply returns the Param, just like accessing the `outputCol` did at the beginning of the section. I believe this is done so that PySpark transformers can have a consistent API with their Java/Scala equivalent.

SETTING PARAMS OF AN INSTANTIATED TRANSFORMER USING GETTERS AND SETTERS

In this section, we modify the Params of a transformer. Simple as that! This is mainly useful in two scenarios:

- You are building your transformer in the REPL, and you want to experiment with different Param-eterizations.
- You are optimizing your ML pipeline Params, like we do in section 13.3.3.

TIP Just like the previous section on getting Params, setting Params works the same for estimators.

How do we change the Params of a transformer? For every getter, there is a *setter*, which is simply putting the word `set`, followed by the name of our Param in CamelCase. Unlike getters, setters take the new value as their sole argument. In listing 13.5, we change the `outputCol` Param to `more_continuous` using the relevant setter method. This operation returns the transformed transformer but also makes the modification in place, which means that you do not have to assign the result of a setter to a variable (see the sidebar at the end of this section for more information and how to avoid potential pitfalls).

Listing 13.5   Setting the `outputCol` Param to `more_continuous`

```
continuous_assembler.setOutputCol("more_continuous")

print(continuous_assembler.getOutputCol())   # => more_continuous
```

While the setOutputCol() method returns a new transformer object, it also makes the modification in place, so we don't have to assign the result to a variable.

If you need to change multiple Params as once (e.g., you want to change the input and output columns in one fell swoop while experimenting with different scenarios), you can use the `setParams()` method. `setParams()` has the same signature as the constructor: you just pass the new values as keywords, as shown in the next listing.

Listing 13.6 Changing multiple Params at once using `setParams()`

```
continuous_assembler.setParams(
    inputCols=["one", "two", "three"], handleInvalid="skip"
)
print(continuous_assembler.explainParams())
# handleInvalid: How to handle invalid data (NULL and NaN values). [...]
#    (default: error, current: skip)
# inputCols: input column names. (current: ['one', 'two', 'three'])
# outputCol: output column name.
#    (default: VectorAssembler_e18a6589d2d5__output, current: continuous)
```

> **Params not passed to setParams keep their previous value (set in listing 13.5).**

Finally, if you want to return a Param to its default value, you can use the `clear()` method. This time, you need to pass the Param object. For instance, in listing 13.7, we reset the `handleInvalid` Param by using `clear()`. We pass the actual Param as an argument, accessed via the attribute slot seen at the beginning of the section, `continuous_assembler.handleInvalid`. This will prove useful if you have a transformer that has both `inputCol`/`outputCol` and `inputCols`/`outputCols` as possible Params. PySpark only allows one set to be active at once, so if you want to move between one column and multiple columns, you need to `clear()` the ones not being used.

Listing 13.7 Clearing the current value of the `handleInvalid` Param with `clear()`

```
continuous_assembler.clear(continuous_assembler.handleInvalid)

print(continuous_assembler.getHandleInvalid())   # => error
```

> **handleInvalid returned to its original value, error.**

This is it, folks! In this section, we learned in greater detail the how and why of a transformer, as well as how to get, set, and clear its Params. In the next section, we apply this useful knowledge to speed through the second building block of an ML pipeline, the estimator.

Transformers and estimators are passed by reference: The copy() method

Thus far, we have been used to a fluent API (see chapter 1), where each data frame transformation generates a new data frame. This enables method chaining, which makes our data transformation code very readable.

When working with transformers (and estimators), remember that they are passed by reference and that setters modify the object in place. If you assign your transformer to a new variable name and then use a setter on either of those variables, it'll modify the Param for both references:

```
new_continuous_assembler = continuous_assembler

new_continuous_assembler.setOutputCol("new_output")

print(new_continuous_assembler.getOutputCol())  # => new_output
print(continuous_assembler.getOutputCol())  # => new_output
```

> **Both the outputCol of continuous_assembler and new_continuous_assembler were modified by the setter.**

> **(continued)**
>
> The solution to this is to `copy()` the transformer and then assign the copy to the new variable:
>
> ```
> copy_continuous_assembler = continuous_assembler.copy()
>
> copy_continuous_assembler.setOutputCol("copy_output")
>
> print(copy_continuous_assembler.getOutputCol())  # => copy_output
> print(continuous_assembler.getOutputCol())  # => new_output      ◁
> ```
>
> **When making a copy, modifications to the Params of copy_continuous_assembler don't impact continuous_assembler.**

13.1.2 *Data comes in, transformer comes out: The Estimator*

This section covers the estimator, the second half of the ML pipeline. Just like with transformers, understanding how to operate and configure an estimator is an invaluable step in creating an efficient ML pipeline. Where a transformer transforms an input data frame into an output data frame, an estimator is fitted on an input data frame and returns an output transformer. In this section, we see that this relationship between transformers and estimators means that they are Param-eterized the same way as explained in section 13.1.1. We focus on estimator usage through the `fit()` method (versus `transform()` for the transformer), which is really the only notable difference for the end user.

Where a transformer uses a `transform()` method, applied to a data frame, to return a transformed data frame, an estimator uses a `fit()` method, applied to a data frame, to return a fully parameterized transformer called a `Model`. This distinction enables estimators to configure transformers based on the input data.

As an example, the `MinMaxScaler` estimator in figure 13.2 takes four parameters, two of which rely on the default value:

- `min` and `max`, which are the minimum and maximum values our scaled column will take. We keep both at their default of `0.0` and `1.0`, respectively.
- `inputCols` and `outputCols` are the input and output column, respectively. They follow the same conventions as the transformer.

In order to scale the values between `min` and `max`, we need to extract from the input column the minimum value (which I call `E_min`), as well as the maximum value (`E_max`). `E_min` is transformed to `0.0`, `E_max` is transformed to `1.0`, and any value in between takes a value between `min` and `max`, using the following formula (see the exercise at the end of the section for a corner [or edge] case when `E_max` and `E_min` are the same):

$$\text{MMS}(e_i) = \left(\frac{e_i - E_{min}}{E_{max} - E_{min}} \times (max - min) \right) + min$$

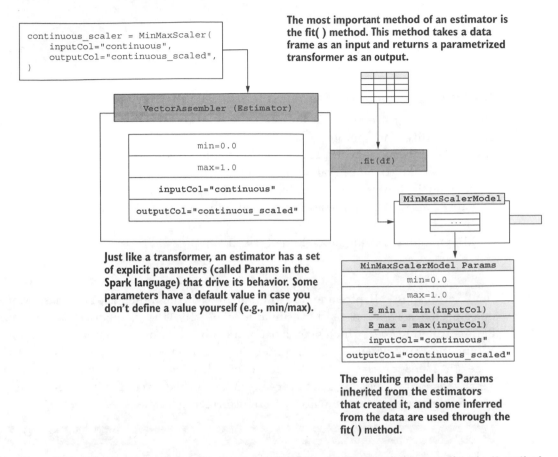

Figure 13.2 The `MinMaxScaler` estimator, along with its Params. The transformer uses the `fit()` method to create and parameterize a `Model` (a subtype of transformer) using the data frame passed as an argument.

Because the transformation relies on actual values from the data, we can't use a plain transformer, which expects to "know" everything (through its Param-eterization) before it can apply the `transform()` method. In the case of the `MinMaxScaler`, we can translate `E_min` and `E_max` as simple operations (`min()` and `max()` come from `pyspark.sql.functions`):

- `E_min = min(inputCol)`
- `E_max = max(inputCol)`

Once these values are computed (during the `fit()` method), PySpark creates, Param-eterizes, and returns a transformer/model.

This `fit()`/`transform()` approach applies for estimators that are far more complex than `MinMaxScaler`. Case in point: ML models are actually implemented as estimators in Spark. In the next section, we assemble our collection of transformers and estimators into a cohesive ML pipeline, complete with machine learning (finally!).

> ### Exercise 13.1
> What happens with the MinMaxScaler when `E_min == E_max`?

13.2 *Building a (complete) machine learning pipeline*

Now that we are strong in our knowledge of transformers and estimators, and can create, modify, and operate them, we are ready to tackle the last element of a successful ML pipeline, the `Pipeline` itself. Pipelines build on transformers and estimators to make training, evaluating, and optimizing ML models much clearer and more explicit. In this section, we build an ML pipeline with the estimators we used for our dessert prediction feature preparation program and add the modeling step in the mix.

ML pipelines are estimators. End of lesson.

…

In all seriousness, ML pipelines are implemented through the `Pipeline` class, which is a specialized version of the estimator. The `Pipeline` estimator has only one Param, called `stages`, which takes a list of transformers and estimators. To illustrate a pipeline, how about we create one? Starting from the `food` data frame from `code/Ch12/end_of_chapter.py`—which is our data set before we applied `Imputer`, `VectorAssembler`, and `MinMaxScaler`—we create a `food_pipeline` in the next listing containing our previous estimators and transformers as stages.

Listing 13.8 The `food_pipeline` pipeline, containing three stages

```
from pyspark.ml import Pipeline
import pyspark.ml.feature as MF

imputer = MF.Imputer(
    strategy="mean",
    inputCols=["calories", "protein", "fat", "sodium"],
    outputCols=["calories_i", "protein_i", "fat_i", "sodium_i"],
)

continuous_assembler = MF.VectorAssembler(
    inputCols=["rating", "calories_i", "protein_i", "fat_i", "sodium_i"],
    outputCol="continuous",
)

continuous_scaler = MF.MinMaxScaler(
    inputCol="continuous",
    outputCol="continuous_scaled",
)

food_pipeline = Pipeline(
    stages=[imputer, continuous_assembler, continuous_scaler]
)
```

The two estimators and the transformer used in chapter 12 for our feature preparation are repeated here for convenience.

The food_pipeline pipeline contains three stages, encoded in the stages Param.

In practical terms, since the pipeline is an estimator, it has a `fit()` method that generates a `PipelineModel`. Under the hood, the pipeline applies each stage in order, calling the appropriate method depending on if the stage is a transformer (`transform()`) or an estimator (`fit()`). By wrapping all of our individual stages into a pipeline, we only have one method to call, `fit()`, knowing that PySpark will do the right thing to yield a `PipelineModel` (figure 13.3). Although PySpark calls the result of a fitted pipeline a pipeline model, we have no machine learning model as a stage (this is covered in section 13.2.2). With a pipeline in place, though, our code becomes more modular and easier to maintain. We can add, remove, and change stages, relying on the pipeline definition to know what work will happen. I often create multiple iterations of transformers and estimators, trying them iteratively (this will also be very useful when we talk about optimizing the model in section 13.3.3) until I am satisfied with the results. I can define a few dozen transformers and estimators and keep some old definitions just in case; as long as my pipeline is clear, I feel confident about how my data gets processed.

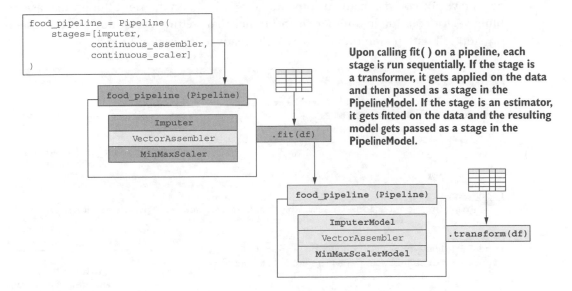

Figure 13.3 Our `food_pipeline` illustrated. When calling `fit()` using a data frame, that data frame gets passed as an argument to the first stage. Each estimator stage gets evaluated (transformers are passed verbatim), and the resulting transformers/models form the stages of the `PipelineModel`.

When using pipelines, remember that the data frame will travel each stage. For instance, the `continuous_scaler` stage will have the output of the data frame transformed by `continuous_scaler`. For estimator stages, the data frame stays identical, as `fit()` does not transform the data frame but returns a `Model` instead.

This section introduced the `Pipeline` object as an estimator with a special purpose: running other transformers and estimators. In the next section, we finish assembling our data before getting ready to model.

13.2.1 Assembling the final data set with the vector column type

This section explores the vector column type and the `VectorAssembler` in the context of model preparation. PySpark requires all the data fed into a machine learning estimator, as well as some other estimators like the `MinMaxScaler`, to be in a single-vector column. We review the variables inputted in the model and how to assemble them seamlessly using the `VectorAssembler`. I finally introduce the ML metadata PySpark imputes when assembling columns so that we can easily remember what's where.

We already know how to assemble data into a vector: use the `VectorAssembler`. Nothing is new here; we can create a `VectorAssembler` stage to assemble all the columns we want to be provided to our ML training. In listing 13.9, we assemble all of our `BINARY_COLUMNS`, the `_ratio` columns we created in chapter 12, and the `continuous_scaled` vector column from our pipeline. PySpark will do the right thing when assembling vector columns in another vector: rather than getting nested vectors, the assembly step will flatten everything into a single, ready-to-use vector.

Listing 13.9   Creating the vector assembler and updating stages of the `food_pipeline`

```
preml_assembler = MF.VectorAssembler(
    inputCols=BINARY_COLUMNS
    + ["continuous_scaled"]
    + ["protein_ratio", "fat_ratio"],
    outputCol="features",
)

food_pipeline.setStages(
    [imputer, continuous_assembler, continuous_scaler, preml_assembler]
)

food_pipeline_model = food_pipeline.fit(food)
 food_features = food_pipeline_model.transform(food)
```

food_pipeline_model becomes
a PipelineModel . . .

. . . that can then
transform() a data frame.

Our data frame is ready for machine learning! We have a number of records, each with

- A *target* (or *label*) column, `dessert`, containing a binary input (`1.0` if the recipe is a dessert, `0.0` otherwise)
- A vector of *features*, called `features`, containing all the information we want to train our machine learning model with

Let's look at our work, shall we? When we look at the relevant columns in our data frame, like in listing 13.10, we see that the `features` column looks very different than anything we've seen before. We provide 513 distinct features (see the `513` at the beginning of the `features` column value) with a large number of zeroes. This is called a *sparse* features set. When storing vectors, PySpark has two choices for representing vectors:

- A *dense* representation, where a `Vector` in PySpark is simply a NumPy (a high-performance multidimensional array library for Python) single-dimensional array object
- A *sparse* representation, where a `Vector` in PySpark is an optimized sparse vector compatible with the SciPy (a scientific computing library in Python) `scipy.sparse` matrix.

Listing 13.10   Displaying the `features` column with sparse vector representation

```
food_features.select("title", "dessert", "features").show(5, truncate=30)
# +-----------------------------+-------+-----------------------------+
# |                        title|dessert|                     features|
# +-----------------------------+-------+-----------------------------+
# |          Swiss Honey-Walnut Tart |    1.0|(513,[30,47,69,154,214,251,...|
# |Mascarpone Cheesecake with ...|    1.0|(513,[30,47,117,154,181,188...|
# |          Beef and Barley Soup |    0.0|(513,[7,30,44,118,126,140,1...|
# |                      Daiquiri |    0.0|(513,[49,210,214,408,424,50...|
# |Roast Beef and Watercress W...|    0.0|(513,[12,131,161,173,244,25...|
# +-----------------------------+-------+-----------------------------+
# only showing top 5 rows
```

> Since we have **513 elements in our vector**, with a majority of zeroes, **PySpark uses a sparse vector representation to save some space.**

In practice, you don't decide if a `Vector` is sparse or dense: PySpark will convert between the two as needed. I bring the difference up since they look different when you `show()` them within a data frame. We already saw the dense vector representation (just like an array) in chapter 12 when we looked at the correlation matrix. To illustrate a sparse vector with less that 513 elements, I wrote the same sample vector twice, using the two different notations. A sparse vector is a triple containing

- The length of a vector
- An array of positions where the elements are nonzero
- An array of nonzero values

```
Dense:  [0.0, 1.0, 4.0, 0.0]
Sparse: (4, [1,2], [1.0, 4.0])
```

TIP   In case you need them, `pyspark.sql.linalg.Vectors` has functions and methods for creating your vectors from scratch.

Now that everything is in a vector, how do we remember what's where? In chapter 6, I mentioned briefly that PySpark allows for a metadata dictionary to be attached to a column, and that this metadata is used when using PySpark's machine learning capabilities. Well, now's the time! Let's look at that metadata.

Listing 13.11   Getting PySpark to unfold the metadata

```
print(food_features.schema["features"])

# StructField(features,VectorUDT,true)

print(food_features.schema["features"].metadata)
# {
#     "ml_attr": {
#         "attrs": {
#             "numeric": [
#                 {"idx": 0, "name": "sausage"},
#                 {"idx": 1, "name": "washington_dc"},
#                 {"idx": 2, "name": "poppy"},
#                 [...]
#                 {"idx": 510, "name": "continuous_scaled_4"},
#                 {"idx": 511, "name": "protein_ratio"},
#                 {"idx": 512, "name": "fat_ratio"},
#             ]
#         },
#         "num_attrs": 513,
#     }
# }
```

The column schema for an assembled vector will keep track of the features making its composition under the metadata attribute.

For scaled variables, since they originate from a VectorAssembler, PySpark gives them a generic name, but you can track their name from the original vector column (here continuous_assembled) as needed.

This section covered the assembly into a final feature vector, the last stage before sending our data for training. We revisited and explored the `Vector` data structure in greater detail, interpreting its dense and sparse representation. Finally, we used the `VectorAssembler` transformer to combine all our features, including those already in a `Vector`, and presented the metadata contained in the `features` vector. Ready to model?

13.2.2 *Training an ML model using a LogisticRegression classifier*

This section covers machine learning in PySpark. OK, I might sell it a little too much. This section covers *the addition of an ML model stage into a pipeline*. In PySpark, training an ML model is nothing more than adding a stage in our ML pipeline. Still, since we don't do things just because, we take the time to review our algorithm selection. While it's easy to take every algorithm available in PySpark and try them every time, each one has properties that make it more suitable for certain types of problems. Often, the business problem you are trying to solve will provide hints about what properties your model should have. Do you want an easily explainable model, one that is robust to outliers (data points that are out of the normal expected range), or do you chase pure model accuracy? In this section, we take our original ask—is this recipe a dessert or not?—and select a first model type to integrate into our ML pipeline.

Because our target is binary (`0.0` or `1.0`), we restrict ourselves to a *classification algorithm*. Like the name suggests, classification algorithms are made for predicting a finite series of outcomes. If your target has a relatively small number of distinct values and there is no specific order between them, you are facing a classification problem. On the flip side, should we want to predict the number of calories in a recipe,[1] we would use a *regression algorithm*, which can predict a target taking any numerical value.

The *logistic regression* algorithm, despite its name, is a classification algorithm that belongs to the family of generalized linear models. This family of models is well understood and quite powerful, yet easier to explain than other models, such as decision trees and neural networks. Despite its simplicity, logistic regression is omnipresent in a classification setting. The most famous example is the credit score, which to this day is powered by logistic regression models. While we didn't really need explainability for our specific use case here, looking at the biggest drivers for our model (section 13.4) informs us about the most impactful inputs of our prediction.

NOTE Logistic regression is not without its faults. Linear models are less flexible than other families of models. They also require the data to be scaled, meaning that the range of each feature should be consistent. In our case, all of our features are either binary or scaled between 0.0 and 1.0, so this is not a problem. For an ML-centric approach to model selection, see the sidebar at the beginning of chapter 12 for some excellent references.

Before integrating our logistic regression into our pipeline, we need to create the estimator. This estimator is called `LogisticRegression` and comes from the `pyspark.ml.classification` module. The API documentation page for the `LogisticRegression` (available in iPython/Jupyter via `LogisticRegression?` or online at http://mng.bz/XWr6) lists 21 Params we can set. To get things started, we use as many default settings as we can, focusing on making the plumbing work. We revisit some of those Params when we talk about hyper-parameter optimization in section 13.3.3. The only three Params we set are the following:

- `featuresCol`: the column containing our features vector
- `labelCol`: the column containing our label (or target)
- `predictionCol`: the column that will contain the predictions of our model

Listing 13.12 Adding a `LogisticRegression` estimator to our pipeline

```
from pyspark.ml.classification import LogisticRegression

lr = LogisticRegression(
    featuresCol="features", labelCol="dessert", predictionCol="prediction"
)

food_pipeline.setStages(
    [
        imputer,
        continuous_assembler,
        continuous_scaler,
        preml_assembler,
```

---

[1] This is a very simple model since the calories are directly tied to carbs, proteins, and fat. See chapter 12 for the formula.

```
        lr,
    ]
)
```

Up next, we `fit()` our pipeline, as shown in listing 13.13. Before doing so, we need to split our data set into two portions using `randomSplit()`: one for *training*, which we feed to our pipeline, and one for *testing*, which is what we use to evaluate our model fit. This allows us to have some confidence about our model's ability to generalize over data that it has never seen before. Think of the training set as the study material and the testing set as the exam: if you give the exam as part of the study material, the grades are going to be much higher, but that does not accurately reflect the students' performance.

Finally, before fitting our pipeline, we `cache()` the training data frame. As you'll remember from chapter 11, we do this because machine learning uses the data frame repeatedly, so caching in memory provides an increase in speed if your cluster has enough memory.

> **WARNING** Although PySpark will use the same seed, which should guarantee that the split will be consistent across runs, there are some cases where PySpark will break that consistency. If you want to be 100% certain about your splits, split your data frame, write each one to disk, and then read them from the disk location.

Listing 13.13 Splitting our data frame for training and testing

```
train, test = food.randomSplit([0.7, 0.3], 13)
```

> randomSplit() takes a list of partitions, each containing the fraction of the data set. The second attribute is a seed for the random number generator.

```
train.cache()

food_pipeline_model = food_pipeline.fit(train)
results = food_pipeline_model.transform(test)
```

> This time, we fit() on train and transform() on test rather than using the same data frame for both operations.

With a model now trained and a prediction made on a testing set, we're ready for the last stage of our model: evaluating and dissecting our model.

The logistic regression in a nutshell

Feel free to skip this sidebar if math is not your cup of tea.

It's easier to think about the logistic regression if we understand the linear regression model first. In school, you probably have learned about the simple one-variable regression displayed. In this case, y is the dependent variable/target, x is the dependent variable/feature, and m is x's `coefficient`, while b is the *intercept* (or the value of the coefficient is zero):

```
y = m * x + b
```

A linear regression takes this simple formula and applies it to multiple features. In other words, x and m become vectors of value. If we use an index-based notation, it would look like this (some statistics textbooks might use a different but equivalent notation):

```
y = b + (m0 * x0) + (m1 * x1) + (m2 * x2) + ... + (mn * xn)
```

Here, we have *n* features and coefficients. This linear regression formula is called the *linear component* and is usually written $x\beta$ (x for the observations, β [beta] for the coefficients vector). A linear regression's prediction can span any number, from negative infinity to infinity—there are no boundaries to the formula.

How do we get a classification model out of this? Behold, the logistic regression!

The logistic regression takes its name from the *logit* transformation. The logit transformation takes our linear component $x\beta$ and yields a function that is between zero and one. The formula is the expanded form of the logistic function. Note the location of the linear component. It looks like an arbitrary choice of function, but there is a lot of theory behind it, and this form is very convenient:

```
y = 1 / (1 + exp(-xβ))
```

The y of the logistic function will return, for any value of $x\beta$, a number from zero to one. For turning this into a binary feature, we apply a simple threshold: `1 if y >/= 0.5, else 0`. If you want your model to be more or less sensitive, you can change this threshold. If you are curious about the raw y result of logistic regression, see the `rawPrediction` column of your prediction data set: you'll get a vector containing $[x\beta, -x\beta]$. The `probability` column will contain the y as defined in the logit formula for both values in `rawPrediction`:

```
results.select("prediction", "rawPrediction", "probability").show(3, False)
# +----------+---------------------+--------------------+
# |prediction|rawPrediction        |probability         |
# +----------+---------------------+--------------------+
# |0.0       |[11.98907,-11.9890722]|[0.9999937,6.2116-6]|
# |0.0       |[32.94732,-32.947325] |[0.99999,4.88498-15]|
# |1.0       |[-1.32753,1.32753254] |[0.209567,0.7904]   |
# +----------+---------------------+--------------------+
```

13.3 *Evaluating and optimizing our model*

Modeling is done. How do we know how good of a job we did? In this section, we perform a crucial step of data science: reviewing our model results and tuning their implementation. Both steps are crucial in making sure we are producing the best model we can with the input we're provided, maximizing the odds that our model will be useful.

PySpark provides a clear API that dovetails with the ML pipeline abstraction (how fortunate!). We start by reviewing out first naive model performance through a tailored evaluator object that provides relevant metrics for our binary classifier. We then try to improve on our model's accuracy by turning some dials (called *hyperparameters*) through a process called cross-validation. By the end of this section, you'll have a reproducible blueprint for evaluating and optimizing models.

13.3.1   *Assessing model accuracy: Confusion matrix and evaluator object*

This section covers two popular metrics when evaluating a binary classification algorithm. At the core, we want to accurately predict our label (dessert or not?) column. There are multiple ways to slice and dice our model's results; for instance, is predicting "dessert" on a liver mousse worse than predicting "not dessert" on a tiramisu? Selecting and optimizing for the appropriate metric is crucial in yielding an impactful model. We focus on two different ways to review our model results:

- The *confusion matrix*, which gives us a 2 × 2 matrix of predictions versus labels and makes it easy to get metrics like precision (how good are we at identifying desserts?) and recall (how good are we at identifying not desserts?)
- The *receiver operating characteristic curve* (or ROC curve), which shows the diagnostic ability of our model as we change its prediction threshold (more on this later)

CONFUSION MATRIX: A SIMPLE WAY TO REVIEW CLASSIFICATION RESULTS

In this section, we create a confusion matrix of our results versus the true label to assess the ability of our model to accurately predict desserts. Confusion matrices are very simple formats for presenting classification results and therefore are very popular when communicating results. On the flip side, they do not provide any guidance on the actual performance of the model, which is why we usually combine them with a set of metrics.

The easiest way to picture a confusion matrix for our dessert classification model is to make a 2 × 2 table where the rows are the label (true) results and columns are the predicted values, just like in figure 13.4. This also gives us four measures that are useful for creating performance metrics:

- *True negative (TN)*—Both the label and the prediction are zero. We accurately identified a nondessert.
- *True positive (TP)*—Both the label and the prediction are one. We accurately identified a dessert.
- *False positive (FP)*—We predicted dessert (1) when the dish was not a dessert (0). This is also called a *type I error*.
- *False negative (FN)*—We predicted nondessert (0) when the dish was a dessert (1). This is also called a *type II error*.

From those four measures, we can craft a multitude of metrics to evaluate our model. The two most popular are *precision* and *recall*, as depicted in figure 13.4. Before getting into performance metrics, let's create our confusion matrix. PySpark only provides a confusion matrix through the legacy `pyspark.mllib` module, which is now in maintenance mode. Truth be told, for such a simple operation, I'd rather do it by hand, like in listing 13.14. For this, we group by the label (`dessert`) and then `pivot()` on the

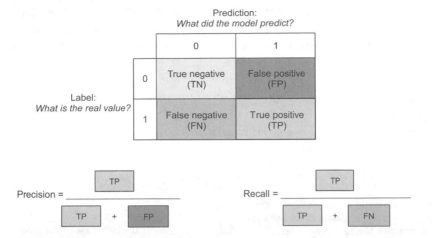

Figure 13.4 A visual depiction of precision and recall, as seen in a confusion matrix. The precision of a model measures how many of the model's predictions (prediction = 1) are legitimate (label = 1). The recall of a model measures how many of the true positives (label = 1) are caught by the model (prediction = 1).

prediction column, using `count()` as the cells' value. `pivot()` takes every value from the column passed as an argument and creates a column out of it.

Listing 13.14 Creating a confusion matrix for our model using `pivot()`

```
results.groupby("dessert").pivot("prediction").count().show()
# +-------+----+----+
# |dessert| 0.0| 1.0|          Prediction values
# +-------+----+----+          are the columns . . .
# |    0.0|4950|  77|
# |    1.0| 104|1005|
# +-------+----+----+          . . . and label values (dessert) are the
#                              rows—our confusion matrix, by hand.
```

NOTE   The confusion matrix shows that our data set has a lot more non-desserts than desserts. In the classification world this is called a *class imbalanced data set* and is often pretty undesirable for model training. In this specific case, the class imbalance is manageable: for a thorough review of the topic, check out *Learning from imbalanced data: open challenges and future directions* by Bartosz Krawczyk (2016, http://mng.bz/W7Yd).

Now that the confusion matrix is under our belt, let's tackle the precision and recall. Before Spark 3.1, you needed to rely (again) on the legacy RDD-based MLlib (`pyspark.mllib.evaluation.MulticlassMetrics`) to get precision and recall. In Spark 3.1, we now have access to a new `LogisticRegressionSummary` object that avoids the trip to the RDD world. Because it is a recent addition, I provide the code for both, focusing on the future-proof data frame approach.

For the data frame approach (Spark 3.1+), we need to first extract our fitted model from the pipeline model. For this, we can use the `stages` attribute of `pipeline_food_model` and access just the last item. From that model, called `lr_model` in listing 13.15, we call `evaluate()` on the `results` data set. `evaluate()` will error out any prediction columns that exist, so I simply give the relevant ones (dessert, features) to it. It's a small price to pay to avoid computing the metrics by hand. Note that PySpark does not know which label we consider positive and negative. Because of this, the precision and recall are accessible through `precisionByLabel` and `recallByLabel`, which both return lists of precision/recall for each label in order.

Listing 13.15   Computing the precision and recall (Spark 3.1+)

Since PySpark has no notion of which label is the positive one, it'll compute precision and recall for both and put them in a list. We pick the second one (dessert == 1.0).

The last stage of the pipeline model is the fitted ML model.

```
lr_model = food_pipeline_model.stages[-1]      ◄
metrics = lr_model.evaluate(results.select("title", "dessert", "features"))
# LogisticRegressionTrainingSummary

print(f"Model precision: {metrics.precisionByLabel[1]}")
print(f"Model recall: {metrics.recallByLabel[1]}")

# Model precision: 0.9288354898336414
# Model recall: 0.9062218214607755
```

Over 90% precision and recall on the first try: pop the champagne (is champagne a dessert?)!

For those using the legacy RDD-based MLLib, the process is quite similar, but we first need to move our data to an RDD containing pairs of (prediction, label). Then, we need to pass the RDD to the `pyspark.ml.evaluation.MulticlassMetrics` and extract the relevant metric. This time, `precision()` and `recall()` are *methods*, so we need to pass the positive label (1.0) as an argument.

Listing 13.16   Computing precision and recall through an RDD-based API

```
from pyspark.mllib.evaluation import MulticlassMetrics

predictionAndLabel = results.select("prediction", "dessert").rdd

metrics_rdd = MulticlassMetrics(predictionAndLabel)

print(f"Model precision: {metrics_rdd.precision(1.0)}")
print(f"Model recall: {metrics_rdd.recall(1.0)}")

# Model precision: 0.9288354898336414
# Model recall: 0.9062218214607755
```

In this section, we covered useful metrics for evaluating our binary classification model. The next section introduces another useful perspective when evaluating a binary classifier: the ROC curve.

13.3.2 *True positives vs. false positives: The ROC curve*

This section covers another common metric used when evaluating binary classification models. The *receiver operating characteristic curve*, commonly known as a ROC (pronounced like "rock") curve, provides a visual cue of the performance of the model. We also discuss the main metric that leverages the ROC curve: the area under the ROC curve. This alternate way of showcasing performance models provides hints on how we can optimize the model, discriminating power by tweaking the decision boundary. This will prove useful when we want to optimize our model for our use case (see section 13.3.3).

The logistic regression (this applies to most classification models as well) predicts a value between 0 and 1 (see the "The Logistic Regression in a Nutshell" sidebar for more information) where PySpark stores a column named `probability`. By default, any probability equal or over `0.5` will yield a prediction of `1.0`, while any probability under `0.5` will yield a `0.0`. It turns out that we can change that threshold by, you guessed it, changing the `threshold` Param of the `LogisticRegression` object.

Because this threshold is such an important concept in discriminating the power of a classification model, PySpark stores the raw prediction (for those math-inclined folks, the linear component xβ as seen in "The Logistic Regression in a Nutshell" sidebar) in a `rawPrediction` column. By using this raw prediction and changing the threshold without retraining the model, we can have a sense of the performance of the model according to a different sensitivity. Because ROC curves are much better explained visually, I skip a few steps and present the result in figure 13.5, along with some relevant elements. The code to generate this chart follows later in this section.

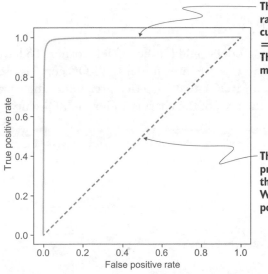

The solid line is our ROC curve. For a given false positive rate, it show the corresponding true positive rate. The curve will always start at (0.0, 0.0) (every prediction == 0.0) and end at (1.0, 1.0) (every prediction == 1.0). The closer we get to (0.0, 1.0), the more accurate the model.

This dotted line represents a model that assigns a prediction based on the rate of 0/1 in the testing sample: the true positive rate is equal to the false positive rate. We strive to have a curve as far (to the left and up) as possible to that line.

Figure 13.5 The ROC curve for our model. We want the solid curve to hit the top-left corner as much as possible.

In a nutshell, the ROC curve maps false positive rates (FPRs) to true positive rates (TPRs). A perfectly accurate model will have a TPR of 100% and an FPR of 0%, meaning that every prediction is on point. We therefore want the curve shown in figure 13.5 to hit the top-left corner as much as possible. A less-precise model will get close to the dotted line, which echoes what we consider a *random* model (FPR = TPR).

Okay, we saw our ROC curve. How do we create one?

The ROC curve is obtained through the `BinaryClassificationEvaluator` object. In listing 13.17, we instantiate said object, asking explicitly for the `areaUnderROC` metric, which yields the ROC curve. Our evaluator takes the raw prediction as an input. The evaluator generates a single measure, which is the area under the ROC curve, a number between zero and one (higher is better). We're doing great, but it would be nice to know what this number means.

> **TIP** The other option we can use for the metric is `areaUnderPR`, which will give us the area under the precision-recall curve. This is useful when the classes are very imbalanced or when dealing with rare events.

Listing 13.17　Creating and evaluating a `BinaryClassificationEvaluator` object

```
from pyspark.ml.evaluation import BinaryClassificationEvaluator

evaluator = BinaryClassificationEvaluator(
    labelCol="dessert",
    rawPredictionCol="rawPrediction",
    metricName="areaUnderROC",
)

accuracy = evaluator.evaluate(results)
print(f"Area under ROC = {accuracy} ")
# Area under ROC = 0.9927442079816466
```

We pass our label (or target) and the rawPrediction column generated by our model.

As seen earlier in this section, a perfect model would hit the top-left corner. To have a sense numerically of how close we are to this, the area under the ROC curve is used: it's the ratio of the chart that is under our ROC curve. An AUC (area under the curve) score of 0.9929 means that 99.29% of the area of the chart is under the ROC curve.

Listing 13.18　Using `matplotlib` to display the ROC curve

```
import matplotlib.pyplot as plt

plt.figure(figsize=(5, 5))
plt.plot([0, 1], [0, 1], "r--")
plt.plot(
    lr_model.summary.roc.select("FPR").collect(),
    lr_model.summary.roc.select("TPR").collect(),
)
plt.xlabel("False positive rate")
plt.ylabel("True positive rate")
plt.show()
```

For the first run, our model did amazingly. This does not mean that our job is over: initial model fitting is the first step in having a production-ready model. Our code looks a little artisanal and could use a cup or two of robustness. We also need to make sure that our model will stay accurate as time goes by, which is why having an automated metrics pipeline is important.

The last section looks at optimizing some aspect of our model training to yield better performance.

13.3.3 *Optimizing hyperparameters with cross-validation*

This section covers how we can optimize some of the Params provided by the `Logistic-Regression`. By fine-tuning some aspects of the model training (how Spark builds the fitted model), we can hope to yield better model accuracy. For this, we use a technique called *cross-validation*. Cross-validation resamples the data set into training and testing sets to assess the ability of the model to generalize over new data.

In section 13.2.2, we saw that we split our data set into two parts: one for training and one for testing. With cross-validation, we subdivide the training set one more time to try to find the optimal set of Params for our `LogisticRegression` estimator. In ML terms, those Params are called hyperparameters since they are the parameters we use to train the model (which will internally contain parameters to make a prediction). We call hyperparameter optimization the process of selecting the best hyperparameters for a given situation/data set.

Before digging into the details of how cross-validation works, let's select a hyperparameter to optimize against. To keep the example simple and computationally manageable, we only build a simple grid with a single hyperparameter: `elasticNetParam`. This hyperparameter (called α) can take any value between `0.0` and `1.0`. To start, I keep myself to two values, namely `0.0` (the default) and `1.0`.

> **TIP** For more information about α, check out *Introduction to Statistical Learning*, by Gareth James, Daniela Witten, Trevor Hastie, and Rob Tibshirani (Springer, 2013). Trevor Hastie co-invented the concept of *Elastic Net*, which is what this α is about!

To build the set of hyperparameters we wish to evaluate our model against, we use the `ParamGridBuilder`, which assists in creating a Param Map, as shown in listing 13.19. For this, we start with the builder class (just like we did with `SparkSession.builder` in chapter 2). This builder class can take a series of `addGrid()` methods taking two parameters:

- The Param of the stage we want to modify. In this case, our `LogisticRegression` estimator was assigned to the variable `lr`, so `lr.elasticNetParam` is the Param in question.
- The values we wish to assign the hyperparameter on, passed as a list.

Once we are done, we call build(), and a list of *Param Maps* is returned. Each element of the list is a dictionary (called `Map` in Scala, hence the name) of the Params that will be passed to our pipeline when fitting. Often, we want to set the hyperparameters for the model estimator, but nothing prevents us from changing the Params from another stage, for instance the `preml_assembler`, should we want to remove features (see the exercises). Just be sure to be consistent if you meddle with `inputCol`/`outputCol` to avoid missing column errors.

Listing 13.19   Using `ParamGridBuilder` to build a set of hyperparameters

```
from pyspark.ml.tuning import ParamGridBuilder

grid_search = (
    ParamGridBuilder()          ◀──────────────          ParamGridBuilder() is
    .addGrid(lr.elasticNetParam, [0.0, 1.0])      ◀──    a builder class ...
    .build()          ◀──
)                                    ... until we call build()      ... to which we can append
                                     to finalize the grid!          addGrid() methods, setting
print(grid_search)                                                  an α of 0.0 and 1.0 ...
# [
#     {Param(parent='LogisticRegression_14302c005814',
#            name='elasticNetParam',
#            doc='...'): 0.0},
#     {Param(parent='LogisticRegression_14302c005814',      ◀──    I've edited the output to
#            name='elasticNetParam',                                keep only the relevant
#            doc='...'): 1.0}          ◀──                          elements.
# ]
```

Grid, done. Now onto cross-validation. PySpark provides out-of-the-box *K-fold cross-validation* through the `CrossValidator` class. In a nutshell, cross-validation tries every combination of hyperparameters by splitting the data set into a set of nonoverlapping, randomly partitioned sets (called *folds*), which are used as separate training and validation[2] data sets. In figure 13.6, I demonstrate an example with k = 3 folds. For each element of the grid, PySpark will perform three train-validation splits, fit the model on the train portion (which contains 2/3 of the data), and then evaluate the performance metric selected on the validation set (which contains the remaining 1/3).

Code-wise, the `CrossValidator` object combines everything under a single abstraction. To build a cross-validator, we need three elements, all of which we've encountered so far:

- An `estimator`, which contains the model we wish to evaluate (here: `food_pipeline`)
- An `estimatorParamMaps` set, which is the list of Param Maps we created earlier in the section
- An `evaluator`, which carries the metric we wish to optimize against (here, we reuse the one we created in listing 13.17)

In listing 13.20, we also provide a few parameters: the `numFolds` = 3, setting our number of folds k to 3, a seed (13) for keeping the random number generator consistent

---

[2] The documentation calls them train and test, but I prefer to be unambiguous and reserve the "test" moniker for the split we did before running the data through the pipeline.

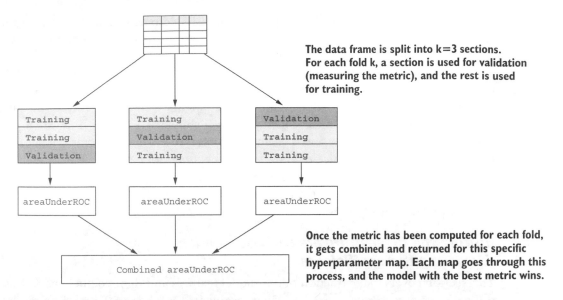

The data frame is split into k=3 sections. For each fold k, a section is used for validation (measuring the metric), and the rest is used for training.

Once the metric has been computed for each fold, it gets combined and returned for this specific hyperparameter map. Each map goes through this process, and the model with the best metric wins.

Figure 13.6 Three-fold cross-validation. For each Param map, we perform three train/validation cycles, each time using a different third as a validation set. The selected metric `areaUnderROC` is then combined (averaged), and this becomes the performance metric for the resulting model plus Param Map.

between runs, and `collectSubModels=True` to keep a version of every model being trained (to compare the results). The resulting cross-validator follows the same conventions as an estimator, so we apply the `fit()` method to start the cross-validation process.

Listing 13.20 Creating and using a `CrossValidator` object

```
from pyspark.ml.tuning import CrossValidator

cv = CrossValidator(
    estimator=food_pipeline,
    estimatorParamMaps=grid_search,
    evaluator=evaluator,
    numFolds=3,
    seed=13,
    collectSubModels=True,
)

cv_model = cv.fit(train)      ◁── We use the fit() method on
                                  a CrossValidator, just like
                                  with any pipeline.

print(cv_model.avgMetrics)
# [0.9899971586317382, 0.9899992947698821]    ◁── elasticNetParam
                                                  == 1.0 wins by a
                                                  razor-thin margin.

pipeline_food_model = cv_model.bestModel
```

To extract the `areaUnderROC` (which is the metric our evaluator was tracking) from the models trained, we use the `avgMetrics` attribute. Here, we are really splitting some hairs: both models are basically indistinguishable performance-wise, with the `elasticNetParam == 1.0` model winning by a thin margin. Finally, we extract the `bestModel` so we can use it as a pipeline model.

We have done a lot in this section. Thanks to PySpark's friendly and consistent API, we were able to evaluate our model two ways (precision versus recall, as well as area under the ROC curve) and then optimize our pipeline's hyperparameters through cross-validation. Knowing which model to use, which metric to select, and which process to follow could fill many books (it already has!), but I find doing data science with PySpark very pleasing. It's nice to know that syntax does not get in the way!

In the next and final section of the chapter, we brush against model interpretability. We explore the coefficients of the model's features and discuss some improvements based on our findings.

13.4 Getting the biggest drivers from our model: Extracting the coefficients

This section covers the extraction of our model features and their coefficients. We use those coefficients to get a sense of the most important features of the model and plan some improvements for a second iteration.

In section 13.2.1, I explained that the features in a vector built via the `VectorAssembly` object keep the feature names in the column's metadata dictionary, and showed how to access them. We can access the schema through the `StructField` (see chapter 6 for a deep dive into the schema and the `StructField`) contained in the top-level `StructField`. Then we just need to match the variables to the coefficient in the right order. In listing 13.21, I show the metadata for the `features` column and extract the relevant fields. I then extract the coefficients from my `lrModel` through the `coefficient.values` attribute. Note that PySpark keeps the intercept of the model under the `intercept` slot: because I like to show everything in one fell swoop, I tend to add it as another "feature" in my table.

> **TIP** If you have non-numeric features, PySpark will store the metadata for the features in a `binary` key instead of a `numeric` one. In our case, since we knew the features were binary, we did not treat them as special, and PySpark lumped them into the numeric metadata key.

Listing 13.21 Extracting the feature names from the `features` vector

```
import pandas as pd

feature_names = ["(Intercept)"] + [          ◁─┐ I add the intercept
    x["name"]                                   │ manually from the
    for x in (                                  │ intercept slot.
        food_features
        .schema["features"]
        .metadata["ml_attr"]["attrs"]["numeric"]
    )
]
```

```
feature_coefficients = [lr_model.intercept] + list(
    lr_model.coefficients.values
)
```

◁─┐ **I add the intercept manually from the intercept slot.**

```
coefficients = pd.DataFrame(
    feature_coefficients, index=feature_names, columns=["coef"]
)

coefficients["abs_coef"] = coefficients["coef"].abs()
```

◁── **Since negative and positive values are equally important in logistic regression, I create an absolute value column for easy ordering.**

```
print(coefficients.sort_values(["abs_coef"]))
#                              coef     abs_coef
# kirsch                   0.004305     0.004305
# jam_or_jelly            -0.006601     0.006601
# lemon                   -0.010902     0.010902
# food_processor          -0.018454     0.018454
# phyllo_puff_pastry_dough -0.020231    0.020231
# ...                          ...          ...
# cauliflower            -13.928099    13.928099
# rye                    -13.987067    13.987067
# plantain               -15.551487    15.551487
# quick_and_healthy      -15.908631    15.908631
# horseradish            -17.172171    17.172171

# [514 rows x 2 columns]
```

In chapter 12, I explained that having features on the same scale (here from zero to one) helps with the interpretability of the coefficients. Each coefficient gets multiplied by a value between 0 and 1, so they are all consistent with one another. By ordering them by their absolute value, we can see which coefficients have the greatest impact on our model.

A coefficient close to zero, like `kirsch`, `lemon`, and `food_processor`, means that this feature is not very predictive of our model. On the flip side, a very high or low coefficient, like `cauliflower`, `horseradish`, and `quick_and_healthy`, means that this feature is highly predictive. When using a linear model, a positive coefficient means that the feature will predict toward a `1.0` (the dish is a dessert). Our results are not too surprising; looking at the very negative features, it seems that the presence of horseradish or a "quick and healthy" recipe means "not a dessert!"

Unsurprisingly, data science revolves very much around one's ability to process, extract information, and apply the right abstractions on the data. Statistical know-how becomes very useful when you need to know the why of specific models. PySpark provides functionality for a growing number of models, but each one will use a similar estimator/transformer setup. Now that you understand how the different components work, applying a different model will be a *piece of cake*!

Portability of ML pipelines: Read and write

Serializing and deserializing an ML pipeline is as simple as writing and reading a data frame. A Spark `PipelineModel` has a `write` method that works just like the one for the data frame (with the exception of the `format`, as the pipeline format is predefined). Setting the `overwrite()` option allows you to overwrite any existing model:

```
pipeline_food_model.write().overwrite().save("am_I_a_dessert_the_model")
```

The result is a directory named `am_I_a_dessert_the_model`. To read it back, we need to import the `PipelineModel` class and call the `load()` method:

```
from pyspark.ml.pipeline import PipelineModel

loaded_model = PipelineModel.load("am_I_a_dessert_the_model")
```

Summary

- Transformers are objects that, through a `transform()` method, modify a data frame based on a set of Params that drives its behavior. We use a transformer stage when we want to deterministically transform a data frame.

- Estimators are objects that, through a `fit()` method, take a data frame and return a fully parameterized transformer called a model. We use an estimator stage when we want to transform a data frame using a data-dependent transformer.

- ML pipelines are like estimators, as they use the `fit()` method to yield a pipeline model. They have a single Param, `stages`, that carries an ordered list of transformers and estimators to be applied on a data frame.

- Before training a model, every feature needs to be assembled in a vector using the `VectorAssembler` transformer. This provides a single optimized (sparse or dense) column containing all the features for machine learning.

- PySpark provides useful metrics for model evaluation through a set of evaluator objects. You select the appropriate one based on your type of prediction (binary classification = `BinaryClassificationEvaluator`).

- With a Param Map grid, an evaluator, and an estimator, we can perform model hyperparameter optimization to try different scenarios and try to improve model accuracy.

- Cross-validation is a technique that resamples the data frame into different partitions before fitting/testing the model. We use cross-validation to test if the model performs consistently when it sees different data.

Building custom ML transformers and estimators

This chapter covers

- Creating your own transformers using Params for parameterization
- Creating your own estimators using the companion model approach
- Integrating custom transformers and estimators in an ML Pipeline

In this chapter, we cover how to create and use custom transformers and estimators. While the ecosystem of transformers and estimators provided by PySpark covers a lot of frequent use cases and each version brings new ones to the table, sometimes you just need to go off trail and create your own. The alternative is to cut your pipeline in half and insert a data transformation function into the mix. This basically nullifies all the advantages (portability, self-documentation) of the ML pipeline that we covered in chapters 12 and 13.

Because of how similar transformers and estimators are, we start with in-depth coverage of the transformer and its fundamental building block, the Param. We then move on to creating estimators, focusing on the differences in the transformer. Finally, we conclude with the integration of custom transformers and estimators in an ML pipeline, paying attention to serialization.

Before jumping into the content of this chapter, I strongly recommend reading chapters 12 and 13 and working through the examples and exercises. It is much easier to build a robust and useful transformer/estimator if you know how it is being used. I see custom transformers and estimators as a tool best used sparingly; always leverage the predefined PySpark components. Should you need to go off script, this chapter will guide you.

14.1 *Creating your own transformer*

This section covers how to create and use a custom transformer. We implement a `ScalarNAFiller` transformer that fills the `null` values of a column with a scalar value instead of the `mean` or `median` when using the `Imputer`. Thanks to this, our dessert pipeline from chapter 13 will have a `ScalarNAFiller` stage that we'll be able to use when running different scenarios—when optimizing hyperparameters, for instance—without changing the code itself. This improves the flexibility and robustness of our ML experiments.

Creating a custom transformer is not hard, but there are a lot of moving parts and a set of conventions to follow to make it consistent with the other transformers provided by PySpark. Our blueprint for this section follows this plan:

1 Design our transformer: Params, inputs, and outputs.
2 Create the Params, inheriting some preconfigured ones as necessary.
3 Create the necessary getters and setters to get.
4 Create the initialization function to instantiate our transformer.
5 Create the transformation function.

NOTE Because we will be implementing the class in stages, some of the code blocks will not be able to be run in the REPL as is. Refer to the end of each section for an updated definition of the transformer with the new elements.

The PySpark `Transformer` class (`pyspark.ml.Transformer`; http://mng.bz/y4Jq) provides many of the methods we used in chapter 13, such as `explainParams()` and `copy()`, plus a handful of other methods that will prove useful for implementing our own transformers. By sub-classing `Transformer`, we inherit all of this functionality for free, like we do in the following listing. This gives us a starting point!

Listing 14.1   The shell for the `ScalarNAFiller` transformer

```
from pyspark.ml import Transformer


class ScalarNAFiller(Transformer):
    pass
```

The ScalarNAFiller class sub-classes the Transformer class, inheriting its generic methods.

Before we start to code the rest of the transformer, let's outline its parameterization and functionality. The next section reviews how to design a great transformer using Params and the transformation function.

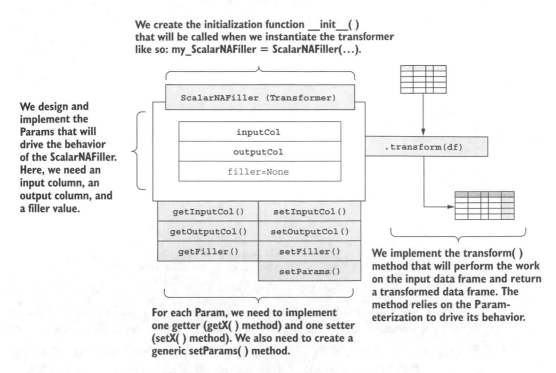

**We create the initialization function __init__( )
that will be called when we instantiate the transformer
like so: my_ScalarNAFiller = ScalarNAFiller(...).**

**We design and
implement the
Params that will
drive the behavior
of the ScalarNAFiller.
Here, we need an
input column, an
output column, and
a filler value.**

ScalarNAFiller (Transformer)

inputCol

outputCol

filler=None

.transform(df)

getInputCol()	setInputCol()
getOutputCol()	setOutputCol()
getFiller()	setFiller()
	setParams()

**We implement the transform( )
method that will perform the work
on the input data frame and return
a transformed data frame. The
method relies on the Param-
eterization to drive its behavior.**

**For each Param, we need to implement
one getter (getX( ) method) and one setter
(setX( ) method). We also need to create a
generic setParams( ) method.**

Figure 14.1 Our custom `ScalarNAFiller` blueprint, step 1

14.1.1 Designing a transformer: Thinking in terms of Params and transformation

This section explains the relationship between the transformer, its Params, and the transformation function. By designing a transformer using these moving parts, we can ensure that our transformer is correct, robust, and consistent with the rest of the API pipeline.

In chapters 12 and 13, we saw that a transformer (and, by extension, an estimator) is configured through a collection of Params. The `transform()` function always takes a data frame as an input and returns a transformed data frame. We want to stay consistent with our design to avoid problems at use time.

When designing a custom transformer, I always start by implementing a function that reproduces the behavior of my transformer. For the `ScalarNAFiller`, we leverage the `fillna()` function. I also create a sample data frame to test the behavior of my function.

Listing 14.2 Creating a function that reproduces the transformer's desired behavior

```
import pyspark.sql.functions as F
from pyspark.sql import Column, DataFrame

test_df = spark.createDataFrame(
    [[1, 2, 4, 1], [3, 6, 5, 4], [9, 4, None, 9], [11, 17, None, 3]],
```

```
        ["one", "two", "three", "four"],
)


def scalarNAFillerFunction(
    df: DataFrame, inputCol: Column, outputCol: str, filler: float = 0.0
):
    return df.withColumn(outputCol, inputCol).fillna(
        filler, subset=outputCol
    )


scalarNAFillerFunction(test_df, F.col("three"), "five", -99.0).show()
# +---+---+-----+----+----+
# |one|two|three|four|five|
# +---+---+-----+----+----+
# |  1|  2|    4|   1|   4|
# |  3|  6|    5|   4|   5|
# |  9|  4| null|   9| -99|
# | 11| 17| null|   3| -99|
# +---+---+-----+----+----+
```

> null in column three has been
> replaced by -99, our filler value.

Through our design of the transformation function (which will prove useful in section 14.1.5), we immediately see that we need three Params in our `ScalarNAFiller`:

- `inputCol` and `outputCol` are for the input and output columns, following the same behavior as the other transformers and estimators we've encountered thus far.

- `filler` contains a floating-point number for the value that `null` will be replaced with during the `transform()` method.

The data frame (`df` in listing 14.2) would get passed as an argument to the `transform()` method. Should we want to map this into the transformer blueprint introduced in chapter 13, it would look like figure 14.2.

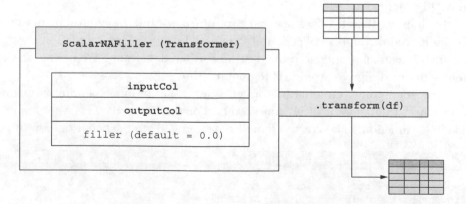

Figure 14.2   A blueprint for `ScalarNAFiller`. Three Params (`inputCol`, `outputCol`, `filler`) are necessary to configure its behavior. The `transform()` method provides the data frame, as with other transformers.

I believe we are now ready to start coding on the `ScalarNAFiller` class. In this section, we designed our transformer by outlining the Params and created a function that reproduced the expected behavior of the `transform()` function. In the next section, we create the Params necessary for our transformer to operate.

14.1.2 Creating the Params of a transformer

In this section, we create the three Params (`inputCol`, `outputCol`, `filler`) for the `ScalarNAFiller` transformer. We learn how to define a Param from scratch that will play well with other Params. We also leverage the predefined Param classes PySpark provides for common Params. Params drive the behavior of the transformer and estimator, and allow for easy customization when running a pipeline (e.g., the cross-validation in chapter 13 where we provide Param maps to test different ML hyperparameters). It is therefore very important that we create them in a way that allows for that customization and self-documentation.

First, we start with the creation of a custom Param, our filling value `filler`. To create a custom Param, PySpark provides a `Param` class with four attributes:

- A `parent`, which carries the value of the transformer once the transformer is instantiated.
- A `name`, which is the name of our Param. By convention, we set it to the same name as our Param.
- A `doc`, which is the documentation of our Param. This allows us to embed documentation for our Param when the transformer will be used.
- A `typeConverter`, which governs the type of the Param. This provides a standardized way to convert an input value to the right type. It also gives a relevant error message if, for example, you expect a floating-point number, but the user of the transformer provides a string.

In listing 14.3, we create a fully configured `filler`. Every custom Param we create needs to have `Params._dummy()` as a parent; this ensures that PySpark will be able to copy and change transformers' Params when you use or change them, for instance, during cross-validation (chapter 13). The name and doc are self-explanatory, so let's spend a little more time on the `typeConverter`.

Type converters are the way we instruct the Param about the type of value it should expect. Think of them like value annotations in Python, but with the option to try to convert the value. In the case of the `filler`, we want a floating-point number, so we use `TypeConverters.toFloat`. There are many other options that are available. (Check the API reference to find the right one for your use case: http://mng.bz/M2vn.)

Listing 14.3 Creating the `filler` Param using the `Param` class

```
from pyspark.ml.param import Param, Params, TypeConverters

filler = Param(
    Params._dummy(),        ◁── The parent is set to Params._dummy()
                               to be consistent with other Params.
```

This is the documentation for our Param.

```
    "filler",
    "Value we want to replace our null values with.",
    typeConverter=TypeConverters.toFloat,
)
```

Our Param name is set to the string value of the variable (filler).

We expect a floating point-like value for our Param.

```
filler
# Param(parent='undefined', name='filler',
#       doc='Value we want to replace our null values with.')
```

With three Params for our transformer, we would expect to repeat this process two more times, which is tedious, but feasible. Fortunately for us, PySpark provides some accelerated means to include commonly used Params without writing custom Param definitions. Since every transformer needs input and output columns, inputCol and outputCol, they belong in that category.

Commonly used Params are defined in special classes called *Mixin* under the pyspark.ml.param.shared module. There is, at time of writing, no public documentation about this module, so you have to resort to reading the source code to see the Mixins available (http://mng.bz/aDZB). As of Spark 3.2.0, 34 are defined. The class for inputCol and outputCol Params are HasInputCol and HasOutputCol, respectively. The class in itself is nothing magical: it defines the Param (see the next listing for the complete code for HasInputCol) and provides an initialization and a getter function, which we cover in section 14.1.3.

Listing 14.4   The `HasInputCol` class looks very familiar

```
class HasInputCols(Params):
    """Mixin for param inputCols: input column names."""

    inputCols = Param(
        Params._dummy(),
        "inputCols", "input column names.",
        typeConverter=TypeConverters.toListString,
    )

    def __init__(self):
        super(HasInputCols, self).__init__()

    def getInputCols(self):
        """Gets the value of inputCols or its default value. """
        return self.getOrDefault(self.inputCols)
```

The Param definition follows the same set of conventions as seen in a custom Param.

To use these accelerated Param definitions, we simply have to sub-class them in our transformer class definition. Our updated class definition now has all three Params defined: two of them through a Mixin (inputCol, outputCol), and one custom (filler).

Listing 14.5 The `ScalarNAFiller` transformer with its three Params defined

```
from pyspark.ml.param.shared import HasInputCol, HasOutputCol


class ScalarNAFiller(Transformer, HasInputCol, HasOutputCol):

    filler = Param(
        Params._dummy(),
        "filler",
        "Value we want to replace our null values with.",
        typeConverter=TypeConverters.toFloat,
    )


    pass
```

> inputCol and outputCol are defined through Mixin classes, HasInputCol and HasOutputCol.

> filler, as defined, has a custom Param.

Our `ScalarNAFiller` is getting closer to being usable now that the Params are defined. Following our plan outlined at the beginning of the section, the next logical step—and the subject of the next section—is to create the different getters and setters.

TIP What if you need more than one input/output column? See section 14.3.1, where we expand `ScalarNAFiller` to work on more than one column.

14.1.3 Getters and setters: Being a nice PySpark citizen

This section covers how to create getters and setters for a custom transformer. As seen in chapter 13, getters and setters are useful when we want to get or change the value of a Param. They provide a consistent interface to interact with the Param-eterization of a transformer or estimator.

Based on the design of every PySpark transformer we have used so far, the simplest way to create setters is as follows: we first create a general method, `setParams()`, that allows us to change multiple parameters passed as keyword arguments (seen on the `continuous_assembler` transformer in chapter 13). Then, creating the setter for any other Param will simply call `setParams()` with the relevant keyword argument.

The `setParams()` method is difficult to get right at first; it needs to accept any Params our transformer has and then update only those we are passing as arguments. Fortunately for us, we can leverage the approach the PySpark developers have used for other transformers and estimators. In listing 14.6, I provide the code for `set-Params()`, adjusted for the `ScalarNAFiller`. If you look at the source code for any transformer or estimator provided by PySpark, you'll see the same body of code, but with different arguments to the function.

The `keyword_only` decorator provides the attribute `_input_kwargs`, which is a dictionary of the arguments passed to the function. For instance, if we were to call `setParams(inputCol="input", filler=0.0)`, `_input_kwargs` would be equal to `{"inputCol": "input", "filler": 0.0}`. This attribute allows us to capture only the arguments we pass explicitly to `setParams()`, even if we pass `None` explicitly.

The `Transformer` class[1] has a `_set()` method that will update the relevant Params when passed a dictionary in the format `_input_kwargs` accepts. Handy!

> **Listing 14.6   The `setParams()` method for the `ScalarNAFiller`**

```
from pyspark import keyword_only


@keyword_only
def setParams(self, *, inputCol=None, outputCol=None, filler=None):
    kwargs = self._input_kwargs
    return self._set(**kwargs)
```

The keyword_only decorator provides the _input_kwargs attribute containing a dictionary of the arguments provided to setParams().

Our setParams() signature contains only the Params ScalarNAFiller has.

We finally use the _set() method provided by the superclass to update every Params from the _input_kwargs dictionary.

The setParams() method may look like magic when you first encounter it. Why not just use `**kwargs` and `_set()` directly? I think that the signature of `setParams()` is more clear when it contains only the Params that our transformer has. Also, if we input a typo (I often wrongly type `inputcol`—no capital letter—instead of `inputCol`), it'll be caught at the function call rather than much later when we call `_set()`. I think that the trade-offs are worthwhile.

> **TIP**   If you create a custom transformer and you forget how to create `set-Params()`, check out any transformer in PySpark's source code: they all implement this method the same way!

With `setParams()` cleared out, it's time to create the individual setters. That couldn't be easier: simply call `setParams()` with the appropriate argument! In listing 14.4, we saw that, while the getter for `inputCol` is provided, the setter is not because it would imply creating a generic `setParams()` that we'd override anyway. Fear not, it's just a few more lines of boilerplate code.

> **Listing 14.7   Individual setters for `ScalarNAFiller`**

```
def setFiller(self, new_filler):
    return self.setParams(filler=new_filler)


def setInputCol(self, new_inputCol):
    return self.setParams(inputCol=new_inputCol)


def setOutputCol(self, new_outputCol):
    return self.setParams(outputCol=new_outputCol)
```

All three setX() methods use the setParams() blueprint.

---

[1]   Theoretically, it is provided by the `Params` class, from which both `Transformer` and `Estimator` inherit.

The setters are done! Now it's time for the getters. Unlike setters, getters for Mixin are already provided, so we only have to create `getFiller()`. We also do not have to create a generic `getParams()`, since the `Transformer` class provides `explainParam` and `explainParams` instead.

The Mixin definition of listing 14.4 kind of spoiled the surprise for us by providing a blueprint for the getter's syntax. We leverage the `getOrDefault()` method provided by the superclass to return the relevant value to the caller in the next listing.

Listing 14.8 The `getFiller()` method of `ScalarNAFiller`

```
def getFiller(self):
    return self.getOrDefault(self.filler)
```

If we put out code together, our transformer looks like the code in listing 14.9. We have our Param definition (elided to avoid cluttering the listing), as well as a general setter (`setParam()`), three individual setters (`setInputCol()`, `setOutputCol()`, `setFiller()`), and an explicit getter (`getFiller()`; `getInputCol()` and `getOutputCol()` are provided by the Mixin classes).

Listing 14.9 The `ScalarNAFiller` with its getters and setters defined

```
class ScalarNAFiller(Transformer, HasInputCol, HasOutputCol):

    filler = [...]  # elided for terseness

    @keyword_only
    def setParams(self, inputCol=None, outputCol=None, filler=None):
        kwargs = self._input_kwargs
        return self._set(**kwargs)

    def setFiller(self, new_filler):
        return self.setParams(filler=new_filler)

    def getFiller(self):
        return self.getOrDefault(self.filler)

    def setInputCol(self, new_inputCol):
        return self.setParams(inputCol=new_inputCol)

    def setOutputCol(self, new_outputCol):
        return self.setParams(outputCol=new_outputCol)
```

In this section, we covered the creation of getters and setters for our custom transformer, leveraging some of the templates and Mixin classes PySpark provides to reduce boilerplate code. The next section covers the initialization function that will enable us to instantiate and therefore use our transformer.

14.1.4 *Creating a custom transformer's initialization function*

This section covers the initialization code for our transformer. If we want to create an instance of a class in Python, an initialization method is the simplest and most common way to proceed. We cover how to interact with the Param map and how to use the PySpark helper function to create an API consistent with the other PySpark transformers.

At the core, initializing a transformer means nothing more than initializing the superclasses of the transformer and setting the Param map accordingly. Just like set-Params(), __init__() is defined for every transformer and estimator, so we can take inspiration from the ones provided by PySpark.

The __init__() method of the SparkNAFiller, shown in listing 14.10, performs the following tasks:

1 Instantiate every superclass ScalarNAFiller inherits from via the super() function.
2 Call setDefault() on the custom Param we created. Because of the keyword_only decorator, we need setDefault() to set the default value for the filler Param. inputCol and outputCol are covered by the __init__() method in HasInputCol and HasOutputCol, respectively (see listing 14.4).
3 Extract the _input_kwargs and call setParams() to set the Params passed to the __init__() method to set the Params to the value passed to the class constructor.

Listing 14.10   The ScalarNAFiller initializer

This will call the __init__() method of Transformer,
then HasInputCol, then HasOutputCol.

```
class ScalarNAFiller(Transformer, HasInputCol, HasOutputCol):
    @keyword_only
    def __init__(self, inputCol=None, outputCol=None, filler=None):
        super().__init__()
        self._setDefault(filler=None)
        kwargs = self._input_kwargs
        self.setParams(**kwargs)

    @keyword_only
    def setParams(self, *, inputCol=None, outputCol=None, filler=None):
        kwargs = self._input_kwargs
        return self._set(**kwargs)

    # Rest of the methods
```

We set the default value for the Param filler, since keyword_only hijacks the regular default argument capture.

Here, we could have called _set(), but other PySpark transformers use setParams(). Both would work.

All the boilerplate code for our custom transformer is done! Just like for getters and setters, taking inspiration from the existing PySpark transformers ensures that our code is consistent and easy to deduce. The next section covers the transformation function; our transformer will then be fully functional!

14.1.5 *Creating our transformation function*

This section covers the creation of our transformation function. This function is certainly the most important of our transformer, as it performs the actual work of transforming the data frame. I explain how to create a robust transformation function using the Params values and how to deal with improper inputs.

In chapters 12 and 13, I explained how a transformer modifies the data via the transform() method. The Transformer class, on the other hand, expects the programmer to provide a _transform() method (note the trailing underscore). The difference is subtle: PySpark provides a default implementation for transform() that allows for an optional argument, params, in case we want to pass a Param map at transformation time (similar to the Param maps we encountered in chapter 13 with the ParamGridBuilder and the CrossValidator). transform() ends up calling _transform(), which takes a single argument, dataset, and performs the actual data transformation.

Because we already have a working function (scalarNAFillerFunction that we created in listing 14.2), implementing the _transform() method is a piece of cake! The method is shown in listing 14.11, with a few details worth going over.

First, should we want to validate any Param (e.g., making sure that inputCol is set), we would do it at _transform() time by using the isSet() method (provided by the superclass) and throwing an exception if it hasn't been explicitly set. If we do it earlier, we risk running into problems when writing/loading custom transformers, like we do in section 14.3.2.

We then set some explicit variables for the three Params of the transformer using the individuals getters. output_column and na_filler represent the outputCol and filler Params , respectively. For input_column, representing the inputCol Param value (a string), we promote it to a column object on the dataset using the bracket notation; this makes it consistent with our prototype function and simplifies the return clause of our method. Since the filler Param is meant to be a double, I explicitly cast input_column as a double to ensure that the fillna() method will work. Since outputCol and filler have default values, we just need to test for inputCol being set by the user, throwing an exception if not.

Listing 14.11 The _transform() method of the ScalarNAFiller transformer

```
def _transform(self, dataset):                    We raise a ValueError
                                                   if inputCol isn't set by
    if not self.isSet("inputCol"):                 the user.
        raise ValueError(              ◁─────
            "No input column set for the ScalarNAFiller transformer."
        )
    input_column = dataset[self.getInputCol()]
    output_column = self.getOutputCol()
    na_filler = self.getFiller()
    return dataset.withColumn(
        output_column, input_column.cast("double")
    ).fillna(na_filler, output_column)
```

With the _transform() method done, we have a fully functional transformer! The entire code is displayed in the next listing. The next section demonstrates that our transformer works as expected, so we can congratulate ourselves on a job well done.

Listing 14.12 The source code for the `ScalarNAFiller`

```
class ScalarNAFiller(Transformer, HasInputCol, HasOutputCol):

    filler = Param(                                        Custom Param definition
        Params._dummy(),                                   (section 14.1.2)
        "filler",
        "Value we want to replace our null values with.",
        typeConverter=TypeConverters.toFloat,
    )
                                                           Initializer method
                                                           (section 14.1.4)
    @keyword_only
    def __init__(self, inputCol=None, outputCol=None, filler=None):
        super().__init__()
        self._setDefault(filler=None)
        kwargs = self._input_kwargs
        self.setParams(**kwargs)
                                                           General setParams()
                                                           method (section 14.1.3)
    @keyword_only
    def setParams(self, inputCol=None, outputCol=None, filler=None):
        kwargs = self._input_kwargs
        return self._set(**kwargs)

    def setFiller(self, new_filler):
        return self.setParams(filler=new_filler)

    def setInputCol(self, new_inputCol):                   Individuals setters
        return self.setParams(inputCol=new_inputCol)       (section 14.1.3)

    def setOutputCol(self, new_outputCol):
        return self.setParams(outputCol=new_outputCol)

    def getFiller(self):                                   Individual getter (only for the
        return self.getOrDefault(self.filler)              custom Param, section 14.1.3)

    def _transform(self, dataset):                         Transformation method
        if not self.isSet("inputCol"):                     (section 14.1.5)
            raise ValueError(
                "No input column set for the "
                "ScalarNAFiller transformer."
            )
        input_column = dataset[self.getInputCol()]
        output_column = self.getOutputCol()
        na_filler = self.getFiller()
        return dataset.withColumn(
            output_column, input_column.cast("double")
        ).fillna(na_filler, output_column)
```

14.1.6 Using our transformer

Now that we have a custom transformer in our pocket, it's time to use it! In this section, we ensure that the `ScalarNAFiller` transformer works as expected. To do so, we'll instantiate it, set its Params, and use the transformation method. I don't think I need to convince you that you need try your code once written.

We already saw how a transformer is instantiated and used in chapter 12 and 13, so we can jump right in.

Listing 14.13 Instantiating and testing the `ScalarNAFiller` transformer

```
test_ScalarNAFiller = ScalarNAFiller(
    inputCol="three", outputCol="five", filler=-99
)

test_ScalarNAFiller.transform(test_df).show()
# +---+---+-----+----+-----+
# |one|two|three|four| five|
# +---+---+-----+----+-----+
# |  1|  2|    4|   1|  4.0|
# |  3|  6|    5|   4|  5.0|
# |  9|  4| null|   9|-99.0|
# | 11| 17| null|   3|-99.0|
# +---+---+-----+----+-----+
```

Because we inherit from `HasInputCol` and `HasOutputCol`, for conciseness, I skip the testing of changing `inputCol` or `outputCol` and instead focus on `filler`. In listing 14.14 and figure 14.3, I show two methods of changing the Params, which should yield the same behavior:

- Using the explicit `setFiller()`, which calls `setParams()` under the hood
- Passing a Param map to the `transform()` method, which overrides the default Param map

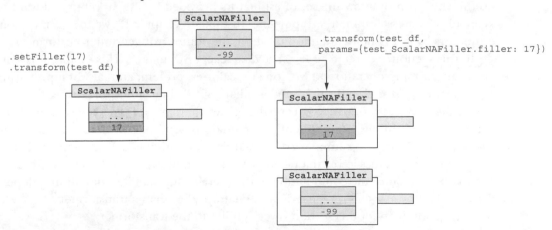

Figure 14.3 By setting the `filler` Param explicitly, we modify the transformer in place permanently. We can also temporarily set new Params in the `transform()` method to test different scenarios without modifying the original transformer.

In practice, both scenarios yield the same results; the difference is in what the transformer looks like after the operation. When using setFiller() explicitly, we modify test_ScalarNAFiller in place, setting filler to 17 before performing the transformation. In the transform() approach, with a Param map, we temporarily override the filler Param without changing the test_ScalarNAFiller in place.

Listing 14.14 Testing changes to the `filler` Param

```
test_ScalarNAFiller.setFiller(17).transform(test_df).show()      ◁── We modify
                                                                     test_ScalarNAFiller
                                                                     in place.
test_ScalarNAFiller.transform(
    test_df, params={test_ScalarNAFiller.filler: 17}      ◁──┐
).show()                                                     │
# +---+---+-----+----+----+          We temporarily override the
# |one|two|three|four|five|          filler Param without changing
# +---+---+-----+----+----+          test_ScalarNAFiller in place.
# |  1|  2|    4|   1| 4.0|
# |  3|  6|    5|   4| 5.0|
# |  9|  4| null|   9|17.0|
# | 11| 17| null|   3|17.0|
# +---+---+-----+----+----+
```

The transformer is done! Not only have we learned how to create a custom transformer from scratch, but we have a head start on the next section, where we cover how to create a custom estimator.

14.2 Creating your own estimator

Transformers and estimators goes hand in hand in an ML pipeline. In this section, we build on the knowledge of creating custom transformers (Params, getters/setters, initializers, and transform functions) to build a custom estimator. Custom estimators are useful when you outgrow the set of estimators provided by PySpark, but still want to keep all your steps within an ML pipeline. Just like in chapter 13, we focus on custom estimators by giving more attention to where they differ from custom transformers.

In this section, we create an ExtremeValueCapper estimator. This estimator is similar to the capping operation we've done on calories, protein, and fat when preparing data for our dessert classification model (chapter 12), but rather than using the 99th percentile, ExtremeValueCapper caps the values that are beyond the average of the column, plus or minus a multiple of the standard deviation. For instance, if the average of the values in our column is 10, the standard deviation is 2, and the multiple is 3, we will floor the values lower than 4 (or $10 - 2 \times 3$) and cap the values larger than 16 (or $10 + 2 \times 3$). Since the computation of the average and standard deviation is dependent on the input column, we need an estimator rather than a transformer.

Our action plan for this section is very similar to the transformer:

1 Outline the design or the estimator, taking into account the resulting model: inputs, outputs, fit(), and transform().

2 Create the companion model class as a `Model` (which is a specialized `Transformer`) subclass.

3 Create the estimator as an `Estimator` subclass.

Let's start with the design.

14.2.1 Designing our estimator: From model to params

This section covers the design of the estimator before we start coding. Just like the design of a custom transformer (section 14.1.1), I cover how to design your estimator from the desired outputs to the inputs, making sure that the design is logical and sound.

For an estimator to be a transformer-creating machine, we need the `fit()` method to return a fully parameterized transformer. When designing an estimator, it therefore makes sense to start the design of an estimator by building the returned `Model`, which I call the "companion model," which dictates how the estimator needs to be configured, not the other way around.

In the case of our `ExtremeValueCapper`, the resulting transformer is akin to a boundary guard: given a floor and a cap value

- Any value in our column lower than the floor will be changed with the floor value
- Any value in our column higher than the cap will be changed with the cap value

In figure 14.4, I draw my transformer flow, called `ExtremeValueCapperModel`, illustrating the relevant Params, named `inputCol`, `outputCol`, `cap`, and `floor`. I also highlight the Params in two categories:

- The *implicit* Params, which are inferred from the data itself
- the *explicit* Params, which are not data-dependent and need to be provided explicitly via the construction of the estimator

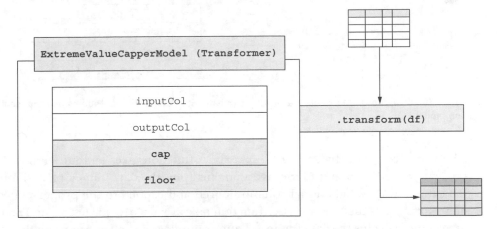

Figure 14.4 The high-level design of `ExtremeValueCapperModel`, showing the explicit and implicit Params

For the `ExtremeValueCapperModel`, `cap` and `floor` are implicit Params since they are computed using the average and standard deviation of the input column. The `input-Col` and `outputCol` Params are explicit.

With the model design out of the way, we can backtrack to the estimator design itself. Our estimator needs to have all the explicit Params required by the companion model, so it can pass them through. For our model-implicit Params, they need to be computed from the input column(s) and the Params of the estimator. In our case, we only need a single additional Param, which I name `boundary`, to compute both the `cap` and `floor` of the `ExtremeValueCapperModel`. The design is displayed in figure 14.5, and the test functions (just like we did for the transformer in section 14.1.1) are in listing 14.15. This time, I create two functions: one for the functionality of the `fit()` method of the estimator and one for the functionality of the `transform()` method of the companion model.

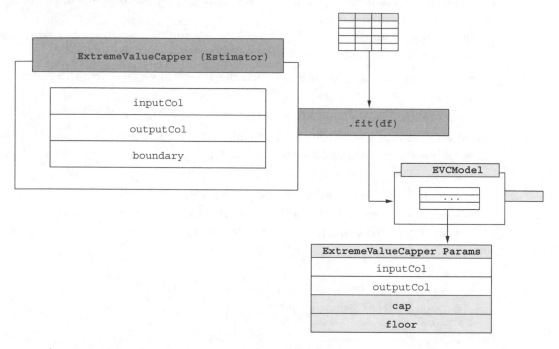

Figure 14.5   The design of the `ExtremeValueCapper` estimator, along with its Params and the resulting companion model

The `test_ExtremeValueCapper_transform()` function takes all four Params, `input-Col`, `outputCol`, `cap`, and `floor`, as arguments (plus the data frame `df`), and returns a data frame with an additional column floored and capped to the proper values. The `test_ExtremeValueCapper_fit()` function takes `inputCol`, `outputCol`, and `boundary` as arguments (plus the data frame `df`) and computes `cap` and `floor` using the average (`avg`) and standard deviation (`stddev`) of the input column. The function returns `test_ExtremeValueCapper_transform()` applied to the same data frame, with all the Params, both implicit and explicit, computed.

> **TIP** If we wanted `fit()` to return a `test_ExtremeValueCapper_transform()` function pre-Param-eterized and ready to apply to a new data frame, we could have used the same mechanics as a transform-enabled function. This very useful functionality requires a little more Python gymnastics and is covered in appendix C, under "Transform-Enabled Function: Functions Returning Functions."

Listing 14.15 Blueprint functions for the `ExtremeValueCapper` companion model

```
def test_ExtremeValueCapperModel_transform(
    df: DataFrame,
    inputCol: Column,
    outputCol: str,
    cap: float,
    floor: float,
):
    return df.withColumn(
        outputCol,
        F.when(inputCol > cap, cap)
        .when(inputCol < floor, floor)
        .otherwise(inputCol),
    )
```

Using when() makes our code more verbose, but more explicit than using F.min(F.max(inputCol, floor), cap).

```
def test_ExtremeValueCapper_fit(
    df: DataFrame, inputCol: Column, outputCol: str, boundary: float
):
    avg, stddev = df.agg(
        F.mean(inputCol), F.stddev(inputCol)
    ).head()
    cap = avg + boundary * stddev
    floor = avg - boundary * stddev
    return test_ExtremeValueCapperModel_transform(
        df, inputCol, outputCol, cap, floor
    )
```

We return the application of the companion model.

head() returns the first (and only) record of the aggregated data frame as a Row object, which we can bind to each field using de-structuring.

We compute cap and floor using avg and stddev, which depend on the data, and boundary, one of the estimator's Params.

With the design of both our estimator and companion model in the bag, we can now get to coding. In the next section, we implement the companion model class, using a trick for separating Params from implementation code.

14.2.2 *Implementing the companion model: Creating our own Mixin*

In this section, we implement the companion model, `ExtremeValueCapperModel`, which is akin to a transformer. Because this is an identical process to the implementation of the `ScalarNAFiller` from section 14.1.1, we introduce an additional trick to make our code more modular by separating Params from implementation and creating our own Param Mixin. When creating an estimator and its companion model, it is customary to propagate the Params of the estimator to the companion model, even if they are not used. In our case, it means that `boundary` will be added to the Params of `ExtremeValueCapperModel`. In order to make our code clearer and more terse, we can implement a Mixin (which in Python is a regular class) for both `ExtremeValueCapper` and `ExtremeValueCapperModel` to inherit from.

> **NOTE** We won't implement a `setBoundary()` method on the companion model, as we do not want to change that Param once we've computed the cap and floor values.

Creating a Mixin is very similar to creating half a transformer:

1 Inherit from any Mixin we wish to add the Params from (e.g. `HasInputCol`, `HasOutputCol`).
2 Create the custom Param(s) and their getter(s).
3 Create the `__init__()` function.

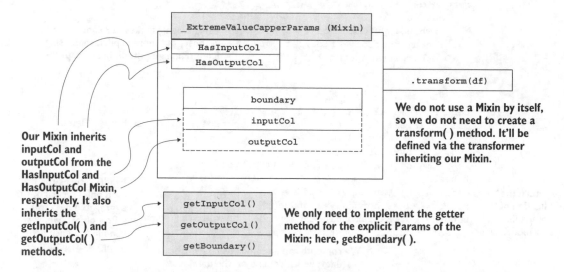

Figure 14.6 The design of our `_ExtremeValueCapperParams` Mixin, complete with inheritance from two Mixins

The only slight difference here is in the signature of the `__init__()` method. Because this Mixin will not be directly called—the call will come from when we call `super()` in a class that inherits from our Mixin—we need to accept the arguments of any downstream transformer, model, or estimator. In Python, we simply do this by passing `*args` to our initializer. Because each transformer calling this Mixin as a superclass might have different arguments (and we don't use them), we capture them under `*args` and call `super()` with those same arguments. Finally, we `_setDefault()` for our custom Param `boundary`.

Listing 14.16 The `_ExtremeValueCapperParams` Mixin implementation

```
class _ExtremeValueCapperParams(HasInputCol, HasOutputCol):

    boundary = Param(
        Params._dummy(),
        "boundary",
        "Multiple of standard deviation for the cap and floor. Default = 0.0.",
        TypeConverters.toFloat,
    )

    def __init__(self, *args):
        super().__init__(*args)
        self._setDefault(boundary=0.0)

    def getBoundary(self):
        return self.getOrDefault(self.boundary)
```

Ensure proper superclass call hierarchy by capturing them all under *args.

Just like when initializing a transformer, we use _setDefault() to set the default value of the boundary Param.

Mixin customarily provides the getter as part of the class definition. We reuse the same plumbing as with any getter.

TIP The syntax for the `__init()__` method for a Mixin is the same (besides `_setDefault()`, which will take the Param(s) of the Mixin(s) for every one of them, including those provided by PySpark). You can refer to the source code of an existing Mixin as a reminder.

Now we can now implement the full model, inheriting from `Model` (rather than the transformer, since we want the added knowledge that this is a model) and `_Extreme-ValueCapperParams`. To keep things a little more clean, I've elided the getters and setters. The full code for every transformer and estimator in this chapter is available in the book's companion repository.

Listing 14.17 The source code for the `ExtremeValueCapperModel`

```
from pyspark.ml import Model


class ExtremeValueCapperModel(Model, _ExtremeValueCapperParams):

    cap = Param(
        Params._dummy(),
        "cap",
        "Upper bound of the values `inputCol` can take."
        "Values will be capped to this value.",
        TypeConverters.toFloat,
    )
    floor = Param(
        Params._dummy(),
        "floor",
        "Lower bound of the values `inputCol` can take."
        "Values will be floored to this value.",
        TypeConverters.toFloat,
    )
```

We inherit from the Model superclass, as well as our Mixin (which includes HasInputCol and HasOutputCol), so we don't have to list them again here.

```
@keyword_only
def __init__(
    self, inputCol=None, outputCol=None, cap=None, floor=None
):
    super().__init__()
    kwargs = self._input_kwargs
    self.setParams(**kwargs)

def _transform(self, dataset):
    if not self.isSet("inputCol"):
        raise ValueError(
            "No input column set for the "
            "ExtremeValueCapperModel transformer."
        )
    input_column = dataset[self.getInputCol()]
    output_column = self.getOutputCol()
    cap_value = self.getOrDefault("cap")
    floor_value = self.getOrDefault("floor")

    return dataset.withColumn(
        output_column,
        F.when(input_column > cap_value, cap_value).when(input_column <
floor_value, floor_value).otherwise(input_column),
    )
```

Although our model is not meant to be used as is—it should only be the output of the fit() method—nothing prevents our users or ourselves from importing Extreme-ValueCapperModel and using it directly, passing direct values to cap and floor rather than computing them. Because of this, I code my companion models just like any free-standing transformer, checking the appropriate Params in the transform() method.

In this section, we created the companion model ExtremeValueCapperModel, as well as an _ExtremeValueCapperParams Mixin. Now we are ready to tackle the creation of the ExtremeValueCapper estimator.

14.2.3 *Creating the ExtremeValueCapper estimator*

This section covers the creation of the ExtremeValueCapper. Just like with creating a transformer/companion model class, the estimator borrows heavily from the set of conventions we have encountered so far. The only difference is in the return value of the fit() method: instead of returning a transformed data frame, we return a fully-Param-eterized model. And, just like with transformers, custom estimators allow for the implementation of functionality not provided outright by PySpark. This makes our ML pipelines more clean and robust.

We are already working with a significant body of raw material. We have our Params defined in a Mixin and have a companion model handy (section 14.2.2). We simply have to provide the __init__() method, the setters, and the fit() method. Because the first two are completed the same way as the transformer, our focus will be on the fit() method.

For the `fit()` method, illustrated in figure 14.7, we already have a sample function we can borrow heavily from in listing 14.15. In listing 14.18, the `fit()` method reproduces the functionality of our sample function, using the Params of the estimator as necessary. The return value is a fully Param-eterized `ExtremeValueCapperModel`. Note that, just like `_transform()`, PySpark asks us to create the `_fit()` method, providing a `fit()` wrapped, which allows for overriding Params at call time.

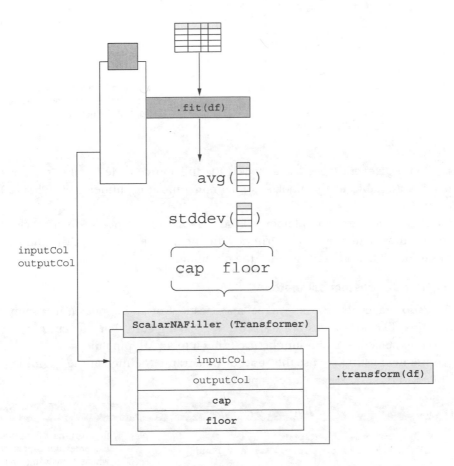

Figure 14.7 The `fit` method of the `ExtremeValueCapper` estimator. For the companion model, we generate the `cap` and `floor` Params based on the data passed as input, where `inputCol` and `outputCol` are passed verbatim by the estimator instantiation.

Listing 14.18 The `_fit()` method of the `ExtremeValueCapper`

```
from pyspark.ml import Estimator
```
> We inherit from the Estimator class and the _ExtremeValueCapperParams Mixin to reduce boilerplate code.

```
class ExtremeValueCapper(Estimator, _ExtremeValueCapperParams):
```

```
# [... __init__(), setters definition]

def _fit(self, dataset):
    input_column = self.getInputCol()        We set the relevant
    output_column = self.getOutputCol()      variables from the
    boundary = self.getBoundary()            Params.

    avg, stddev = dataset.agg(               ◁── We compute the
        F.mean(input_column), F.stddev(input_column)   average (avg) and the
    ).head()                                 standard deviation
                                             (stddev) from the
    cap_value = avg + boundary * stddev      data frame passed
    floor_value = avg - boundary * stddev    as argument.
    return ExtremeValueCapperModel(
        inputCol=input_column,               We return a fully Param-eterized
        outputCol=output_column,             ExtremeValueCapperModel as an
        cap=cap_value,                       output of the method.
        floor=floor_value,
    )
```

Just like the ExtremeValueCapperModel, the full source code for the ExtremeValue-Capper is available in the book's companion repository under code/Ch14/custom_feature.py

In this section, we've implemented the ExtremeValueCapper estimator, closing the loop in our custom estimator journey. In the next section, we test-drive our estimator on a sample data set to sanity-check the plumbing.

14.2.4   *Trying out our custom estimator*

This section takes the ExtremeValueCapper estimator and applies it to a sample data frame. Just like with a custom transformer, making sure that our custom estimator works as expected is paramount before using it in an ML pipeline.

In the next listing, we use the test_df data frame (defined at the beginning of the chapter) to try the ExtremeValueCapper.

Listing 14.19   Trying out the ExtremeValueCapper on a sample data frame

```
test_EVC = ExtremeValueCapper(                  fit() returns a Param-eterized
    inputCol="one", outputCol="five", boundary=1.0   ExtremeValueCapperModel,
)                                               whose transform() method is
                                                then called. The result is a
test_EVC.fit(test_df).transform(test_df).show()  ◁── transformed data frame.
# +---+---+-----+----+------------------+
# |one|two|three|four|              five|
# +---+---+-----+----+------------------+
# |  1|  2|    4|   1|1.2390477143047667|     ◁── 1 is lower than the floor, while
# |  3|  6|    5|   4|               3.0|         11 is higher than the cap. Both
# |  9|  4| null|   9|               9.0|         cases work as expected.
# | 11| 17| null|   3|10.760952285695232|  ◁──
# +---+---+-----+----+------------------+
```

In this very short section, we ensured that our `ExtremeValueCapper` was functioning as expected. With the development of two new pipeline member candidates, the next section covers their inclusion in our original dessert prediction model.

14.3   *Using our transformer and estimator in an ML pipeline*

What's the point of creating custom transformers and estimators if we don't plan on using them? In this section, we apply both `ScalarNAFiller` and `ExtremeValueCapper` to the dessert classification modeling pipeline. This custom transformer and estimator will help make our ML pipeline more portable and remove some of the pre-processing work we need to perform (filling `null` and capping numerical values) before we can run the pipeline.

When writing an ML program, we get to choose whether we want to integrate an operation into a pipeline (through custom transformers/estimators) or leave it as a data transformation. I like the testability and the portability of pipelines and tend to err on the "pipeline more than less" camp. When building ML models, we often want to cap/floor values, or impute a scalar value for `null` ones; with our custom transformer/estimator, there is no need to rewrite that transformation code.

If we were to use `ScalarNAFiller` as is, we would have to apply one transformer for every binary column we wished to fill. Not on my watch! We start this section by extending the `ScalarNAFiller` to accept more than one column.

14.3.1   *Dealing with multiple inputCols*

> **NOTE**   From this section onward, I use the word *transformer* for succinctness. The concepts apply identically to transformers, estimators, and companion models.

In this section, we tackle the common issue of dealing with multiple input and output columns when building custom transformers. We introduce the `HasInputCols` and `HasInputCols` Mixins and how to deal with transformers that can accept one or more columns as inputs or outputs. A transformer accepting multiple columns as inputs or outputs yields less repetition versus using one transformer for each column. Furthermore, the `VectorAssembler`, encountered for the first time in chapter 12, requires, by definition, multiple input columns (`inputCols`) and a single Vector output column (`outputCol`). At the end of this section, you'll be able to create robust transformers that work on single and multiple columns.

Just like `HasInputCol` and `HasOutputCol`, PySpark provides the `HasInputCols` and `HasOutputCols` Mixins that we can use. In listing 14.20, we get the new class definition for `ScalarNAFiller` with the additional Mixins' inheritance. Since we want `ScalarNA-Filler` to work with either a single column as inputs/outputs or with multiple columns, we inherit from both the singular and plural Mixins.

Listing 14.20   Adding `HasInputCols` and `HasOutputCols` to `ScalarNAFiller`

```python
from pyspark.ml.param.shared import HasInputCols, HasOutputCols


class ScalarNAFiller(
    Transformer,
    HasInputCol,
    HasOutputCol,
    HasInputCols,
    HasOutputCols,
):
    pass
```

> Just like their singular counterparts, accepting multiple columns is just about inheriting from the appropriate Mixins.

> **NOTE**   We need to create the appropriate setters and update the arguments to `setParams()` and `__init__` as well. The code for the full `ScalarNAFiller` is available in the book's companion repository, under `code/Ch14/custom_feature.py`.

Dealing with `inputCol`/`inputCols`/`outputCol`/`outputCols` means that we have to ensure we are using the right Params at the right time. This also means that we have to validate that

- The right Params are defined
- We can unambiguously determine which ones should be used

In the case of the `ScalarNAFiller`, we either want to apply the transformer on a single column (`inputCol`/`outputCol`) or multiple columns (`inputCols`/`outputCols`). From this, we can derive three use cases we want to defend ourselves against:

- If `inputCol` and `inputCols` are both set, we should raise an error, as we don't know if the transformer should be applied to a single or multiple columns.
- Inversely, we should also raise an error if neither of them are set.
- Finally, if `inputCols` is set, `outputCols` should be set as a list of the same length (*N* columns in, *N* columns out).

> **NOTE**   `outputCol` is set to a default value, so we don't need to test for `isSet()`.

We wrap those three test cases in a `checkParams()` method within the transformer definition.

Listing 14.21   Checking for the validity of the Params

```python
def checkParams(self):

    if self.isSet("inputCol") and (self.isSet("inputCols")):
        raise ValueError(
            "Only one of `inputCol` or `inputCols`" "must be set."
        )

    if not (self.isSet("inputCol") or self.isSet("inputCols")):
        raise ValueError("One of `inputCol` or `inputCols` must be set.")
```

Test 1: Either inputCol or inputCols can be set, but not both.

Test 2: At least one (inputCol or inputCols) must be set.

```
if self.isSet("inputCols"):
    if len(self.getInputCols()) != len(self.getOutputCols()):
        raise ValueError(
            "The length of `inputCols` does not match"
            " the length of `outputCols`"
        )
```

Test 3: If inputCols is set, then outputCols must be a list of the same len().

The third aspect of the updated `ScalarNAFiller` is the `_transform()` method itself. In listing 14.22, the new method has a few new moving parts.

First, we `checkParams()` using the method defined in listing 14.21. I like putting all the checks under a single method so the `_transform()` method is more squarely focused on the actual transformation work.

Second, since `inputCols`/`outputCols` are lists of strings and `inputCol`/`outputCol` are strings, and our transformation routine needs to accommodate both, we wrap the singular Param (when used) in a single-item list that we can iterate over later. This way, we can use a for loop over `input_columns`/`output_columns` without worrying if we are in the singular or plural case.

Finally, in the transformation routine itself, we first test to see if `input_columns` is identical to `output_columns`: when this is the case, we have no need to create new columns with `withColumn()` as they already exist in the data frame. We will address all the columns in the `output_columns` list with `na_filler`.

Listing 14.22 The modified `_transform()` method

```
def _transform(self, dataset):
    self.checkParams()
```

We check for the validity of the Params first before performing any work.

```
    input_columns = (
        [self.getInputCol()]
        if self.isSet("inputCol")
        else self.getInputCols()
    )
    output_columns = (
        [self.getOutputCol()]
        if self.isSet("outputCol")
        else self.getOutputCols()
    )
```

Because the plural Params are in lists, we keep the same behavior by wrapping the singular Param in a (single-item) list so that we can iterate over it.

```
    answer = dataset

    if input_columns != output_columns:
        for in_col, out_col in zip(input_columns, output_columns):
            answer = answer.withColumn(out_col, F.col(in_col))

    na_filler = self.getFiller()
    return dataset.fillna(na_filler, output_columns)
```

To save a few operations, when input_columns equal output_columns, we overwrite the existing columns; there is no need to create new ones.

Transitioning a single-column transformer to a multiple-columns one is pretty straightforward; we still need to make sure we design the usage of Params appropriately so they work appropriately, or fail with an informative error message. In the next section, we put our custom transformers to good use in our dessert prediction pipeline.

14.3.2 *In practice: Inserting custom components into an ML pipeline*

In this last section of the chapter, we look into applying a custom transformer/estimator to our dessert ML pipeline, introduced in chapter 13. Furthermore, we look at serializing and deserializing an ML pipeline containing custom transformers and estimators, ensuring the same portability as the made-out-of-stock components. This section has a faster pace because we reuse the same plumbing encountered in chapter 13; as a matter of fact, this shows how consistent our custom transformers and estimators are with the PySpark ML API.

To instantiate custom transformers and estimators, we simply call the class constructor with the relevant parameters. Just like with any PySpark stock components, our custom ones take fully keyworded attributes, just like in the next listing.

Listing 14.23   Instantiating custom transformers and estimators for our pipeline

```
scalar_na_filler = ScalarNAFiller(
    inputCols=BINARY_COLUMNS, outputCols=BINARY_COLUMNS, filler=0.0
)
extreme_value_capper_cal = ExtremeValueCapper(
    inputCol="calories", outputCol="calories", boundary=2.0
)
extreme_value_capper_pro = ExtremeValueCapper(
    inputCol="protein", outputCol="protein", boundary=2.0
)
extreme_value_capper_fat = ExtremeValueCapper(
    inputCol="fat", outputCol="fat", boundary=2.0
)
extreme_value_capper_sod = ExtremeValueCapper(
    inputCol="sodium", outputCol="sodium", boundary=2.0
)
```

inputCols, outputCols, and filler are passed as explicit keyworded arguments.

Now we can define (in listing 14.24) a `food_pipeline`, which contains our new components as stages. Our new pipeline contains a handful of new stages because of our custom transformers and estimators, but the rest is copied on the one we used in chapter 13.

Listing 14.24   The new and improved `food_pipeline`

```
from pyspark.ml.pipeline import Pipeline

food_pipeline = Pipeline(
    stages=[
        scalar_na_filler,
        extreme_value_capper_cal,
        extreme_value_capper_pro,
        extreme_value_capper_fat,
        extreme_value_capper_sod,
```

The new processing stages are listed like any other stage.

```
        imputer,
        continuous_assembler,
        continuous_scaler,
        preml_assembler,
        lr,
    ]
)
```

Unsurprisingly, the updated food_pipeline works using the same methods (fit()/transform()). In listing 14.25, we follow the same logical steps as when running our previous version of the pipeline:

1 Split the data set into train and test partitions.
2 Fit the pipeline on the train data frame.
3 Classify the observations on the test data frame.
4 Evaluate the AUC (area under the curve) and print the results.

Listing 14.25 Transforming food_pipeline on our training data set

```
from pyspark.ml.evaluation import BinaryClassificationEvaluator

train, test = food.randomSplit([0.7, 0.3], 13)

food_pipeline_model = food_pipeline.fit(train)

results = food_pipeline_model.transform(test)


evaluator = BinaryClassificationEvaluator(
    labelCol="dessert",
    rawPredictionCol="rawPrediction",
    metricName="areaUnderROC",
)

accuracy = evaluator.evaluate(results)
print(f"Area under ROC = {accuracy} ")
# Area under ROC = 0.9929619675735302
```

Confident with our pipeline working from beginning to end, let's look at serialization and deserialization. In the next listing, our pipeline does not save, throwing a Value-Error with an informative message: one stage (ScalarNAFiller) is not MLWritable. So close!

Listing 14.26 Attempting to serialize our model to disk

```
food_pipeline_model.save("code/food_pipeline.model")
# ValueError: ('Pipeline write will fail on this pipeline because
# stage %s of type %s is not MLWritable',
# 'ScalarNAFiller_7fe16120b179', <class '__main__.ScalarNAFiller'>)
```

Fortunately for us, we can add the capability of serializing a transformer (or estimator) just by inheriting from a Mixin. In this specific case, we want our custom components to inherit from `DefaultParamsReadable` and `DefaultParamsWritable`, both from the `pyspark.ml.util` module. In listing 14.27, we add those Mixins to `ScalarNAFiller` and `_ExtremeValueCapperParams` so that both the `ExtremeValueCapper` estimator and its companion model inherit from them. Doing so takes care of serializing the metadata of the transformer or estimator so that another instance of Spark can read them back and then apply the Param-eterization from your pipeline definition or fitting.

Listing 14.27   Adding the two Mixins for writing/reading the transformer

```
from pyspark.ml.util import DefaultParamsReadable, DefaultParamsWritable

class ScalarNAFiller(
    Transformer,
    HasInputCol,
    HasOutputCol,
    HasInputCols,
    HasOutputCols,
    DefaultParamsReadable,
    DefaultParamsWritable,
):
    # ... rest of the class here

class _ExtremeValueCapperParams(
    HasInputCol, HasOutputCol, DefaultParamsWritable, DefaultParamsReadable
):
    # ... rest of the class here
```

This takes care of the serialization. What about reading back a pipeline with custom components? PySpark, when reading a serialized pipeline, will perform the following steps:

1 Create a shell of the pipeline, with the default Param-eterization.
2 For each component, apply the Param-eterization from the serialized configuration.

In many cases, the serialization environment is not the same as the deserialized one. For instance, we usually train an ML pipeline on a powerful Spark cluster, serializing the fitted pipeline. We can then predict, on a different (less powerful and/or costly) setup, as needed. In those scenarios, you need to provide the deserialized Spark environment an indication about where to find the classes that implement transformers and estimators. Those included with PySpark will be found without explicit importing, but any custom ones need to be imported explicitly.

Listing 14.28   Reading the serialized pipeline from disk

```
from pyspark.ml.pipeline import PipelineModel
from .custom_feature import ScalarNAFiller, ExtremeValueCapperModel

food_pipeline_model.save("code/food_pipeline.model")
food_pipeline_model = PipelineModel.read().load("code/food_pipeline.model")
```

In this section, we reviewed practical steps in using custom transformers and estimators. By taking a few precautions, such as making sure to inherit the appropriate Mixins and importing the necessary custom classes, we can ensure that our pipelines are portable and therefore usable in multiple Spark environments.

Summary

- Behind transformers and estimators, PySpark has the concept of Param/Params, self-documenting attributes that govern how a transformer or estimator behaves.
- When creating custom transformers/estimators, we create their Param first, and then use them in `transform()`-/`fit()`-like instance attributes. PySpark provides standard Params for frequent use cases in the `pyspark.ml.param.shared` module.
- For often-used Params or functionalities, such as writing and reading, PySpark provides Mixins, classes containing specific methods to simplify and reduce boilerplate code for transformers and estimators.
- When deserializing a Pipeline containing custom stages, you need to ensure the underlying classes are imported within the program's name space.

Conclusion: Have data, am happy!

This concludes our overview of the PySpark ecosystem for data analysis. I hope that, through the different use cases and questions we asked ourselves, you gained an appreciation for the Spark data model and operating engine. At the beginning of this book, I summarized every data job as akin to an *ingest, transform, and export* process. Throughout this book, we did the following:

- Ingested a variety of data sources, from text (chapter 2) to CSV (chapter 4) to JSON (chapter 6) to parquet (chapter 10)
- Transformed data using a SQL-esque data manipulation framework (chapters 4 and 5), even resorting to actual SQL code (chapter 7). We also used Python and pandas code (chapters 8 and 9) to combine the power of Python and the scalability of Spark.
- Learned about Spark data types, schema, and how to build multidimensional data models using the data frame (chapter 6).
- Flipped the data frame model on its head and delved into the lower-level RDD, gaining full control over the distributed data model. We understood the trade-offs between complexity, performance, and flexibility using the RDD versus the data frame (chapter 8).
- Analyzed how Spark processes data and manages compute and memory resources through the Spark UI (chapter 11).

- Prepared data for machine learning (chapter 12), built ML pipelines for reproducible ML experimentation (chapter 13), and created custom components for
  more flexible and powerful pipelines (this chapter).

While PySpark is a moving target, I hope that the information in this book will make
using PySpark today (and tomorrow) easier, more productive, and more enjoyable. As
data continues to grows faster than our hardware, I believe that distributed processing
has much more value to provide.

Thank you for giving me the chance to accompany you on this journey. I look forward to hearing about the insights you derive from data using Python and PySpark.

appendix A
Solutions to the exercises

This appendix contains the solutions to the exercises presented in the book. If you have not solved them, I encourage you to do so. Reading the API doc and searching in other chapters of the book is fair game, but merely reading the answers won't do any good!

Unless specified, each code block assumes the following:

```
from pyspark.sql import SparkSession
import pyspark.sql.functions as F
import pyspark.sql.types as T

spark = SparkSession.builder.getOrCreate()
```

Chapter 2

Exercise 2.1

Eleven records. `explode()` generates one record for each element of each array of the exploded column. The `numbers` column contains two arrays, one with five elements, one with six: $5 + 6 = 11$.

```
from pyspark.sql.functions import col, explode

exo_2_1_df = spark.createDataFrame(
    [
        [[1, 2, 3, 4, 5]],
        [[5, 6, 7, 8, 9, 10]]
    ],
    ["numbers"]
)

solution_2_1_df = exo_2_1_df.select(explode(col("numbers")))
```

```
print(f"solution_2_1_df contains {solution_2_1_df.count()} records.")
# => solution_2_1_df contains 11 records.

solution_2_1_df.show()
# +---+
# |col|
# +---+
# |  1|
# |  2|
# |  3|
# |  4|
# |  5|
# |  5|
# |  6|
# |  7|
# |  8|
# |  9|
# | 10|
# +---+
```

Exercise 2.2

Using a list comprehension (see appendix C), we can iterate over each dtypes of our data frame. Because dtypes is a list of tuple, we can destructure to x, y, where x maps to the name of the columns and y to the type. We only need to keep the ones where y != "string".

```
print(len([x for x, y in exo2_2_df.dtypes if y != "string"]))   # => 1
```

Exercise 2.3

Rather than creating a column through function application and then renaming it, we can use alias() directly on the resulting column.

```
exo2_3_df = (
    spark.read.text("./data/gutenberg_books/1342-0.txt")
    .select(length(col("value")).alias("number_of_char"))
)
```

Exercise 2.4

The data frame has one column after the first select() statement: maximum_value. We then try to select key and max_value, which fails.

Exercise 2.5

a)

We just have to filter our column (using filter() or where()) to keep the word that is not equal (!=) to "is".

```
words_without_is = words_nonull.where(col("word") != "is")
```

b)

```
from pyspark.sql.functions import length

words_more_than_3_char = words_nonull.where(length(col("word")) > 3)
```

Exercise 2.6

Remember that the negation sign in PySpark is ~.

```
words_no_is_not_the_if = (
    words_nonull.where(~col("word").isin(
        ["no", "is", "the", "if"])))
```

Exercise 2.7

By assigning book.printSchema() to our book variable, we lose the data frame: print-Schema() returns None, which we assign to book. NoneType does not have a select() method.

Chapter 3

Exercise 3.1

Answer: b

(a) is missing the "length" alias, so the groupby() clause won't work. (c) groups by a column that does not exist.

```
from pyspark.sql.functions import col, length

words_nonull.select(length(col("word")).alias("length")).groupby(
    "length"
).count().show(5)

# +------+-----+
# |length|count|
# +------+-----+
# |    12|  815|
# |     1| 3750|
# |    13|  399|
# |     6| 9121|
# |    16|    5|
# +------+-----+
# only showing top 5 rows
```

Exercise 3.2

PySpark does not necessarily preserve order during operations. In this specific case, we do the following:

- Order by the column count.
- Group by the length of each (unique) word.
- count again, generating a new count column (different from the one in 1).

The count column we ordered by in 1 does not exist anymore.

Exercise 3.3

1)

```
results = (
    spark.read.text("./data/gutenberg_books/1342-0.txt")
    .select(F.split(F.col("value"), " ").alias("line"))
    .select(F.explode(F.col("line")).alias("word"))
    .select(F.lower(F.col("word")).alias("word"))
    .select(F.regexp_extract(F.col("word"), "[a-z']*", 0).alias("word"))
    .where(F.col("word") != "")
    .groupby(F.col("word"))
    .count()
    .count()              ◁        The data frame had only one record per word through the
)                                  groupby()/count(). Counting the number of records again will
                                   give the number of records, or the number of distinct words.
print(results)  # => 6595
```

Alternatively, we can remove the `groupby()`/`count()` and replace it with a `distinct()` that will keep only distinct records.

```
results = (
    spark.read.text("./data/gutenberg_books/1342-0.txt")
    .select(F.split(F.col("value"), " ").alias("line"))
    .select(F.explode(F.col("line")).alias("word"))
    .select(F.lower(F.col("word")).alias("word"))
    .select(F.regexp_extract(F.col("word"), "[a-z']*", 0).alias("word"))
    .where(F.col("word") != "")
    .distinct()           ◁        distinct() removes the
    .count()                       need for a groupby()/
)                                  count().

print(results)  # => 6595
```

2)

```
def num_of_distinct_words(file):
    return (
        spark.read.text(file)
        .select(F.split(F.col("value"), " ").alias("line"))
        .select(F.explode(F.col("line")).alias("word"))
        .select(F.lower(F.col("word")).alias("word"))
        .select(
            F.regexp_extract(F.col("word"), "[a-z']*", 0).alias("word")
        )
        .where(F.col("word") != "")
        .distinct()
        .count()
    )


print(num_of_distinct_words("./data/gutenberg_books/1342-0.txt"))  # => 6595
```

Exercise 3.4

After the groupby()/count(), we can use the count column like any other column. In this case, we filter the count values to keep only the 1s.

```
results = (
    spark.read.text("./data/gutenberg_books/1342-0.txt")
    .select(F.split(F.col("value"), " ").alias("line"))
    .select(F.explode(F.col("line")).alias("word"))
    .select(F.lower(F.col("word")).alias("word"))
    .select(F.regexp_extract(F.col("word"), "[a-z']*", 0).alias("word"))
    .where(F.col("word") != "")
    .groupby(F.col("word"))
    .count()
    .where(F.col("count") == 1)          ◁──── We only keep the
)                                              records with a count
                                               value of 1.

results.show(5)
# +------------+-----+
# |        word|count|
# +------------+-----+
# |    imitation|    1|
# |      solaced|    1|
# |premeditated|    1|
# |      elevate|    1|
# |     destitute|    1|
# +------------+-----+
# only showing top 5 rows
```

Exercise 3.5

Assuming that results is available (from words_count_submit.py):

```
results = (
    spark.read.text("./data/gutenberg_books/1342-0.txt")
    .select(F.split(F.col("value"), " ").alias("line"))
    .select(F.explode(F.col("line")).alias("word"))
    .select(F.lower(F.col("word")).alias("word"))
    .select(F.regexp_extract(F.col("word"), "[a-z']*", 0).alias("word"))
    .where(F.col("word") != "")
    .groupby(F.col("word"))
    .count()
)
```

1)

```
results.withColumn(
    "first_letter", F.substring(F.col("word"), 1, 1)
).groupby(F.col("first_letter")).sum().orderBy(
    "sum(count)", ascending=False
).show(
    5
)
```

```
# +------------+----------+
# |first_letter|sum(count)|
# +------------+----------+
# |           t|     16101|
# |           a|     13684|
# |           h|     10419|
# |           w|      9091|
# |           s|      8791|
# +------------+----------+
# only showing top 5 rows
```

2)

```
results.withColumn(
    "first_letter_vowel",
    F.substring(F.col("word"), 1, 1).isin(["a", "e", "i", "o", "u"]),
).groupby(F.col("first_letter_vowel")).sum().show()
# +------------------+----------+
# |first_letter_vowel|sum(count)|
# +------------------+----------+
# |              true|     33522|
# |             false|     88653|
# +------------------+----------+
```

Exercise 3.6

After using groupby()/count(), we get a data frame. The DataFrame object has no sum() method (see chapter 5 for a broader introduction to the GroupedData object).

Chapter 4

Exercise 4.1

```
sample = spark.read.csv("sample.csv",
                        sep=",",
                        header=True",
                        quote="$",
                        inferSchema=True)
```

Explanation:

1 sample.csv is the name of the file we want to ingest.
2 The record delimiter is the comma. Since we are asked to provide a value there, I pass the comma character , explicitly, knowing it is the default.
3 The file has a header row, so I input header=True.
4 The quoting character is the dollar sign character, $, so I pass it as an argument to quote.
5 Finally, since inferring the schema is nice, I pass True to inferSchema.

Exercise 4.2

c

Explanation: Both item and UPC match as columns, while prices doesn't. PySpark will ignore the nonexistent columns passed to drop().

Exercise 4.3

```
DIRECTORY = "./data/broadcast_logs"
logs_raw = spark.read.csv(os.path.join(
    DIRECTORY, "BroadcastLogs_2018_Q3_M8.CSV"),)

logs_raw.printSchema()
# root
#  |-- _c0: string (nullable = true)

logs_raw.show(5, truncate=50)
# +--------------------------------------------------+
# |                                               _c0|
# +--------------------------------------------------+
# |BroadcastLogID|LogServiceID|LogDate|SequenceNO|...|
# |1196192316|3157|2018-08-01|1|4||13|3|3|||10|19|...|
# |1196192317|3157|2018-08-01|2||||1|||||20|||00:0...|
# |1196192318|3157|2018-08-01|3||||1|||||3|||00:00...|
# |1196192319|3157|2018-08-01|4||||1|||||3|||00:00...|
# +--------------------------------------------------+
# only showing top 5 rows
```

Two major differences:

- PySpark put everything into a single string column, since it did not encounter the default delimiter (,) consistently in the records.
- It names the record _c0, the default convention when it has no information about column names.

Exercise 4.4

```
logs_clean = logs.select(*[x for x in logs.columns if not x.endswith("ID")])

logs_clean.printSchema()
# root
#  |-- LogDate: timestamp (nullable = true)
#  |-- SequenceNO: integer (nullable = true)
#  |-- Duration: string (nullable = true)
#  |-- EndTime: string (nullable = true)
#  |-- LogEntryDate: timestamp (nullable = true)
#  |-- ProductionNO: string (nullable = true)
#  |-- ProgramTitle: string (nullable = true)
#  |-- StartTime: string (nullable = true)
#  |-- Subtitle: string (nullable = true)
#  |-- Producer1: string (nullable = true)
#  |-- Producer2: string (nullable = true)
#  |-- Language1: integer (nullable = true)
#  |-- Language2: integer (nullable = true)
```

Explanation: I use the list comprehension trick on the data frame's columns, using the filtering clause `if not x.endswith("ID")` to keep only the columns that do not end with "ID."

Chapter 5

Exercise 5.1

This is a left join between one and two.

Explanation: A `left_semi` join only keeps the records on the left, where the `my_column` value is also present in the `my_column` column on the `right`. A `left_anti` join is the opposite: it will keep the records not present. Unioning these results in the original data frame, `left`.

Exercise 5.2

c: inner

Exercise 5.3

b: right

Exercise 5.4

```
left.join(right, how="left",
        on=left["my_column"] == right["my_column"]).where(
        right["my_column"].isnull()
        ).select(left["my_column"]).
```

Explanation: When performing an inner join, all the records from the left data frame are kept in the joined data frame. If the predicate is unsuccessful, then the column values from the right table are all set to `null` for the affected records. We just have to filter to keep only the unmatched records and then select the `left["my_column"]` column.

Exercise 5.5

First, we need to read the `Call_Signs.csv` file. Since the delimiter is the comma, we can keep the default parameterization for the reader, with the exception of `header=True`. Then we see that both tables share `LogIdentifierID`, which we can equi-join over.

```
import pyspark.sql.functions as F

call_signs = spark.read.csv(
    "data/broadcast_logs/Call_Signs.csv", header=True
).drop("UndertakingNo")

answer.printSchema()
# root
```

```
#  |-- LogIdentifierID: string (nullable = true)
#  |-- duration_commercial: long (nullable = true)
#  |-- duration_total: long (nullable = true)
#  |-- commercial_ratio: double (nullable = false)

call_signs.printSchema()
# root
#  |-- LogIdentifierID: string (nullable = true)
#  |-- Undertaking_Name: string (nullable = true)
```

We can do an equi-join on those columns.

```
exo5_5_df = answer.join(call_signs, on="LogIdentifierID")

exo5_5_df.show(10)
# +---------------+-------------------+--------------+--------------------+--------------------+
# |LogIdentifierID|duration_commercial|duration_total|    commercial_ratio|    Undertaking_Name|
# +---------------+-------------------+--------------+--------------------+--------------------+
# |           CJCO|             538455|       3281593| 0.16408341924181336|Rogers Media Inc....|
# |          BRAVO|             701000|       3383060|  0.2072088582525879|              Bravo!|
# |           CFTF|                665|         45780|0.01452599388379205|Télévision MBS in...|
# |           CKCS|             314774|       3005153| 0.10474475010091|Crossroads Televi...|
# |           CJNT|             796196|       3470359| 0.22942756066447303|Rogers Media Inc....|
# |           CKES|             303945|       2994495| 0.1015012548025627|Crossroads Televi...|
# |           CHBX|             919866|       3316728| 0.27734140393785683|Bell Media Inc., ...|
# |           CASA|             696398|       3374798| 0.20635249872733125|Casa - (formerly ...|
# |           BOOK|             607620|       3292170| 0.18456519560047022|Book Television (...|
# |         MOVIEP|             107888|       2678400|0.040280764635603344|STARZ (formerly T...|
# +---------------+-------------------+--------------+--------------------+--------------------+
# only showing top 10 rows
```

Exercise 5.6

We can reuse the same plumbing for generating our final answer, slightly changing the when() chause to remove "PRC" from the "pure" (1.0) commercials. Then we chain an additional when() to account for the different treatment of "PRC".

```
PRC_vs_Commercial = (
    F.when(
        F.trim(F.col("ProgramClassCD")).isin(
            ["COM", "PGI", "PRO", "LOC", "SPO", "MER", "SOL"]
        ),
        F.col("duration_seconds"),
    )
    .when(
        F.trim(F.col("ProgramClassCD")) == "PRC",
        F.col("duration_seconds") * 0.75,
    )
    .otherwise(0)
)

exo5_6_df = (
    full_log.groupby("LogIdentifierID")
    .agg(
        F.sum(PRC_vs_Commercial).alias("duration_commercial"),
```

We separate the when() clauses into separate variable for neatness (optional).

Here is the second when() clause for "PRC".

```
        F.sum("duration_seconds").alias("duration_total"),
    )
    .withColumn(
        "commercial_ratio",
        F.col("duration_commercial") / F.col("duration_total"),
    )
)

exo5_6_df.orderBy("commercial_ratio", ascending=False).show(5, False)
```

Exercise 5.7

We can create our round() predicate directly in the groupby() clause, making sure to alias our new columns.

```
exo5_7_df = (
    answer
        .groupby(F.round(F.col("commercial_ratio"),
    1).alias("commercial_ratio"))
        .agg(F.count("*").alias("number_of_channels"))
)

exo5_7_df.orderBy("commercial_ratio", ascending=False).show()
# +----------------+------------------+
# |commercial_ratio|number_of_channels|
# +----------------+------------------+
# |             1.0|                24|
# |             0.9|                 4|
# |             0.8|                 1|
# |             0.7|                 1|
# |             0.5|                 1|
# |             0.4|                 5|
# |             0.3|                45|
# |             0.2|               141|
# |             0.1|                64|
# |             0.0|                38|
# +----------------+------------------+
```

Chapter 6

Exercise 6.1

For this solution, I create a dictionary copy of the JSON document that I then dump using the json.dump function. Because spark.read.json can only read files, we use a neat trick where we create an RDD (see chapter 8) that can be read via our spark.read.json (see http://mng.bz/g41E for more information).

```
import json
import pprint

exo6_1_json = {
    "name": "Sample name",
    "keywords": ["PySpark", "Python", "Data"],
}
```

```
exo6_1_json = json.dumps(exo6_1_json)

pprint.pprint(exo6_1_json)
# '{"name": "Sample name", "keywords": ["PySpark", "Python", "Data"]}'

sol6_1 = spark.read.json(spark.sparkContext.parallelize([exo6_1_json]))

sol6_1.printSchema()
# root
#  |-- keywords: array (nullable = true)
#  |    |-- element: string (containsNull = true)
#  |-- name: string (nullable = true)
```

Exercise 6.2

Although we have a number in our list/array of keywords, PySpark will default to the lowest common denominator and create an array of strings. The answer is the same as exercise 6.1.

```
import json
import pprint

exo6_2_json = {
    "name": "Sample name",
    "keywords": ["PySpark", 3.2, "Data"],
}

exo6_2_json = json.dumps(exo6_2_json)

pprint.pprint(exo6_2_json)
# '{"name": "Sample name", "keywords": ["PySpark", 3.2, "Data"]}'

sol6_2 = spark.read.json(spark.sparkContext.parallelize([exo6_2_json]))

sol6_2.printSchema()
# root
#  |-- keywords: array (nullable = true)
#  |    |-- element: string (containsNull = true)
#  |-- name: string (nullable = true)

sol6_2.show()
# +--------------------+-----------+
# |            keywords|       name|
# +--------------------+-----------+
# |[PySpark, 3.2, Data]|Sample name|
# +--------------------+-----------+
```

Exercise 6.3

A StructType() will take a list of StructField(), not the types directly. We need to wrap T.StringType(), T.LongType(), and T.LongType() into a StructField(), giving them an appropriate name.

Exercise 6.4

To illustrate the problem, let's create a column, info.status, in a data frame that already has an info struct, containing a status field. By creating an info.status, the column becomes unreachable because Spark defaults to picking status from the info struct column.

```
struct_ex = shows.select(
    F.struct(
        F.col("status"), F.col("weight"), F.lit(True).alias("has_watched")
    ).alias("info")
)

struct_ex.printSchema()
# root
#  |-- info: struct (nullable = false)
#  |    |-- status: string (nullable = true)
#  |    |-- weight: long (nullable = true)
#  |    |-- has_watched: boolean (nullable = false)

struct_ex.show()
# +-----------------+
# |             info|
# +-----------------+
# |{Ended, 96, true}|
# +-----------------+

struct_ex.select("info.status").show()
# +------+
# |status|
# +------+
# | Ended|
# +------+

struct_ex.withColumn("info.status", F.lit("Wrong")).show()
# +-----------------+-----------+
# |             info|info.status|
# +-----------------+-----------+
# |{Ended, 96, true}|      Wrong|
# +-----------------+-----------+

struct_ex.withColumn("info.status", F.lit("Wrong")).select(
    "info.status"
).show()
# +------+
# |status|
# +------+            Ended,
# | Ended|  <---|     not Wrong
# +------+
```

Exercise 6.5

```
import pyspark.sql.types as T

sol6_5 = T.StructType(
    [
        T.StructField("one", T.LongType()),
        T.StructField("two", T.ArrayType(T.LongType())),
    ]
)
```

Exercise 6.6

Depending on your Spark version, the interval might be displayed differently. When selecting an element of a column of type array of struct, you get an array of elements without the need to explode. We can then use array_min() and array_max() to compute the first and last airdate.

```
sol6_6 = three_shows.select(
    "name",
    F.array_min("_embedded.episodes.airdate").cast("date").alias("first"),
    F.array_max("_embedded.episodes.airdate").cast("date").alias("last"),
).select("name", (F.col("last") - F.col("first")).alias("tenure"))

sol6_6.show(truncate=50)
```

Exercise 6.7

```
sol6_7 = shows.select(
    "_embedded.episodes.name", "_embedded.episodes.airdate"
)

sol6_7.show()
# +--------------------+--------------------+
# |                name|             airdate|
# +--------------------+--------------------+
# |[Minimum Viable P...|[2014-04-06, 2014...|
# +--------------------+--------------------+
```

Exercise 6.8

```
sol6_8 = (
    exo6_8.groupby()
    .agg(
        F.collect_list("one").alias("one"),
        F.collect_list("square").alias("square"),
    )
    .select(F.map_from_arrays("one", "square"))
)

# sol6_8.show(truncate=50)
# +---------------------------+
# |map_from_arrays(one, square)|
# +---------------------------+
# |    {1 -> 2, 2 -> 4, 3 -> 9}|
# +---------------------------+
```

Chapter 7

Exercise 7.1

b

Note that d could work as well, but it returns an integer value and not a data frame like the example.

```
elements.where(F.col("Radioactive").isNotNull()).groupby().count().show()
```

```
# +-----+
# |count|
# +-----+
# |   37|
# +-----+
```

Exercise 7.2

Looking at the `failures` table, we can see that we `count` the records where `failure = 1`. A useful trick when working with Booleans (`True/False`) as integers (`1/0`) is that we can combine the filtering and counting clauses into a `sum` operation (the count of all records equaling 1 is the same as the sum of all records). Using the `sum` operation also removes the need for using `fillna` for the values from the left join because we don't filter any records. Because of this, the code is greatly simplified.

```
sol7_2 = (
    full_data.groupby("model", "capacity_GB").agg(
        F.sum("failure").alias("failures"),
        F.count("*").alias("drive_days"),
    )
).selectExpr("model", "capacity_GB", "failures / drive_days failure_rate")
```

```
sol7_2.show(10)
# +-----------------+-------------------+--------------------+
# |            model|        capacity_GB|        failure_rate|
# +-----------------+-------------------+--------------------+
# |      ST12000NM0117|            11176.0|0.006934812760055479|
# |      WDC WD5000LPCX|   465.7617416381836|1.013736124486796...|
# |        ST6000DX000|-9.31322574615478...|                 0.0|
# |        ST6000DM004|    5589.02986907959|                 0.0|
# |      WDC WD2500AAJS|  232.88591766357422|                 0.0|
# |        ST4000DM005|   3726.023277282715|                 0.0|
# |HGST HMS5C4040BLE641|   3726.023277282715|                 0.0|
# |      ST500LM012 HN|   465.7617416381836|2.290804285402249...|
# |      ST12000NM0008|            11176.0|3.112598241381993...|
# |HGST HUH721010ALE600|-9.31322574615478...|                 0.0|
# +-----------------+-------------------+--------------------+
# only showing top 10 rows
```

Exercise 7.3

This problem warrants a little more thought. When looking at the reliability of each drive model, we can use drive days as a unit and count the failures versus drive days. Now we need to compute the age of each drive. We can break down this function into a few components:

1 Create a date of death for each drive.
2 Compute the age of each drive.
3 Group by model; get the average age.
4 Return the drives per average age.

I provide the code from the raw data frame data.

```
common_columns = list(
    reduce(
        lambda x, y: x.intersection(y), [set(df.columns) for df in data]
    )
)

full_data = (
    reduce(
        lambda x, y: x.select(common_columns).union(
            y.select(common_columns)
        ),
        data,
    )
    .selectExpr(
        "serial_number",
        "model",
        "capacity_bytes / pow(1024, 3) capacity_GB",
        "date",
        "failure",
    )
    .groupby("serial_number", "model", "capacity_GB")
    .agg(
        F.datediff(
            F.max("date").cast("date"), F.min("date").cast("date")
        ).alias("age")
    )
)

sol7_3 = full_data.groupby("model", "capacity_GB").agg(
    F.avg("age").alias("avg_age")
)

sol7_3.orderBy("avg_age", ascending=False).show(10)
# +-------------------+-----------------+------------------+
# |               model|      capacity_GB|           avg_age|
# +-------------------+-----------------+------------------+
# |       ST1000LM024 HN|931.5133895874023|             364.0|
# |HGST HMS5C4040BLE641|3726.023277282715|             364.0|
# |          ST8000DM002|7452.036460876465| 361.1777375201288|
# |Seagate BarraCuda...|465.7617416381836| 360.8888888888889|
# |        ST10000NM0086|           9314.0| 357.7377450980392|
# |         ST8000NM0055|7452.036460876465|  357.033857892227|
# |        WDC WD5000BPKT|465.7617416381836| 355.3636363636364|
# |HGST HUS726040ALE610|3726.023277282715| 354.0689655172414|
# |        WDC WD5000LPCX|465.7617416381836|352.42857142857144|
# |HGST HUH728080ALE600|7452.036460876465| 349.7186311787072|
# +-------------------+-----------------+------------------+
# only showing top 10 rows
```

Exercise 7.4

In SQL, you can use the extract(day from COLUMN) to get the day out of a date. This is equivalent to the dayofmonth() function.

```
common_columns = list(
    reduce(
        lambda x, y: x.intersection(y), [set(df.columns) for df in data]
    )
)

sol7_4 = (
    reduce(
        lambda x, y: x.select(common_columns).union(
            y.select(common_columns)
        ),
        data,
    )
    .selectExpr(
        "cast(date as date) as date",
        "capacity_bytes / pow(1024, 4) as capacity_TB",
    )
    .where("extract(day from date) = 1")
    .groupby("date")
    .sum("capacity_TB")
)

sol7_4.orderBy("date").show(10)
# +----------+-----------------+
# |      date| sum(capacity_TB)|
# +----------+-----------------+
# |2019-01-01|732044.6322980449|
# |2019-02-01|745229.8319376707|
# |2019-03-01|760761.8200763315|
# |2019-04-01|784048.2895324379|
# |2019-05-01| 781405.457732901|
# |2019-06-01|834218.0686636567|
# |2019-07-01|833865.5910149883|
# |2019-08-01|846133.1006234661|
# |2019-09-01|858464.0372464955|
# |2019-10-01|884306.1266535893|
# +----------+-----------------+
# only showing top 10 rows
```

Exercise 7.5

To solve this problem, we need to extract the most common capacity in bytes and then keep only the top record for each capacity (if there is more than one, we keep both). We do this by counting all the capacities for a given drive model and keeping only the one that occurrs most often (see most_common_capacity and capacity_count). Following this, we join the most common capacity to our original data.

```
common_columns = list(
    reduce(
        lambda x, y: x.intersection(y), [set(df.columns) for df in data]
    )
)
```

```
data7_5 = reduce(
    lambda x, y: x.select(common_columns).union(y.select(common_columns)),
    data,
)

capacity_count = data7_5.groupby("model", "capacity_bytes").agg(
    F.count("*").alias("capacity_occurence")
)

most_common_capacity = capacity_count.groupby("model").agg(
    F.max("capacity_occurence").alias("most_common_capacity_occurence")
)

sol7_5 = most_common_capacity.join(
    capacity_count,
    (capacity_count["model"] == most_common_capacity["model"])
    & (
        capacity_count["capacity_occurence"]
        == most_common_capacity["most_common_capacity_occurence"]
    ),
).select(most_common_capacity["model"], "capacity_bytes")

sol7_5.show(5)
# +--------------------+--------------+
# |               model|capacity_bytes|
# +--------------------+--------------+
# |       WDC WD5000LPVX|   500107862016|
# |        ST12000NM0117|12000138625024|
# |  TOSHIBA MD04ABA500V|  5000981078016|
# |HGST HUS726040ALE610|  4000787030016|
# |HGST HUH721212ALE600|12000138625024|
# +--------------------+--------------+
# only showing top 5 rows

full_data = data7_5.drop("capacity_bytes").join(sol7_5, "model")
```

Chapter 8

Exercise 8.1

Let's create a simple RDD to solve the exercise.

```
exo_rdd = spark.sparkContext.parallelize(list(range(100)))

from operator import add

sol8_1 = exo_rdd.map(lambda _: 1).reduce(add)
print(sol8_1)  # => 100
```

Explanation:

I start by mapping each element to the value 1, regardless of the input. The _ in the lambda function doesn't bind the elements because we don't process the element; we just care that it exists. After the map operation, we have an RDD containing only the value 1. We can `reduce(sum)` to get the sum of all the 1s, which yields the number of elements in the RDD.

Exercise 8.2

a

Filter will drop any values when the predicate (the function passed as an argument) returns a falsey value. In Python, `0`, `None`, and empty collections are falsey. Since the predicate returns the value unchanged, `0`, `None`, `[]` and `0.0` are falsey and filtered out, leaving only `[1]` as the answer.

Exercise 8.3

Because C and K are the same (minus a constant), and F and R are the same (minus another constant), we can reduce the decision tree of our function. If we pass a string value that isn't F, C, K, or R to the `from_temp` and/or `to_temp`, we return `None`.

```
from typing import Optional


@F.udf(T.DoubleType())
def temp_to_temp(
    value: float, from_temp: str, to_temp: str
) -> Optional[float]:

    acceptable_values = ["F", "C", "R", "K"]
    if (
        to_temp not in acceptable_values
        or from_temp not in acceptable_values
    ):
        return None

    def f_to_c(value):
        return (value - 32.0) * 5.0 / 9.0

    def c_to_f(value):
        return value * 9.0 / 5.0 + 32.0

    K_OVER_C = 273.15
    R_OVER_F = 459.67

    # We can reduce our decision tree by only converting from C and F
    if from_temp == "K":
        value -= K_OVER_C
        from_temp = "C"
    if from_temp == "R":
        value -= R_OVER_F
        from_temp = "F"

    if from_temp == "C":
        if to_temp == "C":
            return value
```

```
        if to_temp == "F":
            return c_to_f(value)
        if to_temp == "K":
            return value + K_OVER_C
        if to_temp == "R":
            return c_to_f(value) + R_OVER_F
    else:  # from_temp == "F":
        if to_temp == "C":
            return f_to_c(value)
        if to_temp == "F":
            return value
        if to_temp == "K":
            return f_to_c(value) + K_OVER_C
        if to_temp == "R":
            return value + R_OVER_F
```

```
sol8_3 = gsod.select(
    "stn",
    "year",
    "mo",
    "da",
    "temp",
    temp_to_temp("temp", F.lit("F"), F.lit("K")),
)
sol8_3.show(5)
# +------+----+---+---+----+-----------------------+
# |   stn|year| mo| da|temp|temp_to_temp(temp, F, K)|
# +------+----+---+---+----+-----------------------+
# |359250|2010| 03| 16|38.4|      276.7055555555555|
# |725745|2010| 08| 16|64.4|                 291.15|
# |386130|2010| 01| 24|42.4|      278.92777777777775|
# |386130|2010| 03| 21|34.0|      274.26111111111106|
# |386130|2010| 09| 18|54.1|      285.42777777777775|
# +------+----+---+---+----+-----------------------+
# only showing top 5 rows
```

Exercise 8.4

There are three things to fix:

- Variable usage: we use value consistently instead of t and answer.
- Because we multiply our value by 3.14159, our function needs to be annotated float → float rather than str → str.
- We change the return type of the UDF to DoubleType().

```
@F.udf(T.DoubleType())
def naive_udf(value: float) -> float:
    return value * 3.14159
```

Exercise 8.5

```
@F.udf(SparkFrac)
def add_fractions(left: Frac, right: Frac) -> Optional[Frac]:
```

```
    left_num, left_denom = left
    right_num, right_denom = right
    if left_denom and right_denom:  # avoid division by zero
        answer = Fraction(left_num, left_denom) + Fraction(right_num, right_denom)
        return answer.numerator, answer.denominator
    return None

test_frac.withColumn("sum_frac", add_fractions("reduced_fraction",
    "reduced_fraction")).show(5)
# +--------+----------------+--------+
# |fraction|reduced_fraction|sum_frac|
# +--------+----------------+--------+
# | [0, 1]|          [0, 1]|  [0, 1]|
# | [0, 2]|          [0, 1]|  [0, 1]|
# | [0, 3]|          [0, 1]|  [0, 1]|
# | [0, 4]|          [0, 1]|  [0, 1]|
# | [0, 5]|          [0, 1]|  [0, 1]|
# +--------+----------------+--------+
# only showing top 5 rows
```

Exercise 8.6

```
def py_reduce_fraction(frac: Frac) -> Optional[Frac]:
    """Reduce a fraction represented as a 2-tuple of integers."""
    MAX_LONG = pow(2, 63) - 1
    MIN_LONG = -pow(2, 63)
    num, denom = frac
    if not denom:
        return None
    left, right = Fraction(num, denom).as_integer_ratio()
    if left > MAX_LONG or right > MAX_LONG or left < MIN_LONG or right < MIN_LONG:
        return None
    return left, right
```

We do not need to change the return type from `Optional[Frac]`: the return value of the updated `py_reduce_fraction` is still either a `Frac` or `None`.

Chapter 9

Exercise 9.1

```
WHICH_TYPE = T.IntegerType()
WHICH_SIGNATURE = pd.Series
```

Exercise 9.2

Compared to the identical exercise in chapter 8, we need to return a `pd.Series` instead of a scalar value. The `null` value here (if we pass an unacceptable unit) is a Series of `None`.

```
def temp_to_temp(
    value: pd.Series, from_temp: str, to_temp: str
) -> pd.Series:
```

```
        acceptable_values = ["F", "C", "R", "K"]
        if (
            to_temp not in acceptable_values
            or from_temp not in acceptable_values
        ):
            return value.apply(lambda _: None)

        def f_to_c(value):
            return (value - 32.0) * 5.0 / 9.0

        def c_to_f(value):
            return value * 9.0 / 5.0 + 32.0


        K_OVER_C = 273.15
        R_OVER_F = 459.67

        # We can reduce our decision tree by only converting from C and F
        if from_temp == "K":
            value -= K_OVER_C
            from_temp = "C"
        if from_temp == "R":
            value -= R_OVER_F
            from_temp = "F"

        if from_temp == "C":
            if to_temp == "C":
                return value
            if to_temp == "F":
                return c_to_f(value)
            if to_temp == "K":
                return value + K_OVER_C
            if to_temp == "R":
                return c_to_f(value) + R_OVER_F
        else:  # from_temp == "F":
            if to_temp == "C":
                return f_to_c(value)
            if to_temp == "F":
                return value
            if to_temp == "K":
                return f_to_c(value) + K_OVER_C
            if to_temp == "R":
                return value + R_OVER_F
```

Exercise 9.3

The output is the same. The normalization process does not change based on the
units of temperature.

```
def scale_temperature_C(temp_by_day: pd.DataFrame) -> pd.DataFrame:
    """Returns a simple normalization of the temperature for a site, in Celcius.

    If the temperature is constant for the whole window, defaults to 0.5."""

    def f_to_c(temp):
        return (temp - 32.0) * 5.0 / 9.0
```

```
    temp = f_to_c(temp_by_day.temp)
    answer = temp_by_day[["stn", "year", "mo", "da", "temp"]]
    if temp.min() == temp.max():
        return answer.assign(temp_norm=0.5)
    return answer.assign(
        temp_norm=(temp - temp.min()) / (temp.max() - temp.min())
    )
```

Exercise 9.4

Because of the way we defined our function, our data frame returns a six-columned data frame, where we expect only four. The faulty line is answer = temp_by_day[["stn", "year", "mo", "da", "temp"]], where we hardcode the columns.

```
sol9_4 = gsod.groupby("year", "mo").applyInPandas(
    scale_temperature_C,
    schema=(
        "year string, mo string, "
        "temp double, temp_norm double"
    ),
)


try:
    sol9_4.show(5, False)
except RuntimeError as err:
    print(err)


# RuntimeError: Number of columns of the returned pandas.DataFrame doesn't match
# specified schema. Expected: 4 Actual: 6
```

Exercise 9.5

```
from sklearn.linear_model import LinearRegression
from typing import Sequence


@F.pandas_udf(T.ArrayType(T.DoubleType()))
def rate_of_change_temperature_ic(
    day: pd.Series, temp: pd.Series
) -> Sequence[float]:
    """Returns the intercept and slope of the daily temperature for a given
     period of time."""
    model = LinearRegression().fit(
        X=day.astype(int).values.reshape(-1, 1), y=temp
    )
    return model.intercept_, model.coef_[0]


gsod.groupby("stn", "year", "mo").agg(
    rate_of_change_temperature_ic("da", "temp").alias("sol9_5")
).show(5, truncate=50)
# +------+----+---+------------------------------------------+
# |   stn|year| mo|                                    sol9_5|
# +------+----+---+------------------------------------------+
```

```
# |008268|2010|  07| [135.79999999999973, -2.1999999999999877]|
# |008401|2011|  11| [67.51655172413793, -0.30429365962180205]|
# |008411|2014|  02| [82.69682539682537, -0.02662835249042155]|
# |008411|2015|  12|  [84.03264367816091, -0.0476974416017797]|
# |008415|2016|  01|[82.10193548387099, -0.013225806451612926]|
# +------+----+---+--------------------------------------+
# only showing top 5 rows
```

Chapter 10

Exercise 10.1

c

```
sol10_1 = Window.partitionBy("year", "mo", "da")

res10_1 = (
    gsod.select(
        "stn",
        "year",
        "mo",
        "da",
        "temp",
        F.max("temp").over(sol10_1).alias("max_this_day"),
    )
    .where(F.col("temp") == F.col("max_this_day"))
    .drop("temp")
)

res10_1.show(5)
# +------+----+---+---+------------+
# |   stn|year| mo| da|max_this_day|
# +------+----+---+---+------------+
# |406370|2017| 08| 11|       108.3|
# |672614|2017| 12| 10|        93.8|
# |944500|2018| 01| 04|        99.2|
# |954920|2018| 01| 12|        98.9|
# |647530|2018| 10| 01|       100.4|
# +------+----+---+---+------------+
# only showing top 5 rows
```

Exercise 10.2

Let's create a data frame with 1,000 records (250 distinct index values and the value column), all equal to 2.

```
exo10_2 = spark.createDataFrame(
    [[x // 4, 2] for x in range(1001)], ["index", "value"]
)

exo10_2.show()
# +-----+-----+
# |index|value|
# +-----+-----+
```

```
# |      0|     2|
# |      0|     2|
# |      0|     2|
# |      0|     2|
# |      1|     2|
# |      1|     2|
# |      1|     2|
# |      1|     2|
# |      2|     2|
# |      2|     2|
# |      2|     2|
# |      2|     2|
# |      3|     2|
# |      3|     2|
# |      3|     2|
# |      3|     2|
# |      4|     2|
# |      4|     2|
# |      4|     2|
# |      4|     2|
# +-----+-----+
# only showing top 20 rows

sol10_2 = Window.partitionBy("index").orderBy("value")

exo10_2.withColumn("10_2", F.ntile(3).over(sol10_2)).show(10)
# +-----+-----+----+
# |index|value|10_2|
# +-----+-----+----+
# |   26|    2|   1|
# |   26|    2|   1|
# |   26|    2|   2|
# |   26|    2|   3|
# |   29|    2|   1|
# |   29|    2|   1|
# |   29|    2|   2|
# |   29|    2|   3|
# |   65|    2|   1|
# |   65|    2|   1|
# +-----+-----+----+
# only showing top 10 rows
```

The result might appear counterintuitive, but following our definition (illustrated in figure A.1), we can see that PySpark does the right thing by trying to split every partition window into three (as even as it can) buckets.

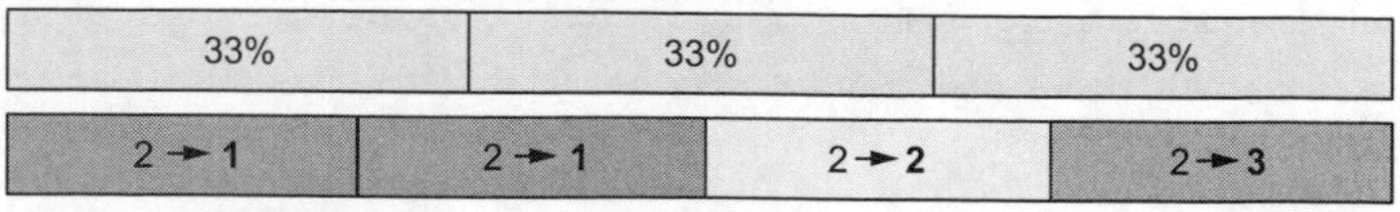

Figure A.1   Three-tiling with all the same `values`. We follow the same behavior: splitting across records.

Exercise 10.3

The rowsBetween() window partitions contain five records. Because the first and second records of the data don't have two preceding records, we see 3 and 4 for the first and second records, respectively.

The rangeBetween() window partitions uses the 10 value (always the same) to compute the window frame boundaries. The result is 1,000,001 everywhere.

```
exo10_3 = spark.createDataFrame([[10] for x in range(1_000_001)], ["ord"])

exo10_3.select(
    "ord",
    F.count("ord")
    .over(Window.partitionBy().orderBy("ord").rowsBetween(-2, 2))
    .alias("row"),
    F.count("ord")
    .over(Window.partitionBy().orderBy("ord").rangeBetween(-2, 2))
    .alias("range"),
).show(10)
# +---+---+-------+
# |ord|row|  range|
# +---+---+-------+
# | 10|  3|1000001|
# | 10|  4|1000001|
# | 10|  5|1000001|
# | 10|  5|1000001|
# | 10|  5|1000001|
# | 10|  5|1000001|
# | 10|  5|1000001|
# | 10|  5|1000001|
# | 10|  5|1000001|
# | 10|  5|1000001|
# +---+---+-------+
# only showing top 10 rows
```

Exercise 10.4

We have multiple records with the highest temperature: PySpark will show all of them.

```
(
    gsod.withColumn("max_temp", F.max("temp").over(each_year))
    .where("temp = max_temp")
    .select("year", "mo", "da", "stn", "temp")
    .withColumn("avg_temp", F.avg("temp").over(each_year))
    .orderBy("year", "stn")
    .show()
)
# +----+---+---+------+-----+--------+
# |year| mo| da|   stn| temp|avg_temp|
# +----+---+---+------+-----+--------+
# |2017| 07| 06|403770|110.0|   110.0|
# |2017| 07| 24|999999|110.0|   110.0|
# |2018| 06| 06|405860|110.0|   110.0|
# |2018| 07| 12|407036|110.0|   110.0|
```

```
# |2018| 07| 26|723805|110.0|   110.0|
# |2018| 07| 16|999999|110.0|   110.0|
# |2019| 07| 07|405870|110.0|   110.0|
# |2019| 07| 15|606030|110.0|   110.0|
# |2019| 08| 02|606450|110.0|   110.0|
# |2019| 07| 14|999999|110.0|   110.0|
# +----+---+---+------+-----+--------+
```

Exercise 10.5

While we can tackle this multiple ways, the simplest (in my opinion) is to create a record number (which will always be increasing) to break the ties.

```
temp_per_month_asc = Window.partitionBy("mo").orderBy("count_temp")
temp_per_month_rnk = Window.partitionBy("mo").orderBy(
    "count_temp", "row_tpm"
)

gsod_light.withColumn(
    "row_tpm", F.row_number().over(temp_per_month_asc)
).withColumn("rank_tpm", F.rank().over(temp_per_month_rnk)).show()
# +------+----+---+---+----+----------+-------+--------+
# |   stn|year| mo| da|temp|count_temp|row_tpm|rank_tpm|
# +------+----+---+---+----+----------+-------+--------+
# |949110|2019| 11| 23|54.9|        14|      1|       1|
# |996470|2018| 03| 12|55.6|        12|      1|       1|
# |998166|2019| 03| 20|34.8|        12|      2|       2|
# |998012|2017| 03| 02|31.4|        24|      3|       3|
# |041680|2019| 02| 19|16.1|        15|      1|       1|
# |076470|2018| 06| 07|65.0|        24|      1|       1|
# |719200|2017| 10| 09|60.5|        11|      1|       1|
# |994979|2017| 12| 11|21.3|        21|      1|       1|
# |917350|2018| 04| 21|82.6|         9|      1|       1|
# |998252|2019| 04| 18|44.7|        11|      2|       2|
# +------+----+---+---+----+----------+-------+--------+
```

These records are 1 and 2.

Exercise 10.6

We can convert the date into a `unix_timestamp` (the number of seconds since the UNIX epoch; see http://mng.bz/enPv) and then use a 7-day window (or 7 days × 24 hours × 60 minutes × 60 seconds).

```
seven_days = (
    Window.partitionBy("stn")
    .orderBy("dtu")
    .rangeBetween(-7 * 60 * 60 * 24, 7 * 60 * 60 * 24)
)
sol10_6 = (
    gsod.select(
        "stn",
        (F.to_date(F.concat_ws("-", "year", "mo", "da"))).alias("dt"),
        "temp",
    )
    .withColumn("dtu", F.unix_timestamp("dt").alias("dtu"))
    .withColumn("max_temp", F.max("temp").over(seven_days))
```

```
    .where("temp = max_temp")
    .show(10)
)
# +------+----------+----+----------+--------+
# |   stn|        dt|temp|       dtu|max_temp|
# +------+----------+----+----------+--------+
# |010875|2017-01-08|46.2|1483851600|    46.2|
# |010875|2017-01-19|48.0|1484802000|    48.0|
# |010875|2017-02-03|45.3|1486098000|    45.3|
# |010875|2017-02-20|45.7|1487566800|    45.7|
# |010875|2017-03-14|45.7|1489464000|    45.7|
# |010875|2017-04-01|46.8|1491019200|    46.8|
# |010875|2017-04-20|46.1|1492660800|    46.1|
# |010875|2017-05-02|50.5|1493697600|    50.5|
# |010875|2017-05-27|51.4|1495857600|    51.4|
# |010875|2017-06-06|53.6|1496721600|    53.6|
# +------+----------+----+----------+--------+
# only showing top 10 rows
```

Exercise 10.7

Assuming there are always 12 months in a year, we can create a pseudo index, num_mo, with year * 12 + mo. With this, we can use an exact range of ± 1 month.

```
one_month_before_and_after = (
    Window.partitionBy("year").orderBy("num_mo").rangeBetween(-1, 1)
)


gsod_light_p.drop("dt", "dt_num").withColumn(
    "num_mo", F.col("year").cast("int") * 12 + F.col("mo").cast("int")
).withColumn(
    "avg_count", F.avg("count_temp").over(one_month_before_and_after)
).show()
# +------+----+---+---+----+----------+------+------------------+
# |   stn|year| mo| da|temp|count_temp|num_mo|         avg_count|
# +------+----+---+---+----+----------+------+------------------+
# |041680|2019| 02| 19|16.1|        15| 24230|             15.75|
# |998012|2019| 03| 02|31.4|        24| 24231|13.833333333333334|
# |996470|2019| 03| 12|55.6|        12| 24231|13.833333333333334|
# |998166|2019| 03| 20|34.8|        12| 24231|13.833333333333334|
# |917350|2019| 04| 21|82.6|         9| 24232|              13.6|
# |998252|2019| 04| 18|44.7|        11| 24232|              13.6|
# |076470|2019| 06| 07|65.0|        24| 24234|              24.0|
# |719200|2019| 10| 09|60.5|        11| 24238|              12.5|
# |949110|2019| 11| 23|54.9|        14| 24239|15.333333333333334|
# |994979|2019| 12| 11|21.3|        21| 24240|              17.5|
# +------+----+---+---+----+----------+------+------------------+
```

Chapter 11

Exercise 11.1

No. We would still have one job (the program, triggered by showString()) and two stages.

Exercise 11.2

The first plan has no action attached to it (`show()`), so we do not have a last action.

Exercise 11.3

a and b are operations on a single record at a time; they are narrow operations. The other ones need to shuffle the data to collocate the relevant records and therefore are wide operations. c, d, and e need the matching keys to be on the same node at one point.

Chapter 13

Exercise 13.1

When `E_max == E_min`, every value becomes `0.5 * (max + min)`

appendix B
Installing PySpark

This appendix covers the installation of standalone Spark and PySpark on your own computer, whether it's running Windows, macOS, or Linux. I also briefly cover cloud offerings, should you want to easily take advantage of PySpark's distributed nature.

Having a local PySpark cluster means that you'll be able to experiment with the syntax using smaller data sets. You don't have to acquire multiple computers or spend money on managed PySpark on the cloud until you're ready to scale your programs. Once you're ready to work on a larger data set, you can easily transfer your program to a cloud instance of Spark for additional power.

B.1 Installing PySpark on your local machine

This section covers installing Spark and Python on your own computer. Spark is a complex piece of software, and, while the installation process is simple, most guides out there overcomplicate the installation process. We'll take a much simpler approach by installing the bare minimum to start and building from there. Our goals are as follows:

- Install Java (Spark is written in Scala, which runs on the Java Virtual Machine, or JVM).
- Install Spark.
- Install Python 3 and IPython.
- Launch a PySpark shell using IPython.
- (Optional) Install Jupyter and use it with PySpark.

In the next sections, we cover instructions for Windows, macOS, and Linux OSes.

> **NOTE** When working with Spark locally, you might get a `21/10/26 17:49:14 WARN NativeCodeLoader: Unable to load native-hadoop library for`

your platform... using builtin-java classes where applicable message. You do not need to worry about it; it simply means that Hadoop isn't found on your system (it is only available on *nix platforms). As we are working locally, it does not matter.

B.2 Windows

When working on Windows, you have the option to either install Spark directly on Windows or to use WSL (Windows Subsystem for Linux). If you want to use WSL, follow the instructions at https://aka.ms/wslinstall and then follow the instructions for GNU/Linux. If you want to install on plain Windows, follow the rest of this section.

B.2.1 Install Java

The easiest way to install Java on Windows is to go to https://adoptopenjdk.net and follow the download and installation instructions for downloading Java 8 or 11.

> **WARNING**   Because Java 11 is incompatible with certain third-party libraries, I recommend staying on Java 8. Spark 3.0+ works using Java 11+ as well, but some third-party libraries trail behind.

B.2.2 Install 7-zip

Spark is available as a GZIP archive (.tgz) file on Spark's website. By default, Windows doesn't provide a native way to extract those files. The most popular option is 7-zip (https://www.7-zip.org/). Simply go to the website, download the program, and follow the installation instructions.

B.2.3 Download and install Apache Spark

Go on the Apache website (https://spark.apache.org/) and download the latest Spark release. Accept the default options, but figure B.1 displays those I see when I navigate to the download page. Make sure you download the signatures and checksums if you want to validate the download (step 4 on the page).

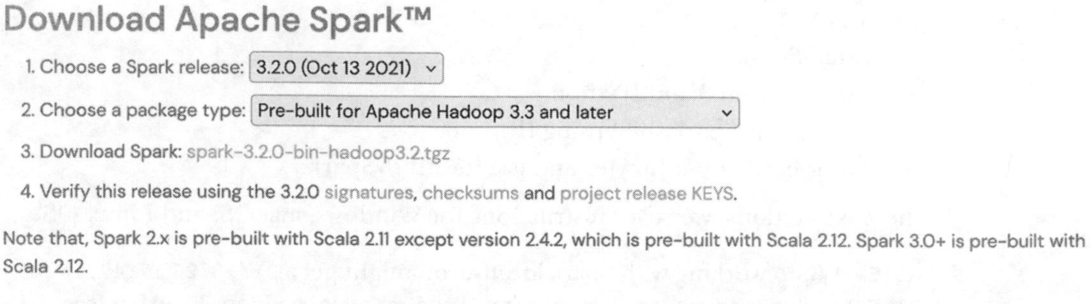

Download Apache Spark™

1. Choose a Spark release: | 3.2.0 (Oct 13 2021) ⌄ |

2. Choose a package type: | Pre-built for Apache Hadoop 3.3 and later   ⌄ |

3. Download Spark: spark-3.2.0-bin-hadoop3.2.tgz

4. Verify this release using the 3.2.0 signatures, checksums and project release KEYS.

Note that, Spark 2.x is pre-built with Scala 2.11 except version 2.4.2, which is pre-built with Scala 2.12. Spark 3.0+ is pre-built with Scala 2.12.

Figure B.1   The options to download Spark

Once you have downloaded the file, unzip the file using 7-zip. I recommend putting the directory under `C:\Users\[YOUR_USER_NAME]\spark`.

Next, we need to download a `winutils.exe` to prevent some cryptic Hadoop errors. Go to the https://github.com/cdarlint/winutils repository and download the winutils.exe file in the `hadoop-X.Y.Z/bin` directory where X.Y matches the Hadoop version that was used for the selected Spark version in figure B.1. Keep the `README.md` of the repository handy. Place the `winutils.exe` in the `bin` directory of your Spark installation (`C:\Users\[YOUR_USER_NAME\spark]`).

Next, we set two environment variables to provide our shell knowledge about where to find Spark. Think of environment variables as OS-level variables that any program can use; for instance, `PATH` indicates where to find executables to run. Here, we set `SPARK_HOME` (the main directory where the Spark executables are located), and we append the value of `SPARK_HOME` to the `PATH` environment variable. To do so, open the Start menu and search for "Edit the system environment variables." Click on the Environment variables button (see figure B.2), and then add them there. You will also need to set `SPARK_HOME` to the directory of your Spark installation (`C:\Users\[YOUR-USER-NAME]\spark`). Finally, add the `%SPARK_HOME%\bin` directory to your `PATH` environment variable.

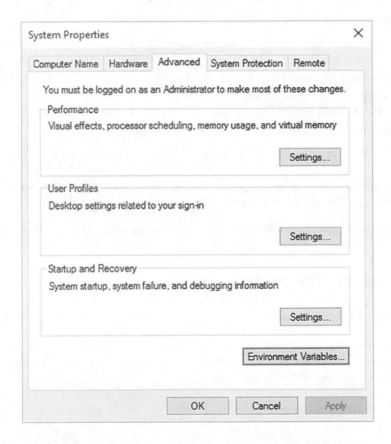

Figure B.2 Setting environment variables for Hadoop on Windows

> **NOTE**   For the PATH variable, you most certainly will already have some values in there (akin to a list). To avoid removing other useful variables that might be used by other programs, double click on the PATH variable and append %SPARK_HOME%\bin.

B.2.4   *Configure Spark to work seamlessly with Python*

If you are using Spark 3.0+ with Java 11+, you need to input some additional configuration to seamlessly work with Python. To do so, we need to create a spark-defaults.conf file under the $SPARK_HOME/conf directory. When reaching this directory, there should be a spark-defaults.conf.template file already there, along with some other files. Make a copy of spark-defaults.conf.template, and name it spark-defaults.conf. Inside this file, include the following:

```
spark.driver.extraJavaOptions="-Dio.netty.tryReflectionSetAccessible=true"
spark.executor.extraJavaOptions="-Dio.netty.tryReflectionSetAccessible=true"
```

This will prevent the pesky java.lang.UnsupportedOperationException: sun.misc.Unsafe or java.nio.DirectByteBuffer.(long, int) not available error that happens when you try to pass data between Spark and Python (chapter 8 onward).

B.2.5   *Install Python*

The easiest way to get Python 3 is to use the Anaconda Distribution. Go to https://www.anaconda.com/distribution and follow the installation instructions, making sure you're getting the 64-bits graphical installer for Python 3.0 and above for your OS.

   Once Anaconda is installed, we can activate the Python 3 environment by selecting the Anaconda PowerShell Prompt in the Start menu. If you want to create a dedicated virtual environment for PySpark, use the following command:

```
$ conda create -n pyspark python=3.8 pandas ipython pyspark=3.2.0
```

> **WARNING**   Python 3.8+ is only supported using Spark 3.0+. If you use Spark 2.4.X or older, be sure to specify Python 3.7 in your environment creation.

Then, to select your newly created environment, just input conda activate pyspark in the Anaconda prompt.

B.2.6   *Launching an IPython REPL and starting PySpark*

If you have configured the SPARK_HOME and PATH variables, your Python REPL will have access to a local instance of PySpark. Follow the next code block to launch IPython:

> **TIP**   If you aren't comfortable with the Command Line or PowerShell, I recommend *Learn Windows PowerShell in a Month of Lunches* by Don Jones and Jeffery D. Hicks (Manning, 2016).

```
conda activate pyspark
ipython
```

Then, within the REPL, you can import PySpark and start it:

```
from pyspark.sql import SparkSession

spark = SparkSession.builder.getOrCreate()
```

> **NOTE** Spark provides a `pyspark.cmd` helper command through the `bin` directory of your Spark installation. I prefer accessing PySpark through a regular Python REPL when working locally, as I find it easier to install libraries and know exactly which Python you're using. It also interfaces well with your favorite editor.

B.2.7 *(Optional) Install and run Jupyter to use a Jupyter notebook*

Since we have configured PySpark to be imported from a regular Python process, we don't have any further configuration to do to use it with a notebook. In your Anaconda PowerShell window, install Jupyter using the following command:

```
conda install -c conda-forge notebook
```

You can now run a Jupyter notebook server using the following command. Use `cd` to move to the directory where your source code is before doing so:

```
cd [WORKING DIRECTORY]
jupyter notebook
```

Start a Python kernel, and get started the same way you would using IPython.

> **NOTE** Some alternate installation instructions will create a separate environment for Python programs and PySpark programs, which is where you might see more than one kernel option. Using this set of instructions, use the `Python 3` kernel.

B.3 *macOS*

With macOS, the easiest option—by far—is to use the Homebrew `apache-spark` package. It takes care of all dependencies (I still recommend using Anaconda for managing Python environments for simplicity).

B.3.1 *Install Homebrew*

Homebrew is a package manager for OS.X. It provides a simple command-line interface to install many popular software packages and keep them up to date. While you can follow the manual's download and install steps that you'll find on the Windows OS with little change, Homebrew will simplify the installation process to a few commands.

To install Homebrew, go to https://brew.sh and follow the installation instructions. You'll be able to interact with Homebrew through the `brew` command.

> **Apple M1: Rosetta or no Rosetta**
>
> If you are using a Mac with the new Apple M1 chip, you have the option to run using Rosetta (an emulator for x64 instrutions). The instructions in this section will work.
>
> If you want to use a JVM specialized for the Apple M1, I use the Azul Zulu VM that you can download using Homebrew (https://github.com/mdogan/homebrew-zulu). All the code in the book works (faster than on an equivalent Intel Mac, dare I say), with the exception of the Spark BigQuery Connector, which fails on an ARM platform (see http://mng.bz/p298).

B.3.2   *Install Java and Spark*

Input the following command in a terminal:

```
$ brew install apache-spark
```

You can specify the version you want; I recommend getting the latest by passing no parameters.

   If Homebrew did not set `$SPARK_HOME` when installing Spark on your machine (test by restarting your terminal and typing `echo $SPARK_HOME`), you will need to add the following to your `~/.zshrc`:

```
export SPARK_HOME="/usr/local/Cellar/apache-spark/X.Y.Z/libexec"
```

Make sure you are inputting the right version number in lieu of `X.Y.Z`.

> **WARNING**   Homebrew will update Spark the moment it has a new version installed. When you install a new package, watch for a "rogue" upgrade of `apache-spark` and change the `SPARK_HOME` version number as needed. While writing this book, it happened to me a few times!

B.3.3   *Configure Spark to work seamlessly with Python*

If you are using Spark 3.0+ with Java 11+, you need to input some additional configurations to seamlessly work with Python. To do so, we need to create a spark-defaults.conf file under the `$SPARK_HOME/conf` directory. When reaching this directory, there should be a spark-defaults.conf.template file already there, along with some other files. Make a copy of spark-defaults.conf.template, and name it spark-defaults.conf. Inside this file, include the following:

```
spark.driver.extraJavaOptions="-Dio.netty.tryReflectionSetAccessible=true"
spark.executor.extraJavaOptions="-Dio.netty.tryReflectionSetAccessible=true"
```

This will prevent the pesky `java.lang.UnsupportedOperationException: sun.misc`
`.Unsafe` or `java.nio.DirectByteBuffer.(long, int) not available` error that happens when you try to pass data between Spark and Python (chapter 8 onward).

B.3.4 Install Anaconda/Python

The easiest way to get Python 3 is to use the Anaconda Distribution. Go to https://
www.anaconda.com/distribution and follow the installation instructions, making sure
you're getting the 64-bits Graphical installer for Python 3.0 and above for your OS:

```
$ conda create -n pyspark python=3.8 pandas ipython pyspark=3.2.0
```

If it's your first time using Anaconda, follow the instructions to register your shell.

> **WARNING** Python 3.8+ is supported only using Spark 3.0. If you use Spark
> 2.4.X or before, be sure to specify Python 3.7 in your environment creation.

Then, to select your newly created environment, just input `conda activate pyspark`
in the terminal.

B.3.5 Launching an IPython REPL and starting PySpark

Homebrew should have the `SPARK_HOME` and `PATH` environment variables, so your
Python shell (also called REPL, or *read eval print loop*) will have access to a local
instance of PySpark. You just have to type the following:

```
conda activate pyspark
ipython
```

Then, within the REPL, you can import PySpark and get rolling:

```
from pyspark.sql import SparkSession

spark = SparkSession.builder.getOrCreate()
```

B.3.6 (Optional) Install and run Jupyter to use Jupyter notebook

Since we have configured PySpark to be discovered from a regular Python process, we
don't have to do any further configuration to use it with a notebook. In your Anaconda PowerShell window, install Jupyter using the following command:

```
conda install -c conda-forge notebook
```

You can now run a Jupyter notebook server using the following command. Use `cd` to
move to the directory where your source code is before doing so:

```
cd [WORKING DIRECTORY]
jupyter notebook
```

Start a Python kernel, and get started the same way you would using IPython.

> **NOTE** Some alternate installation instructions will create a separate environment for Python programs and PySpark programs, which is where you might see more than one kernel option. Using this set of instructions, use the `Python 3` kernel.

B.4   GNU/Linux and WSL

B.4.1   Install Java

> **WARNING** Because Java 11 is incompatible with certain third-party libraries, I recommend staying on Java 8. Spark 3.0 and above works using Java 11 and above as well, but some libraries might trail behind.

Most GNU/Linux distributions provide a package manager. OpenJDK version 11 is available through the software repository:

```
sudo apt-get install openjdk-8-jre
```

B.4.2   Installing Spark

Go on the Apache website and download the latest Spark release. You shouldn't have to change the default options, but figure B.1 displays the ones I see when I navigate to the download page. Make sure to download the signatures and checksums if you want to validate the download (step 4 on the page).

> **TIP** On WSL (and sometimes Linux), you don't have a graphical user interface available. The easiest way to download Spark is to go to the website, follow the line, copy the link of the nearest mirror, and pass it along with the `wget` command:

```
wget [YOUR_PASTED_DOWNLOAD_URL]
```

If you want to know more about using the command line on Linux (and Os.X) proficiently, a good free reference is *The Linux Command Line* by William Shotts (http://linuxcommand.org/). It is also available as a paper or e-book (No Starch Press, 2019).

Once you have downloaded the file, unzip it. If you are using the command line, the following command will do the trick. Make sure you're replacing `spark-[…].gz` with the name of the file you just downloaded:

```
tar xvzf spark-[...].gz
```

This will unzip the content of the archive into a directory. You can now rename and move the directory to your liking. I usually put it under `/home/[MY-USER-NAME]/bin/spark-X.Y.Z/` (and rename it if the name is not identical), and the instructions will use that directory.

WARNING Make sure to replace X.Y.Z with the appropriate Spark version.

Set the following environment variables:

```
echo 'export SPARK_HOME="$HOME/bin/spark-X.Y.Z"' >> ~/.bashrc
echo 'export PATH="$SPARK_HOME/bin/spark-X.Y.Z/bin:$PATH"' >> ~/.bashrc
```

B.4.3   Configure Spark to work seamlessly with Python

If you are using Spark 3.0 and above with Java 11 and above, you need to input some additional configuration to seamlessly work with Python. To do so, we need to create a spark-defaults.conf file under the $SPARK_HOME/conf directory. When reaching this directory, there should be a spark-defaults.conf.template file already there, along with some other files. Make a copy of spark-defaults.conf.template, and name it spark-defaults.conf. Inside this file, include the following:

```
spark.driver.extraJavaOptions="-Dio.netty.tryReflectionSetAccessible=true"
spark.executor.extraJavaOptions="-Dio.netty.tryReflectionSetAccessible=true"
```

This will prevent the pesky java.lang.UnsupportedOperationException: sun.misc .Unsafe or java.nio.DirectByteBuffer.(long, int) not available error that happens when you try to pass data between Spark and Python (chapter 8 onward).

B.4.4   Install Python 3, IPython, and the PySpark package

Python 3 is already provided; you just have to install IPython. Input the following command in a terminal:

```
sudo apt-get install ipython3
```

TIP You can also use Anaconda on GNU/Linux. Follow the instructions in the macOS section.

Then install PySpark using pip. This will allow you to import PySpark in a Python REPL:

```
pip3 install pyspark==X.Y.Z
```

B.4.5   Launch PySpark with IPython

Launch an IPython shell:

```
ipython3
```

Then, within the REPL, you can import PySpark and get started:

```
from pyspark.sql import SparkSession

spark = SparkSession.builder.getOrCreate()
```

B.4.6   *(Optional) Install and run Jupyter to use Jupyter notebook*

Since we have configured PySpark to be discovered from a regular Python process, we don't have to do any further configuration to use it with a notebook. In your terminal, input the following to install Jupyter:

```
pip3 install notebook
```

You can now run a Jupyter notebook server using the following command. Use `cd` to move to the directory where your source code is before doing so:

```
cd [WORKING DIRECTORY]
jupyter notebook
```

Start a Python kernel, and get started the same way you would using IPython.

> **NOTE**   Some alternate installation instructions will create a separate environment for Python programs and PySpark programs, which is where you might see more than one kernel option. Using this set of instructions, use the `Python 3` kernel.

B.5   *PySpark in the cloud*

We finish this appendix with a very quick review of the main options for using PySpark in the cloud. There are many options—too many to review—but I decided to limit myself to the three main cloud providers (AWS, Azure, GCP). For completeness, I also added a section on Databricks since they are the team behind Spark and provide a great cloud option for managed Spark that spans all three major clouds.

Cloud offerings are very much moving targets. While writing this book, every provider adjusted their API, sometimes in a significant fashion. Because of this, I provide direct links to the relevant articles and the knowledge base I used to get Spark running with each provider. With most of them, the documentation evolves quickly, but the concepts remain the same. At their core, they all provide Spark access; the differences are in the UIs provided for creating, managing, and profiling clusters. I recommend, once you pick your preferred option, that you read through the documentation to understand some of the idiosyncrasies of a given provider.

> **NOTE**   A lot of cloud providers provide some small VM with Spark for you to test. They are useful if you can't install Spark locally on your machine (because of work limitations or some other reason). Check options for "single-node" when creating your cluster.

> **A (small) difference when working with cloud Spark**
>
> When working with a Spark cluster, especially on the cloud, I strongly recommend that you install the libraries you wish to use (pandas, scikit-learn, etc.) at *cluster creation time*. Managing dependencies on a running cluster is annoying at best, and most often you are better off destroying the whole thing and creating a new one.
>
> Each cloud provider will give you instructions on how to create startup actions to install libraries. If this is something you end up doing repeatedly, check into opportunities for automation, such as Ansible, Puppet, Terraform, and so on. When working on personal projects, I usually create a simple shell script. Most cloud providers provide a CLI interface to interact with their API in a programmatic way.

B.6 AWS

Amazon offers two products with Spark: EMR (Elastic Map-Reduce) and Glue. While they are pretty different and cater to different needs, I find that Spark is usually more up to date on EMR, and the pricing is also better if you are running sporadic jobs in the context of getting familiar.

EMR provides a complete Hadoop environment with a trove of open source tools, including Spark. The documentation is available through https://aws.amazon.com/emr/resources/.

Glue is advertised as a serverless ETL service, which includes Spark as part of the tools. Glue extends Spark with some AWS-specific notions, such as `DynamicFrame` and `GlueContext`, which are pretty powerful but not usable outside of Glue itself. The documentation is available through https://aws.amazon.com/glue/resources/.

B.7 Azure

Azure provides a managed Spark service through the HDInsight umbrella. The documentation for the product is available through https://docs.microsoft.com/en-us/azure/hdinsight/. Microsoft really segments the different products offered on a Hadoop cluster, so make sure you follow the Spark instructions. With Azure, I usually prefer using the GUI: the instructions on http://mng.bz/OGQR are very easy to follow, and for exploring large-scale data processing, Azure will give you hourly pricing as you build your cluster.

Azure also offers single-node Spark through its Data Science Virtual Machine for Linux (documentation available through http://mng.bz/YgwB). This is a lower-cost option to use if you don't want to bother with setting up an environment.

B.8 GCP

Google offers managed Spark through Google Dataproc. The documentation is available through https://cloud.google.com/dataproc/docs. I've used GCP Dataproc for most of the "scaled-out" examples in the book, as I find the command-line utilities very easy to learn and that the documentation works well.

The easiest way to get up and running when learning Spark with Google Dataproc is to use the option for single-node clusters that Google offers. The documentation for single-node clusters is a little hard to find; it is available at http://mng.bz/GGOv.

B.9   *Databricks*

Databricks was founded in 2013 by the creator of Apache Spark. Since then, they have grown a complete ecosystem around Spark, which spans data warehousing (Delta Lake), a solution for MLOps (MLFlow), and even a secure data interchange functionality (Delta Share).

> **TIP**   If you just want to get started on Databricks with a minimum amount of fuss, check out the Databricks community edition at https://community .cloud.databricks.com/login.html. This provides a small cluster for you to get started, with no installation up front. This section covers using a full-blown (paid) Databricks instance for when you need more power.

Databricks anchors its Spark distribution around *Databricks Runtime*, which is a cohesive set of libraries (Python, Java, Scala, R) tied to a specific Spark version. Their runtimes are available in a few flavors:

- Databricks runtime is the standard option, which features a complete ecosystem for running Spark on Databricks (https://docs.databricks.com/runtime/dbr .html).
- Databricks runtime for machine learning provides a curated set of popular ML libraries (such as TensorFlow, PyTorch, Keras, and XGBoost) on top of the standard options. This runtime ensures you have a cohesive set of ML libraries that play well with one another (https://docs.databricks.com/runtime/mlruntime.html).
- Photon is a new, faster, but feature-incomplete reimplementation of the Spark query engine in C++. It already is becoming a seductive option because of its increased performance (https://docs.databricks.com/runtime/photon.html).

Databricks prices their services based on DBU (*Databricks Units*), which are analog to a "standard compute node for one hour." The more powerful the cluster (either by having more nodes or by making them more powerful), the more DBUs you consume, and the more expensive it gets. You also need to factor in the price of the underlying cloud resources (VM, storage, network, etc.). This can make the pricing quite opaque; I usually use a pricing estimator (both Databricks's and the cloud provider's) to get a sense of the hourly cost.

> **NOTE**   Review each cloud provider's page for a price per DBU. They are not consistent between providers.

For the rest of this appendix, I'll walk through the main steps to set up, use, and destroy a workspace in Databricks. I use Google Cloud Platform, but the general steps apply to Azure and AWS as well. You won't find a complete guide to administering Databricks, but this should provide you with a working environment to run and scale the book's examples.

> **WARNING** Using Databricks costs money the moment you create a workspace. Using a powerful cluster will cost a lot of money. Be sure to shut down your clusters and your workspace once you're done!

To start with Databricks, we have to enable the service and create a workspace. For this, search for Databricks in the search bar and activate the trial. Carefully read the terms and conditions, as well as the permissions required to use the service. Once you are done, click on the Manage on Provider button and sign in with your GCP account. You will reach a screen like figure B.3, which has an empty list and a Create workspace button.

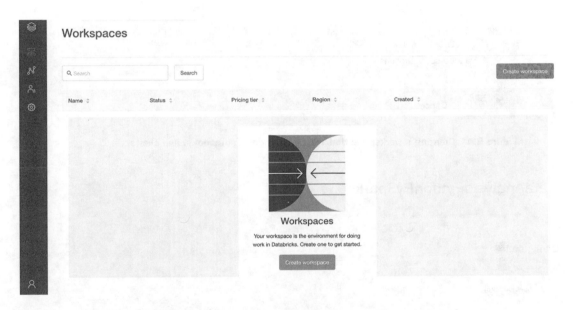

Figure B.3 The landing page for the Databricks Workspace (here using GCP)

To start using Databricks, we need to create a workspace, which serves as an umbrella for clusters, notebooks, pipelines, and so on. Organizations typically use workspaces as logical separations (by team, project, environment, etc.). In our case, we just need one; in figure B.4, we see the simple form to create a new workspace. If you don't have your Google Cloud Project ID, go to the landing page for the GCP console and check the top left box: mine is `focus-archway-214221`.

Once the workspace is created, Databricks will provide a page with a URL to reach the workbench; check the right section of figure B.5 for a unique URL ending with

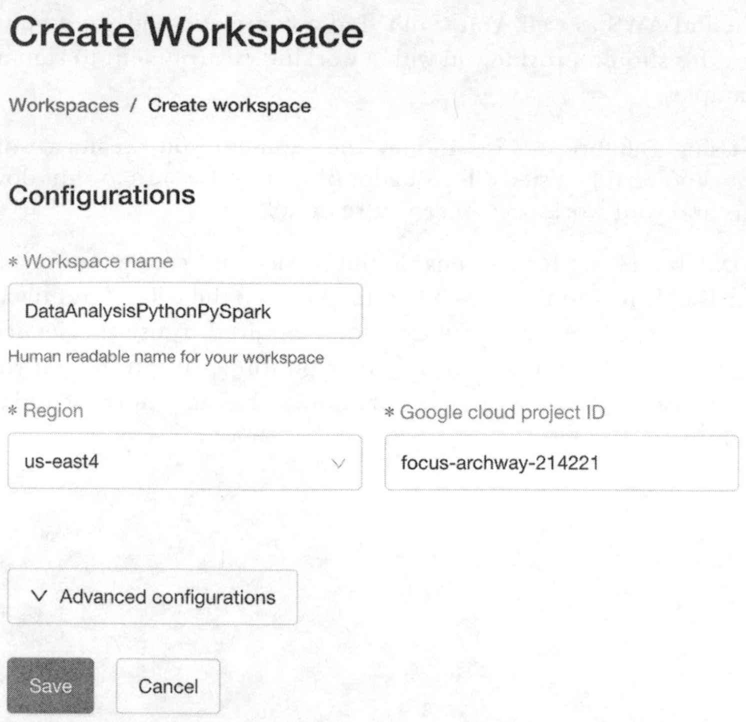

Create Workspace

Workspaces / Create workspace

Configurations

* Workspace name

DataAnalysisPythonPySpark

Human readable name for your workspace

* Region

us-east4 ∨

* Google cloud project ID

focus-archway-214221

∨ Advanced configurations

Save		Cancel

Figure B.4 Creating a workspace that will hold our data, notebooks, and clusters

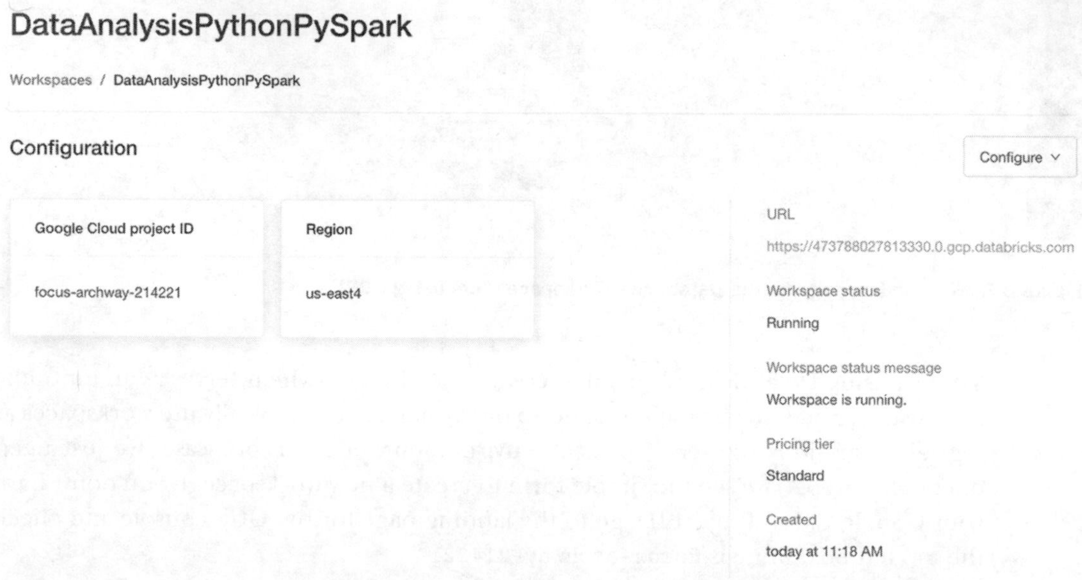

DataAnalysisPythonPySpark

Workspaces / DataAnalysisPythonPySpark

Configuration

Configure ∨

Google Cloud project ID	Region
focus-archway-214221	us-east4

URL

https://473788027813330.0.gcp.databricks.com

Workspace status

Running

Workspace status message

Workspace is running.

Pricing tier

Standard

Created

today at 11:18 AM

Figure B.5 Our new workspace created and ready for action. Click the unique URL on the right to access the workbench.

gcp.databricks.com. On the top right of this page, pay attention to the dropdown Configure menu. We will use it to destroy the workspace once done.

The workbench is really where we start working with Databricks. If you work in a corporate environment, you probably have your workspace(s) configured for you. You start using Databricks through the screen displayed in figure B.6. For this simple example, we limit ourselves to the Spark-centric functionalities of Databricks: notebooks/code, clusters, and data. As discussed at the beginning of the section, Databricks contains a complete ecosystem for ML experiments, data management, data sharing, data exploration/business intelligence, and version control/library management. As you get familiar with the general workflow, seek the documentation for those additional components.

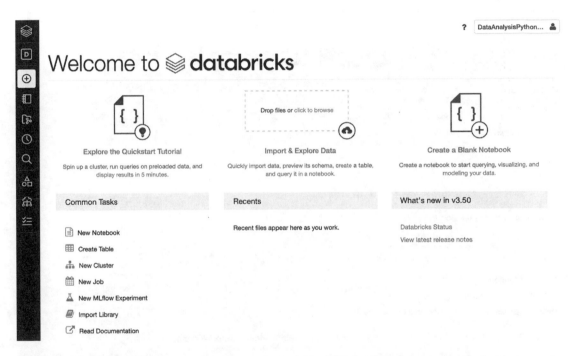

Figure B.6   The landing page for our workspace workbench. From this landing page, we can create, access, and manage clusters, as well as run jobs and notebooks.

It's time to start a cluster. Click on New Cluster (or the Cluster menu on the sidebar) and fill in the instructions for the cluster configuration. The menu, displayed in figure B.5, is pretty self-explanatory. If you are working with small data sets, I recommend the single-node Cluster Mode option, which will emulate the setup on your local machine (driver plus worker on the same machine). If you want to experiment with a larger cluster, set the min/max workers to appropriate values. Databricks will start with the min value, scaling automatically, up to max as needed.

NOTE By default, GCP has pretty strict usage quotas. When I started using Databricks, I had to request for two additional quotas to be increased so that I could launch a cluster. I asked for `SSD_TOTAL_GB` to be set to `10000` (10,000 GB of SSD usable) and `CPUS` for the relevant region (`us-east4`; see figure B.2) to `100` (100 CPUs). If you run into issues where the cluster gets destroyed upon creation, check the logs; chances are you've busted your quota.

For most use cases, the default configuration, displayed in figure B.7 (`n1-highmem-4`, with 26 GB of RAM and 4 cores), is plenty. If necessary, for instance, when performing a lot of joins, you can beef up the machines to something more powerful. For GCP, I have found that high-memory machines provide the sweetest spot performance-cost-wise. Remember that DBU costs are *in addition to* the VM costs GCP will charge you.

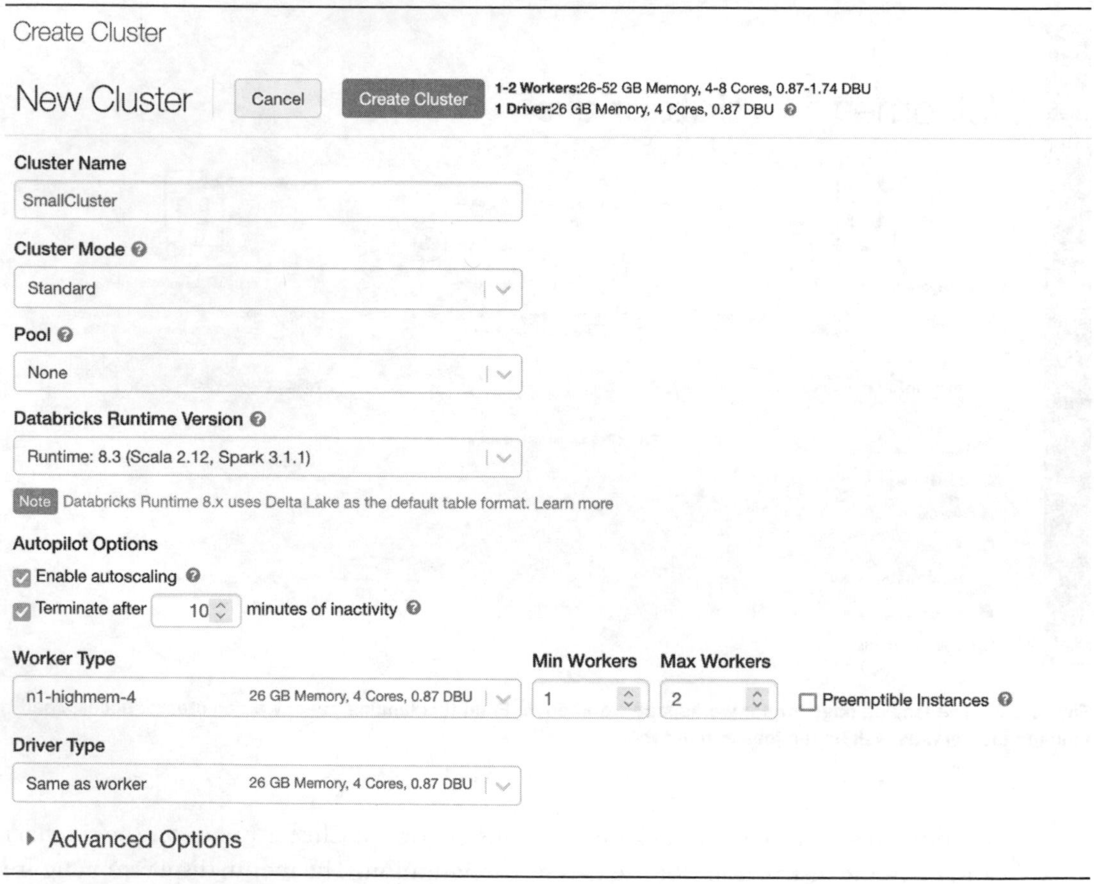

Figure B.7 Creating a small cluster with one to two worker nodes, each containing 26 GB of RAM and 4 cores. Each node costs 0.87 DBU.

While the cluster is creating (it will take a few minutes), let's upload the data for running our program. I picked the Gutenberg books, but any data follows the same process.

Click Create Table on the workbench landing page, choose Upload File, and drag and drop the files you want to upload. Pay attention to the DBFS Target Directory (here, /FileStore/tables/gutenberg_books), which we need to reference when reading the data in PySpark.

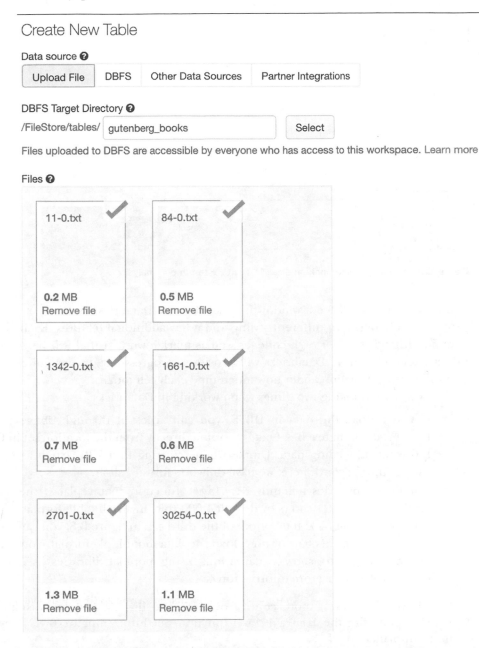

Figure B.8 Upload data (here, the Gutenberg books from chapters 2 and 3) in DBFS (Databricks File System)

Once the cluster is operational and the data is in DBFS, we can create a notebook to start coding. Click Create Notebook on the workbench landing page and select the name of your cluster, which your notebook will be attached to (like in figure B.9).

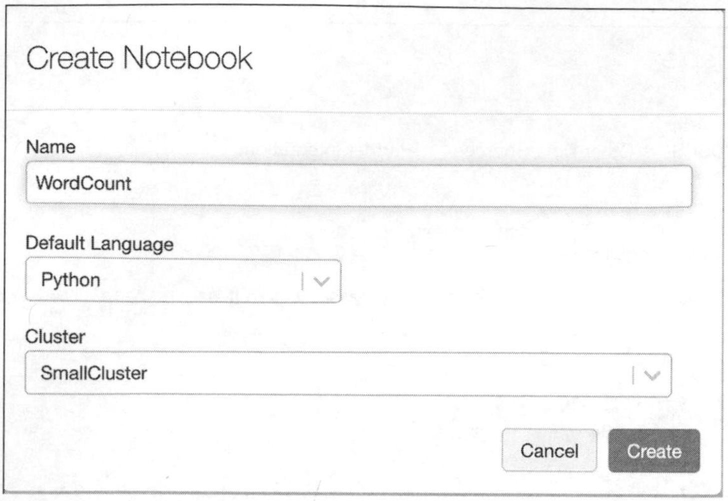

Figure B.9   Creating a notebook on `SmallCluster` to run our analysis

Upon creation, you'll see a window like figure B.10. Databricks notebooks look like Jupyter notebooks, with different styling and a few additional features. Each cell can contain either Python or SQL code, as well as markdown text that will be rendered. When executing a cell, Databricks will provide a progress bar during the execution and will give information about how much time each cell took.

It's worth mentioning two things when working in Databricks:

- If you upload the data in DBFS, you can access it through `dbfs:/[DATA-LOCATION]`. In figure B.8, I take the value directly from the location set in figure B.6 when uploading data. Unlike when referring to a URL (such as https://www.manning.com), here, we have only one forward slash.
- Databricks provides a handy `display()` function that replaces the `show()` method. `display()` shows by default 1,000 rows in a rich table format that you can scroll through. At the bottom of the third cell in figure B.8, you can also see buttons to create a chart or download the data in multiple format. You can also use `display()` to show visualizations using popular libraries (see http://mng.bz/zQEB for more information).

TIP   If you want even more control over what to display, you can display HTML code using the `displayHTML()` function. See http://mng.bz/0w1N for more information.

Figure B.10 Our notebook, operational and ready to rumble! Databricks notebooks look like Jupyter notebooks, with a few Spark-specific additions.

Once you are done with your analysis, you should turn off your cluster by pressing the Stop button in the cluster page of the workbench. If you don't plan to use Spark/Databricks for a longer period of time (more than a few hours) and are using a personal subscription, I recommend destroying the workspace, as Databricks spins off a few VMs to manage it. You can also go in GCP's Storage tab and delete the buckets Databricks created for hosting data and cluster metadata if you want to bring your cloud expenditure to zero dollars.

Databricks provides an attractive way to interact with PySpark in the cloud. Each vendor has a different approach to managed Spark in the cloud, from close-to-the-metal (GCP Dataproc, AWS EMR) to auto-piloted (AWS Glue). From a user perspective, the differences are mostly in how much you are expected to configure your environment (and how expensive it is). Just like with Databricks, some additional bundle tools are provided to simplify code and data management or provide optimized code to speed up key operations. Fortunately, Spark is the common denominator between those environments. What you learn in this book should apply regardless of your favorite Spark flavor.

appendix C
Some useful
Python concepts

Python is a fascinating and complex language. While there is a trove of beginners guides to learn the basics of the language, some new or more complex aspects of Python are less discussed. This appendix is a nonexhaustive compendium of intermediate to advanced Python concepts that will be useful when working with PySpark.

C.1 List comprehensions

List comprehensions are one of Python's constructs that, once you understand, you'll wonder how you were able to code without using them. At the core, they are nothing more than iterations over a list. Their power comes from their conciseness and how readable they are. We start using them in chapter 4 when providing multiple columns to methods like `select()` and `drop()`, most often to select/drop a subset of columns.

When working with lists, tuples, and dictionaries, it'll often happen that you want to apply an operation to every element in the list. For this, you can use the `for` loop, like in the first half of listing C.1 where I create a list of columns to delete in my data frame. This is completely valid, if a little long, at five lines of code.

We can also use a list comprehension as a replacement for the list creation and iteration. This way, we can avoid useless variable assignment, like in the second half of listing C.1. The focus is also squarely on the `drop()` method, compared to the loop approach, where we focus more on creating the subset of columns.

Listing C.1 Applying a function to every column of my data frame

```
# Without a list comprehension

to_delete = []
for col in df.columns:
    if "ID" in col:
        to_delete.append(col)

df = f.drop(*to_delete)

# With a list comprehension

df = df.drop(*[col for col in df.columns if "ID" in col])
```

List comprehensions can be especially useful when you consider that PySpark can store computations aside from the main code using the Column object. In listing C.2, for instance, using the gsod data at the end of chapter 9, we can compute the maximum of the temp and temp_norm without having to resort to typing everything. We also use argument unpacking through the star operator. (See section C.2 for more details on this.)

Listing C.2 Computing the maximum of the `temp` and `temp_norm`

```
maxes = [F.max(x) for x in ["temp", "temp_norm"]]

gsod_map.groupby("stn").agg(*maxes).show(5)    ◁─────   The star prefix operator
                                                        unpacks the list (see
                                                        section C.2).
# +------+---------+--------------+
# |   stn|max(temp)|max(temp_norm)|
# +------+---------+--------------+
# |296450|     77.7|           1.0|
# |633320|     81.4|           1.0|
# |720375|     79.2|           1.0|
# |725165|     83.5|           1.0|
# |868770|     94.6|           1.0|
# +------+---------+--------------+
# only showing top 5 rows
```

Visually, in figure C.1, we can envision the process in which the new list gets built out of the previous list passed as input (through the keyword in within the list

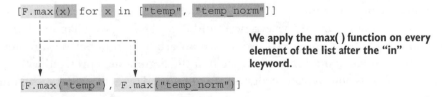

We apply the max( ) function on every element of the list after the "in" keyword.

The result is a list with every element transformed. There is no need to create an empty list and append the elements one by one.

Figure C.1 Using a simple list comprehension for computing the max of multiple columns

comprehension). The result is a new list, where each element comes from the input list, processed through the function at the start.

List comprehension can be much more complex. Here is an artificial example with two input lists and an `if` clause to filter out the result.

Listing C.3 A more ambitious list comprehension

```
print([x + y for x in [0, 1, 2] for y in [0, 1, 2] if x != y])
```
⟵

```
# => [1, 2, 1, 3, 2, 3]
```

Including multiple lists to iterate over will yield a cartesian product of the input lists. Here, we have nine elements before the filtering.

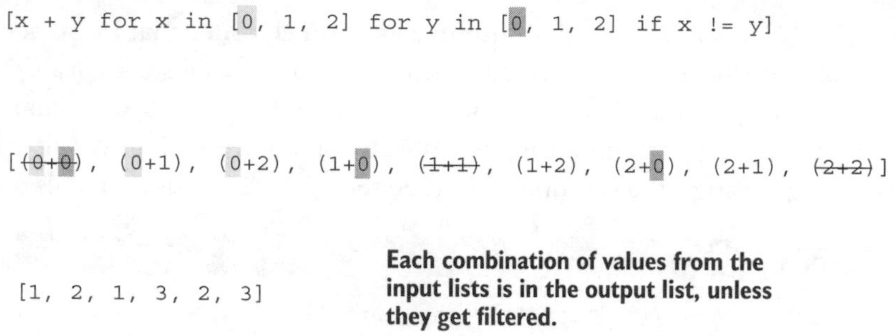

```
[x + y for x in [0, 1, 2] for y in [0, 1, 2] if x != y]
```

```
[(0+0), (0+1), (0+2), (1+0), (1+1), (1+2), (2+0), (2+1), (2+2)]
```

```
[1, 2, 1, 3, 2, 3]
```
Each combination of values from the input lists is in the output list, unless they get filtered.

Figure C.2 A more ambitious list comprehension. Each combination of elements from the input list are in the output list, unless they get filtered by the `if` clause.

C.2 *Packing and unpacking arguments (*args and **kwargs)*

A number of Python and PySpark functions and methods work with a variable number of arguments. As an example, in PySpark, we can `select()` one, two, three, and so on columns using the same method: the `select()` method. Under the hood, Python uses argument packing and unpacking to allow this flexibility. This section introduces argument packing and unpacking in the context of PySpark operations. Knowing when and how to leverage those techniques goes a long way toward making your code more robust and simple.

As a matter of fact, some of PySpark's most common data frame methods, such as `select()`, `groupby()`, `drop()`, `summary()`, and `describe()` (see chapters 4 and 5 for more content on those methods), work with an arbitrary number of arguments. By going into the documentation, we can see that the argument is prefixed with a `*`, just like `drop()`. This is how we can recognize that a method/function works with multiple arguments:

```
drop(*cols)
```

This syntax can look a little confusing if you've never encountered it. On the other hand, it is so useful, especially in the context of PySpark, that it's worth internalizing it.

Taking the `drop()` example, let's assume that we have a simple four-column data frame like in listing C.4. The columns are named `feat1`, `pred1`, `pred2`, and `feat2`; imagine that `feat` columns are features and the `pred` columns are predictions from an ML model. In practice, we might have an arbitrarily large number of columns we wish to delete, and not just two ML models.

Listing C.4 A simple data frame with four columns

```
sample = spark.createDataFrame(
    [[1, 2, 3, 4], [2, 2, 3, 4], [3, 2, 3, 4]],
    ["feat1", "pred1", "pred2", "feat2"],
)
sample.show()
# +-----+-----+-----+-----+
# |feat1|pred1|pred2|feat2|
# +-----+-----+-----+-----+
# |    1|    2|    3|    4|
# |    2|    2|    3|    4|
# |    3|    2|    3|    4|
# +-----+-----+-----+-----+
```

What is the best way to delete *every* column that has the `pred` prefix? One solution is to pass the names of the columns directly to drop, like `sample.drop("pred1", "pred2")`. This will work as long as we have those two columns named this way. What if we have `pred3` and `pred74`?

For a given data frame `sample`, we saw in chapter 5 that we can use a list comprehension (see section C.1 for more information on the topic) to work with the list of columns using `sample.columns`. With that, we can easily get the columns, starting with pred.

Listing C.5 Filtering the columns of the `sample` data frame

```
to_delete = [c for c in sample.columns if str.startswith(c, "pred")]
print(to_delete)  # => ['pred1', 'pred2']
```

If we try to perform the `sample.drop(to_delete)` operation, we'll get a `TypeError: col should be a string or a Column` message. `drop()` takes multiple arguments that each are either a string or a Column, and we have a list of strings. Enter `*args`, also called *argument packing and unpacking*.

The `*` prefix operator operates in two directions: when using it in a function, it *unpacks* the argument so it looks like it was individually passed. Used in a function definition, it *packs* all the arguments of the function call into a tuple.

C.2.1   *Argument unpacking*

Let's start with the unpacking, as it is the situation we face right now. We have a list of strings that we need to extract from each element to pass as arguments to `drop()`. Prefixing `to_delete` with a star in `drop()`, just like in the next listing, does the trick.

> **Listing C.6   Dropping multiple columns at once using the argument unpacking operator**

```
sample.drop(*to_delete).printSchema()
# root
# |-- feat1: long (nullable = true)
# |-- feat2: long (nullable = true)
```

pred1 and pred2 are no more!

I like to think of argument unpacking as a *syntax-ic transformation*, where the star "eats" the container of a tuple or list, leaving the elements bare. This is best seen visually. In figure C.3, we see the duality: adding the star as a prefix to `*to_delete` is equivalent to passing each element of the list as a distinct argument.

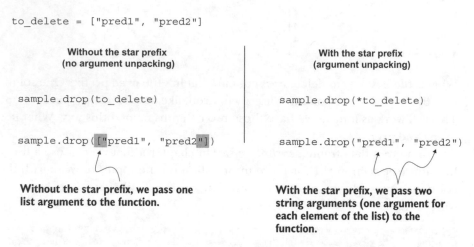

```
to_delete = ["pred1", "pred2"]
```

| **Without the star prefix** (no argument unpacking) | **With the star prefix** (argument unpacking) |

```
sample.drop(to_delete)                  sample.drop(*to_delete)

sample.drop(["pred1", "pred2"])         sample.drop("pred1", "pred2")
```

Without the star prefix, we pass one list argument to the function.

With the star prefix, we pass two string arguments (one argument for each element of the list) to the function.

Figure C.3   Prefixing a list/tuple argument with a stat "unpacks" each element into a distinct argument.

C.2.2   *Argument packing*

Now that unpacking has been covered, what about packing? For this, let's create a simple implementation of `drop()`. In chapter 4, we saw that drop is equivalent to `select()`-ing the columns we don't want to drop. `drop()` needs to take a variable number of arguments. A simple implementation is shown in the next listing.

> **Listing C.7   Implementing a simple equivalent of the `drop()` method**

```
def my_drop(df, *cols):
    return df.select(*[x for x in df.columns if x not in cols])
```

We pack every argument (other than the first, called df) into a tuple called cols.

With the function defined, we can see how Python packs the `"pred1"` and `"pred2"` arguments into a tuple called `cols` to be used within the function. Again, we can use the same `*` prefix to unpack an argument list, as shown on the right of figure C.4.

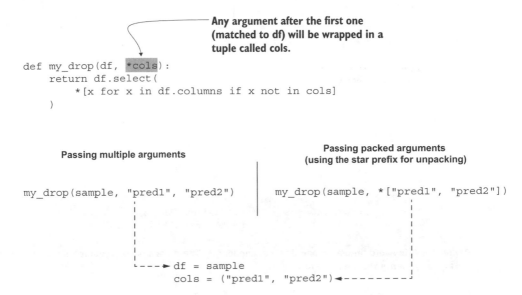

Figure C.4 Using `*args` in a function definition. Every argument after the first gets lumped into a tuple named `cols`.

C.2.3 Packing and unpacking keyword arguments

Python also accepts packing and unpacking keyword arguments through the `**` prefix operator. If you see a function with `**kwargs` in its signature as illustrated in figure C.5, it means it will pack named arguments into a `dictionary` named `kwargs` (you don't have to name it `kwargs`, just like you don't have to name the classical un/packing `args`). PySpark doesn't use it as much, reserving it for optional named parameters for methods taking options. `DataFrame.orderBy()` is the best example, where `ascending` is captured as a keyword argument.

Argument packing and unpacking make Python functions more flexible: we don't have to implement `select1()`, `select2()`, `select3()`, for selecting one, two, or three columns. It also makes the syntax easier to remember, as we don't have to pack the columns we wish to select in a list just to make the function happy. It also helps with making Python-static typing tools happier, which happens to be the topic of the next section.

C.3 Python's typing and mypy/pyright

Python is a strongly, yet dynamically typed language. When I was learning to program, I recall many more experienced developers chanting this like a mantra. I also recall many puzzled looks when I asked, "What does that mean?" The inclusion of typing

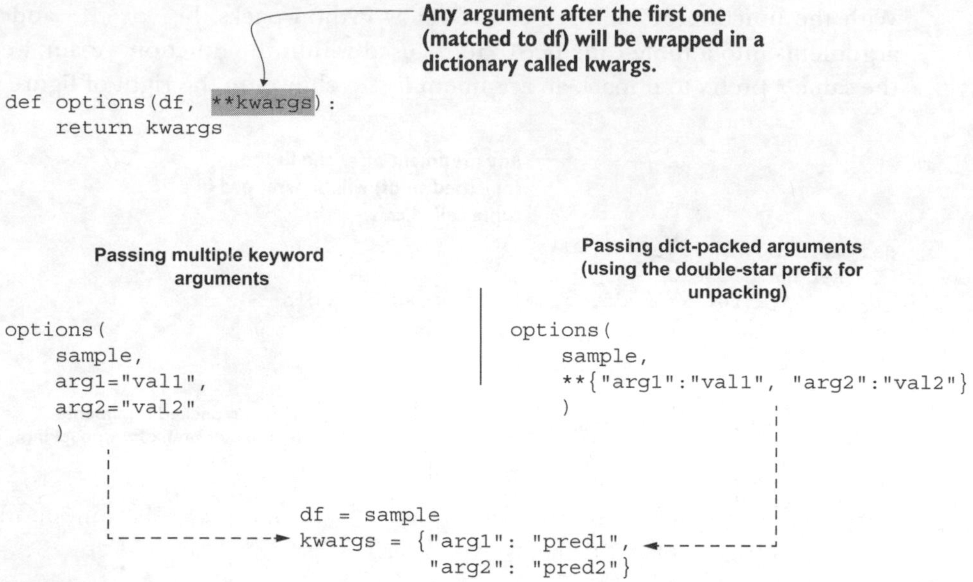

Any argument after the first one (matched to df) will be wrapped in a dictionary called kwargs.

```
def options(df, **kwargs):
    return kwargs
```

Passing multiple keyword arguments

```
options(
    sample,
    arg1="val1",
    arg2="val2"
)
```

Passing dict-packed arguments (using the double-star prefix for unpacking)

```
options(
    sample,
    **{"arg1":"val1", "arg2":"val2"}
)
```

```
df = sample
kwargs = {"arg1": "pred1",
          "arg2": "pred2"}
```

Figure C.5   Keyword argument packing and unpacking: The names of the arguments are dict keys, and the arguments themselves are values.

tools—the topic of this section—added a layer of mystique to Python's type story. This section starts with a working definition of strong and dynamic typing, before reviewing how Python, and more specifically PySpark, use types to simplify and increase the robustness of data-processing and analysis code.

Strong typing, in the context of a programming language, means that every variable has a type. As an example, in Python, the statement a = "the letter a" assigns the string the letter a to the variable a. This means that any operation we perform on a needs to have an implementation that will work on a string. Some languages, such as Python, are more flexible in their typing, where they'll allow some function to apply to many types, as long as a behavior is defined. Let's take our string example: in listing C.8, we see that, while we can't add 1 to a, we can "add" a string to make a longer string. In Python, every variable has a type, and this type matters when performing operations: the + operator won't work with an int and a str, but will work with two ints or two strs.

Listing C.8   Addition between numbers and between strings (concatenation)

```
>>> a = "the letter a"

>>> a + 1
Traceback (most recent call last):
  File "<stdin>", line 1, in <module>
TypeError: cannot concatenate 'str' and 'int' objects
```

```
>>> a + " but not the letter b"
'the letter a but not the letter b'
```

A weakly typed language could perform something when passed a + 1 rather than throwing a type error. Weak and strongly typed languages form a gradient rather than two clans; the clear boundary between weak and strong typing is still up for debate. In our specific case, it is enough to remember that Python carries a type for every variable. The type of a variable matters when performing an operation, and performing an operation on incompatible types, such as adding 1 to a string, will yield a type error.

Python is also dynamically typed, which means that type resolution/errors are found at runtime, or when the program runs. This is in contrast to *static* typing, which means that types are inferred (or known) during compilation. Languages like Haskell, OCaml, and even Java are great examples of statically typed languages: where Python will throw a runtime error when performing type-incompatible operations, a statically typed language will refuse to run the program outright or even compile the source code. Whether strict or dynamic typing is best is a matter of personal preference. Some argue that strict typing ensures better discipline when coding and eliminating type errors. It is also believed that dynamic types help get things done without getting sidetracked with extraneous ceremony from the type verification. Like many things in programming, it is a topic that is heavily debated, mostly by people who have not tried both sides extensively.

Python 3.5 changed the game slightly by introducing type hints within the language. While they do not mean that Python is now a statically typed language, the inclusion of optional type checking means that we can reap some of the benefits of static checking without having to contend with the very rigid framework they can force.

To start with type checking, you need to get a type checker. The easiest way to start is with mypy (http://mypy-lang.org/); I use it for the examples in this section. You can also check pytype (from Google), Pyright/Pylance (from Microsoft, bundled with VS Code), and Pyre (from Facebook) for alternatives. PyCharm also bundles a type-checking tool out of the box. Refer to your editor/type-checker documentation for installation instructions.

Let's create a small example where the types do not match. In the following code, we have an obvious type error, where we (again!) add an integer value to a string (I'll never learn).

> **Listing C.9** `type_error.py`**: Creating a type error on purpose**

```
def add_one(value: float):
    return value + 1
```
⟵ **By annotating value as a float, we indicate that we can pass an int or float (every int is a float, but not every float is an int).**

```
add_one("twenty")
```
⟵ **"twenty" is not a float. This is a type error.**

If you have configured your editor to do type checking as you type, you should get an error pretty much right after you type the last line of listing C.9. If not, use the command line tool `mypy` to check your file, as in the following listing.

Listing C.10 Using the `mypy` command line tool to identify the type error

```
$ mypy type_error.py
type_error.py:8: error: Argument 1 to "add_one"
has incompatible type "str"; expected "float"

Found 1 error in 1 file (checked 1 source file)
```

This is a very simple example, but type hints can be helpful when you design your own functions. Not only do they serve as indications about the kind of arguments to expect (and return) for the function's potential users, but they can help enforce some desired behavior and explain `TypeError`. In PySpark, they are used to dispatch a type of pandas UDF (see chapter 9) without requiring any special annotations beyond the types. As an example, I reproduced the f_to_c function in listing C.11: the signature of the function is `(degrees: pd.Series) -> pd.Series`, meaning that it takes a single argument that must be a pandas Series and return a pandas Series. PySpark takes that typing information and knows automatically that it is a Series to Series UDF. Before the introduction of type hints for pandas UDFs, you needed to add a second argument to the decorator (see section C.5) to help with the dispatch.

Listing C.11 Typing hints in the `f_to_c` function

```
import pandas as pd
import pyspark.sql.types as T
import pyspark.sql.functions as F


@F.pandas_udf(T.DoubleType())
def f_to_c(degrees: pd.Series) -> pd.Series:        ◁──  f_to_c takes a Series and
    """Transforms Farhenheit to Celcius."""              returns a Series. We know
    return (degrees - 32) * 5 / 9                         because it's annotated.
```

We end this section with useful typing constructors to use when building your own functions. (For more information, refer to PEP484—Type Hints [https://www.python .org/dev/peps/pep-0484/].) All five constructors, `Iterator`, `Union`, `Optional`, `Tuple`, and `Callable`, are imported from the `typing` module when using Python 3.8 (the semantics changed slightly in Python 3.9, and they are available without explicit importing; see PEP585—Type Hinting Generics In Standard Collections [https:// www.python.org/dev/peps/pep-0585/]):

```
from typing import Iterator, Union, Optional, Callable
```

We've encountered `Iterator` from the Iterator of Series (single and multiple) in chapter 9. The `Iterator` type hint means that you are dealing with a collection that can be iterated over, for instance a list, a dict, a tuple, or even the content of a file. It suggests that this variable will be iterated over, probably by using a `for` loop.

A `Union` type hint means that the variable can be either type within the union. For instance, many PySpark functions have a signature of `Union[Column, str]`, meaning that they accept either a `Column` object (seen in `pyspark.sql`) or a string as an argument. `Optional[…]` is equivalent to `Union[…, None]`, where we put a type in the ellipsis.

`Tuple` is used in the Iterator of multiple Series UDF. Since tuples are immutable in Python (you can't change them in place), we can enforce a strict type through annotations. A tuple of three pandas Series would be `Tuple[pd.Series, pd.Series, pd.Series]`.

`Callable` is addressed in the next section, where we talk about Python closure and the `transform()` method. It refers to the type of a function (an object that takes arguments to return another object). For instance, the type of the `add_one` function in listing C.11 is `Callable[[float], float]`: the list in first position is the input parameters, and the second is the return value.

Before ending this section, I encourage you to use type hints as a tool: no more, no less. Because type checking is a recent addition to Python, there are some rough edges, and we have uneven coverage between different type checkers. It is too easy to become obsessed with finding the perfect type signature, which will steal precious time from doing useful work.

C.4   *Python closures and the PySpark transform() method*

If I were to summarize this section in a few words, I would say that you can create functions in Python that return functions. This can prove useful when you are using higher-order functions (such as `map()` and `reduce()`, seen in chapter 8), but it also unlocks a very useful—but optional—code pattern when transforming data in PySpark.

In chapter 1, I introduced method chaining as the preferred way of organizing data transformation code. The code we submitted as a job in chapter 3, reproduced in the next listing, illustrates this concept well: we see a column of dots, each a method called on the data frame returned via the previous application.

Listing C.12 The word count submit program, with its series of method chaining

```
results = (
    spark.read.text("./data/gutenberg_books/1342-0.txt")
    .select(F.split(F.col("value"), " ").alias("line"))
    .select(F.explode(F.col("line")).alias("word"))
    .select(F.lower(F.col("word")).alias("word"))
    .select(F.regexp_extract(F.col("word"), "[a-z']*", 0).alias("word"))
    .where(F.col("word") != "")
    .groupby(F.col("word"))
    .count()          ⊲───┐   The alignment of the
)                         │   code highlights the
    ^                     │   method chaining.
```

What if you need to go beyond select(), where(), groupby(), count(), or any of the methods available out of the box via the data frame API?

Enter the transform() method. The transform() method takes one argument: a function that takes a single parameter. It returns the result of applying the function to the data frame. As an example, let's say we want to compute the modulo of a given column. Let's create a function that takes a data frame as an argument and returns the modulo of a column as a new column. Our function takes four arguments:

- The data frame itself
- The name of the old column
- The name of the new column
- The modulo value

Listing C.13   The `modulo_of` function taking four parameters

```
def modulo_of(df, old_column, new_column, modulo_value):
    return df.withColumn(new_column, F.col(old_column) % modulo_value)
```

If we want to apply this function to a data frame, we need to apply the function like a regular function, such as modulo_of(df, "old", "new", 2). This breaks the chain of methods, cluttering the code between function application and method application. To use the transform() method with modulo_of(), we need to make it a function of a single parameter, the data frame.

In listing C.14, we rewrite our modulo_of function to fulfill this contract. The return value of modulo_of() is a function/callable, taking a data frame as an argument and returning a data frame. To have a function to return, we create an _inner_ func() that takes a data frame as an argument and returns a transformed data frame. _inner_func() has access to the parameters passed to modulo_of(), namely new_name, old_col, and modulo_value.

Listing C.14   Rewriting the `modulo_of` function

```
from typing import Callable
from pyspark.sql import DataFrame


def modulo_of(
    new_name: str, old_col: str, modulo_value: int
) -> Callable[[DataFrame], DataFrame]:
    """Return the value from the column mod `modulo_value`

    Transform-enabled function."""

    def _inner_func(df: DataFrame) -> DataFrame:
        # Function knows about new_name and old_col and modulo_value
        return df.withColumn(new_name, F.col(old_col) % modulo_value)

    return _inner_func
```

modulo_of() returns a function from a DataFrame to a DataFrame.

_inner_func() has access to the parameters passed to modulo_of(), namely new_name, old_col, and modulo_value.

We return the function as if it was any other object (it is).

How does it work?

- In Python, functions can return functions, as they are just like any other object.
- A function created inside a function in Python has access to the environment (defined variables) where it was defined. In the case of _inner_func(), the helper function DataFrame → DataFrame we created to return has access to new_name, old_col, and modulo_value. This will work even after we end the enclosing function block. This is called *closing on a function*, and the resulting function is called a *closure*.
- The result is akin to partially evaluating a function, where we set all the parameters in the first "application," and then set the data frame in the second data frame.

Now we can simply use transform() with our newly created "transform-enabled" function.

Listing C.15 Applying the modulo_of() function to a sample data frame

```
df = spark.createDataFrame(
    [[1, 2, 4, 1], [3, 6, 5, 0], [9, 4, None, 1], [11, 17, None, 1]],
    ["one", "two", "three", "four"],
)

(
    df.transform(modulo_of("three_mod2", "three", 2))
    .transform(modulo_of("one_mod10", "one", 10))
    .show()
)

# +---+---+-----+----+----------+---------+
# |one|two|three|four|three_mod2|one_mod10|
# +---+---+-----+----+----------+---------+
# |  1|  2|    4|   1|         0|        1|
# |  3|  6|    5|   0|         1|        3|
# |  9|  4| null|   1|      null|        9|
# | 11| 17| null|   1|      null|        1|
# +---+---+-----+----+----------+---------+
```

To close the loop, what if we wanted to use our new modulo_of() function like a function, without transform()? We just need to apply it two times: the first application will return a function taking a data frame as sole argument. The second application will return the transformed data frame:

```
modulo_of("three_mod2", "three", 2)(df)
```

Transform-enabled functions are not necessary to write performant and maintainable programs. On the other hand, they enable us to embed arbitrary logic through the transform method, which keeps the method-chaining code organization pattern. This yields cleaner, more readable code.

C.5   *Python decorators: Wrapping a function to change its behavior*

Decorators, at least in the context we encounter them, are a construction that allow modification of a function without changing the body of the code. They are pretty simple constructions that look complex because of their rather unique syntax. Decorators rely on Python's ability to treat functions as objects: you can pass them as arguments and return them from functions (see section C.4). Put simply, a decorator is a simplified syntax to wrap a function around a function passed as an argument.

Decorators can do a lot of things. Because of this, it's best to focus on how they are used in PySpark. In PySpark, we use Python decorators to transform a function into a UDF (regular or vectorized/pandas). As an example, let's review the `f_to_c()` UDF we created in chapter 9. If we recall how the `pandas_udf` decorator works, when applied to a function, here `f_to_c()`, the function no longer applies to a pandas Series. The decorator transforms it into a UDF that can be applied to a Spark `Column`.

Listing C.16   The `f_to_c` UDF

```
@F.pandas_udf(T.DoubleType())
def f_to_c(degrees: pd.Series) -> pd.Series:
    """Transforms Farhenheit to Celcius."""
    return (degrees - 32) * 5 / 9
```

Upon applying the decorator, the f_to_c function is no longer a simple function on a pandas Series, but a vectorized UDF to be used on a Spark data frame.

Under the hood, creating UDFs requires some JVM (Java Virtual Machine, as Spark is written in Scala, and PySpark leverages the Java API) gymnastics. We can use the pseudocode of the `pandas_udf()` decorator to better understand how decorators work and how to create one, if needed.

Decorators are functions—for completeness, we can have decorator classes, but they are not used in the user-facing API for PySpark—that take at least a function `f` as an argument. Usually, the decorator perform additional work around the function `f` before returning (its return value).

Listing C.17   The pseudocode for the `pandas_udf` decorator function

```
def pandas_udf(f, returnType, functionType):

    Step 1: verify the returnType to ensure its validity (either
        `pyspark.sql.types.*` or a string representing a PySpark data type).

    Step 2: assess the UDF type (functionType) based on the signature (Spark 3)
    or the PandasUDFType (Spark 2.3+))

    Step 3: Create the UDF object wrapping the function `f` passed as an
    argument (in PySpark, this is done through the
            `pyspark.sql.udf._create_udf()` function)

    Return: the newly formed UDF from step 3.
```

Let's create a decorator `record_counter` that will count and print the number of records before and after transforming our data frame. `record_counter` takes only one argument, the function we want to decorate, and returns a wrapper that counts the number of records, applies the function, counts the number of records of the result of the function, and returns the result of the function.

Listing C.18 A simple decorator function

We apply the function and save the value to return at the end of the wrapper function.

We create a function inside the decorator function, just like with the transform-enabled function. This function will be the one returned from applying the decorator.

```
def record_counter(f):

    def _wrapper(value):
        print("Before: {} records".format(value.count()))
        applied_f = f(value)
        print("After: {} records".format(applied_f.count()))
        return applied_f

    return _wrapper
```

Before actually applying the function passed as argument, we print the number of records.

We return the result of the function. Forgetting this would mean that decorating a function with record_counter would return nothing.

We return the wrapper as a result of the decorator function.

To apply a decorator to a function, we prefix the function definition with `@record_counter`. Python assigns the function on the line right after the decorator as the first argument to `record_counter`. When applying a decorator with no additional parameter than the function, we don't have to add parentheses `()` at the end of the decorator name.

Listing C.19 Applying the `record_counter` to a function

```
@record_counter
def modulo_data_frame(df):
    return (
        df.transform(modulo_of("three_mod2", "three", 2))
        .transform(modulo_of("one_mod10", "one", 10))
        .show()
    )
```

We put the decorator on top of the function definition. Since our decorator takes no additional parameters, we don't need to add the parentheses at the end.

Since a decorated function is a function, we can use it in the same way we would use any function. In the case of the pandas UDF, the decorator actually changes the nature of the object, so it's being used differently, but still has that function flavor.

Listing C.20 Using our decorated function like any other function

```
modulo_data_frame(df)
# Before: 4 records
# +---+---+-----+----+----------+---------+
# |one|two|three|four|three_mod2|one_mod10|
# +---+---+-----+----+----------+---------+
# |  1|  2|    4|   1|         0|        1|
```

We see the before and after counting on top of the show() method of the function passed as argument.

```
# |  3|  6|    5|   0|        1|       3|
# |  9|  4| null|   1|     null|       9|
# | 11| 17| null|   1|     null|       1|
# +---+---+-----+----+---------+--------+

# After: 4 records
```

We see the before and after counting on top of the show() method of the function passed as argument.

Since a decorator function is a function, we can also use it without resorting to the @ pattern. For this, we use `record_counter()` as a regular function and assign the result to a variable. I personally find the decorator pattern quite attractive and clean, as it avoids having two variables: one for the original function (`modulo_data_frame2`) and one for the decorated one (`modulo_data_frame_d2`).

> **Listing C.21   Avoiding the decorator pattern by using a regular function application**

```python
def modulo_data_frame2(df):
    return (
        df.transform(modulo_of("three_mod2", "three", 2))
        .transform(modulo_of("one_mod10", "one", 10))
        .show()
    )


modulo_data_frame_d2 = record_counter(modulo_data_frame2)
```

Finally, when working with UDFs, you can still access the original function (the one working on Python or pandas objects) through the `func` attribute. This is useful when unit testing a function that is already user-defined. It can also ensure consistent behavior between pandas and PySpark.

> **Listing C.22   Accessing the original function from the UDF through the `func` attribute**

```python
print(f_to_c.func(pd.Series([1,2,3])))
# 0    -17.222222
# 1    -16.666667
# 2    -16.111111
# dtype: float64
```

Decorators are useful in PySpark for signaling that a function is user-defined (as well as in signaling its type). Because decorators are regular Python language constructions, we are not limited to using them solely for UDFs: whenever you want to add new functionality (we demonstrated logging) to a set of functions, decorators are a very readable option.

index